T0184305

Lecture Notes in Computer Science   11399

Commenced Publication in 1973
Founding and Former Series Editors:
Gerhard Goos, Juris Hartmanis, and Jan van Leeuwen

Editorial Board

More information about this series at http://www.springer.com/series/7407

Thomas Hinze · Grzegorz Rozenberg
Arto Salomaa · Claudio Zandron (Eds.)

Membrane Computing

19th International Conference, CMC 2018
Dresden, Germany, September 4–7, 2018
Revised Selected Papers

 Springer

Editors
Thomas Hinze
Friedrich Schiller University Jena
Jena, Germany

Arto Salomaa
Turku Center for Computer Science (TUCS)
Turku, Finland

Grzegorz Rozenberg
Leiden Centre of Advanced Computer
Science (LIACS)
Leiden University
Leiden, The Netherlands

Claudio Zandron
Informatics, Systems and Communication
University of Milano-Bicocca
Milan, Italy

ISSN 0302-9743   ISSN 1611-3349 (electronic)
Lecture Notes in Computer Science
ISBN 978-3-030-12796-1   ISBN 978-3-030-12797-8 (eBook)
https://doi.org/10.1007/978-3-030-12797-8

Library of Congress Control Number: 2019930657

LNCS Sublibrary: SL1 – Theoretical Computer Science and General Issues

This Springer imprint is published by the registered company Springer Nature Switzerland AG
The registered company address is: Gewerbestrasse 11, 6330 Cham, Switzerland

Preface

The present volume contains the invited contributions and a selection of papers presented at the 19th International Conference on Membrane Computing (CMC 19), which was held in Dresden, Germany, during September 4–7, 2018 (further information can be found on the website at the following address: http://cmc19.uni-jena.de/) as well as one selected paper from the Workshop on Membrane Computing that was held in Fontainebleau, France, on June 25, 2018 (website address: https://ucnc2018.lacl.fr/wmc-ucnc-2018/) as a satellite event of the UCNC conference (Unconventional Computation and Natural Computation).

The CMC series started with three workshops that were organized in Curtea de Argeş, Romania, in 2000, 2001, and 2002. The workshops were then held in Tarragona, Spain (2003), Milan, Italy (2004), Vienna, Austria (2005), Leiden, The Netherlands (2006), Thessaloniki, Greece (2007), and in Edinburgh, UK (2008).

The tenth edition was organized again in Curtea de Argeş, in 2009, where it was decided to continue the series as the Conference on Membrane Computing (CMC). The following editions were held in Jena, Germany (2010), Fontainebleau, France (2011), Budapest, Hungary (2012), Chişinău, Moldova (2013), Prague, Czech Republic (2014), Valencia, Spain (2015), Milan, Italy (2016), and Bradford, UK (2017).

A regional version of CMC, the Asian Conference on Membrane Computing, ACMC, started in 2012 in Wuhan (China), and continued in Chengdu, China (2013), Coimbatore, India (2014), Hefei, Anhui, China (2015), Bangi, Selangor, Malaysia (2016), and Chengdu, (China), 2017.

CMC 19 was organized, under the auspices of the International Membrane Computing Society, by the Friedrich Schiller University of Jena, Germany.

The invited lectures were given by Erzsébet Csuhaj-Varjú (ELTE Eötvös Loránd University, Budapest, Hungary), Alberto Leporati (University Milan-Bicocca, Italy), Gheorghe Păun (Romanian Academy, Bucharest, Romania), Thomas Preußer (Accemic Technologies GmbH Dresden, Germany), and Stefan Schuster (Friedrich Schiller University Jena, Germany).

The Best Student Paper Award, sponsored by Springer, was given to the paper "Testing Identifiable Kernel P Systems Using an X-machine Approach," by Marian Gheorghe, Florentin Ipate, Raluca Lefticaru, and Ana Turlea.

The Best Paper Award was given to the paper "Solving QSAT in Sublinear Depth," by Alberto Leporati, Luca Manzoni, Giancarlo Mauri, Antonio E. Porreca, and Claudio Zandron.

The editors express their gratitude to the Program Committee, the invited speakers, the authors of the papers, the reviewers, and all the participants for their contributions to the success of CMC 19.

The support of the Friedrich Schiller University of Jena and the prize for the Best Student Paper award granted by Springer are gratefully acknowledged.

December 2018

Thomas Hinze
Grzegorz Rozenberg
Arto Salomaa
Claudio Zandron

Organization

Steering Committee of CMC and ACMC

Henry Adorna	Quezon City, Philippines
Artiom Alhazov	Chişinău, Moldova
Bogdan Aman	Iaşi, Romania
Matteo Cavaliere	Edinburgh, UK
Erzsébet Csuhaj-Varjú	Budapest, Hungary
Rudolf Freund	Vienna, Austria
Marian Gheorghe (Honorary Member)	Bradford, UK
Thomas Hinze	Jena, Germany
Florentin Ipate	Bucharest, Romania
Shankara N. Krishna	Bombay, India
Alberto Leporati	Milan, Italy
Taishin Y. Nishida	Toyama, Japan
Linqiang Pan (Co-chair)	Wuhan, China
Gheorghe Păun (Honorary Member)	Bucharest, Romania
Mario J. Pérez-Jiménez	Seville, Spain
Agustín Riscos-Núñez	Seville, Spain
Petr Sosík	Opava, Czech Republic
Kumbakonam Govindarajan Subramanian	Penang, Malaysia
György Vaszil	Debrecen, Hungary
Sergey Verlan	Paris, France
Claudio Zandron (Co-chair)	Milan, Italy
Gexiang Zhang	Chengdu, China

Organizing Committee of CMC 19

Thomas Hinze	Jena and Dresden, Germany
Jörn Behre	Jena, Germany

Program Committee of CMC 19

Henry Adorna	Quezon City, Philippines
Bogdan Aman	Iasi, Romania
Jörn Behre	Jena, Germany
Matteo Cavaliere	Manchester, UK
Erzsébet Csuhaj-Varjú	Budapest, Hungary
Lucas Eberhardt	Leipzig, Germany

Abstracts of Invited Papers

Membrane Computing, After Twenty Years (Extended Abstract)

Gheorghe Păun

Romanian Academy, Bucureşti, Romania
gpaun@us.es, curteadelaarges@gmail.com

1 A Quick View over MC

The presentation will be a quick glimpse on the evolution of membrane computing, with an autobiographical character, starting with the initial motivation, briefly describing the main research directions, the bibliography, the dedicated meetings, the more active research groups.

A special attention is pais to the recently organized International Membrane Computing Society, its *Bulletin* (available at http://membranecomputing.net/IMCSBulletin/) and the forthcoming *Journal of Membrane Computing* (JMeC), to be published by Springer-Verlag (www.springer.com/41965, waiting for submissions at www.editorialmanager.com/JMEC).

Membrane computing is a research area (a branch of natural computing) aiming to abstract computing models from the structure and the functioning of the biological cell, considered alone or cooperating in tissues, colonies (e.g., of bacteria), organs (in particular, the brain). A large variety of models (called P systems) is obtained, most of them equivalent in power with the Turing machine; for many classes of P systems (especially, but not only when possibilities to create an exponential workspace in a polynomial time is provided, e.g., by means of cell division), then computationally hard problems (typically, **NP**-complete problems) can be solved in a feasible time (polynomial, or even linear). Several applications were reported (biology and bio-medicine, ecology, approximate optimization/distributed evolutionary computing, economics, linguistics, robot control and other technology issues, cryptography, computer graphics, and so on) and several software products were developed, including a dedicated programming language, *P-lingua*.

Three yearly dedicated international meetings are organized: *Conference on Membrane Computing - CMC* (from 2000 to 2009 it was called *Workshop on Membrane Computing WMC*, and from 2019 on *European CMC - ECMC*), the *Asian Conference on Membrane Computing - ACMC*, and the *Brainstorming Week on Membrane Computing - BWMC*. Also a *Workshop on Membrane Computing* started recently to be organized in China.

The bibliography of the domain is rather large: over 2500 papers, more than 100 PhD theses, about 10 monographs, about 50 collective volumes and special issues of journals – including the comprehensive *The Oxford Handbook of Membrane Computing*, OUP, 2010.

Although so developed, membrane computing is still an active research area, with many open problems and research directions waiting for further efforts. Among the branches of this kind, I mention here spiking neural P systems, numerical P systems, generalizations (such as kernel P systems), complexity issues, hypercomputation, membrane algorithms, software and implementation (e.g., on dedicated or on parallel existing hardware), applications in general - and especially in biology related areas.

2 Basic References in MC

A comprehensive source of information in MC is the website from http://ppage. psystems.eu hosted in Vienna, Austria: bibliographies, addresses of authors and groups, software, conferences, and so on. (Before it, a similar site was hosted in Milan, Italy, at http://psystems.disco.unimib.it.)

Here are a few **papers** (chronologically ordered) where various types of P systems were introduced:

1. Gh. Păun: Computing with Membranes. *Journal of Computer and System Sciences*, 61, 1 (2000), 108–143, and *Turku Center for Computer Science-TUCS Report* No 208, 1998 (www.tucs.fi).
2. Gh. Păun: P systems with active membranes: Attacking NP-complete problems, *J. Automata, Languages, and Combinatorics*, 6, 1 (2001), 75–90.
3. Andrei Păun, Gh. Păun: The power of communication: P systems with symport/antiport, *New Generation Computing*, 20, 3 (2002), 295–306.
4. Carlos Martín-Vide, Juan Pazos, Gh. Păun, Alfonso Rodriguez-Patón: Tissue P systems, *Theoretical Computer Sci.*, 296, 2 (2003), 295–326.
5. Gh. Păun, Radu Păun: Membrane computing and economics: Numerical P systems, *Fundamenta Informaticae*, 73, 1–2 (2006), 213–227.
6. Mihai Ionescu, Gh. Păun, Takashi Yokomori: Spiking neural P systems, *Fundamenta Informaticae*, 71, 2–3 (2006), 279–308.
7. Gh. Păun, Mario J. Pérez-Jiménez: Solving problems in a distributed way in membrane computing: dP systems, *Int. J. of Computers, Communication and Control*, 5, 2 (2010), 238–252.

I mention only these papers because I am involved in them and because they introduced solid research directions in MC; of course, there are several other research directions which deserve to be mentioned (similarly, they deserve to be mentioned the initiating papers), but the reader is referred to the MC bibliography for references: colonies, population, kernel, multi environment, polymorphic P systems, membrane algorithms, generalizations, arrays or other complex objects, formal verification and model checking, semantics and algebraic approaches, and so on and so forth.

Part of these issues can be found in the **monographs and collective volumes** in this area (including the massive handbook – number 5 below): I mention most of them – without conference volumes or special issues of journals devoted to MC:

1. Gh. Păun: *Membrane Computing. An Introduction.* Springer, 2002 (translated in Chinese in 2012).
2. Gabriel Ciobanu, Gh. Păun, M.J. Pérez-Jiménez, eds.: *Applications of Membrane Computing.* Springer, 2006.
3. Pierluigi Frisco: *Computing with Cells. Advances in Membrane Computing.* Oxford Univ. Press, 2009.
4. Gabriel Ciobanu: *Membrane Computing. Biologically Inspired Process Calculi.* The Publ. House of Al.I. Cuza Univ., Iaşi, 2010.
5. Gh. Păun, Grzegorz Rozenberg, Arto Salomaa, eds.: *The Oxford Handbook of Membrane Computing.* Oxford Univ. Press, 2010.
6. Vincenzo Manca: *Infobiotics. Information in Biotic Systems.* Springer, 2013.
7. Pierluigi Frisco, Marian Gheorghe, Mario J. Pérez-Jiménez, eds.: *Applications of Membrane Computing in Systems and Synthetic Biology.* Springer, 2014.
8. Gexiang Zhang, Jixiang Cheng, Tao Wang, Xueyuan Wang, Jie Zhu: *Membrane Computing: Theory and Applications.* Science Press, Beijing, 2015.
9. Gexiang Zhang, M.J. Pérez-Jiménez, M. Gheorghe: *Real-Life Applications with Membrane Computing.* Springer, 2017.
10. Andrei George Florea, Cătălin Buiu: *Membrane Computing for Distributed Control of Robotic Swarms: Emerging Research and Opportunities*, IGI Global, 2017.

Recent (hence comprehensive) bibliographies of several branches of MC as well as several lists of open problems can be found in the *Bulletin of IMCS*, at http://membranecomputing.net/IMCSBulletin/.

Algebra Meets Biology

Stefan Schuster

Matthias Schleiden Institute, Department of Bioinformatics,
Friedrich Schiller University, Ernst-Abbe-Platz 2, 07743 Jena, Germany
stefan.schu@uni-jena.de

Abstract. Fibonacci numbers and the Golden Section occur in many instances in Biology. We have recently found that the potential number of fatty acids increases with their chain length according to the famous Fibonacci series, when *cis/trans* isomerism is neglected. Since the ratio of two consecutive Fibonacci numbers tends to the Golden section, 1.618…, organisms can increase fatty acid variability approximately by that factor per carbon atom invested. Moreover, we show that, under consideration of *cis/trans* isomerism, modification by hydroxy and/or oxo groups, triple bonds or adjacent double bonds, diversity can be described by generalized Fibonacci numbers (e.g. Pell numbers). Similar calculations can be applied to aliphatic amino acids. Our results should be of interest for mass spectrometry, combinatorial chemistry, synthetic biology, patent applications, use of fatty acids as biomarkers and the theory of evolution.

A second example of the role of algebra in biology discussed in this talk concerns intracellular calcium oscillations. Such oscillations are transformed (in a sense, decoded) in the cell by phosphorylation of proteins. In this way, an approximate temporal integral of the signal is computed. This implies that the number of spikes in the oscillation can be counted. In plant cells, an effect is often triggered only if a certain number of spikes (e.g., five) occurred. Some techniques for the mathematical modelling of such phenomena are reviewed here.

References

1. Schuster, S., Fichtner, M., Sasso, S.: Use of Fibonacci numbers in lipidomics – Enumerating various classes of fatty acids. Sci. Rep. **7**, 39821 (2017)
2. Fichtner, M., Voigt, K., Schuster, S.: The tip and hidden part of the iceberg: proteinogenic and non-proteinogenic aliphatic amino acids. Biochim. Biophys. Acta - Gen. Subj. **1861**, 3258–3269 (2017)
3. Bodenstein, C., Knoke, B., Marhl, M., Perc, M., Schuster, S.: Using Jensen's inequality to explain the role of regular calcium oscillations in protein activation. Phys. Biol. **7**, 036009 (2010)

Contents

Invited Papers

Impacts of Membrane Computing on Theoretical Computer Science (Extended Abstract)

Erzsébet Csuhaj-Varjú[✉]

Department of Algorithms and Their Applications,
Faculty of Informatics, ELTE Eötvös Loránd University,
Pázmány Péter sétány 1/c, Budapest 1117, Hungary
csuhaj@inf.elte.hu

Abstract. We present some ideas about impacts of Membrane Computing, a vivid research area of Natural Computing, on Theoretical Computer Science.

1 Introduction

This extended abstract was prepared on the base of ideas of the talk "How Membrane Computing Influences Theoretical Computer Science?", presented by the author at the Nineteenth International Conference on Membrane Computing, CMC19, 4–7, September, 2018, Dresden, Germany.

Membrane Computing has been an active research area since 1998 when the notion of a membrane system (later also called a P system) was introduced by Gheorghe Păun (the seminal paper was published in 2000, [8]). The original concept aimed at providing a distributed computing device inspired by architecture and functioning of living cells. Later the notion was extended to model the organization of cells in tissues, neural systems, organs, or in higher order structures like colonies of bacteria.

In the last decades, there has been an increasing demand for computing devices and computational methods which exceed the boundaries of Turing machines and significantly differ from them from the point of view of architecture and functioning. This is due to, among others, technological and social challenges as the need for treating extremely huge amount of data, having tools for efficient information and data processing in large networks, or simulation of large complex systems.

Natural Computing attempts to provide approaches to solving these problems. By [4], it is "the field of research that investigates models and computational techniques inspired by nature and, dually, attempts to understand the world around us in terms of information processing". Subfields of natural computing are motivated by various natural phenomena: self-reproduction, functioning of brain, characteristics of life, group behavior, cell membranes, tissue organization, only to mention a few. Examples for scientific areas that belong

© Springer Nature Switzerland AG 2019
T. Hinze et al. (Eds.): CMC 2018, LNCS 11399, pp. 3–9, 2019.
https://doi.org/10.1007/978-3-030-12797-8_1

to (or belong in part to) Natural Computing are Cellular Automata, Neural Networks, Evolutionary Computation, Swarm Intelligence, Artificial Life, DNA Computing, and Membrane Computing.

2 P Systems

A P system (a membrane system) consists of the membrane structure (a virtual graph, originally a tree), multisets of objects that are placed in the compartments (nodes) of the membrane structure, and rules that describe the change of the objects in the compartments (including communication) and the change of the membrane structure. In the standard, tree-like case compartments are usually called regions. The actual configuration (the actual state) of a P system consists of the current membrane structure and the current multisets of objects in the compartments. Using its rules and the prescribed way of rule application, the P system changes its states. A sequence of configurations starting from the so-called initial state, directly following each other and ending with a halting state is called a computation. A state of the membrane system is halting if no rule of the system can be applied. The way of the application of rules is called the computation mode. P systems are usually used as computing devices. The result of the computation usually is the number of objects in a distinguished compartment, the output region, but the number of objects which leave the system in the course of computation can also be considered as result.

These characteristics describe the generic model that has been extended or modified in various manner; the reader may find a lot of variants in the literature.

In the following, we provide the reader with a brief description of certain important variants of membrane systems and their properties, based on summaries [3,5,9,10]. We note that our summary is given without the aim of completeness.

P systems can operate with different types of objects as symbols, strings, spikes, arrays, trees which can be located in the regions (in the compartments), in the nodes, on the membranes separating the regions, on the edges of the underlying graph of the P system. The data structures built from objects are usually multisets or sets (languages). (We note that the objects of the same P system are of the same type.) The form of the rules used to change the multisets of objects and their locations can be multiset rewriting rules, communication rules, rules with membrane creation, division, dissolution, or can be spike processing, and several other variants. The application of these rules can be controlled in various manner: by catalyst objects, by priority, by promoters and/or inhibitors, or so-called channels. The membrane architecture can be cell-like (tree), tissue-like (arbitrary graph), and tissue-like with static or dynamic communication channels (population P systems). The membrane structure can be static or dynamically changing under functioning, or it can be precomputed. The membrane system works in discrete time steps driven by a clock; these steps can be synchronized, or asynchronous, or time-free.

Usually, the rules can be applied in the so-called maximally parallel manner (roughly, as many rule is applied in parallel as possible), but there are other computation modes as well: minimal parallelism, bounded parallelism, sequential rule application, etc.

Successful computation can be defined by global halting, local halting, final states. The P systems can work in generating or in accepting mode, the types of the output can be sets of numbers, set of vectors of numbers, languages, or yes/no answers.

During the years, P systems have been investigated from various points of view. A lot of research has been devoted to their computing power, computational complexity (computational efficiency), descriptional complexity, normal forms, hierarchies. Several implementations have been made, and P systems have been related to algorithms, modelling, simulations, semantics, model checking, verifications, dynamical systems, and other research fields or directions.

Applications of P systems have been demonstrated in, among others, Biology/Biomedicine, Ecosystems, Economics, Optimization, Computer Graphics, Linguistics, Cryptography, and further fields of Computer Science.

P systems demonstrate structural and functional similarities to other models in Computer Science, thus they have been related to Petri nets, process algebra, X-machines, lambda calculus, ambient calculus, brane calculi, etc.

3 Membrane Computing and Theoretical Computer Science

Most of the variants of membrane systems are distributed multiset processing systems that work in a massively parallel manner. These basic properties would not be sufficient to maintain the permanent interest in investigating P systems and their applications in different areas. Membrane systems have further significant characteristics. Since P systems have been inspired by Biology, Bio-Chemistry and several other scientific areas in natural and social sciences, Membrane Computing abstracts and adopts concepts or methods in the motivating areas into its rigorous mathematical framework. This fact implies that Membrane Computing and Theoretical Computer Science are connected.

Theoretical Computer Science is a research area that belongs to both Computer Science (general computer science) and Mathematics. It focuses on (more) mathematical aspects and topics of computing and treat problems with mathematical rigour. Research areas that belong to theoretical computer science are, among others: Algorithms, Data Structures, Foundations of Computing, Computational Complexity, Parallel and Distributed Computation, Information Theory, Cryptography, Program Semantics and Verification, Machine Learning, etc.

What kind of the impacts Membrane Computing on Theoretical Computer Science can have? How Membrane Computing influences developments in Theoretical Computer Science? Recently, it is difficult to provide any precise answer to these question. However, by the developments in P Systems Theory some observations can be made.

Membrane Computing, by using non-standard, unconventional approaches can contribute to better understand the nature of (classical) computational models, algorithms, computing, and it can introduce new, more efficient, more complex models, equivalent to classical computational models of Theoretical Computer Science. P Systems Theory can also provide non-standard tools to solve problems for certain well-known problems in Theoretical Computer Science.

4   Impacts of Membrane Computing on Theoretical Computer Science

A lot of research has been devoted to study P systems as computing devices, in particular to those variants which are as powerful as Turing machines. Many classes of P systems are able to simulate Turing machines, and a lot of proofs are based on simulating register machines. Since these proofs are constructive, universal P systems (in the same sense as universal Turing machines) can also be obtained. As a consequence, these membrane system variants are programmable devices. These investigations have contributed to understand better what computation and universal computing devices, in particular register (counter) machines mean. (For more information the reader is referred to [3, 9, 10].)

During the years, it has also been established that membrane systems are not only powerful computing devices, but their computing efficiency is rather high. For example, due to their construction and usually used functioning (computation) mode (massive parallelism) they are suitable for solving computationally hard problems in a feasible time. Furthermore, the large power and efficiency can be obtained with P systems having restricted, small syntactic complexity parameters. Studying P systems as computing devices certainly enhanced the tool set of Theoretical Computer Science and contributed to developing new approaches to Turing complete computing devices. For computational complexity aspects of Membrane Computing, the reader is referred to [10] and the recent literature. In this subfield, a large amount of important results have been obtained and complexity concepts have been developed in terms of P systems.

The applicability of membrane systems in several other areas of Theoretical Computer Science has also been demonstrated. Well-known algorithms were interpreted in P Systems Theory, Boolean circuits, several well-known parallel architectures have been represented in terms of membrane system. Links of P systems to Petri nets, process algebra, X-machines have been examined. The interested reader is referred to consult the corresponding chapters and parts of [2, 10] and the recent literature.

5   Examples for New Approaches

We briefly describe two cases where characteristics of P systems inspire new approaches in Theoretical Computer Science.

Membrane algorithms were introduced as a new type of approximate algorithms applying P systems theory to evolutionary computing [7,10]. The basic idea was to use membrane computing in devising approximate algorithms for hard optimization problems, as a new class of distributed evolutionary algorithms. The concept is the following: candidate solutions evolve in compartments of a (dynamically changing) membrane structure according to their own local algorithms. The better solutions move down in the membrane structure. When a specified halting condition holds, the current best solution is extracted as the result of the algorithm. This notion enhances the concept of the evolutionary algorithms, since membrane algorithms are high level evolutionary algorithms which are distributed and their structure dynamically evolves during the computation.

P automata are purely communicating, accepting variants of P systems which combine properties of classical automata and membrane systems. Briefly, a P automaton is a P system receiving input in each computational step from its environment which affects its operation, by changing its configuration and thus, affects its functioning. Certain sequences of inputs are distinguished as accepted sequences. The input is given as a multiset of objects. The P system that receives the input is called the underlying P system of the P automaton. Usually, the underlying P system is an antiport P systems, a P system with only communication. The accepted multiset sequences of a P automaton can be encoded to strings, thus making possible to assign languages to the P automaton. It is shown that P automata working sequential mode describe languages that can be computed by Turing machines with restricted logarithmic space, and P automata working in the maximally parallel mode describe context-sensitive languages. Some variants of P automata are Turing complete. (For more information we refer to the corresponding chapter of [10].)

Similarities between P automata and classical automata can immediately be noticed, but differences between the two types of constructs can also easily be observed: for example, classical automata have separate state sets while in the case of P automata the actual state is represented by the actual configuration of the underlying P system. Another property which makes P automata different from classical automata is that the workspace that they can use for computation is provided by the objects of the already consumed input multisets. The objects which enter the system become part of the description of the machine, that is, the input, the object of the computation and the machine which executes the computation cannot be separated as it can be done in the case of usual automata in Theoretical Computer Science. We note that these properties resemble properties of natural processes. Natural processes, in particular bio-processes can be considered as computational processes with the following characteristics: Usually, the object of the computation and the "machine" which executes the computation cannot be separated and it can use only existing objects for computation. Natural processes are not necessarily composed from a set of elements bounded by a constant. Notice that P automata also have this property.

In addition to Turing equivalent models, membrane computing also provides P systems "going beyond Turing". Examples for these computing devices are red-green P automata [1]. The concept is the counterpart of the notion of red-green Turing machines [6]. In case of red-green Turing machines the set of states is divided into two disjoint sets: red states and green states. Acceptance and recognizability of finite strings by a red-green Turing machine are defined via infinite runs of the machine on the input string and the way how to distinguish between red and green states. Via infinite runs that are allowed to change between red and green states more than once, more than the recursively enumerable sets of strings can be obtained, i.e., we can "go beyond Turing".

6   Conclusions

Although only a few models and concepts of membrane computing were briefly recalled in this extended abstract, the reader can see that they contribute to extend the boundaries, enhance the semantics of certain important standard, classical computing models and methods in Theoretical Computer Science. The new approaches can launch new research fields as well. Possible new research directions are expected in utilizing the fact that parts of P Systems Theory can be considered as subfields of the theory of multiset rewriting systems. Further connections between Membrane Computing and Data Science are expected to be explored; the multiset of objects in the compartments can be considered as multisets of data, thus they can be investigated by tools of Data Science as well. Other challenging areas, connected to Theoretical Computer Science are P systems with infinite computations (hypercomputation) or numerical P systems. Finally, complexity theory of P systems is expected to provide further new, significant results, to help better understand how complexity notions, concepts can be formalized.

Acknowledgement. This work was supported by the National Research, Development, and Innovation Office - NKFIH, Hungary, Grant no. K 120558.

References

1. Aman, B., Csuhaj-Varjú, E., Freund, R.: Red–Green P automata. In: Gheorghe, M., Rozenberg, G., Salomaa, A., Sosík, P., Zandron, C. (eds.) CMC 2014. LNCS, vol. 8961, pp. 139–157. Springer, Cham (2014). https://doi.org/10.1007/978-3-319-14370-5_9
2. Gheorghe, M., Păun, G., Pérez-Jiménez, M.-J., Rozenberg, G.: Research frontiers of membrane computing: open problems and research topics. Int. J. Found. Comput. Sci. 24(5), 547–624 (2013)
3. Ibarra, O.H., Păun, G.: Membrane computing - a general view. Ann. Eur. Acad. Sci. (2006–2007), 83–101 (2007)
4. Kari, L., Rozenberg, G.: The many facets of natural computing. Commun. ACM 51(10), 72–83 (2008)

5. Krishna, S.N.: An overview of membrane computing. In: Natarajan, R., Ojo, A. (eds.) ICDCIT 2011. LNCS, vol. 6536, pp. 1–14. Springer, Heidelberg (2011). https://doi.org/10.1007/978-3-642-19056-8_1
6. van Leeuwen, J., Wiedermann, J.: Computation as an unbounded process. Theor. Comput. Sci. **429**, 202–212 (2012)
7. Nishida, T.Y.: Membrane algorithms. In: Freund, R., Păun, G., Rozenberg, G., Salomaa, A. (eds.) WMC 2005. LNCS, vol. 3850, pp. 55–66. Springer, Heidelberg (2006). https://doi.org/10.1007/11603047_4
8. Păun, G.: Computing with membranes. J. Comput. Syst. Sci. **61**(1), 108–143 (2000)
9. Păun, G.: From cells to (silicon) computers, and back. In: Cooper, B.S., Lowe, B., Sorbi, A. (eds.) New Computational Paradigms. Changing Conceptions of what is Computable, pp. 343–371. Springer, New York (2008). https://doi.org/10.1007/978-0-387-68546-5_15
10. Păun, G., Rozenberg, G., Salomaa, A. (eds.): The Oxford Handbook of Membrane Computing. Oxford University Press Inc., New York (2010)

Time and Space Complexity of P Systems — And Why They Matter

Alberto Leporati[✉]

Dipartimento di Informatica, Sistemistica e Comunicazione,
Università degli Studi di Milano-Bicocca,
Viale Sarca 336/14, 20126 Milano, Italy
alberto.leporati@unimib.it

Abstract. Computational complexity theory allows one to investigate the amount of resources (usually, time and/or space) which are needed to solve a given computational problem. Indeed, since the appearance of P systems several computational complexity techniques have been applied to study their computational power and efficiency. In this paper, starting from some results which have been obtained in the last few years by the group of Membrane Computing at the University of Milan-Bicocca (also known as the "Milano Team"), sometimes in collaboration with colleagues from the Membrane Computing community, I will make some observations on what is the relevance (in my opinion) of time and space complexity theory for P systems. Speaking about the results, I will focus in particular on the *ideas* lying behind them, without delving into technical details. I will also comment on the importance of these results for applications, such as modelling complex systems and implementing decentralized applications. I will finally conclude with some (somewhat provocative) connections with other Computer Science subjects, related with Cryptography, Computer and Network Security, and Decentralized Applications.

1 Introduction

P systems constitute an incredibly rich and interesting framework for defining parallel and distributed models of computation. Since their introduction in 1998 (see [20] for the first presentation of P systems in a peer-reviewed scientific journal), several variants have been proposed, among which symport/antiport, tissue-like, neural-like and numerical P systems. Most of these variants are synchronous, but also asynchronous versions of P systems have been defined.

Computational complexity theory can be used to study the computing capabilities and the computational features of these systems, usually with two goals in mind: (1) understanding what kind of problems can or cannot be solved, and (2) how much time and space the P systems need to solve a given problem. We thus discover very soon that most of the P systems mentioned above have the same computing power of Turing machines – and hence are also *universal* – usually even with a very small number of cells. Indeed, one of the research lines

© Springer Nature Switzerland AG 2019
T. Hinze et al. (Eds.): CMC 2018, LNCS 11399, pp. 10–22, 2019.
https://doi.org/10.1007/978-3-030-12797-8_2

which have been most successful since the appearance of P systems is the investigation of what combinations of computational features – such as the number of membranes, the number of polarizations, the number of objects moved by communication rules – constitute a *border* for Turing-completeness, in the sense that P systems are Turing-complete with those features but are less powerful than Turing machines without them. Similarly, also *complexity borders* are investigated: What computational features do allow to solve in polynomial time (that is, in an efficient way) computationally hard (**NP**-complete, **PSPACE**-complete, ...) problems? Finally, another area of investigation concerns the use of P systems as a modelling tool, for the simulation of physical and natural systems; indeed, as Konur et al. say in [9], computational models in general (and P systems in particular) are perceived as an attractive alternative to mathematical models, such as ordinary differential equations.

In this paper – related with the invited talk I have given at CMC 19 in Dresden – I will mainly cover the second aspect, that is, the role of computational complexity in the study of P systems. I will not delve into the technical details, but I will instead discuss over the significance, both at the theoretical level and in the view of possible applications, of complexity theory in the area of P systems.

2   First Considerations

Establishing the computing power of a model of P systems is usually performed through *simulations*, basing upon the fact that if a model A is able to simulate a model B, then A is at least as powerful as B. So, many simulations of Turing machines, register machines, Petri nets, and Boolean circuits by (some variant of) P systems have been presented in the literature. So doing, very soon one realizes that it is very easy to obtain the computational power of Turing machines. Consider *deterministic register machines*, whose programs are ordered lists of instructions of the following two types:

- $j : (INC(r), k)$, with $j, k \in \{0, 1, \ldots, m - 1\}$ and $r \in \{0, 1, \ldots, n - 1\}$
  This instruction, labelled with j, increments the value contained in register r, and then jumps to instruction k.
- $j : (DEC(r), k, l)$, with $j, k, l \in \{0, 1, \ldots, m - 1\}$ and $r \in \{0, 1, \ldots, n - 1\}$
  If the value contained in register r is positive then decrement it and jump to instruction k. If the value of r is zero then jump to instruction l (without altering the contents of the register).

Here m is the number of instructions in the program, and n is the number of registers. Each register contains a non-negative integer number. Computations start by executing the first instruction (labelled with 0), and terminate when the instruction currently executed tries to jump to label m. For a formal definition of *configurations* and *computations* we refer the reader to [4]. As stated in [4, Proposition 1], deterministic register machines provide a simple universal computational model. Hence, to prove that a P system reaches the computing power of Turing machines it just suffices to simulate deterministic register machines.

In particular, the ability to test whether the value stored in a register is zero or positive (implicitly used in the DEC instruction) turns out to be the key for reaching Turing-completeness.

So, since Turing machines and register machines are *universal*, also the P systems which are able to simulate them are universal too. This means that they can simulate any other P system, albeit in a very *indirect* way: Given a universal P system U_Π, and another P system Π to be simulated, the simulation is performed as follows:

– Π is encoded as a positive integer number in a non-ambiguous and appropriate way, and then it is given as input to a register machine R_Π that simulates it, using an appropriate program;
– each increment and decrement operation of R_Π is then simulated by the universal P system U_Π.

As far as I know, no class of P systems that contains a universal P system U_Π which is able to simulate any other P system Π of the same class in a *direct* way – that is, by feeding an encoded version of Π as input to U_Π, without passing from the simulation of any other intermediate universal computation model – has been proposed in the literature. In my opinion, this constitutes an interesting open problem.

Since many variants of P systems are Turing-complete, in principle we can use them to compute *anything*. But passing from theory to practice presents many problems. Think about the applications we have mentioned above: Imagine we have a physical system to be simulated, because we want to investigate some property of its dynamics. So we encode the system description as a positive integer number in a non-ambiguous way, and we define a register machine which is able to simulate it (this requires implementing the simulation algorithm as a program for a register machine); finally, we simulate the register machine with a P system of the chosen family. Clearly, this process is unsatisfactory from many points of view. First of all, programming a register machine can be a tedious task; then, when we encode the physical system as an integer number we loose information about its structure and the relationships between the parts that compose it. Finally, the working of the register machine (and thus of the simulating P system) may not be intuitive at all. Consider, for example, the (small) universal register machine defined in [10] and reported in Fig. 1. Being universal, this register machine can compute anything, but how does it work? Understanding the dynamic behavior of this system – as well as of many other universal systems – may be difficult. Even representing each increment and decrement instruction as nodes of a graph, and the jumps between instructions as edges between the nodes (see Fig. 2) does not help. Last, but not the least, so doing the whole simulation is performed in a *sequential* way, rather than in parallel. The reason why we would like to use P systems to perform these kinds of simulations is that they are a *parallel* and *distributed* model of computation; moreover, they are by far more *expressive* than register machines or even Turing machines. This expressiveness could be pushed even further, in my opinion, by designing a *descriptive language* that is able to describe the features of the applicative

$0 : (DEC(1), 1, 2)$ $1 : (INC(7), 0)$

$2 : (INC(6), 3)$ $3 : (DEC(5), 2, 4)$

$4 : (DEC(6), 5, 3)$ $5 : (INC(5), 6)$

$6 : (DEC(7), 7, 8)$ $7 : (INC(1), 4)$

$8 : (DEC(6), 9, 0)$ $9 : (INC(6), 10)$

$10 : (DEC(4), 0, 11)$ $11 : (DEC(5), 12, 13)$

$12 : (DEC(5), 14, 15)$ $13 : (DEC(2), 18, 19)$

$14 : (DEC(5), 16, 17)$ $15 : (DEC(3), 18, 20)$

$16 : (INC(4), 11)$ $17 : (INC(2), 21)$

$18 : (DEC(4), 0, 22)$ $19 : (DEC(0), 0, 18)$

$20 : (INC(0), 0)$ $21 : (INC(3), 18)$

Fig. 1. The small universal deterministic register machine defined in [10]

domain, and that can be "compiled" to working P systems. Of course, such a high-level language should be able to describe communicating processes that are executed in parallel.

Another difficulty is that determining the dynamic properties of a Turing-complete system is in general *undecidable*, hence it becomes impossible to reason about the behavior of the system: will an object of some type ever be inside a region of the P system? Will the number of elements of the physical system under simulation go over or under certain thresholds? Will the value of a given register of a register machine be an odd number?

For all these reasons, *non-universal* systems are much more interesting both from a theoretical and from an applicative point of view. This leads us to the focus of this paper: the role of computational complexity. When we investigate about the possibility to solve in polynomial time a computationally hard problem, say an **NP**-complete problem, we are indeed looking whether the computational features of our P systems allow them to cross the border between *tractability* (the realm of problems that can be solved in polynomial time) and *intractability*. Albeit the techniques used to prove or disprove that such a border can be crossed are quite different from the case of Turing-completeness, the two kinds of results share some similarities: in the case of Turing-completeness we ask whether we can solve all recursively enumerable problems (that form the so called class **RE**), whereas in the case of **NP**-completeness (**PSPACE**-completeness, etc.) we ask whether we can solve all the problems in the complexity class **NP** (**PSPACE**, etc., respectively).

Another merit of computational complexity is that sometimes it is able to tell us what kind of problems we can solve with a given model of computation, and – even more importantly – what kind of problems we *cannot* solve. This may be an important help in case we have a problem, and we want to try to solve it with a given model of computation: if it is known that such kind of problems cannot be solved, we can avoid trying and save a lot of unnecessary time and effort.

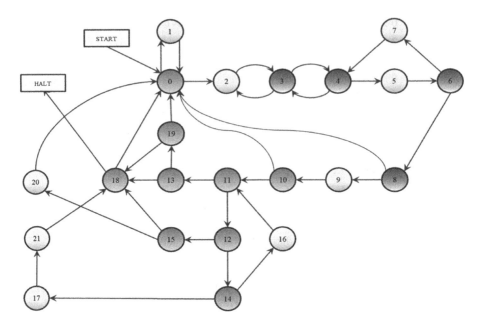

Fig. 2. A graph representation of the jumps between the instructions of Fig. 1. Increment instructions are drawn as blue nodes, while decrement instructions are depicted in light brown (Color figure online)

A comparative example which involves Boolean circuits is instructive: let us assume that you are asked (or would like) to compute the PARITY Boolean function with a family of polynomial-size constant-depth AND/OR/NOT Boolean circuits. The n-input PARITY function is simply the XOR between its inputs: $\text{PARITY}(x_1, \ldots, x_n) = x_1 \oplus \ldots \oplus x_n$, so the problem does not seem difficult at all. However, as proved in [5] this task is actually *impossible*: there is no family of polynomial-size constant-depth AND/OR/NOT circuits that can compute the PARITY function.

Of course, the answers given by computational complexity are not precise and should be taken with care and criticism. The fact that a problem can be solved in polynomial time *does not mean* at all that the problem can be *practically* solved. After all, even *constant* complexity may be inaccessible when implemented in practice: think about Cryptography, where *computational security* is often reached through functions that could be inverted (meaning that a valid input value can be determined) in a constant amount of time steps, thus breaking the system. For example, if we have a plaintext message and a corresponding ciphertext message computed using the standard symmetric cryptosystem AES-128, then a brute-force attack that recovers the secret key takes at most 2^{128} time steps: we just try to encrypt the plaintext message with every possible key, and compare the result with the ciphertext message. This attack requires a constant number of time steps, but it is inaccessible in practice.

Also, we must take into account the fact that using a *non-universal* model of computation for which the dynamic properties are decidable, does not imply that determining such properties is a feasible task: the corresponding problem could be decidable but (for example) **NP**-complete, and thus once again inaccessible. As an example, in [16] it is shown that deciding whether a neuron will fire in the next computation step – in a spiking neural P system that uses arbitrary regular expressions – may entail solving an **NP**-complete problem.

In the next sections I will make some considerations – and recall some results obtained recently by the so called "Milano Team" – about the time and space complexity of P systems. I will consider in particular time complexity problems defined over spiking neural P systems, and space complexity problems related to P systems with active membranes. I will finally conclude this paper by proposing some connections between the theory of Membrane Computing and other Computer Science subjects, related with Cryptography, Computer and Network Security, and Decentralized Applications.

3   Time Complexity: The Case of Spiking Neural P Systems

To speak about *time* complexity, I will consider spiking neural P systems (SN P systems, for short) as the reference model. The definition and working of these systems is inspired from the way biological neurons communicate by means of *spikes*, electrical impulses of identical shape. Since their introduction [7], the possibility to use them for solving computationally difficult problems has been extensively studied: see for example Chap. 23 of [23] for a comprehensive review, as well [31] for further recent developments.

In my talk, after briefly recalling the relevant definitions taken from [7], I have discussed how to solve the **NP**-complete problems SAT and SUBSET SUM by SN P systems, as explained in [14]. In particular, due to the fact that SN P systems take their input in unary form, it is interesting to see how they can solve so called *numerical* **NP**-complete problems, such as SUBSET SUM, whose difficulty is also related to the magnitude of the numbers which are contained into the instances to be solved. On the other side we have *strongly* **NP**-complete problems, that remain hard to solve even when the numbers that occur in the instance are expressed in unary form; the underlying idea is that such numbers are just labels, such as for example the indexes of variables in SAT instances (which is in fact a strongly **NP**-complete problem). Let us also recall that there exists a pseudo-polynomial solution to SUBSET SUM [3], in which an instance $(\{v_1, \ldots, v_n\}, S)$ is solved by using a Boolean matrix M of n rows and $S + 1$ columns; the value of $M[i, j]$ is set to TRUE if and only if there exists a subset of $\{v_1, \ldots, v_i\}$ whose sum is equal to j, and the solution is read from $M[n, S]$ at the end of the execution. The time (and space) complexity of the algorithm is $\Theta(nS)$, which is proportional to the value of S, one of the elements of the instance. The *instance size* of SUBSET SUM is the number of bits needed to express each value that occurs in the instance in binary form, so if we define $K = \max\{v_1, \ldots, v_n, S\}$

then the instance size is $\Theta(n \log K)$. On the other hand, if the values in the instance are expressed in unary form then we obtain a description of the instance whose length is *exponential* in the instance size, and we obtain a time complexity for the solving algorithm which is comparable with the time complexity of the above pseudo-polynomial algorithm. This makes trying to solve SUBSET SUM (and several other numerical **NP**-complete problems) by SN P systems (or by any other kind of computational model) that take their input in unary form a useless effort. The interested reader can find further details in [15], where a semi-uniform and a uniform families of SN P systems that solve the SUBSET SUM problem in polynomial time are presented. Note, however, that the SN P systems used in [15] are not standard: they use *extended rules*, take all the numbers as input simultaneously, and the output of the computation is encoded as the presence or absence of a spike at a given time step.

Perhaps the most surprising result concerning SN P systems is that we can solve the SUBSET SUM problem in *one step*, by using a single neuron containing a *single rule* [16]. This result is based on the fact that the regular expressions that control the activation of firing rules in the neurons are defined over the singleton alphabet $\{a\}$, where the symbol a denotes the spike. Since unary strings are in one-to-one correspondence with their length, they constitute another way to represent positive integer numbers in unary form. A regular expression thus denotes a regular set of positive integer numbers, and a regular expression of the kind $(\lambda + \{a^{v_1}\}) \circ \cdots \circ (\lambda + \{a^{v_n}\})$ denotes the set of all possible subsets of $\{v_1, \ldots, v_n\}$. A firing rule with this regular expression, that requires the presence of S spikes to be enabled, can then fire if and only if there exists a subset of $\{v_1, \ldots, v_n\}$ whose sum of the elements is S; this is equivalent to solving the instance $(\{v_1, \ldots, v_n\}, S)$ of SUBSET SUM.

This, of course, raises the question about how powerful SN P systems are, and whether they constitute a *fair* model of computation (where *fair* in this context means that the system does not contain any "hidden" mechanism which is able to solve a computationally hard problem in a constant number of time steps). In [16] we have tried to give an answer to these questions by showing a simulation of SN P systems by deterministic Turing machines. It turns out that the simulation can be performed in polynomial time with respect to the *description size* of the simulated system – which is defined as the length of a non-ambiguous encoding of the system, where all the numerical values are encoded in binary form – only if the regular expressions used in such a system are of very restricted forms (which are however sufficient to make the resulting model of SN P systems Turing-complete).

4 Space Complexity of P Systems with Active Membranes

We now move to *space* complexity. Here the reference model will be that of P systems with *active membranes* (see [23], Chaps. 11–12 for a survey), which has been introduced in [21] to solve computationally difficult problems.

In this variant of P systems, also the membranes play an active role in the computations: they possess an electrical charge that can inhibit or activate the rules that govern the evolution of the system, and they can also increase exponentially in number via division rules. This latter feature makes them extremely efficient from a computational complexity standpoint: using exponentially many membranes that evolve in parallel, they can be used to solve **NP**-complete and even **PSPACE**-complete problems [1, 32] in polynomial time. Surprisingly, polarizations are not even needed (provided that division rules are powerful enough) to solve these kinds of problems [11, 39]. On the other hand, when the ability of dividing membranes is limited the efficiency apparently decreases: the so called Milano theorem [38] tells us that no **NP**-complete problem can be solved in polynomial time without using division rules, unless **P** = **NP** holds.

In this part of my talk I have surveyed some recent results obtained by the so called "Milano Team" on the space complexity of P systems with active membranes (see also [18] for a less recent but comprehensive review). Here we just recall that the space complexity of a P system is defined as the maximum number of objects and membranes that can occur during the computation. Referring to [36], I have first recalled that a deterministic single-tape Turing machine, operating in polynomial space with respect to the input length, can be efficiently simulated – both in terms of time and space – by a semi-uniform family of P systems with active membranes and three polarizations, using only communication rules. The computing power of polynomial-time P systems with division rules operating only on *elementary* membranes (that is, membranes not containing other membranes) is possibly the most interesting case. It is a known fact that elementary division rules suffice to efficiently solve **NP**-complete problems (and, due to closure under complement, also **coNP**-complete ones). This result dates back to 2000 in the semi-uniform case [38], and to 2003 in the uniform case [24]. Since these results do not require membrane dissolution rules, they hold also for the so called *P systems with restricted elementary active membranes* [1]. Although a **PSPACE** upper bound was proved in 2007 [33], no significant improvement on the **NP** ∪ **coNP** lower bound for these P systems has been found until 2010. Following [26] and [27], it is possible to show that there exists a uniform family of P systems with restricted elementary active membranes that solves the **PP**-complete problem SQRT-3SAT, which is formulated as follows: Given a Boolean formula of m variables in 3CNF, do at least $\sqrt{2^m}$ among the 2^m possible truth assignments satisfy it? The ability to solve all decision problems in the complexity class **PP** will follow by an analogous solution of the **NP**-hard problem THRESHOLD-3SAT, whose statement is: Given a Boolean formula of m variables in 3CNF, and a non-negative integer $k < 2^m$, do more than k assignments (out of 2^m) satisfy it? Note that the complexity class **PP** appears to be larger than **NP**, since it contains **NP** as a subset and it is closed under complement: thus **NP** ∪ **coNP** ⊆ **PP**.

The existence of the uniform family of P systems with restricted elementary active membranes shown in [26, 27] has an interesting consequence. As shown in [29], it is possible to use the P systems that solve THRESHOLD-3SAT (presented in [27]) as modules inside a larger P system; this allows us to simulate subroutines or oracles. In this way, the class $\mathbf{P}^{\mathbf{PP}}$ turns out to be solvable in polynomial time by P systems, without requiring nonelementary division or dissolution rules. This result, together with Toda's theorem [35], allows us to conclude that P systems with restricted elementary active membranes are able to solve all the decision problems residing in the *polynomial hierarchy* $\mathbf{PH}$ [34].

We can then consider computations of P systems with active membranes occurring in *polynomial, exponential, logarithmic*, and *constant* space.

Concerning polynomial space, we can focus our attention on recognizer P systems with active membranes (that, in this context, means associating three polarizations to the membranes, whereas division and dissolution rules are forbidden). Following [25], we can show that these P systems are able to efficiently simulate deterministic register machines, using only communication and evolution rules. Such a simulation will then be used to illustrate the following result: recognizer P systems with active membranes are able to solve, in a uniform way, the $\mathbf{PSPACE}$-complete problem QUANTIFIED-3SAT, using a polynomial amount of space (and an arbitrary amount of time—in a sense, we are here trading time for space). This means that the complexity class $\mathbf{PSPACE}$ is contained into the class of decision problems which can be solved in polynomial space by the above kind of recognizer P systems; furthermore, such P systems can solve in arbitrary time (and polynomial space) problems which cannot be solved in polynomial time unless $\mathbf{P} = \mathbf{PSPACE}$. On the contrary, in [28] it has been proved that P systems with active membranes can be simulated by Turing machines with only a polynomial increase in space complexity. By combining this result with the above stated ability of P systems to solve $\mathbf{PSPACE}$-complete problems in polynomial space, we obtain a *characterization* of $\mathbf{PSPACE}$ in terms of membrane systems. An interesting aspect is that this result holds for both confluent and non-confluent systems, and even when strong features such as division rules are used.

A similar result can be obtained for P systems with active membranes working in *exponential* space. In particular, in [2] we have shown that exponential-space P systems with active membranes *characterise* the complexity class $\mathbf{EXPSPACE}$. This result is proved by simulating Turing machines working in exponential space via uniform families of P systems with restricted elementary active membranes; the simulation is efficient, in the sense that the time and space required are at most polynomial with respect to the resources employed by the simulated Turing machine. Moreover, as shown in [2], this simulation can be extended to any amount of space (doubly exponential, triple exponential, and so on) which is at least polynomial.

When considering P systems with active membranes working in *logarithmic* space, a new notion of uniformity is needed, which is weaker than the P systems themselves, otherwise one could cheat by letting the Turing machine that builds the P systems solve the problem. Inspired by Boolean circuit complexity [19] we have thus introduced $\mathbf{DLOGTIME}$-uniformity [30], and we have proved that $\mathbf{DLOGTIME}$-uniform families of P systems with active membranes working in logarithmic space (not counting their input) can simulate logarithmic-space deterministic Turing machines. This result only represents a lower bound for the power of logarithmic-space P systems; as a matter of fact, already in [30] it was conjectured that such a bound could be improved, since P systems working in logarithmic space have an *exponential* number of different configurations, which could possibly be used to efficiently solve harder problems than those in the class **L**. It turned out [13] that this is the case, and that polynomial-space deterministic Turing machines can be simulated by means of P systems with active membranes using only logarithmic auxiliary space, thus characterising once again **PSPACE**.

After considering P systems with active membranes working in logarithmic space, a natural question arises concerning the power of such systems using only a constant amount of space. Surprisingly, it turns out that constant space is sufficient to simulate polynomial-space bounded deterministic Turing machines [12], thus providing a further (unexpected) characterization of **PSPACE**.

We conclude this section by observing that [17] offers many equivalences between computational ingredients used by P systems, that help when we have to design a P system that solves a specific problem. For example, we can set a priority between rules and use any number of membrane charges without loss of generality, as the obtained systems can be simulated by standard P systems with active membranes, in particular using only two charges. Also some "non-standard" halting conditions can be used, without changing the computation power of the model.

5   Bridges to Other Areas of Computer Science

In the last part of the talk I have proposed some (perhaps – and hopefully – provocative) bridges towards other Computer Science topics, related with Cryptography, Computer and Network Security, and Decentralized Applications. Indeed, since many variants of P systems are Turing-complete they can be considered a general-purpose parallel and distributed model of computation. This opens up a number of (still unexplored) possibilities.

For example, as far as I know very few papers deal with the use of P systems to compute cryptographic functions or cryptographic protocols. Consider that Craig Gentry showed in 2009 the theoretical feasibility of *Fully Homomorphic Encryption* (FHE) [6]: in practice, this means that one can delegate computations to another (possibly malicious) party, giving him encrypted inputs and obtaining as a result the correct encrypted output; the party that actually performs the computation will never be able to decrypt anything during the process. On the other hand, the result of the computation comes with a proof of correctness, so that it is also impossible for the computing party to cheat. The original FHE scheme runs on a particular variant of arithmetic circuits; it has later been extended to several other kinds of circuits, and also to Turing machines [8]. So why not considering P systems as a model to perform fully homomorphic computations? Differently from Turing machines we could exploit parallelism, whereas differently from arithmetic circuits they would be easier to design.

Since encryption can be seen as a particular kind of coding, this suggests the possibility to encode P systems as appropriate multisets and perform operations on them, thus obtaining two kinds of behaviors: (1) a *simulation* of encoded P systems, like it happens in the direct construction of the universal Turing machine, and (2) *hiding* "executable" P systems into "data" multisets, and executing them "covertly" by another P system – that is, without the user being aware of it while using the simulating P system – like it happens with computer malware. It would be nice to show an explicit example of such an encoding, and indirect (covert) execution.

Finally, Decentralized Applications (DApps) is a subject whose interest is currently growing, also due to its connection with blockchains. Briefly stated, a decentralized application allows some mutually untrusted parties to collaborate in order to compute an agreed upon result, without the possibility to cheat. The most famous framework and environment to design and run DApps is Ethereum [37], which provides a P2P network of virtual machines that communicate over encrypted channels. These machines can run arbitrary programs written in Solidity, a high-level programming language which is compiled into the machine-level code of the virtual machines. All this inspires the following idea: why not using a network of P systems, like in dP systems [22], as the formal model of computation that supports the membrane computing version of DApps? Why not defining a high-level programming language that, when compiled, produces these kinds of networks?

References

1. Alhazov, A., Martín-Vide, C., Pan, L.: Solving a PSPACE-complete problem by recognizing P systems with restricted active membranes. Fundam. Informaticae **58**(2), 67–77 (2003)
2. Alhazov, A., Leporati, A., Mauri, G., Porreca, A.E., Zandron, C.: Space complexity equivalence of P systems with active membranes and Turing machines. Theor. Comput. Sci. **529**, 69–81 (2014)
3. Cormen, T.H., Leiserson, C.H., Rivest, R.L.: Introduction to Algorithms. MIT Press, Cambridge (1990)
4. Freund, R., Leporati, A., Oswald, M., Zandron, C.: Sequential P systems with unit rules and energy assigned to membranes. In: Margenstern, M. (ed.) MCU 2004. LNCS, vol. 3354, pp. 200–210. Springer, Heidelberg (2005). https://doi.org/10.1007/978-3-540-31834-7_16
5. Furst, M., Saxe, J.B., Sipser, M.: Parity, circuits, and the polynomial-time hierarchy. Math. Syst. Theory **17**, 13–27 (1984)
6. Gentry, C.: Fully homomorphic encryption using ideal lattices. In: Mitzenmacher, M. (ed.) Proceedings of the 41st Annual ACM Symposium on Theory of Computing, STOC 2009, pp. 169–178. ACM (2009)
7. Ionescu, M., Păun, G., Yokomori, T.: Spiking neural P systems. Fundam. Informaticae **71**(3), 279–308 (2006)
8. Goldwasser, S., Kalai, Y.T., Popa, R.A., Vaikuntanathan, V., Zeldovich, N.: How to run turing machines on encrypted data. In: Canetti, R., Garay, J.A. (eds.) CRYPTO 2013. LNCS, vol. 8043, pp. 536–553. Springer, Heidelberg (2013). https://doi.org/10.1007/978-3-642-40084-1_30

9. Konur, S., Gheorghe, M., Dragomir, C., Mierla, L., Ipate, F., Krasnogor, N.: Qualitative and quantitative analysis of systems and synthetic biology constructs using P systems. ACS Synth. Biol. **4**(1), 83–92 (2015)
10. Korec, I.: Small universal register machines. Theor. Comput. Sci. **168**, 267–301 (1996)
11. Leporati, A., Ferretti, C., Mauri, G., Pérez-Jiménez, M.J., Zandron, C.: Complexity aspects of polarizationless membrane systems. Nat. Comput. **8**, 703–717 (2009)
12. Leporati, A., Manzoni, L., Mauri, G., Porreca, A.E., Zandron, C.: Constant-space P systems with active membranes. Fundam. Informaticae **134**(1–2), 111–128 (2014)
13. Leporati, A., Mauri, G., Porreca, A.E., Zandron, C.: A gap in the space hierarchy of P systems with active membranes. J. Automata Lang. Comb. **19**(1–4), 173–184 (2014)
14. Leporati, A., Mauri, G., Zandron, C., Păun, G., Péréz-Jiménez, M.J.: Uniform solutions to SAT and Subset Sum by spiking neural P systems. Nat. Comput. **8**, 681–702 (2009)
15. Leporati, A., Zandron, C., Ferretti, C., Mauri, G.: Solving numerical NP-complete problems with spiking neural P systems. In: Eleftherakis, G., Kefalas, P., Păun, G., Rozenberg, G., Salomaa, A. (eds.) WMC 2007. LNCS, vol. 4860, pp. 336–352. Springer, Heidelberg (2007). https://doi.org/10.1007/978-3-540-77312-2_21
16. Leporati, A., Zandron, C., Ferretti, C., Mauri, G.: On the computational power of spiking neural P systems. Int. J. Unconventional Comput. **5**, 459–473 (2009)
17. Leporati, A., Manzoni, L., Mauri, G., Porreca, A.E., Zandron, C.: A toolbox for simpler active membrane algorithms. Theor. Comput. Sci. **673**, 42–57 (2017)
18. Mauri, G., Leporati, A., Porreca, A.E., Zandron, C.: Recent complexity-theoretic results on P systems with active membranes. J. Logic Comput. **25**(4), 1047–1071 (2015)
19. Mix Barrington, D.A., Immerman, N., Straubing, H.: On uniformity within NC[1]. J. Comput. Syst. Sci. **41**(3), 274–306 (1990)
20. Păun, G.: Computing with membranes. J. Comput. Syst. Sci. **1**(61), 108–143 (2000)
21. Păun, G.: P systems with active membranes: attacking NP-complete problems. J. Automata Lang. Comb. **6**(1), 75–90 (2001)
22. Păun, G., Pérez-Jiménez, M.J.: Solving Problems in a distributed way in membrane computing: dP systems. Int. J. Comput. Commun. Control **5**(2), 238–250 (2010)
23. Păun, G., Rozenberg, G., Salomaa, A. (eds.): The Oxford Handbook of Membrane Computing. Oxford University Press, Oxford (2010)
24. Pérez-Jiménez, M.J., Romero Jiménez, A., Sancho Caparrini, F.: Complexity classes in models of cellular computing with membranes. Nat. Comput. **2**(3), 265–285 (2003)
25. Porreca, A.E., Leporati, A., Mauri, G., Zandron, C.: P systems with active membranes: trading time for space. Nat. Comput. **10**(1), 167–182 (2011)
26. Porreca, A.E., Leporati, A., Mauri, G., Zandron, C.: P systems with elementary active membranes: beyond NP and coNP. In: Gheorghe, M., Hinze, T., Păun, G., Rozenberg, G., Salomaa, A. (eds.) CMC 2010. LNCS, vol. 6501, pp. 338–347. Springer, Heidelberg (2010). https://doi.org/10.1007/978-3-642-18123-8_26
27. Porreca, A.E., Leporati, A., Mauri, G., Zandron, C.: Elementary active membranes have the power of counting. Int. J. Nat. Comput. Res. **2**(3), 35–48 (2011)
28. Porreca, A.E., Leporati, A., Mauri, G., Zandron, C.: P systems with active membranes working in polynomial space. Int. J. Found. Comput. Sci. **2**(1), 65–73 (2011)

29. Porreca, A.E., Leporati, A., Mauri, G., Zandron, C.: P systems simulating oracle computations. In: Gheorghe, M., Păun, G., Rozenberg, G., Salomaa, A., Verlan, S. (eds.) CMC 2011. LNCS, vol. 7184, pp. 346–358. Springer, Heidelberg (2012). https://doi.org/10.1007/978-3-642-28024-5_23

30. Porreca, A.E., Leporati, A., Mauri, G., Zandron, C.: Sublinear-space P systems with active membranes. In: Csuhaj-Varjú, E., Gheorghe, M., Rozenberg, G., Salomaa, A., Vaszil, G. (eds.) CMC 2012. LNCS, vol. 7762, pp. 342–357. Springer, Heidelberg (2013). https://doi.org/10.1007/978-3-642-36751-9_23

31. Rong, H., Wu, T., Pan, L., Zhang, G.: Spiking neural P systems: theoretical results and applications. In: Bulletin of the International Membrane Computing Society (IMCS), June 2018. http://membranecomputing.net/IMCSBulletin/index.php?page=SNP-review

32. Sosík, P.: The computational power of cell division in P systems: beating down parallel computers? Nat. Comput. 2(3), 287–298 (2003)

33. Sosík, P., Rodríguez-Patón, A.: Membrane computing and complexity theory: a characterization of PSPACE. J. Comput. Syst. Sci. 73(1), 137–152 (2007)

34. Stockmeyer, L.J.: The polynomial hierarchy. Theor. Comput. Sci. 3, 1–22 (1976)

35. Toda, S.: PP is as hard as the polynomial-time hierarchy. SIAM J. Comput. 20(5), 865–877 (1991)

36. Valsecchi, A., Porreca, A.E., Leporati, A., Mauri, G., Zandron, C.: An efficient simulation of polynomial-space turing machines by P systems with active membranes. In: Păun, G., Pérez-Jiménez, M.J., Riscos-Núñez, A., Rozenberg, G., Salomaa, A. (eds.) WMC 2009. LNCS, vol. 5957, pp. 461–478. Springer, Heidelberg (2010). https://doi.org/10.1007/978-3-642-11467-0_31

37. Wood, G.: Ethereum: a secure decentralised generalised transaction ledger. Ethereum Project Yellow Paper (2014). https://github.com/ethereum/yellowpaper

38. Zandron, C., Ferretti, C., Mauri, G.: Solving NP-complete problems using P systems with active membranes. In: Antoniou, I., Calude, C.S., Dinneen, M.J. (eds.) Unconventional Models of Computation, UMC'2K. Discrete Mathematics and Theoretical Computer Science, pp. 289–301. Springer, London (2001). https://doi.org/10.1007/978-1-4471-0313-4_21

39. Zandron, C., Leporati, A., Ferretti, C., Mauri, G., Pérez-Jiménez, M.J.: On the computational efficiency of polarizationless recognizer P systems with strong division and dissolution. Fundam. Informaticae 87(1), 79–91 (2008)

A Brute-Force Solution to the 27-Queens Puzzle Using a Distributed Computation

Thomas Preußer[✉]

Accemic Technologies GmbH, Dresden Office,
Gostritzer Str. 65, 01217 Dresden, Germany
thomas.preusser@utexas.edu

Abstract. The N-Queens Puzzle is an intriguing mathematical riddle that provokes many interesting but hard questions albeit having an astonishingly simple problem statement. One of these questions asks for the number of non-attacking placements of N queens onto a generalized $N \times N$ chessboard. While estimates and bounds can certainly be given, the exact solution counts, so far, have not lent themselves to a reasonable closed-form solution but rather to showcasing the arts of computer programming - and of digital design - in a tedious systematic exploration of the vast solution space. Already, Donald Knuth has made it a classic example illustrating the technique of backtracking. The largest problem sizes with known solution counts are $N = 26$ and $N = 27$. Both of them were first obtained by distributed computations relying on nodes featuring solver engines built within field-programmable hardware. This presentation will briefly introduce the capabilities and opportunities of programmable hardware highlighting its great fit for exploring the N-Queens Puzzle. It will illustrate how the computations were partitioned and how symmetries were used to prune the search spaces before even starting. Finally, the distributed architectures running the actual computations over several months each will be detailed.

1 Overview

The N-Queens Puzzle is a 150-year-old mathematical riddle whose comprehensive history is very well described by Bell and Stevens along with interesting generalizations and practical applications [4].

The chess rules allow a queen to move an arbitrary distance in a horizontal, vertical or diagonal direction. This implies that each of the N columns and each of the N rows of a completed solution must contain exactly one of the N placed queens. Any one of the $2N - 1$ diagonals in both the upward and downward directions may be occupied by at most one queen. The total number of valid solutions is trivially bounded by $N!$. This is the number of possible placements of N non-attacking rooks, which lack the constraining ability to move along a diagonal.

© Springer Nature Switzerland AG 2019
T. Hinze et al. (Eds.): CMC 2018, LNCS 11399, pp. 23–29, 2019.
https://doi.org/10.1007/978-3-030-12797-8_3

Mathematically, an N-Queens solution can be viewed as a permutation matrix that contains its one (1) entries exactly at the coordinates of the validly placed queens. The permutation matrices that correspond to an N-Queens solution shuffle an input vector especially well:

$$\begin{pmatrix} 0\,0\,0\,0\,1 \\ 0\,0\,1\,0\,0 \\ 1\,0\,0\,0\,0 \\ 0\,0\,0\,1\,0 \\ 0\,1\,0\,0\,0 \end{pmatrix} \cdot \begin{pmatrix} 1 \\ 2 \\ 3 \\ 4 \\ 5 \end{pmatrix} = \begin{pmatrix} 5 \\ 3 \\ 1 \\ 4 \\ 2 \end{pmatrix}$$

As no two queens can reside on the same diagonal, the induced permutation does not allow any two elements to maintain their relative position after the shuffle.

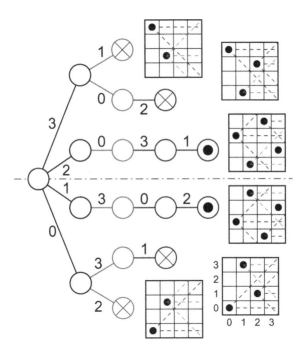

Fig. 1. Backtracking search of the 4-Queens Puzzle

Most interestingly, the last constraint differentiating queens from rooks that complicates the counting of valid solutions. In fact, the only known approach is backtracking search, for which it still is a prominent example as in the upcoming volume 4 of *The Art of Computer Programming – Introduction to Backtracking* by Donald Knuth. The unfolded backtracking search tree for exploring the solutions of the rather tiny 4-Queens puzzle is shown by Fig. 1.

Practical solutions for challenging problem sizes will unfold the initial levels of the backtracking search tree to induce a partitioning of the solution space. Its granularity can be easily tuned by the choice of the unfolded depth so that even the huge solution spaces of larger problem sizes can be chopped into *independent* pieces of a manageable size. This way, the N-Queens Puzzle still remains a computational challenge but also becomes a perfect showcase for massively parallel, high-performance computing. It has, indeed, been used as such for grid computations [2], for Internet computations [3], for supercomputers [1] as well as for FPGA [5,7] and for GPU [10] platforms.

2   Programmable Logic Devices

Programmable logic devices are universal digital circuits that postpone the determining configuration of the interconnect and logic functionality until after the silicon production process. This approach (a) removes the production time of the physical device from the application design loop, (b) increases flexibility making design updates and bug fixes cheaper, and (c) enables low-volume design solutions for small markets or for prototyping to leverage the latest silicon production processes in exchange for an affordable abstraction overhead. On the bottom line, programmable logic devices are key for making real hardware solutions feasible in a wide range of application scenarios.

The pivotal characteristic of physical digital designs is their intrinsic, potentially enormous concurrency. Functionalities are separated in space rather than in processing time. The limits of concurrency are not defined by some fixed, rather small core count but can be pushed to hundreds of processing engines on a single chip if their physical footprints in silicon can be kept small.

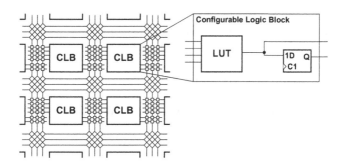

Fig. 2. Basic concept of the generic FPGA fabric

The largest and most powerful among the modern programmable logic devices are SRAM-programmed field-programmable gate arrays (FPGAs). To appreciate the silicon abstraction that they offer refer to Fig. 2. Besides special-purpose structures including general-purpose IO pads, high-performance transceivers, on-chip memory and even whole CPUs, it is the sketched fabric that provides full customization of application designs down to the bitlevel. This fabric is arranged in a grid, which is tiled by configurable routing structures

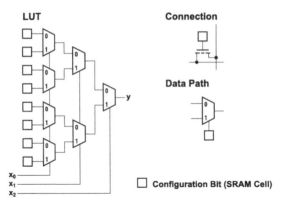

Fig. 3. Universal function implementation using lookup tables (LUTs) and programmed routing

that wire up application circuits connecting the implementing configurable logic blocks (CLBs) appropriately. Those CLBs, in turn, are composed (a) of combinational lookup tables (LUTs) that are able to implement any BOOLEan function of up to some number of k inputs and (b) of registers that can optionally be included on the output data path to implement state. A concrete application circuit is configured into volatile SRAM cells distributed throughout the device. As illustrated in Fig. 3, they are used (a) to store the truth table backing the functionality of a LUT , (b) to configure data-path multiplexers and (c) to connect routing paths.

While programmable hardware devices enable truly structural hardware implementations, they do so by emulating the configured application design. This abstraction layer induces costs in terms of the achievable clock frequency and in terms of the functional density as compared to a true application-specific integrated circuit (ASIC) at the same technology node. Considering the enormous expenses of designing and producing such custom silicon on recent, competitive technology nodes, FPGAs are a precious trade-off for flexible low-volume applications.

3   Conquering 26 and 27 Queens

The N-Queens puzzle and FPGAs are a great fit. The backtracking search to explore the puzzle relies heavily on blocking information encoding which of the rows, diagonals and columns are already occupied by a previously placed queen. This information can be naturally represented by physical bit vectors in FPGA fabric registers. Also, the computation of the next valid placement step or, alternatively, the detection of the need to backtrack are simple, bit-level operations based on this blocking information. This natural fit and its computational simplicity are key to the implementation of small-footprint processing elements that allow an enormous concurrency.

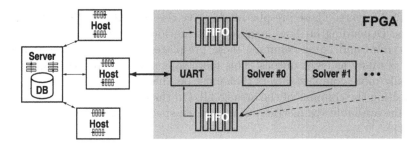

Fig. 4. Infrastructure of the distributed FPGA computations

Both of the two recent computational records of searching an N-Queens solution space where attained by distributed computations relying on FPGA solvers. Scaling the concurrency beyond the capabilities of an individual device, a whole host of FPGAs were joined in a compute network orchestrated by a central database. The database node distributed open subproblems to the clients and collected their corresponding results. This infrastructure is illustrated in Fig. 4.

The 26-Queens computation [7] used a straightforward partitioning of the search space by pre-placing the six queens fitting into the six leftmost columns. The solvers explored and counted the valid completions by processing and backtracking the board column by column. The conclusive total was computed after exploring half of the search space. Leveraging the symmetry of the chessboard about its horizontal center, pre-placements with a queen beyond the thirteenth row in the first column did not have to be considered.

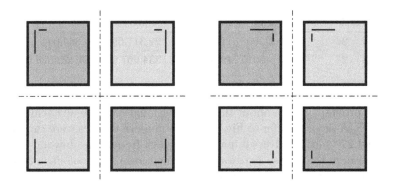

Fig. 5. Maximum 8-element orbit under the symmetry group D_4 of the square

As depicted in Fig. 5, the chessboard exhibits much more powerful symmetry properties. These were exploited for exploring the solution space of the 27-Queens puzzle [5]. For this purpose, coronal pre-placements of queens within the two outer rings of the chessboard were computed for the completion by the distributed solvers. These pre-placements give rise to 2 024 110 796 independent subtasks. Depending on how many queens are located within the intersection of outer rows and outer columns, these pre-placement may involve as few as four or as many as eight queens. This more sophisticated approach resulted in marginally more complex solvers that must be able to honor pre-placed queens also affecting the columns of the area to fill. On the other, the rigorous exploitation of the available symmetries cut the search space roughly down to an eighth (Table 1).

Table 1. Compute power of selected off-the-shelf FPGA boards used for $N = 27$

Board	Device	Solvers	Clock	SE
VC707	XC7VX485T-2	325	250.0 MHz	812
KC705	XC7K325T-2	250	284.4 MHz	711
DNK7_F5_PCIe	5× XC7K325T-1	5× 240	220.0 MHz	2640
ML605	XC6VLX240T-1	127	171.4 MHz	217
ML505	XC5VLX50T-1	22	177.7 MHz	39
S3SK	XC3S1000-4	9	84.6 MHz	7
DE4	EP4SGX230KF40C2	125	250.0 MHz	312

SE (Solver Equivalent): one solver slice running at 100 MHz

Table 2. Durations and results of the 26- and 27-queens explorations

Puzzle size	Start date	Finish date	Solution count
$N = 26$	14-Oct-2008	11-Jul-2009	22,317,699,616,364,044
$N = 27$	03-Sep-2015	19-Sep-2016	234,907,967,154,122,528

So as to provide an idea about the computational concurrency achieved even on single FPGA devices, refer to Fig. 1. Larger modern devices were running several hundred 27-Queens solvers in parallel at clock frequencies beyond 200 MHz. Carefully observe that these hardware implementations do not have to process any instruction overhead at all. This means that really every single clock cycle, each of those solvers either places a valid queen or tracks back. The finally determined solution totals and the durations of the two compute projects are tabulated in Table 2. Note that the solution count obtained for $N = 26$ was confirmed by a Russian supercomputer effort already in August 2009. A confirmation of the result for $N = 27$ is still pending.

4 Future FPGA Story

FPGAs are true hardware platforms, on which computations are unfolded in space and at the finest level of granularity. i.e. bits. Given the resource supply on a device, it is the structural complexity of the core compute kernel that directly determines the achievable concurrency. Some applications, such as the exploration of the N-Queens Puzzle or many cryptography applications, are a natural fit for an implementation on FPGAs as they rely heavily on bit-level operations. Other applications must be tuned for this platform. A prominent example for the latter are neural networks. Traditionally computed with floating-point hardware, they have been demonstrated to work well with numeric data formats quantized to a few or even a single bit [8,9]. FPGA implementations benefit immediately from such a simplification as lower-precision arithmetic translates directly into more operations per silicon area and, hence, more concurrency achievable on a given device. So, before trying to conquer the 28-Queens problem, there are many other interesting alternative applications to explore, such as the object detection in life video by a quantized Tiny YOLO neural network on an embedded Ultra96 platform [6].

References

1. MC#. http://www.mcsharp.net/
2. nQueens: n=25. http://www-sop.inria.fr/oasis/ProActive2/apps/nqueens25.html
3. NQueens@Home. http://www.rechenkraft.net/wiki/NQueens@Home
4. Bell, J., Stevens, B.: A survey of known results and research areas for n-queens. Discrete Math. **309**(1), 1–31 (2009). https://doi.org/10.1016/j.disc.2007.12.043, http://www.sciencedirect.com/science/article/pii/S0012365X07010394
5. Preußer, T.B., Engelhardt, M.R.: Putting queens in carry chains, No. 27. J. Signal Process. Syst. 1–17 (2016). https://doi.org/10.1007/s11265-016-1176-8
6. Preußer, T.B., Gambardella, G., Fraser, N., Blott, M.: Inference of quantized neural networks on heterogeneous all-programmable devices. In: Design, Automation and Test in Europe (DATE 2018), pp. 833–838, March 2018. https://doi.org/10.23919/DATE.2018.8342121
7. Preußer, T.B., Nägel, B., Spallek, R.G.: Putting queens in carry chains. In: 3rd HIPEAC Workshop on Reconfigurable Computing, pp. 83–92, January 2009
8. Sung, W., Shin, S., Hwang, K.: Resiliency of deep neural networks under quantization. In: CoRR abs/1511.0 (2015)
9. Umuroglu, Y., et al.: FINN: a framework for fast, scalable binarized neural network inference. In: Proceedings of the 2017 ACM/SIGDA International Symposium on Field-Programmable Gate Arrays (FPGA 2017), FPGA, pp. 65–74. ACM, New York, February 2017. https://doi.org/10.1145/3020078.3021744
10. Zhang, T., Shu, W., Wu, M.-Y.: Optimization of N-queens solvers on graphics processors. In: Temam, O., Yew, P.-C., Zang, B. (eds.) APPT 2011. LNCS, vol. 6965, pp. 142–156. Springer, Heidelberg (2011). https://doi.org/10.1007/978-3-642-24151-2_11

Regular Papers

Tissue P Systems with Point Mutation Rules

Artiom Alhazov[1], Rudolf Freund[2(✉)], Sergiu Ivanov[3], and Sergey Verlan[4]

[1] Institute of Mathematics and Computer Science,
Academiei 5, 2028 Chişinău, Moldova
`artiom@math.md`
[2] Faculty of Informatics, TU Wien, Favoritenstraße 9–11, 1040 Vienna, Austria
`rudi@emcc.at`
[3] IBISC, Université Évry, Université Paris-Saclay,
23 Boulevard de France, 91025 Évry, France
`sergiu.ivanov@univ-evry.fr`
[4] Laboratoire d'Algorithmique, Complexité et Logique, Université Paris Est Créteil,
61 Avenue du Général de Gaulle, 94010 Créteil, France
`verlan@u-pec.fr`

Abstract. We consider tissue P systems working in the sequential mode on vesicles of multisets with the very simple operations of insertion, deletion, and substitution of single objects. In a computation step, one rule is to be applied if possible, and then, in any case, the whole multiset being enclosed in a vesicle moves to one of the cells as indicated by the underlying graph structure of the system. The target cell is chosen in a non-deterministic way and does not depend on the possibly applied rule. With defining halting as reaching the final cell with a vesicle only containing terminal symbols, computational completeness can be obtained. Imposing the restriction that in each derivation step one rule has to be applied, we only reach the computational power of matrix grammars for multisets. Moreover, we also discuss variants for computations on strings. Finally, we outline a way how to "go beyond Turing" like with red-green register machines.

1 Introduction

Membrane systems were introduced at the end of the last century by Păun, e.g., see [11] and [32], motivated by the biological interaction of molecules between cells and their surrounding environment. In the basic model, the membranes are organized in a hierarchical membrane structure (i.e., the connection structure between the compartments/regions within the membranes being representable as a tree), and the multisets of objects in the membrane regions evolve in a maximally parallel way, with the resulting objects also being able to pass through the surrounding membrane to the parent membrane region or to enter an inner membrane. Since then, a lot of variants of membrane systems, for obvious

© Springer Nature Switzerland AG 2019
T. Hinze et al. (Eds.): CMC 2018, LNCS 11399, pp. 33–56, 2019.
https://doi.org/10.1007/978-3-030-12797-8_4

reasons mostly called *P systems*, have been investigated, most of them being computationally complete, i.e., being able to simulate the computations of register machines. If an arbitrary graph is used as the connection structure between the cells/membranes, the systems are called *tissue P systems*, see [28].

Instead of multisets of plain symbols coming from a finite alphabet, P systems quite often operate on more complex objects (e.g., strings, arrays), too. A comprehensive overview of different variants of (tissue) P systems and their expressive power is given in the handbook which appeared in 2010, see [33]. For a short view on the state of the art of the domain, we refer the reader to the P systems website [37] as well as to the Bulletin series of the International Membrane Computing Society [36].

Very simple biologically motivated operations on strings are the so-called *point mutations*, i.e., *insertion*, *deletion*, and *substitution*, which mean inserting or deleting one symbol in a string or replacing one symbol by another one. For example, graph-controlled insertion-deletion systems have been investigated in [20], and P systems using these operations at the left or right end of string objects were introduced in [25], where also a short history of using these point mutations in formal language theory can be found.

When dealing with multisets of objects, the close relation of insertion and deletion with the increment and decrement instructions in register machines looks rather obvious. The power of changing states in connection with the increment and decrement instructions then can be mimicked by moving the whole multiset representing the configuration of a register machine from one cell to another one in the corresponding tissue system. Yet usually moving the whole multiset of objects in a cell to another one, besides maximal parallelism, requires *target agreement* between all applied rules, i.e., that all results are moved to the same target cell, e.g., see [23].

In this paper we follow a different approach which has been introduced in [3]: in order to guarantee that the whole multiset is moved even if only some point mutations are applied, the multiset is enclosed in a vesicle, and this vesicle is moved from one cell to another one as a whole, no matter if a rule has been applied or not. Running the tissue P system in the sequential mode we obtain computational completeness when allowing even no rule to be applied in a derivation step, i.e., if none of the rules assigned to the cell where the vesicle currently is to be found can be applied to the multiset contained in the vesicle. Requiring that one rule has to be applied in every derivation step, we achieve a characterization of the family of sets of (vectors of) natural numbers defined by partially blind register machines, which itself corresponds with the family of sets of (vectors of) natural numbers obtained as number (Parikh) sets of string languages generated by matrix grammars without appearance checking.

The idea of using vesicles of multisets has already been used in variants of P systems using the operations drip and mate, corresponding with the operations cut and paste well-known from the area of DNA computing, see [21]. Yet in that case, always two vesicles (one of them possibly being an axiom available in an unbounded number) have to interact. In this paper, the rules are always applied to the same vesicle.

The *point mutations*, i.e., *insertion*, *deletion*, and *substitution*, well-known from biology as operations on DNA, have also widely been used in the variants of *networks of evolutionary processors (NEPs)*, which consist of cells (processors) each of them allowing for specific operations on strings. *Networks of Evolutionary Processors* (NEPs) were introduced in [9] as a model of string processing devices distributed over a graph, with the processors carrying out these point mutations. Computations in such a network consist of alternatingly performing two steps – an *evolution step* where in each cell all possible operations on all strings currently present in the cell are performed, and a *communication step* in which strings are sent from one cell to another cell provided specific conditions are fulfilled. Examples of such conditions are (output and input) filters which have to be passed, and these (output and input) filters can be specific types of regular languages or permitting and forbidden context conditions. The set of strings obtained as results of computations by the NEP is defined as the set of objects which appear in some distinguished node in the course of a computation.

In *hybrid networks of evolutionary processors* (HNEPs), each language processor performs only one of these operations at a certain position of a string. Furthermore, the filters are defined by some variants of random-context conditions, i.e., they check the presence and the absence of certain symbols in the strings. For an overview on HNEPs and the best results known so far, we refer the reader to [4].

In *networks of evolutionary processors with polarizations*, each symbol has assigned a fixed integer value; the polarization of a string is computed according to a given evaluation function, and in the communication step the obtained string is moved to any of the connected cells having the same polarization. Networks of polarized evolutionary processors were considered in [7] and [6], and networks of evolutionary processors only using the elementary polarizations $-1, 0, 1$ were investigated in [31]. The number of processors (cells) needed to obtain computational completeness has been improved in a considerable way in [24] making these results already comparable with those obtained in [4] for hybrid networks of evolutionary processors using permitting and forbidden contexts as filters for the communication of strings between cells.

Seen from a biological point of view, networks of evolutionary processors are a collection of cells communicating via membrane channels, which makes them closely related to tissue-like P systems considered in the area of membrane computing. The tissue P systems considered in this paper now take features of several of the devices mentioned above: we use a set of cells, each of them having assigned a set of point mutation rules as in (H)NEPs as well as two substeps in each derivation step – an *evolution step* in which one rule out of the set of rules assigned to the cell is applied (i.e., if possible) to the multiset in the vesicle currently present in the cell, and a *communication step* in which the vesicle is sent from the current cell to another cell.

In contrast to (H)NEPs, which usually deal with strings, we here deal with multisets enclosed in a vesicle. Yet the most important difference is that the communication is not guided by output and input filters or by polarizations, but simply by using a directed graph as the underlying communication structure. On the other hand, in contrast to the well-known control mechanism of graph control with appearance checking (e.g., see [10] and [19]), the target cell does not depend on which rule – if any – has been applied, which resembles the special variant of graph control known as unconditional transfer, for example, see [12].

Another control mechanism closely related to this moving a vesicle through the underling communication structure of a tissue P system is using regular control languages (e.g., see [10]): the directed graph describing the control structure can be interpreted as the graph of a finite automaton for the rule labels; in this model, appearance checking, i.e., allowing some rules to be skipped if they cannot be applied, is modeled by fixing a set of rules which may be skipped when following a control word in the regular control language. An important technical detail to be mentioned here is that in regular control languages the control word usually is composed of single rule labels, whereas in the tissue P systems introduced in this paper the control word would be composed of sets of rule labels.

For comparing the results exhibited in this paper by using the control given by the underlying communication structure of the tissue P system, we recall the general framework for grammars working in the sequential derivation mode, developed in [19]; many relations between various regulating mechanisms can be established in a very general setting without any reference to the underlying objects the rules are working on, as, for example, for graph-controlled, programmed, matrix, random-context, and ordered grammars. Other control mechanisms considered in this paper are grammars with regular control languages and time-varying grammars, which in the context of P systems have been investigated in [2]. In that paper, computational completeness is shown for membrane systems with only one membrane, but using non-cooperative rules and a lot of additional control symbols. Moreover, the number of steps needed without applying a rule in the proof given there was two, whereas our result established in this paper only needs one step without applying a rule.

Finally, we should like to mention that the control given by the underlying communication structure of the tissue P system could also be interpreted as having a P system with only one membrane but using states instead; for a discussion on how to use and interpret features of (tissue) P systems as states we refer to [2], where also an example only using the point mutation rules insertion and deletion is given.

Although dealing with multisets, we can also simulate computations on strings: adding the rules for taking an object from the environment into the vesicle and/or sending an object out of the vesicle allows us to define the input and output strings as the sequence of symbols taken in and sent out, respectively. As an input sequence can be encoded as a number and then processed by only two registers (the folklore result for two-counter automata) and the final result can be encoded as a number and then decoded into a sequence of symbols sent out (e.g., see [13]), the basic result showing how to simulate register machines also allows for simulating computations on strings.

Various possibilities of how one may "go beyond Turing" are discussed in [27]; for example, the definitions and results for red-green Turing machines can be found there. In [5] the notion of red-green automata for register machines with input strings given on an input tape (often also called *counter automata*) is introduced and the concept of *red-green P automata* for several specific models of membrane systems is explained. Via red-green counter automata, the results for acceptance and recognizability of finite strings by red-green Turing machines are carried over to red-green P automata. The basic idea of red-green automata is to distinguish between two different sets of states (red and green states) and to consider infinite runs of the automaton on finite input objects (strings, multisets); allowed to change between red and green states more than once, red-green automata can recognize more than the recursively enumerable sets (of strings, multisets), i.e., in that way one can "go beyond Turing". In the area of P systems, first attempts to do that can be found in [8] and [35]. Computations with infinite words by P automata were investigated in [22].

In [17,18], infinite runs of P automata are considered, taking into account the existence/non-existence of a recursive feature of the current sequence of configurations. In that way, infinite sequences over $\{0,1\}$, called "observer languages", are obtained, where 1 indicates that the specific feature is fulfilled by the current configuration and 0 indicates that this specific feature is not fulfilled. The recognizing runs of red-green automata then correspond to having ω-regular languages over $\{0,1\}$ of a specific form ending with 1^ω as observer languages.

The main problem with finding a red-green variant of the special variant of tissue P systems introduced in this paper is its inherent non-determinism even when simulating deterministic register machines and their red-green variant (again see [5]) – the zero-test case and the decrement case of a SUB-instruction are chosen in a non-deterministic way. Yet there is a possibility to overcome this problem by using ideas as, for example, discussed in [30] and in [1]. In [30], k-determinism of variants of P systems like (purely) catalytic P systems is discussed, i.e., with a look-ahead of (at most) k derivation steps always a deterministic continuation of a derivation can be found, although at some moment several (multisets of) rules could be applied, because all other derivation paths would lead to the introduction of the trap symbol; this technique is used very often in proofs in the area of membrane systems to cause non-halting computations. In [1], the concept of toxic objects is introduced which "kill" any derivation branch producing a toxic object as, for example, the trap symbol. As we will show later, our proof for simulating the SUB-instructions of a register machine only needs a look-ahead of 1, i.e., as the deterministic continuation of a derivation in the tissue P system we can just take the one which does not introduce the trap symbol. In that way, also a red-green variant of the model introduced in this paper can be defined, thus even allowing us to "go beyond Turing".

The rest of the paper is structured as follows: In Sect. 2 we recall some well-known definitions from formal language theory, and in the Sect. 3 we describe the general model for sequential grammars as established in [19] and the control mechanisms we are referring to in this paper within this general framework.

In Sect. 4 we give the definitions of the model of tissue P systems with vesicles of multisets as well as its variants to be considered in this paper. In Sect. 5 we show our main results for tissue P systems with vesicles of multisets using the three operations – insertion, deletion, and substitution – in the sequential derivation mode and moving the vesicle according to the underlying communication structure of the system. Computational completeness can be achieved when allowing also no rule to be applied in a derivation step, whereas otherwise we get a characterization of the families of sets of natural numbers and Parikh sets of natural numbers generated by partially blind register machines. In Sect. 6 we briefly discuss how computations on strings can be simulated with this model of tissue P systems. Moreover, we briefly outline how we even can "go beyond Turing" with such systems by simulating red-green register machines in Sect. 7. A summary of the results and an outlook to future research conclude the paper.

2   Prerequisites

We start by recalling some basic notions of formal language theory. An alphabet is a non-empty finite set. A finite sequence of symbols from an alphabet V is called a *string* over V. The set of all strings over V is denoted by V^*; the *empty string* is denoted by λ; moreover, we define $V^+ = V^* \setminus \{\lambda\}$. The *length* of a string x is denoted by $|x|$, and by $|x|_a$ we denote the number of occurrences of a letter a in a string x. For a string x, $alph(x)$ denotes the smallest alphabet Σ such that $x \in \Sigma^*$.

A *multiset* M with underlying set A is a pair (A, f) where $f : A \to \mathbb{N}$ is a mapping, with $\mathbb{N}$ denoting the set of natural numbers (non-negative integers). If $M = (A, f)$ is a multiset then its *support* is defined as $supp(M) = \{x \in A \mid f(x) > 0\}$. A multiset is empty (respectively finite) if its support is the empty set (respectively a finite set). If $M = (A, f)$ is a finite multiset over A and $supp(M) = \{a_1, \dots, a_k\}$, then it can also be represented by the string $a_1^{f(a_1)} \dots a_k^{f(a_k)}$ over the alphabet $\{a_1, \dots, a_k\}$ (the corresponding vector $(f(a_1), \dots, f(a_k))$ of natural numbers is called Parikh vector of the string $a_1^{f(a_1)} \dots a_k^{f(a_k)}$), and, moreover, all permutations of this string precisely identify the same multiset M (they have the same Parikh vector). The set of all multisets over the alphabet V is denoted by V°.

The family of all recursively enumerable sets of strings is denoted by RE, the corresponding family of recursively enumerable sets of Parikh sets (vectors of natural numbers) and of number sets is denoted by $PsRE$ and NRE, respectively. For more details of formal language theory the reader is referred to the monographs and handbooks in this area, such as [34].

2.1   Insertion, Deletion, and Substitution

For an alphabet V, let $a \to b$ be a rewriting rule with $a, b \in V \cup \{\lambda\}$, and $ab \neq \lambda$; we call such a rule a *substitution rule* if both a and b are different from λ and we also write $S(a, b)$; such a rule is called a *deletion rule* if $a \neq \lambda$ and $b = \lambda$, and it is also written as $D(a)$; $a \to b$ is called an *insertion rule* if $a = \lambda$

and $b \neq \lambda$, and we also write $I(b)$. The set of all insertion rules, deletion rules, and substitution rules over an alphabet V is denoted by Ins_V, Del_V, and Sub_V, respectively. Whereas an insertion rule is always applicable, the applicability of a deletion and a substitution rule depends on the presence of the symbol a. We remark that insertion rules, deletion rules, and substitution rules can be applied to strings as well as to multisets. Whereas in the string case, the position of the inserted, deleted, and substituted symbol matters, in the case of a multiset this only means incrementing the number of symbols b, decrementing the number of symbols a, or decrementing the number of symbols a and at the same time incrementing the number of symbols b.

2.2 Register Machines

Register machines are well-known universal devices for computing (generating or accepting) sets of vectors of natural numbers.

Definition 1. *A register machine is a construct*

$$M = (m, B, l_0, l_h, P)$$

where

- *m is the number of registers,*
- *B is a set of labels bijectively labeling the instructions in the set P,*
- *$l_0 \in B$ is the initial label, and*
- *$l_h \in B$ is the final label.*

  The labeled instructions of M in P can be of the following forms:

- *$p : (ADD\,(r)\,,q,s)$, with $p \in B \setminus \{l_h\}$, $q, s \in B$, $1 \leq r \leq m$.*
  Increase the value of register r by one, and non-deterministically jump to instruction q or s.
- *$p : (SUB\,(r)\,,q,s)$, with $p \in B \setminus \{l_h\}$, $q, s \in B$, $1 \leq r \leq m$.*
  If the value of register r is not zero then decrease the value of register r by one (decrement case) and jump to instruction q, otherwise jump to instruction s (zero-test case).
- *$l_h : HALT$.*
  Stop the execution of the register machine.

  A configuration of a register machine is described by the contents of each register and by the value of the current label, which indicates the next instruction to be executed.

In the accepting case, a computation starts with the input of a k-vector of natural numbers in its first k registers and by executing the first instruction of P (labeled with l_0); it terminates with reaching the $HALT$-instruction. Without loss of generality, we may assume all registers to be empty at the end of the computation.

In the generating case, a computation starts with all registers being empty and by executing the first instruction of P (labeled with l_0); it terminates with reaching the $HALT$-instruction and the output of a k-vector of natural numbers in its first k registers. Without loss of generality, we may assume all registers $> k$ to be empty at the end of the computation. The set of vectors of natural numbers computed by M in this way is denoted by $Ps(M)$. If we want to generate only numbers (1-dimensional vectors), then we have the result of a computation in register 1 and the set of numbers computed by M in this way is denoted by $N(R)$. By NRM and $PsRM$ we denote the families of sets of natural numbers and of sets of vectors of natural numbers, respectively, generated by register machines. It is folklore (e.g., see [29]) that $PsRE = PsRM$ and $NRE = NRM$ (actually, three registers are sufficient in order to generate any set from the family NRE, and, in general, $k + 2$ registers are needed to generate any set from the family $PsRE$).

Partially Blind Register Machines. In the case when a register machine cannot check whether a register is empty we say that it is partially blind: the registers are increased and decreased by one as usual, but if the machine tries to subtract from an empty register, then the computation aborts without producing any result; hence, we may say that the subtract instructions are of the form $p : (SUB\,(r)\,, q, abort)$; instead, we simply will write $p : (SUB\,(r)\,, q)$.

Moreover, acceptance or generation now by definition also requires all registers, except the first k output registers, to be empty (which means all registers $k + 1, \ldots, m$ have to be empty at the end of the computation), i.e., there is an implicit test for zero, at the end of a (successful) computation, that is why we say that the device is partially blind. By $NPBRM$ and $PsPBRM$ we denote the families of sets of natural numbers and of sets of vectors of natural numbers, respectively, computed by partially blind register machines. It is known (e.g., see [16]) that partially blind register machines are strictly less powerful than general register machines (hence than Turing machines); moreover, $NPBRM$ and $PsPBRM$ characterize the number and Parikh sets, respectively, obtained by matrix grammars without appearance checking.

3   A General Model for Sequential Grammars

We first recall the main definitions of the general model for sequential grammars as established in [19].

A *(sequential) grammar* G is a construct $(O, O_T, w, P, \Longrightarrow_G)$ where

- O is a set of *objects*;
- $O_T \subseteq O$ is a set of *terminal objects*;
- $w \in O$ is the *axiom (start object)*;
- P is a finite set of *rules*;

- $\Longrightarrow_G \subseteq O \times O$ is the *derivation relation* of G.

We assume that each of the rules $p \in P$ induces a relation $\Longrightarrow_p \subseteq O \times O$, in sum yielding $\Longrightarrow_G = \bigcup_{p \in P} \Longrightarrow_p$. The reflexive and transitive closure of $\Longrightarrow_G$ is denoted by $\overset{*}{\Longrightarrow}_G$. A rule $p \in P$ is called *applicable* to an object $x \in O$ if and only if there exists at least one object $y \in O$ such that $(x, y) \in \Longrightarrow_p$; we also write $x \Longrightarrow_p y$.

In the following we shall consider different types of grammars depending on the components of G (where the set of objects O is infinite, e.g., V^*, the set of strings over the alphabet V), especially with respect to different types of rules (e.g., context-free string rules). Some specific conditions on the elements of G, especially on the rules in P, may define a special type X of grammars which then will be called *grammars of type X*.

The *language generated by G* is the set of all terminal objects (we also assume $v \in O_T$ to be decidable for every $v \in O$) derivable from the axiom, i.e.,

$$L(G) = \left\{ v \in O_T \mid w \overset{*}{\Longrightarrow}_G v \right\}.$$

The family of languages generated by grammars of type X is denoted by $\mathcal{L}(X)$.

3.1 Specific Types of Objects

As special types of objects, in this paper we consider strings and multisets.

String Grammars. In the general notion as defined above, a *string grammar* G_S is represented as

$$\left((N \cup T)^*, T^*, w, P, \Longrightarrow_{G_S} \right)$$

where N is the alphabet of *non-terminal symbols*, T is the alphabet of *terminal symbols*, $N \cap T = \emptyset$, $w \in (N \cup T)^+$, P is a finite set of *rules* of the form $u \to v$ with $u \in V^*$ (for generating grammars, $u \in V^+$) and $v \in V^*$ (for accepting grammars, $v \in V^+$), with $V := N \cup T$; the derivation relation for $u \to v \in P$ is defined by $xuy \Longrightarrow_{u \to v} xvy$ for all $x, y \in V^*$, thus yielding the well-known derivation relation $\Longrightarrow_{G_S}$ for the string grammar G_S. In the following, we shall also use the common notation $G_S = (N, T, w, P)$ instead, too. We remark that, usually, the axiom w is supposed to be a non-terminal symbol, i.e., $w \in V \setminus T$, and is called the *start symbol*.

As special types of string grammars we consider string grammars with *arbitrary* rules as well as with *context-free* of the form $A \to v$, with $A \in N$ and $v \in V^*$. The corresponding types of grammars are denoted by ARB and CF, thus yielding the families of languages $\mathcal{L}(ARB)$, i.e., the family of recursively enumerable languages (also denoted by RE), as well as $\mathcal{L}(CF)$, i.e., the family of context-free languages, respectively.

We refer to [19] where some examples for string grammars of specific types illustrating the expressive power of this general framework are given.

The subfamily of REG only consisting of 1-star languages of the form W^* for some finite set of strings W is denoted by REG^{1*}; to be more specific, we also consider $REG^{1*}(k,p)$ consisting of all 1-star languages of the form W^* with k being the maximum number of strings in W and p being the maximum lengths of the strings in W. If $W = \{w\}$ for a singleton w, we call the set $\{w\}^*$ *periodic* and $|w|$ its *period*; thus, $REG^{1*}(1,p)$ denotes the family of all periodic sets with period at most p. If any of the numbers k or p may be arbitrarily large, we replace it by $*$.

Multiset Grammars. $G_m = ((N \cup T)^\circ, T^\circ, w, P, \Longrightarrow_{G_m})$ is called a *multiset grammar*; N is the alphabet of *non-terminal symbols*, T is the alphabet of *terminal symbols*, $N \cap T = \emptyset$, w is a non-empty multiset over V, $V := N \cup T$, and P is a (finite) set of multiset rules yielding a derivation relation $\Longrightarrow_{G_m}$ on the multisets over V; the application of the rule $u \to v$ to a multiset x has the effect of replacing the multiset u contained in x by the multiset v. For the multiset grammar G_m we also write $(N, T, w, P, \Longrightarrow_{G_m})$.

As special types of multiset grammars we consider multiset grammars with *arbitrary* rules as well as *context-free* (*non-cooperative*) rules of the form $A \to v$, with $A \in N$ and $v \in V^\circ$; the corresponding types X of multiset grammars are denoted by $mARB$ and mCF, thus yielding the families of multiset languages $\mathcal{L}(X)$.

As is well known, for example, see [26], even with arbitrary multiset rules, it is not possible to get $Ps(\mathcal{L}(ARB))$:

$$\mathcal{L}(mCF) = Ps(\mathcal{L}(CF)) \subsetneqq \mathcal{L}(mARB) \subsetneqq Ps(\mathcal{L}(ARB)).$$

3.2   Graph-Controlled and Programmed Grammars

A *graph-controlled grammar* (with applicability checking) of type X is a construct

$$G_{GC} = (G, g, H_i, H_f, \Longrightarrow_{GC})$$

where $G = (O, O_T, w, P, \Longrightarrow_G)$ is a grammar of type X; $g = (H, E, K)$ is a labeled graph where H is the set of node labels identifying the nodes of the graph in a one-to-one manner, $E \subseteq H \times \{Y, N\} \times H$ is the set of edges labeled by Y or N, $K : H \to 2^P$ is a function assigning a subset of P to each node of g; $H_i \subseteq H$ is the set of initial labels, and $H_f \subseteq H$ is the set of final labels. The derivation relation $\Longrightarrow_{GC}$ is defined based on $\Longrightarrow_G$ and the control graph g as follows: For any $i, j \in H$ and any $u, v \in O$, $(u, i) \Longrightarrow_{GC} (v, j)$ if and only if

 – $u \Longrightarrow_p v$ by some rule $p \in K(i)$ and $(i, Y, j) \in E$ *(success case)*, **or**
 – $u = v$, no $p \in K(i)$ is applicable to u, and $(i, N, j) \in E$ *(failure case)*.

The language generated by G_{GC} is defined by

$$L(G_{GC}) = \left\{ v \in O_T \mid (w, i) \Longrightarrow^*_{G_{GC}} (v, j), \ i \in H_i, j \in H_f \right\}.$$

If $H_i = H_f = H$, then G_{GC} is called a *programmed grammar*. The families of languages generated by graph-controlled and programmed grammars of type X are denoted by $\mathcal{L}(X\text{-}GC_{ac})$ and $\mathcal{L}(X\text{-}P_{ac})$, respectively. If the set E contains no edges of the form (i, N, j), then the graph-controlled or programmed grammar is said to be *without applicability checking*; the corresponding families of languages are denoted by $\mathcal{L}(X\text{-}GC)$ and $\mathcal{L}(X\text{-}P)$, respectively. If for all pairs $(i, j) \in H \times H$ we have $(i, Y, j) \in E$ if and only if $(i, N, j) \in E$, then this regulated grammar is said to be with *unconditional transfer*, as the transitions in the control graph do not depend on the application of a rule; the corresponding families of languages are denoted by $\mathcal{L}(X\text{-}GC_{ut})$ and $\mathcal{L}(X\text{-}P_{ut})$, respectively.

The notions and concepts *with/without applicability checking* were introduced as *with/without appearance checking* in the original definition for string grammars because the appearance of the non-terminal symbol on the left-hand side of a context-free rule was checked, which coincides with checking for the applicability of this rule in our general model; in both cases – applicability checking and appearance checking – we can use the abbreviation *ac*.

The concept of unconditional transfer has only been investigated in a few papers; the most interesting results are to be found in [12], where the following was shown for strings:

Theorem 1. $\mathcal{L}(CF\text{-}GC_{ut}) = \mathcal{L}(CF\text{-}GC_{ac}) = RE$.

3.3 Matrix Grammars

A *matrix grammar* (with applicability checking) of type X is a construct

$$G_M = (G, M, F, \Longrightarrow_{G_M})$$

where $G = (O, O_T, w, P, \Longrightarrow_G)$ is a grammar of type X, M is a finite set of sequences of the form $(p_1, \ldots, p_n)$, $n \geq 1$, of rules in P, and $F \subseteq P$. For $w, z \in O$ we write $w \Longrightarrow_{G_M} z$ if there are a matrix $(p_1, \ldots, p_n)$ in M and objects $w_i \in O$, $1 \leq i \leq n + 1$, such that $w = w_1$, $z = w_{n+1}$, and, for all $1 \leq i \leq n$, either

- $w_i \Longrightarrow_G w_{i+1}$ or
- $w_i = w_{i+1}$, p_i is not applicable to w_i, and $p_i \in F$.

$L(G_M) = \{v \in O_T \mid w \Longrightarrow_{G_M}^* v\}$ is the language generated by G_M. The family of languages generated by matrix grammars of type X is denoted by $\mathcal{L}(X\text{-}MAT_{ac})$. If the set F is empty, then the grammar is said to be *without applicability checking*; the corresponding family of languages is denoted by $\mathcal{L}(X\text{-}MAT)$.

We mention that in this paper we choose the definition where the sequential application of the rules of the final matrix may stop at any moment.

3.4 Grammars with Regular Control and Time-Varying Grammars

Another possibility to capture the idea of controlling the derivation in a grammar as with a control graph is to consider the sequence of rules applied during a computation and to require this sequence to be an element of a regular language:

A *grammar with regular control and appearance checking* is a construct

$$G_C = (G, H_C, L, F)$$

where $G = (O, O_T, w, P, \Longrightarrow_G)$ is a grammar of type X and L is a regular language over H_C, where H_C is the set of labels identifying the non-empty subsets of productions from P in a one-to-one manner, and $F \subseteq H_C$. We will use the notation $H_C(P')$ to refer to the label of the subset $P' \subseteq P$. The language generated by G_C consists of all terminal objects z such that there exist a string $H_C(P_1) \dots H_C(P_n) \in L$ as well as objects $w_i \in O$, $1 \le i \le n+1$, such that $w = w_1$, $z = w_{n+1}$, and, for all $1 \le i \le n$, either

- $w_i \Longrightarrow_G w_{i+1}$ by some production from P_i or
- $w_i = w_{i+1}$, no production from P_i is applicable to w_i, and $H_C(P_i) \in F$.

It is rather easy to see that the model of grammars with regular control is closely related with the model of graph-controlled grammars in the sense that the control graph corresponds to the deterministic finite automaton accepting L. Hence, we may also speak of a *grammar with regular control and without appearance checking* if $F = \emptyset$, and if $F = H_C$ then G_C is said to be a *grammar with regular control and unconditional transfer*. The corresponding families of languages are denoted by $\mathcal{L}(X\text{-}C\,(REG)_{ac})$, $\mathcal{L}(X\text{-}C\,(REG))$, and $\mathcal{L}(X\text{-}C\,(REG)_{ut})$.

Obviously, the control languages can also be taken from another family of languages Y, e.g., $\mathcal{L}(CF)$, thus yielding the families $\mathcal{L}(X\text{-}C\,(Y)_{ac})$, etc., but in this paper we shall restrict ourselves to the cases $Y = REG$ and $Y = REG^{1*}(k,p)$. For $Y = REG^{1*}(1,p)$, these grammars are also known as *(periodically) time-varying grammars*, as the control language $\{H_C(P_1) \dots H_C(P_p)\}^*$ means that the set of productions available at a time t in a derivation is P_i if $t = kp+i$, $k \ge 0$; p is called the *period* of the time-varying system. The corresponding families of languages generated by time-varying grammars with appearance checking, without appearance checking, with unconditional transfer, and with period p, are denoted by $\mathcal{L}(X\text{-}TV_{ac}(p))$, $\mathcal{L}(X\text{-}TV(p))$, and $\mathcal{L}(X\text{-}TV_{ut}(p))$, respectively; if p may be arbitrarily large, p is replaced by $*$ or omitted in these notations.

In many cases it is not necessary to insist that the control string $H_C(P_1) \dots H_C(P_n)$ of a derivation is in L, it usually also is sufficient that $H_C(P_1) \dots H_C(P_n)$ is a prefix of some string in L. We call this control *weak* and replace C by wC and TV by wTV in the notions of the families of languages. We should like to mention that in the case of wTV the control words are just prefixes of the ω-word $(H_C(P_1) \dots H_C(P_p))^\omega$.

In the case of string grammars, from the results stated in [12], we obtain the following, for $\alpha \in \{\lambda, w\}$:

$$
\begin{aligned}
RE &= \mathcal{L}(CF\text{-}GC_{ac}) = \mathcal{L}(CF\text{-}GC_{ut}) \\
&= \mathcal{L}(CF\text{-}P_{ac}) = \mathcal{L}(CF\text{-}MAT_{ac}) \\
&= \mathcal{L}(CF\text{-}\alpha C\,(REG)_{ac}) = \mathcal{L}(CF\text{-}\alpha C\,(REG)_{ut}) \\
&= \mathcal{L}(CF\text{-}\alpha TV_{ac}) = \mathcal{L}(CF\text{-}\alpha TV_{ut}) \\
&\supsetneq \mathcal{L}(CF\text{-}GC) = \mathcal{L}(CF\text{-}P) = \mathcal{L}(CF\text{-}MAT).
\end{aligned}
$$

Remark 1. We would like to mention that in the standard definition only the rules themselves are labeled for the control language and not all the subsets of rules, which corresponds with having only one rule assigned to each node in a graph-controlled grammar and not allowing a set of rules to be assigned. Yet in our more general definition, time-varying grammars are just an easy special case of grammars with regular control.

In [2], time-varying (tissue) P systems with only one cell are considered. As a sequential (tissue) P system with only one cell and no interaction with the environment corresponds with a multiset grammar, the main results obtained in this paper can be expressed as follows:

Theorem 2. *For all* $\alpha \in \{\lambda, w\}$, $\beta \in \{\lambda, ac, ut\}$, *and* $k, p \geq 1$,

$$
\begin{aligned}
\mathcal{L}\left(mARB\text{-}MAT\right) &= \mathcal{L}\left(mCF\text{-}MAT\right) \\
&= Ps\mathcal{L}\left(CF\text{-}MAT\right) \\
&= \mathcal{L}\left(mARB\right) \\
&= \mathcal{L}\left(mARB\text{-}TV\left(p\right)\right) \\
&= \mathcal{L}\left(mARB\text{-}\alpha C\left(REG\right)_\beta\right) \\
&= \mathcal{L}\left(mCF\text{-}\alpha C\left(REG^{1*}\left(*, p+1\right)\right)_\beta\right) \\
&= \mathcal{L}\left(mCF\text{-}\alpha C\left(REG\right)_\beta\right).
\end{aligned}
$$

Theorem 3. *For all* $\alpha \in \{\lambda, w\}$, $\beta \in \{ac, ut\}$, $p \geq 12$, *and* $d \geq 2$,

$$
\mathcal{L}\left(mCF\text{-}\alpha TV_\beta\left(p, d\right)\right) = PsRE.
$$

The additional parameter d – for *delay* – indicates that for at most d steps no rule is applied during any derivation before it stops.

4 Tissue P Systems Working on Vesicles of Multisets With Point Mutation Rules

We now define the model of tissue P systems working on vesicles of multisets in the sequential mode using point mutation rules:

Definition 2. *A tissue P systems working on vesicles of multisets in the sequential derivation mode with point mutation rules (an* stPV *system for short) is a tuple*

$$
\Pi = (L, V, T, R, g, (i_0, w_0), h)
$$

where

- *L is a set of labels identifying in a one-to-one manner the $|L|$ cells of the tissue P system Π;*
- *V is the alphabet of the system,*
- *T is the terminal alphabet of the system,*

- R is a set of rules *of the form* (i,p) *where* $i \in L$ *and* $p \in Ins_V \cup Del_V \cup Sub_V$, *i.e., p is an insertion, deletion or substitution rule over the alphabet V; we may collect all rules from cell i in one set and then write $R_i = \{(i,p) \mid (i,p) \in R\}$, so that $R = \bigcup_{i \in L} R_i$; moreover, for the sake of conciseness, we may simply write $R_i = \{p \mid (i,p) \in R\}$, too;*
- g *is a directed graph describing the underlying communication structure of Π,* $g = (N, E)$ *with $N = L$ being the set of nodes of the graph g and the set of edges $E \subseteq N \times N$;*
- (i_0, w_0) *describes the* initial vesicle *containing the multiset w_0 in cell i_0;*
- h *is the* output cell *for extracting the terminal results.*

The stPV system now works as follows: The computation of Π starts with a vesicle containing the multiset w_0 in cell i_0, and the computation proceeds with derivation steps until a specific output condition is fulfilled, which in all possible cases means that the vesicle has arrived in the output cell h.

In each derivation step, with the vesicle enclosing the multiset w being in cell i, tentatively (i.e., if possible) one rule p from R_i is applied to w and the resulting multiset in its vesicle is moved to a cell j such that $(i,j) \in E$.

As we are dealing with membrane systems, the classic output condition – in the generating case – would be to only consider halting computations; yet as we allow that we also move the vesicle to the next cell even if no rule can be applied to the multiset in the vesicle, the most natural condition is to take as results only those multisets which have arrived in the output cell h enclosed in the vesicle and only consist of terminal symbols.

On the other hand, *halting* still can be defined as follows for vesicles enclosing terminal multisets which have arrived in the output cell h: consider any loopless path from the output cell h through the communication graph g; then halting can be defined as having no such path along which we arrive in a cell where still a rule can be applied.

In [2], the notion *halting with delay d* is used to describe the situation that we allow the system to stay inactive (i.e., without applying a rule) for d steps before a computation is said to halt. We will also use this refinement of halting in this paper to specify how many steps we have to go ahead in order to see that the system halts; according to the definition for halting given above, in the worst case d is the length of the longest loopless path through the communication graph g.

Hence, for the tissue P systems considered in this paper we may specify the following derivation and output strategies:

- *halt*: the only condition is that the system halts in the sense explained above, i.e., no matter which path we followed in the communication graph g, no rule will be applicable any more; the result is the multiset contained in the vesicle to be found in cell h (which in fact means that specifying the terminal alphabet is obsolete);

- $(halt, d)$: the result is the multiset contained in the vesicle to be found in cell h, but the additional condition is that in no successful derivation (i.e., a derivation yielding a result) more than d steps without applying a rule may occur; the special case $d = 0$ means that we do not allow a derivation step where no rule is applied (again specifying the terminal alphabet is obsolete);
- $term$: the resulting multiset contained in the vesicle to be found in cell h consists of terminal symbols only (yet the system need not have reached a halting configuration);
- $(term, d)$: the resulting multiset contained in the vesicle to be found in cell h consists of terminal symbols only (yet the system need not have reached a halting configuration), but, in addition, we require that in any successful derivation at most d steps without applying a rule may occur;
- $(halt, term)$: both conditions must be fulfilled, i.e., the resulting multiset contained in the vesicle to be found in cell h consists of terminal symbols only as well as the system halts in the way defined above;
- $(halt, term, d)$: all three conditions must be fulfilled, i.e., the resulting multiset contained in the vesicle to be found in cell h consists of terminal symbols only, the system halts in the way defined above, and in any successful derivation at most d steps without applying a rule may occur.

Instead of $halt$, $term$, and $(halt, term)$ we may also write $(halt, *)$, $(term, *)$, and $(halt, term, *)$, respectively.

The set of all multisets obtained as results of computations in Π with the output being obtained by using the derivation and output strategy $\beta \in \mathbb{D}$,

$$\mathbb{D} = \{(halt, \alpha), (term, \alpha), (halt, term, \alpha) \mid \alpha \in \mathbb{N} \cup \{*\}\}$$

is denoted by $Ps(\Pi, sequ, gen, \beta)$, with $sequ$ specifying that the tissue P system works in the sequential derivation mode and gen indicating that Π is considered as a generating device; if we are only interested in the number of symbols in the resulting multiset, the corresponding set of natural numbers is denoted by $N(\Pi, sequ, gen, \beta)$. The families of sets of (k-dimensional) vectors of natural numbers and sets of natural numbers generated by stPV systems with at most n cells using the derivation and output strategy β are denoted by $Ps(tPV_n, sequ, gen, \beta)$ and $N(tPV_n, sequ, gen, \beta)$, respectively. If n is not bounded, we simply omit the subscript in these notations.

The tissue P systems defined above can also be used as accepting and as computing devices: the input multiset w then is added to the initial multiset w_0, i.e., we start with the multiset $w w_0$ enclosed in the vesicle to be found in cell i_0 at the beginning of the computation. In the computing case, the results are obtained as described above according to the two different derivation and output strategies β as explained above. In the accepting case, the final multiset can either be required to be empty or else even to be any multiset over V, in which case only getting the vesicle into the output cell is the main acceptance criterion. We here prefer to require the strong condition that the final multiset in the vesicle having arrived in cell h must be the empty multiset. In all the notions defined in the preceding paragraph, gen is replaced by acc or $comp$ in order to indicate that we are considering the tissue P systems as accepting or computing devices, respectively.

5   Simulation Results

Our first results show that without allowing derivation steps where no rule is applied, the computational power of stPV systems is very much reduced, i.e., such systems only have the power of partially blind register machines.

Lemma 1. *For any* $\beta \in \{(term, 0), (halt, term, 0)\}$,

$$PsPBRM \subseteq Ps(stPV, sequ, gen, \beta).$$

Proof. Let $K \in PsPBRM$, i.e., the vector set K can be generated by a partially blind register machine $M = (m, B, l_0, l_h, P)$. We now define an equivalent stPV system Π generating K, i.e., $Ps(\Pi, sequ, gen, (term, 0)) = K$. The number of symbols a_r represents the contents of register r.

$$
\begin{aligned}
\Pi &= (L, V, T, R, g = (L, E), (i_0, w_0), h), \\
L &= B, \\
V &= \{a_r \mid 1 \leq r \leq m\}, \\
T &= \{a_r \mid 1 \leq r \leq k\}, \\
R &= \{(p, I(a_r)) \mid p : (ADD\,(r)\,, q, s) \in P\} \\
&\quad \cup \{(p, D(a_r)) \mid p : (SUB\,(r)\,, q) \in P\}, \\
E &= \{(p, q), (p, s) \mid p : (ADD\,(r)\,, q, s) \in P\} \\
&\quad \cup \{(p, q) \mid p : (SUB\,(r)\,, q) \in P\}, \\
(i_0, w_0) &= (l_0, \lambda), \\
h &= l_h.
\end{aligned}
$$

The simulation of the computations in M by Π works in real time, i.e., one step of the register machine is simulated in one step of Π: incrementing register r by an ADD-instruction is simulated by inserting a symbol a_r, decrementing register r by a SUB-instruction is simulated by deleting a symbol a_r; in case we try to decrement an empty register, the partially blind register machine aborts the computation, which is mimicked in the stPV system with Π getting stuck in cell p, as without applying the rule $D(a_r)$ the vesicle cannot move further and thus will never reach the output cell l_h.

Any halting computation in M finally reaches the halting instruction labeled by l_h, and thus in Π the vesicle obtained so far has also reached the output cell h, and as no rule is assigned to cell h, the computation in Π also halts when a vesicle reaches the output cell h. Provided no non-terminal symbol a_r with $k+1 \leq r \leq m$ is still present, the computation in Π yields the same result as the corresponding computation in M, i.e., we conclude that $Ps(\Pi, sequ, gen, (term, 0)) = K$ and $Ps(\Pi, sequ, gen, (halt, term, 0)) = K$, too.

The construction given in the preceding proof does not need additional symbols, the computation is guided by the communication graph g. Moreover, only insertion and deletion rules are needed.

If we only require halting, we have to guarantee that a vesicle arriving in the output cell can only stay there if its contents entirely consists of terminal symbols; in this case, we not only need an additional symbol (the trap symbol $\#$), but also substitution rules:

Lemma 2. $PsPBRM \subseteq Ps(stPV, sequ, gen, (halt, 0))$.

Proof. Let $K \in PsPBRM$, i.e., the vector set K can be generated by a partially blind register machine $M = (m, B, l_0, l_h, P)$. We now define an equivalent stPV system Π generating K such that $Ps(\Pi, sequ, gen, (halt, 0)) = K$. The number of symbols a_r represents the contents of register r.

The simulation of the computations in M by Π works in real time as described in the preceding proof: incrementing register r by an ADD-instruction is simulated by inserting a symbol a_r, decrementing register r by a SUB-instruction is simulated by deleting a symbol a_r.

$$
\begin{aligned}
\Pi &= (L, V, T, R, g = (L, E), (i_0, w_0), h), \\
L &= B, \\
V &= \{a_r \mid 1 \le r \le m\} \cup \{\#\}, \\
T &= \{a_r \mid 1 \le r \le k\}, \\
R &= \{(p, I(a_r)) \mid p : (ADD\,(r), q, s) \in P\} \\
&\quad \cup \{(p, D(a_r)) \mid p : (SUB\,(r), q) \in P\} \\
&\quad \cup \{(h, S(a_r, \#)) \mid k + 1 \le r \le m\} \\
&\quad \cup \{(h, S(\#, \#))\}, \\
E &= \{(p, q), (p, s) \mid p : (ADD\,(r), q, s) \in P\} \\
&\quad \cup \{(p, q) \mid p : (SUB\,(r), q) \in P\} \\
&\quad \cup \{(h, h)\}, \\
(i_0, w_0) &= (l_0, \lambda), \\
h &= l_h.
\end{aligned}
$$

Any halting computation in M finally reaches the halting instruction labeled by l_h, and thus in Π the vesicle obtained so far has also reached the output cell h. Yet now we have to check by applying trap rules $S(a_r, \#)$ that no non-terminal symbol a_r with $k + 1 \le r \le m$ is still present to guarantee that the computation in Π yields the same result as the corresponding computation in M: If the multiset enclosed in the vesicle which has reached the output cell h only contains terminal symbols a_r with $1 \le r \le k$, then no rule $S(a_r, \#)$ for a non-terminal symbol a_r with $k + 1 \le r \le m$ is applicable, i.e., the computation halts. Otherwise, the application of one of these trap rules $S(a_r, \#)$ forces the the rule $S(\#, \#)$ to be applicable in cell h again and again, i.e., the computation gets trapped in an infinite loop, so no unwanted result will be obtained in that case.

In sum, we conclude that $Ps(\Pi, sequ, gen, (halt, 0)) = K$. $\qquad\square$

We now also show that the computations of an stPV system using the derivation and output strategy $(term, 0)$ can be simulated by a partially blind register machine.

Lemma 3. $Ps(stPV, sequ, gen, (term, 0)) \subseteq PsPBRM$.

Proof (Sketch). Let $(L, V, T, R, g = (L, E), (i_0, w_0), h)$ be an arbitrary stPV system yielding an output in the output cell provided the multiset in the vesicle having arrived there contains only terminal symbols. Without loss of generality we assume $L = \{i \mid 1 \le i \le n\}$.

We now construct a register machine $M = (m, B, l_0, l_h, P)$ generating $Ps(\Pi, sequ, gen, (term, 0))$, yet using a more relaxed definition for the labeling of instructions in M, i.e., one label may be used for different instructions, which does not affect the computational power of the register machine as shown in [16]. For example, instead of a nondeterministic ADD-instruction $p : (ADD(r), q, s)$ we use the two deterministic ADD-instructions $p : (ADD(r), q)$ and $p : (ADD(r), s)$. Moreover, we omit the generation of w_0 in l_0 by a sequence of ADD-instructions finally ending up with label l_0 and the correct values in registers r for the numbers of symbols a_r in cell l_0. In general, the number of symbols a_r in the current multiset enclosed in the vesicle is represented by the corresponding number of symbols in the registers r, $1 \le r \le m$.

We now sketch how the computations in Π can be simulated by the register machine instructions in M:

- for any combination of rules $(p, I(a_r)) \in R$ and edges $(p, q) \in E$ we take the instruction $p : (ADD(r), q)$ into P.
- for any combination of rules $(p, D(a_r)) \in R$ and edges $(p, q) \in E$ we take the instruction $p : (SUB(r), q)$ into P.
- for any combination of rules $(p, S(a_r, a_s)) \in R$ and edges $(p, q) \in E$ we take the sequence of two instructions $p : (SUB(a_r), p')$ and $p' : (ADD(a_s), q)$ into P using an intermediate label p'.

If a vesicle reaches the final cell h with the multiset inside only consisting of terminal symbols, we also have to allow M to have this multiset as a result: this goal can be accomplished by using the final sequence

$$h : \left(ADD(m), \tilde{h} \right),$$

$$\tilde{h} : \left(SUB(m), \hat{h} \right),$$

$$\hat{h} : HALT.$$

We observe that $\tilde{h}, \hat{h}$ are new labels different from all others. The new label $\hat{h}$ now the only halting instruction of M, i.e., $l_h = \hat{h}$. Hence, M must have reset to zero all its working registers before reaching $\hat{h}$ to satisfy the final zero check, which corresponds to Π having produced a multiset consisting exclusively of terminal symbols.

In sum, we conclude that $Ps(M) = Ps(\Pi, sequ, gen, (term, 0))$.

As a consequence of Lemmas 1 and 3 we obtain:

Theorem 4. $PsPBRM = Ps(stPV, sequ, (term, 0))$.

It remains as a challenging open question if a similar characterization result can also be obtained for the derivation and output strategies $(halt, 0)$ and $(term, halt, 0)$ including the condition that no rule can be applied any more in the output cell. This immediately turns out to be true if we require that no rules should be applied in the output cell, which seems to be a very natural condition. In general, without this condition, this need not be true: just consider a loop in the output cell h with an insertion rule leading back to h itself or via an additional cell h' as used in the proof of Lemma 2.

We now turn our attention to stPV systems allowing to continue the computation even if in some derivation step(s) no rule can be applied:

Theorem 5. $PsRE \subseteq Ps(stPV, sequ, gen, \beta)$ *for any* β *with*

$$\beta \in \mathbb{D} \setminus \{(halt, term, 0), (halt, 0), (term, 0)\}.$$

Proof. Let K be an arbitrary recursively enumerable set of k-dimensional vectors of natural numbers. Then K can be generated by a register machine $M = (m, B, l_0, l_h, P)$ with the first k registers being the output registers and the other ones being working registers, which without loss of generality can be assumed to be empty at the end of any successful computation. We now define an stPV system Π generating K, i.e., $Ps(\Pi, sequ, gen, \beta) = K$:

$$
\begin{aligned}
\Pi \ &= \ (L, V, T, R, g = (L, E), (i_0, w_0), h)\,, \\
L \ &= \ B \cup \{p, \bar{p}, \bar{p}', \hat{p}, \hat{p}' \mid p : (SUB\,(r)\,, q, s) \in P\}, \\
V \ &= \ \{a_r \mid 1 \le r \le m\} \cup \{e, \#\}, \\
T \ &= \ \{a_r \mid 1 \le r \le k\}, \\
R \ &= \ \{(p, I(a_r)) \mid p : (ADD\,(r)\,, q, s) \in P\} \\
&\quad \cup \{(p, I(e)), (\hat{p}, S(a_r, \#)), (\hat{p}', D(e)), \\
&\qquad (\bar{p}, S(e, \#)), (\bar{p}, D(a_r)), (\bar{p}', D(e)) \mid p : (SUB\,(r)\,, q) \in P\} \\
&\quad \cup \{(h, S(\#, \#)), (h', S(\#, \#))\}, \\
E \ &= \ \{(p, q), (p, s) \mid p : (ADD\,(r)\,, q, s) \in P\} \\
&\quad \cup \{(p, \bar{p}), (p, \hat{p}), (\bar{p}, \bar{p}'), (\hat{p}, \hat{p}'), (\bar{p}', q), (\hat{p}', s) \mid p : (SUB\,(r)\,, q) \in P\} \\
&\quad \cup \{(h, h'), (h', h)\}, \\
(i_0, w_0) \ &= \ (l_0, \lambda), \\
h \ &= \ l_h.
\end{aligned}
$$

$(ADD\,(r)\,, q, s)$ is simulated by applying the rule $(p, I(a_r))$ and then sending the vesicle from cell p either to cell q or cell s.

$(SUB\,(r)\,, q, s)$ is simulated by first inserting one symbol e, which at the end of a correct simulation path is to be eliminated again in cells $\bar{p}'$ and $\hat{p}'$, respectively. The *decrement case* follows the path $p - \bar{p} - \bar{p}' - q$; if chosen correctly, in cell $\bar{p}$ the rule $D(a_r)$ can be applied, otherwise the trap rule $S(e, \#))$ *must* be applied, in which case instead of eliminating e in cell $\bar{p}'$ no rule will be applicable there.

The *zero-test case* follows the path $p - \hat{p} - \hat{p}' - s$; if chosen correctly, i.e., if no symbol a_r is present (indicating that register r is empty), the rule $S(a_r, \#))$ will not be applicable in cell $\hat{p}$, i.e., the vesicle will move to cell $\hat{p}'$ without a rule having been applied. In cell $\hat{p}'$, the rule $D(e)$ will be applicable in any case.

Any halting computation in M finally reaches the halting instruction labeled by l_h, and thus in Π the vesicle obtained so far has arrived in the output cell h. Provided no trap symbol $\#$ has been generated during the simulation of the computation in M by the stPV system Π, the multiset in this vesicle only contains terminal symbols and the computation in Π halts as well. In case a trap symbol occurs, the computation gets stuck in an infinite loop in cell h.

We observe that by construction in two succeeding derivation steps it may happen at most once that no rule is applicable; hence, we conclude that $Ps(\Pi, smax, \beta) = K$ for any β with

$$\beta \in \mathbb{D} \setminus \{(halt, term, 0), (halt, 0), (term, 0)\}$$

which observation completes the proof.   □

The construction given in the preceding proof could be modified in several ways: for example, we could replace the additional symbol e by $\#$ and replace the rules $(\bar{p}, S(e, \#))$ by the corresponding rules $(\bar{p}, I(\#))$.

Another variant would be to avoid the introduction of e anyway and take two simple paths for the decrement and the zero-test case:

The *decrement case* follows the path $p - q$ with $R_p = \{D(a_r), I(\#))\}$; if chosen correctly, the rule $D(a_r)$ can be applied, otherwise the trap rule $I(\#))$ *must* be applied introducing the trap symbol $\#$.

The *zero-test case* follows the path $p' - s$ with $R_{p'} = \{S(a_r, \#)\}$; if chosen correctly, i.e., if no symbol a_r is present (indicating that register r is empty), the rule $S(a_r, \#)$ will not be applied, otherwise the trap symbol is introduced.

In sum, with this variant we only need two cells p and p' for a SUB-instruction p as well as a simpler communication structure, but from every cell having an edge to p we now need both edges to p *and* p'.

The major drawback of this simpler construction is that we cannot guarantee that the delay between two rule applications is not bigger than one: if the register machine M performs k successful zero checks, then Π in a correct simulation path does not apply any rule to the vesicle for k successive steps.

As already discussed in Sect. 1, the control given by the communication graph in stPV systems nicely corresponds to the control mechanisms in graph-controlled multiset grammars with unconditional transfer and in multiset grammars with regular control and unconditional transfer. The communication graph of an stPV system can be interpreted as the control graph of the corresponding graph-controlled multiset grammar. In a multiset grammar with regular control and unconditional transfer, the communication graph of the stPV system describes a regular control language over L, hence, the proof of Theorem 5 also yields a proof of the following result for graph-controlled multiset grammars with unconditional transfer as well as multiset grammars with regular control and unconditional transfer, both using insertion, deletion, and substitution point mutation rules (we refer to this type of rules by $mIDS$):

Theorem 6. $PsRE = \mathcal{L}\left(mIDS\text{-}C\left(REG\right)_{ut}\right) = \mathcal{L}\left(mIDS\text{-}GC_{ut}\right).$

6   Simulating Computations with Strings

As already discussed in Sect. 1, we can also simulate computations on strings by adding rules for taking an object from the environment into the vesicle and/or sending an object out of the vesicle. We then define the input and output strings as the sequences of symbols taken in and sent out, respectively (for example, see [14,15]). As an input sequence can be encoded as a number and then processed by only two registers (the folklore result for two-counter automata) and the final result can be encoded as a number and then decoded into a sequence of symbols sent out (e.g., see [13]), the basic result how to simulate register machines elaborated in Sect. 5 also allows for simulating computations on strings.

As these additional rules we may use $read(a)$ and $write(a)$ which correspond to taking an object from the environment into the vesicle and sending an object out from the vesicle, respectively.

7   Going Beyond Turing

As already discussed in Sect. 1, a possibility to "go beyond Turing" is to simulate red-green register machines as first introduced in the area of membrane systems in [5], where the concept of *red-green P automata* for several specific models of membrane systems is explained. The basic idea of these red-green automata is to distinguish between two different sets of states (red and green states) and to consider infinite runs of the automaton on finite input objects (strings, multisets); allowed to change between red and green states more than once, red-green automata can recognize more than the recursively enumerable sets (of strings, multisets).

The main problem with finding a red-green variant of the special variant of tissue P systems introduced in this paper is its inherent non-determinism as can be seen from the proof of Theorem 5, even when simulating deterministic register machines and their red-green variant – the zero-test case and the decrement case of a SUB-instruction are chosen in a non-deterministic way. To overcome this problem we now rely on k-determinism (looking ahead k steps in order to know how to proceed in a deterministic way) as, for example, discussed in [30], as well as on the concept of toxic objects, which "kill" any derivation branch that introduces one of the them, as it happens, for example, with the trap symbol, see [1].

As we can see from the proof of Theorem 5, simulating the SUB-instructions of a register machine only needs a look-ahead of 1, i.e., as the deterministic continuation of a derivation in the tissue P system we can just take the one which does not introduce the trap symbol. In that way, also a red-green variant of the model introduced in this paper can be defined, thus even allowing us to "go beyond Turing":

We use the simulation technique as outlined in the proof of Theorem 5, and then all variants of an instruction label p get the same color as p itself. In that way, mind changes are also simulated in a correct way. The only additional trick is to make the infinite run on a finite input deterministic by choosing the branch which does not introduce the trap symbol #.

8 Conclusion and Future Research

In this paper, we have investigated tissue P systems operating on vesicles of multisets with point mutations, i.e., with insertion, deletion, and substitution of single symbols, working in the sequential derivation mode. Without allowing computation steps to not apply a rule, we obtain a characterization of the sets of (vectors of) natural numbers generated by partially blind register machines, whereas otherwise we can generate every recursively enumerable set of (vectors of) natural numbers. Adding the possibility of taking in symbols from the environment and/or sending out symbols to the environment from the vesicle, we are able to simulate computations on strings. Moreover, we even showed how to "go beyond Turing" based on the model of red-green register machines.

Several challenging topics remain for future research: for example, what happens if we are not allowed to use substitution rules (with all possible derivation and output strategies)?

References

1. Alhazov, A., Freund, R.: P systems with toxic objects. In: Gheorghe, M., Rozenberg, G., Salomaa, A., Sosík, P., Zandron, C. (eds.) CMC 2014. LNCS, vol. 8961, pp. 99–125. Springer, Cham (2014). https://doi.org/10.1007/978-3-319-14370-5_7
2. Alhazov, A., Freund, R., Heikenwälder, H., Oswald, M., Rogozhin, Yu., Verlan, S.: Sequential P systems with regular control. In: Csuhaj-Varjú, E., Gheorghe, M., Rozenberg, G., Salomaa, A., Vaszil, Gy. (eds.) CMC 2012. LNCS, vol. 7762, pp. 112–127. Springer, Heidelberg (2013). https://doi.org/10.1007/978-3-642-36751-9_9
3. Alhazov, A., Freund, R., Ivanov, S., Verlan, S.: (tissue) P systems with vesicles of multisets. In: Csuhaj-Varjú, E., Dömösi, P., Vaszil, Gy. (eds.) Proceedings 15th International Conference on Automata and Formal Languages, AFL 2017, Debrecen, Hungary, 4–6 September 2017. EPTCS, vol. 252, pp. 11–25 (2017). https://doi.org/10.4204/EPTCS.252.6
4. Alhazov, A., Freund, R., Verlan, S.: P systems working in maximal variants of the set derivation mode. In: Leporati, A., Rozenberg, G., Salomaa, A., Zandron, C. (eds.) CMC 2016. LNCS, vol. 10105, pp. 83–102. Springer, Cham (2017). https://doi.org/10.1007/978-3-319-54072-6_6

5. Aman, B., Csuhaj-Varjú, E., Freund, R.: Red–green P automata. In: Gheorghe, M., Rozenberg, G., Salomaa, A., Sosík, P., Zandron, C. (eds.) CMC 2014. LNCS, vol. 8961, pp. 139–157. Springer, Cham (2014). https://doi.org/10.1007/978-3-319-14370-5_9

6. Arroyo, F., Gómez-Canaval, S., Mitrana, V., Popescu, Ş.: On the computational power of networks of polarized evolutionary processors. Inf. Comput. **253**(3), 371–380 (2017). https://doi.org/10.1016/j.ic.2016.06.004

7. Arroyo, F., Gómez Canaval, S., Mitrana, V., Popescu, Ş.: Networks of polarized evolutionary processors are computationally complete. In: Dediu, A.-H., Martín-Vide, C., Sierra-Rodríguez, J.-L., Truthe, B. (eds.) LATA 2014. LNCS, vol. 8370, pp. 101–112. Springer, Cham (2014). https://doi.org/10.1007/978-3-319-04921-2_8

8. Calude, C.S., Păun, Gh.: Bio-steps beyond Turing. BioSystems **77**(1–3), 175–194 (2004)

9. Castellanos, J., Martín-Vide, C., Mitrana, V., Sempere, J.M.: Networks of evolutionary processors. Acta Informatica **39**(6–7), 517–529 (2003). https://doi.org/10.1007/s00236-004-0158-7

10. Dassow, J., Păun, Gh.: Regulated Rewriting in Formal Language Theory. Springer, Berlin (1989)

11. Dassow, J., Păun, Gh.: On the power of membrane computing. J. UCS **5**(2), 33–49 (1999). https://doi.org/10.3217/jucs-005-02-0033

12. Fernau, H.: Unconditional transfer in regulated rewriting. Acta Informatica **34**(11), 837–857 (1997). https://doi.org/10.1007/s002360050108

13. Fernau, H., Freund, R., Oswald, M., Reinhardt, K.: Refining the nonterminal complexity of graph-controlled, programmed, and matrix grammars. J. Autom. Lang. Comb. **12**(1–2), 117–138 (2007)

14. Freund, R.: P systems working in the sequential mode on arrays and strings. In: Calude, C.S., Calude, E., Dinneen, M.J. (eds.) DLT 2004. LNCS, vol. 3340, pp. 188–199. Springer, Heidelberg (2004). https://doi.org/10.1007/978-3-540-30550-7_16

15. Freund, R.: P systems working in the sequential mode on arrays and strings. Int. J. Found. Comput. Sci. **16**(4), 663–682 (2005). https://doi.org/10.1142/S0129054105003224

16. Freund, R., Ibarra, O., Păun, Gh., Yen, H.C.: Matrix languages, register machines, vector addition systems. In: Third Brainstorming Week on Membrane Computing, pp. 155–167 (2005)

17. Freund, R., Ivanov, S., Staiger, L.: Going beyond turing with P automata: partial adult halting and regular observer ω-languages. In: Calude, C.S., Dinneen, M.J. (eds.) UCNC 2015. LNCS, vol. 9252, pp. 169–180. Springer, Cham (2015). https://doi.org/10.1007/978-3-319-21819-9_12

18. Freund, R., Ivanov, S., Staiger, L.: Going beyond Turing with P automata: regular observer ω-languages and partial adult halting. IJUC **12**(1), 51–69 (2016)

19. Freund, R., Kogler, M., Oswald, M.: A general framework for regulated rewriting based on the applicability of rules. In: Kelemen, J., Kelemenová, A. (eds.) Computation, Cooperation, and Life. LNCS, vol. 6610, pp. 35–53. Springer, Heidelberg (2011). https://doi.org/10.1007/978-3-642-20000-7_5

20. Freund, R., Kogler, M., Rogozhin, Yu., Verlan, S.: Graph-controlled insertiondeletion systems. In: Proceedings of Twelfth Annual Workshop on Descriptional Complexity of Formal Systems, DCFS 2010, Saskatoon, Canada, 8–10th August 2010, pp. 88–98 (2010). https://doi.org/10.4204/EPTCS.31.11

21. Freund, R., Oswald, M.: Tissue P systems and (mem)brane systems with mateand drip operations working on strings. Electron. Notes Theor. Comput. Sci. **171**(2), 105–115 (2007). https://doi.org/10.1016/j.entcs.2007.05.011

22. Freund, R., Oswald, M., Staiger, L.: ω-P automata with communication rules. In: Martín-Vide, C., Mauri, G., Păun, Gh., Rozenberg, G., Salomaa, A. (eds.) WMC 2003. LNCS, vol. 2933, pp. 203–217. Springer, Heidelberg (2004). https://doi.org/10.1007/978-3-540-24619-0_15

23. Freund, R., Păun, Gh.: How to obtain computational completeness in P systems with one catalyst. In: 2013 Proceedings of Machines, Computations and Universality, MCU 2013, Zürich, Switzerland, 9–11 September 2013, pp. 47–61 (2013). https://doi.org/10.4204/EPTCS.128.13

24. Freund, R., Rogojin, V., Verlan, S.: Computational completeness of networks of evolutionary processors with elementary polarizations and a small number of processors. In: Pighizzini, G., Câmpeanu, C. (eds.) DCFS 2017. LNCS, vol. 10316, pp. 140–151. Springer, Cham (2017). https://doi.org/10.1007/978-3-319-60252-3_11

25. Freund, R., Rogozhin, Yu., Verlan, S.: Generating and accepting P systems with minimal left and right insertion and deletion. Nat. Comput. **13**(2), 257–268 (2014). https://doi.org/10.1007/s11047-013-9396-3

26. Kudlek, M., Martín-Vide, C., Păun, Gh.: Toward a formal macroset theory. In: Calude, C.S., Păun, Gh., Rozenberg, G., Salomaa, A. (eds.) WMC 2000. LNCS, vol. 2235, pp. 123–133. Springer, Heidelberg (2001). https://doi.org/10.1007/3-540-45523-X_7

27. van Leeuwen, J., Wiedermann, J.: Computation as an unbounded process. Theor. Comput. Sci. **429**, 202–212 (2012). https://doi.org/10.1016/j.tcs.2011.12.040

28. Martín-Vide, C., Pazos, J., Păun, Gh., Rodríguez-Patón, A.: A new class of symbolic abstract neural nets: tissue P systems. In: Ibarra, O.H., Zhang, L. (eds.) COCOON 2002. LNCS, vol. 2387, pp. 290–299. Springer, Heidelberg (2002). https://doi.org/10.1007/3-540-45655-4_32

29. Minsky, M.L.: Computation: Finite and Infinite Machines. Prentice Hall, Englewood Cliffs (1967)

30. Oswald, M.: P automata. Ph.D. thesis, Faculty of Computer Science, Vienna University of Technology (2003)

31. Popescu, Ş.: Networks of polarized evolutionary processors with elementary polarization of symbols. In: NCMA 2016, pp. 275–285 (2016)

32. Păun, Gh.: Computing with membranes. J. Comput. Syst. Sci. **61**(1), 108–143 (2000). https://doi.org/10.1006/jcss.1999.1693

33. Păun, Gh., Rozenberg, G., Salomaa, A. (eds.): The Oxford Handbook of Membrane Computing. Oxford University Press, Oxford (2010)

34. Rozenberg, G., Salomaa, A. (eds.): Handbook of Formal Languages, vol. 1–3. Springer, Heidelberg (1997)

35. Sosík, P., Valík, O.: On evolutionary lineages of membrane systems. In: Freund, R., Păun, Gh., Rozenberg, G., Salomaa, A. (eds.) WMC 2005. LNCS, vol. 3850, pp. 67–78. Springer, Heidelberg (2006). https://doi.org/10.1007/11603047_5

36. Bulletin of the International Membrane Computing Society (IMCS). http://membranecomputing.net/IMCSBulletin/index.php

37. The P Systems Website. http://ppage.psystems.eu/

Adaptive P Systems

Bogdan Aman[1,2]([✉]) and Gabriel Ciobanu[1,2]

[1] Institute of Computer Science, Romanian Academy, Iaşi, Romania
bogdan.aman@iit.academiaromana-is.ro
[2] "A.I.Cuza" University of Iaşi, Iaşi, Romania
gabriel@info.uaic.ro

Abstract. In this paper we introduce a membrane system named *adaptive P system* which is able to adjust dynamically its behaviour depending on resource availability. Such a system is defined as a tree of membranes in which the objects are organized in multisets, and the rules are applied in a maximal parallel manner. We use *guards* on the right side of the rules in order to model the biological sensitivity to context, and in this way we are able to describe an adaptive behaviour. The Turing completeness of the adaptive P systems can be obtained only by using non-cooperative rules (with guards) working in the accepting case. Using the adaptive P systems, we provide a polynomially uniform solution for an NP-complete problem (Subset Sum) by using specific membrane computing techniques. The solution employs a linear number of resources and evolution steps.

1 Introduction

Membrane systems (also called P systems) are introduced by Gheorghe Păun as a model of distributed, parallel and non-deterministic systems inspired by cell biology [27]. A membrane system (P system) is a tree-like structure of hierarchically arranged membranes embedded in the *skin* membrane as the outermost part of the system. The membranes can be arranged in a tree (cell-like [28]) structure, or in a graph form (tissue-like [26] and neural-like [19]). In this paper we use the symbol-object P systems [28] in which cells are divided in various regions containing specific objects and evolution rules, each region with a different task and all of them working simultaneously to accomplish a more general task of the whole system. The objects evolve according to the specific rules associated with each region, and the regions cooperate in order to maintain the proper behaviour of the whole system. Several results and variants of membrane systems (inspired by different aspects of living cells like symport and antiport communication through membranes, catalytic objects, membrane charge, etc.) are presented in [28]. There are defined various semantics which express how membrane systems evolve [9,10]. Over the years several books on membrane computing were published presenting the latest results in theory and applications [11,14,25,35,36]. Links between membrane systems and process calculi are presented in [3,8].

© Springer Nature Switzerland AG 2019
T. Hinze et al. (Eds.): CMC 2018, LNCS 11399, pp. 57–72, 2019.
https://doi.org/10.1007/978-3-030-12797-8_5

Besides the degree of non-determinism that appears in the parallel evolution of several biological systems, another important parameter is the degree of context-sensitivity. In most of the biological systems there exists a delicate dynamic balance depending on the context, and due to this mechanism there exist several alternative evolutions for these systems. For example, diabetes can arise through many alternative molecular pathways depending on the context [24]. Inspired by the biological systems in which different evolution paths are taken depending on the existence or absence of certain substances [18], we define in this paper a new class of membrane systems called *adaptive P systems*. These systems use guards in rules to express the dependence to the context (namely on the objects presented in their regions) able to determine dynamically various alternative evolutions. According to [34], designing such systems able to dynamically adapt to resource availability allows to increase the resistance to a variety of failures, and also the expressive power in modelling real systems.

To illustrate a simple adaptive system, Fig. 1 describes the positive and negative tetracycline responsive gene [18]. It is easy to see that tTa is used to activate the transcription in the *absence* of tetracycline, while $rtTa$ is used to activate the transcription in the *presence* of tetracycline. More similar processes in biology can be found in [22].

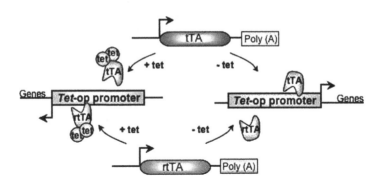

Fig. 1. Positive and negative tetracycline responsive gene [18]

Three main research directions are usually considered in membrane computing: modelling power [1,29], computational power in terms of the classical notion of Turing computability using a minimal quantity of ingredients [2], and efficiency in algorithmically solving (weak [4] or strong [6]) NP-complete problems in polynomial time (by using an exponential quantity of ingredients).

It is easy to see how the adaptive P systems increase the modelling power. We insist in this paper on the efficiency of the adaptive P systems in solving NP-complete problems in linear time (at the cost of using an exponential space). We present a uniform linear solution for a known NP-complete problem, namely Subset Sum, by using a linear number of rules and objects. Solutions for the Subset Sum problem were previously given by using P systems with active membrane [31], spiking neural P systems [23], kernel P systems [21] and tissue P systems [33]. The solution using kernel P systems [21] is closely related to ours due to the form of the rules and systems, but is different as we use only equality to test for the existence of resources.

Regarding computability, the Turing completeness of these adaptive P systems can be obtained only by using non-cooperative rules (with guards) working in the accepting case. As far as we know there are no computability results for kernel P systems to compare with existing results in this formalism. However, note that even if there are certain similarities with the use of promoters and inhibitors in [20], our rules are much simpler and powerful because we do not need the catalysts to obtain Turing completeness.

2 Adaptive P Systems

Let $\mathbb{N}$ be the set of non-negative integers, and consider a finite alphabet O of objects. A multiset over O is a mapping $u : O \rightarrow \mathbb{N}$. The empty multiset is denoted by ε. We use the string representation of multisets that is widely used in the membrane systems; when a multiset is represented by a string u, every permutation of this string is allowed as a representation of the multiset. For an alphabet $O = \{a_1, \ldots, a_n\}$, we denote by O^* the set of all multisets over V, and by $O^+ = O^* \backslash \varepsilon$ the set of all non-empty multisets. An example of such a representation is $u = aabaca$, where $u(a) = 4$, $u(b) = 1$, $u(c) = 1$. Using such a representation, the operations over multisets are defined as operations over strings. Given two multisets u and v over V, for any $a \in O$ we have $(u+v)(a) = u(a) + v(a)$ as the multiset union, and $(u-v)(a) = max\{0, u(a) - v(a)\}$ as the multiset difference. Also, the multiset inclusion is denoted by $u \leq v$ if $u(a) \leq v(a)$ for all $a \in O$. The number of occurrences of a symbol a_i in a string x is denoted by $|x|_{a_i}$, while the length of a string x is denoted by $|x| = \Sigma_{a_i}|x|_{a_i}$.

Inspired by the promoters and inhibitors used in [7,20], in what follows we use guards to decide if a certain rule is applicable: a rule $r : u \rightarrow \{g\}v;w$ could be applied to a multiset x only if $u \leq x$. The guard is satisfied if $g \leq x - u$, and thus u is rewritten to v; otherwise, u is rewritten to w. This means that the guard is used to 'promote' one of the branches, and 'inhibit' the other at the same time.

Definition 1. *An* **adaptive P system** *of degree d is a tuple*

$$\Pi = (O, H, \mu, w_1, \ldots, w_d, R_1, \ldots, R_d, i_0), where:$$

- *O is a finite non-empty alphabet of objects;*
- *H is a finite set of labels for membranes;*
- *μ is a membrane structure with membranes labelled by elements of H;*
- *$w_1, \ldots, w_d \in O^*$ describe the initial multisets of objects placed in μ;*
- *i_0 represents the output membrane where the result of the computation is placed; if $i_0 = e$, then the answer is in the surrounding environment;*
- *R_i (1 ≤ i ≤ d) is a finite set of rules including:*

(a) $u \rightarrow \{g\}v; w$ rewriting and communication rules
with $g, u \in O^+$, $v, w \in O^* \times \{here, out, in_j \mid j \in H\}$.
A multiset of objects u is consumed, and the result depends on the value of the guard g. If the guard is satisfied in the current configuration, then the multiset u is rewritten into the multiset v; otherwise, the multiset u is rewritten into the multiset w. The meaning of the targets $\{here, out, in_j\}$ is that after replacing u with the newly created objects, these objects either remain in the same membrane (here), go out of the current membrane (out), or go to an inner membrane j (in_j). Usually the target "here" is omitted.

(b) $[u]_h \rightarrow \{g\}[v_1]_h[v_2]_h; [w]_h$ division rules
with $g, u \in O^+$, $v_1, v_2, w \in O^*$, $h \in H$.
If an elementary membrane labelled with h contains a non-empty multiset of objects u and the guard g is satisfied in the current configuration, then membrane h is divided into two membranes labelled by h. A copy of each object from the initial membrane h is placed inside the new created membranes, except for the multiset of objects u which is replaced by the multisets of objects v_1 and v_2, respectively. Additionally, a copy of each rule of the initial membrane h is added to the newly created membranes. On the other hand, if the guard g does not hold, then the multiset of objects u is replaced by a multiset of objects w.

These rules are applied in both a non-deterministic maximally parallel manner and a bottom-up manner. Maximally parallel means that at each step it is applied a multiset of applicable rules chosen such that no further rule can be added to this multiset. The application is sequential, meaning that the inner objects not appearing in guards evolve first, then the objects from the guards evolve (in a sequential manner) whenever this is possible, and then the result is duplicated whenever the surrounding membrane is divided. A single step can be seen as a macro-step consisting of several micro-steps. A micro-step corresponds to the application of a rule inside a membrane, while a macro-step consists in applying micro-steps in parallel in all the membranes, as long as a rule can be applied somewhere. A macro-step ends when no further rule is applicable.

Example 1. In this example we show how the new P systems work by building an adaptive P systems to compute the logical AND operation. This means that we have two values (among 0 and 1 values) as input, and produce their AND result as output.

Formally, we define the following adaptive P system:

$$\Pi = (\{0,1\}, \{0,1\}, [[\ ]_1]_2, \varepsilon, \varepsilon, R_1, R_2, e)$$

where:

- $R_1 = \{r_{11} : 0 \rightarrow \{\varepsilon\}(0, out); \varepsilon, \quad r_{12} : 1 \rightarrow \{\varepsilon\}(1, out); \varepsilon\}$,
  $R_2 = \{r_{21} : 0 \rightarrow \{0\}\varepsilon; (0, out), \quad r_{22} : 1 \rightarrow \{1\}(1, out); \varepsilon\}$.

It should be noticed that membrane 1 can be entirely avoided as its only role is to provide the input. Consider that initially two objects 0 are sent from membrane 1 to membrane 2. Even if the rule $r_{21} : 0 \rightarrow \{0\}\varepsilon; (0, out)$ can be applied twice on the multiset 0^2, due to the fact that the guard will be rewritten after the maximal step, the rules are applied in sequence to obtain the next configuration. Namely, we have the evolution:

$$0^2 \xrightarrow{r_{21}} 0 \xrightarrow{r_{21}} (0, out).$$

This evolution is due to the fact that after applying rule r_{21} first, the guard does not hold anymore, namely there are no other 0 objects around, and thus the object 0 is sent to the environment by taking the second branch of the rule. After the object 0 is sent to the environment, the system is restored and can compute other pair of objects 0 and/or 1.

If the multiset communicated to membrane 2 is 01, then the rules r_{21} and r_{22} can be applied in parallel as both guards do not hold, and thus the second branch will be taken for each rule and 01 is rewritten to $(0, out)$. It should be noticed that this is the case regardless of the order of rewriting:

$$01 \xrightarrow{r_{21}} (0, out)1 \xrightarrow{r_{22}} (0, out),$$

$$01 \xrightarrow{r_{22}} 0 \xrightarrow{r_{21}} (0, out).$$

For the case 1^2, the situation is similar with the 0^2, but a different branch is executed even if we apply twice rule r_{22}; namely, the evolution is:

$$1^2 \xrightarrow{r_{22}} (1, out)1 \xrightarrow{r_{22}} (1, out).$$

Remark 1. The guards in these rules depend on some elements present in the system. It is possible that even if a rule satisfies the guard when it is selected to be applied in a macro-step, after performing some micro-steps the guard is not satisfied anymore. By considering dynamic alternatives in our formalism, once a rule is selected, it is applied. This means that an adaptive P system is able to continue its evolution even when the truth values of some guards change during the evolution. In this way the adaptive P systems model the sensitivity to a dynamic context, a property important for most of the biological systems.

To better exemplify this aspect, let us consider a small adaptive P system consisting of the initial configuration $[ab^2]_0$ and the rules $r_1 : b \rightarrow \{\varepsilon\}\varepsilon; \varepsilon$ and $r_2 : [a]_0 \rightarrow \{b\}[a]_0[a]_0; [b]_0$. A maximal multiset of rules to be applied is $r_1^2 r_2$. Using the bottom-up manner, after the r_1 rules are applied, the evaluation of the guard in the r_2 rule changes from *true* (at the initial time) to *false* when the rule r_2 has to be applied. In this case, the rule r_2 is producing $[b]_0$, not $[a]_0[a]_0$.

3 Efficiency of the Adaptive P Systems

Recognizer P systems presented in [30] are associated in a natural way with P systems with input; they are used in the framework of membrane computing to study and solve some decision problems. The encoding of an instance of a decision problem as a multiset placed in an input membrane is provided to a P system in order to compute and send to the environment an answer (*yes* or *no*). The following definitions are adapted from [17].

Definition 2. *A P system with input is a tuple* (Π, Σ, i_Π), *where*

   (a) Π *is an adaptive P system;*
   (b) Σ *is an (input) alphabet strictly contained in the working alphabet O of* Π; *the initial multisets are over* $O - \Sigma$;
   (c) i_Π *is the label of a distinguished (input) membrane.*

Definition 3. *A recognizer adaptive P system is an adaptive P system with input* (Π, Σ, i_Π) *having an external output such that:*

1. *the working alphabet contains two distinguished elements: yes and no;*
2. *all its computations halt;*
3. *if C is a computation of* Π, *then either some object yes or some object no (but not both) must have been released into the environment, only in the last step of the computation.*

C is an accepting (rejecting) computation if the object yes (no) appears in the external environment in the halting configuration of C.

Definition 4. *A decision problem* $X = (I_X, \theta_X)$ *is solved in polynomial time by a family* $\mathbf{\Pi} = \{\mathbf{\Pi}(n) \,|\, n \in \mathbb{N}\}$ *of adaptive P systems whenever the following conditions hold:*

- *The family* $\mathbf{\Pi}$ *is polynomially uniform by Turing machines, namely there exists a deterministic Turing machine constructing* $\Pi(n)$ *from* $n \in \mathbb{N}$ *in polynomial time.*
- *There exists a pair* (cod, s) *of polynomial-time computable functions over* I_X *such that:*
  - *for each instance* $u \in I_X$, $s(u)$ *is a natural number and* $cod(u)$ *is an input multiset of the system* $\Pi(s(u))$;
  - *the family* $\mathbf{\Pi}$ *is polynomially bounded with respect to* (X, cod, s), *namely there exists a polynomial function p such that for each* $u \in I_X$, *each computation of* $\Pi(s(u))$ *with input* $cod(u)$ *performs at most* $p(|u|)$ *steps;*
  - *the family* $\mathbf{\Pi}$ *is sound with respect to* (X, cod, s), *namely for each* $u \in I_X$, *if there exists an accepting computation of* $\Pi(s(u))$ *with input* $cod(u)$, *then* $\theta_X(u) = 1$;
  - *the family* $\mathbf{\Pi}$ *is complete with respect to* (X, cod, s), *namely for each* $u \in I_X$, *if* $\theta_X(u) = 1$, *then every computation of* $\Pi(s(u))$ *with input* $cod(u)$ *is an accepting one.*

3.1   Subset Sum Problem

In this subsection we present a uniform solution for the Subset Sum problem in linear time by using adaptive P systems as confluent deciding devices in which all the computations starting from the initial configuration agree on a final result.

The Subset Sum problem is described in [15] as following: given a finite set $A = \{a_1, \ldots, a_n\}$, a weight function $w : A \to \mathbb{N}$ and a constant $k \in \mathbb{N}$, decide whether or not there exists a non-empty subset B of A such that its weight is equal to k, namely $w(B) = k$.

The solution presented in this paper consists of the following stages:

- *generation and evaluation stage*: using membrane division, all the possible subsets are generated and evaluated;
- *checking stage*: in each membrane, the system checks whether or not the weight is equal to k;
- *output stage*: the systems sends out the answer to the environment.

Theorem 1. *The Subset Sum problem can be solved in linear time by a uniform family of recognizer adaptive P systems.*

Proof. Firstly we consider the function s defined over the set I_{SS} of instances of the Subset Sum problem by $s(u) = ((n + k)(n + k + 1)/2) + n$, with $u = (n, (w_1, \ldots, w_n), k) \in I_{SS}$. It is easy to see that the function $\langle n, k \rangle = s(u)$ is polynomial, primitive recursive and bijective from $\mathbb{N}^2$ onto $\mathbb{N}$ (the inverse is also polynomial). Thus, s is polynomial-time computable.

For each $\langle n, k \rangle \in \mathbb{N}^2$ we consider the recognizer adaptive P system $(\Pi(\langle n, k \rangle), \Sigma(\langle n, k \rangle), i(\langle n, k \rangle))$, where the input alphabet is $E(\langle n, k \rangle) = \{x_l, \ldots, x_n\}$, and the input membrane is $i(\langle n, k \rangle) = 1$. The adaptive P system $\Pi(\langle n, k \rangle) = (O(\langle n, k \rangle), \{0, 1\}, \mu, ans_{n+3}, a_1 \ldots a_n \, ans_{n+1}, R_0(\langle n, k \rangle), R_1(\langle n, k \rangle))$ is defined as follows:

- $O(\langle n, k \rangle) = \{no, yes, b, d, ans'_0\} \cup \{x_i, t_i, f_i \mid 1 \le i \le n\} \cup$
  $\cup \{ans_i \mid 0 \le i \le n + 3\}$;
- $\mu = [[\ ]_1\ ]_0$;
- the sets $R_0(\langle n, k \rangle), R_1(\langle n, k \rangle)$ of the evolution rules are defined by:
  - (i) $[a_i]_1 \to \{b^k\}[\ ]_1; [t_i]_1[f_i]_1 \in R_1(\langle n, k \rangle)$, for $1 \le i \le n$.
    Using these rules, at most 2^n membranes labelled by 1 can be generated containing the subsets over variables $\{x_1, \ldots, x_n\}$ that have at most $k + max_{1 \le i \le n} w(a_i)$ objects b. If the guard is satisfied (there are more than k objects b in membrane 1, meaning that the sum k is exceeded), then the object a_i is simply removed from membrane 1. Otherwise, if the guard is not satisfied (the objects x_i contained in the set B are less than k), then the membrane labelled by 1 is divided into two copies (one containing a multiset t_i signifying that x_i appears in B, and one containing the object f_i signifying that x_i does not appear in B). A similar guard checking for the existence of k objects exists in the algorithm used to solve the Subset Sum in linear time by using kernel P systems [13].

(ii) $x_i \rightarrow \{f_i\}\varepsilon; b \in R_1(\langle n, k \rangle)$, for $1 \le i \le n$.

If no f_i is present, then all the objects x_i are replaced in parallel in one step with objects b. Otherwise, meaning that an object f_i is present, all the objects x_i from the current membrane are removed.

(iii) $ans_i \rightarrow \{\varepsilon\}ans_{i-1}; \varepsilon \in R_1(\langle n, k \rangle)$, for $1 \le i \le n+1$.

This rule is used to count the steps performed. As ε is included in any multiset, only the first branch will be always executed.

(iv) $ans_0 \rightarrow \{b^k\}ans_0'; no \ (no, out) \in R_1(\langle n, k \rangle)$.

$ans_0' \rightarrow \{b^{k+1}\}no \ (no, out); yes \ (yes, out) \in R_1(\langle n, k \rangle)$;

After $n+1$ steps, all the membranes labelled by 1 contain only the objects b, t_i, f_i and ans_0 (as all x_i's are removed by the previous rule). If the guard is satisfied (the number of b objects is at least k), then the object ans_0 is replaced by object ans_0'; otherwise, the object ans_0 is replaced by two objects no. One of the new created objects remains in the current membrane, while the other one is sent outside. If the object ans_0' was created, it means that there are at least k objects b. We have to check if there are exactly k, and this is done by considering the guard b^{k+1}. If the guard is satisfied, then the object ans_0' is replaced by two objects no; otherwise, the object ans_0' is replaced by two objects yes. One of the new created objects remains in the current membrane, while the other one is sent outside.

(v) $ans_i \rightarrow \{\varepsilon\}ans_{i-1}; \varepsilon \in R_0(\langle n, k \rangle)$, for $1 \le i \le n+3$.

This rule is used to count the steps performed.

(iv) $ans_0 \rightarrow \{yes\}(yes, out); (no, out) \in R_0(\langle n, k \rangle)$.

If the guard is $true$ (there exists at least one object yes in membrane 0), then the object ans of membrane 0 is replaced by yes and sent to the environment as the final answer of the problem. Otherwise, the object ans of membrane 0 is replaced by no, and sent to the environment as the final answer of the problem.

Overview of the Computation. First of all, given an instance $u = (n, (w_1, \ldots, w_n), k) \in I_{SS}$ of the problem, we define $s(u) = \langle n.k \rangle$ and $cod(u) = x_1^{w_1} \ldots x_n^{w_n}$. The pair (cod, s) is a pair of polynomial-time computable functions over I_{SS} such that $s(u)$ is a natural number and $cod(u)$ is an input multiset over $\Pi(s(u))$. We describe informally how the adaptive P system $\Pi(s(u))$ with input $cod(u)$ works. The initial configuration is

$$C_0 = [[ans_{n+1} \ a_1 \ldots a_n \ x_1^{w_1} \ldots x_n^{w_n}]_1 ans_{n+3}]_0.$$

The purpose of the membrane division given by rule (i), rule applied in the first n steps of the computation, is to generate a membrane labelled by 1 for each subset B of A. Depending on the weights defined by function w, the number of generated membranes can be much smaller than 2^n, and so the necessary working space is smaller than other existing approaches of the Subset Sum problem in membrane computing (e.g., [31]). This happens because in rule (i) the membrane is replicated only if the weight of the already generated objects is less than or equal with k. Once this limit is exceeded, the division does not take place anymore (as the weight of the generated subset is bigger than k), and the remaining a_i objects are simply removed using the alternative branch.

The evaluation stage takes place in parallel with the generation one. For each subset, the system computes its weight (given by the number of b objects) by replacing the objects x_i either by b whenever object t_i is present (denoting that object a_i is in the subset), or by ε otherwise.

The checking stage happens in step $n+2$, namely after the moment when all the objects x_i were removed from all membranes. The system checks in two steps whether there are exactly k objects b in a membrane labelled 1 by using rule (iv). The rules (iii) and (v) are used to count down the number of performed steps; they are useful in generating the final answer. Once these steps are performed, we are sure that the membranes have finished their checking stage, and so we just check if in membrane 0 arrived either an *yes* or *no* object to be sent to the environment as the final answer of the problem.

Complexity. Let us analyze the necessary resources to construct $\Pi(s(u))$. The number of membranes in the initial configuration is 2, and the number of objects is $n+2$. The size of the working alphabet is $4*n+9$. The number of rules in the above system is: n rules of type (i) and of type (ii), $n+1$ rules of type (iii), 2 rules of type (iv) and (iv) and $n+3$ rules of type (v). Overall, the size of the constructed system is $\mathcal{O}(n)$. Therefore, a Turing machine working in polynomial time can build $\Pi(s(u))$ for the instance u.

It is easy to prove that the system $\Pi(s(u))$ with input $cod(u)$ always halts and sends to the environment either an object *yes* or *no* in the last step of the computation, object corresponding to the correct answer of the instance. The number of steps for such a system is $n+4$ regardless of the answer sent to the environment, namely there exists a linear bound for the number of steps of the computation. Therefore, the family Π of recognizer adaptive P systems solves the Subset Sum problem in linear time (according to Definition 4).

Example 2. Consider the Subset Sum problem with $A = \{a_1, a_2, a_3\}$, $k = 3$, $w(a_1) = 1$, $w(a_2) = 2$ and $w(a_3) = 1$. In this case, $n = 3$, $k = 3$, and the initial configuration of the system after adding the input is

$$[[a_1\ a_2\ a_3\ x_1\ x_2^2\ x_3\ ans_4]_1 ans_6]_0.$$

Graphically, this is illustrated as

The evolution of the system is described by the following steps. The working space is generated in $n = 3$ steps, and the evaluation stage in 4 steps, leading (from the initial configuration) to configuration 4 below:

1. $[[t_1\ a_2\ a_3\ x_1\ x_2^2\ x_3\ ans_3]_1 [f_1\ a_2\ a_3\ x_1\ x_2^2\ x_3\ ans_3]_1 ans_5]_0$

2. $[[b\,t_1\,t_2\,a_3\,x_2^2\,x_3\,ans_2]_1[b\,t_1\,f_2\,a_3\,x_2^2\,x_3\,ans_2]_1$
   $[f_1\,t_2\,a_3\,x_2^2\,x_3\,ans_2]_1[f_1\,f_2\,a_3\,x_2^2\,x_3\,ans_2]_1ans_4]_0$
3. $[[b^3\,t_1\,t_2\,t_3\,x_3\,ans_1]_1[b^3\,t_1\,t_2\,f_3\,x_3\,ans_1]_1[b\,t_1\,f_2\,t_3\,x_3\,ans_1]_1$
   $[b\,t_1\,f_2\,f_3\,x_3\,ans_1]_1[b^2\,f_1\,t_2\,t_3\,x_3\,ans_1]_1[b^2\,f_1\,t_2\,f_3\,x_3\,ans_1]_1$
   $[f_1\,f_2\,t_3\,x_3\,ans_1]_1[f_1\,f_2\,f_3\,x_3\,ans_1]_1ans_3]_0$
4. $[[b^4\,t_1\,t_2\,t_3\,\,ans_0]_1[b^3\,t_1\,t_2\,f_3\,ans_0]_1[b^2\,t_1\,f_2\,t_3\,ans_0]_1$
   $[b\,t_1\,f_2\,f_3\,ans_0]_1[b^3\,f_1\,t_2\,t_3\,ans_0]_1\,[b^2\,f_1\,t_2\,f_3\,ans_0]_1$
   $[b\,f_1\,f_2\,t_3\,ans_0]_1[f_1\,f_2\,f_3\,ans_0]_1ans_2]_0$

The resulting configuration is described by the following picture:

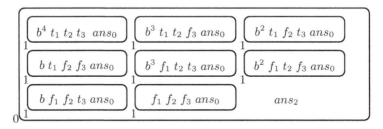

In the next two steps, all ans_0 objects placed in the membranes labelled by 1 are replaced to either yes or no, depending on the number of b objects existing in membranes 1. A copy of each such object is sent to the surrounding membrane 0.

5. $[[b^4\,t_1\,t_2\,t_3\,\,ans_0']_1[b^3\,t_1\,t_2\,f_3\,ans_0']_1[b^2\,t_1\,f_2\,t_3\,no]_1$
   $[b\,t_1\,f_2\,f_3\,no]_1[b^3\,f_1\,t_2\,t_3\,ans_0']_1\,[b^2\,f_1\,t_2\,f_3\,no]_1$
   $[b\,f_1\,f_2\,t_3\,no]_1[f_1\,f_2\,f_3\,no]_1no^5ans_1]_0$
6. $[[b^4\,t_1\,t_2\,t_3\,\,no]_1[b^3\,t_1\,t_2\,f_3\,yes]_1[b^2\,t_1\,f_2\,t_3\,no]_1$
   $[b\,t_1\,f_2\,f_3\,no]_1[b^3\,f_1\,t_2\,t_3\,yes]_1\,[b^2\,f_1\,t_2\,f_3\,no]_1$
   $[b\,f_1\,f_2\,t_3\,no]_1[f_1\,f_2\,f_3\,no]_1no^6yes^2ans_0]_0$

In the final step, the remaining ans_0 object placed in the membrane labelled by 0 is replaced by yes and sent to the environment, signalling a positive answer of the problem.

7. $[[b^4\,t_1\,t_2\,t_3\,\,no]_1[b^3\,t_1\,t_2\,f_3\,yes]_1[b^2\,t_1\,f_2\,t_3\,no]_1$
   $[b\,t_1\,f_2\,f_3\,no]_1[b^3\,f_1\,t_2\,t_3\,yes]_1\,[b^2\,f_1\,t_2\,f_3\,no]_1$
   $[b\,f_1\,f_2\,t_3\,no]_1[f_1\,f_2\,f_3\,no]_1no^6yes^2]_0yes$

The final configuration of the system is described by the following picture:

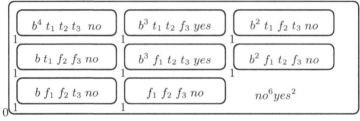

yes

4   Computational Universality

The Parikh vector associated with a string x with respect to objects $a_1, \ldots, a_n$ is $(|x|_{a_1}, \ldots, |x|_{a_n})$. The Parikh image of an arbitrary language L over $\{a_1, \ldots, a_n\}$ is the set of all Parikh vectors of strings in L, and is denoted by $Ps(L)$. For a family of languages FL, the family of Parikh images of languages in FL is denoted by $PsFL$. The family of recursively enumerable string languages is denoted by RE. For more details regarding the formal language theory the reader is referred to the monographs and handbooks in this area as [12] and [32].

A *register machine* is a tuple $M = (m, B, l_0, l_h, P)$, where m is the number of registers, B is a set of labels, $l_0 \in B$ is the initial label, $l_h \in B$ is the final label, and P is the set of instructions bijectively labelled by elements of B. The instructions of M can be of the following forms:

- $l_1 : (ADD(j), l_2, l_3)$, with $l_1 \in B \backslash \{l_h\}$, $l_2, l_3 \in B$, $1 \leq j \leq m$.
  Increases the value of register j by one, followed by a non-deterministic jump to instruction l_2 or l_3. This instruction is usually called *increment*.
- $l_1 : (SUB(j), l_2, l_3)$, with $l_1 \in B \backslash \{l_h\}$, $l_2, l_3 \in B$, $1 \leq j \leq m$.
  If the value of register j is zero then jump to instruction l_3; otherwise, the value of register j is decreased by one, followed by a jump to instruction l_2. The two cases of this instruction are usually called *zero-test* and *decrement*, respectively.
- $l_h : HALT$. Stops the execution of the register machine.

A *configuration* of a register machine is described by the content of each register and by the value of the current label which indicates the next instruction to be executed. Computations start by executing the instruction l_0 of P, and terminate when reaching the HALT-instruction l_h.

The set of (Parikh) vectors of non-negative integers accepted by an automaton as results of halting computations in Π is denoted by $Ps_{acc}(\Pi)$. In the accepting case, a P systems accept all (vectors of) non-negative integers whose input leads to a halting computation. The families of sets $Ps_{acc}(\Pi)$ computed by adaptive P systems (with guards) with at most m membranes is denoted by $Ps_{acc}OP_m(guard)$.

The following theorem illustrates the computational universality (in their accepting variants) of adaptive P systems by simulating a register machine. The rules of adaptive P systems are powerful enough, even we do not use any catalyst.

Theorem 2. *For any $m \geq 1$, $Ps_{acc}OP_m(guard) = PsRE$.*

Proof. Let $M = (m, B, l_0, l_h, P)$ be a register machine. In order to simulate M, we construct a one-membrane adaptive P system

$$\Pi = (O, H, \mu, w_1, R_1, i_0)$$

with

- $O = \{a_r, a'_r, a''_r \mid 1 \le r \le m\} \cup \{l, l' \mid l \in B\};$
  $\cup \{a'_{rl}, a''_{rl} \mid 1 \le r \le m, l \in B\}$
- $H = \{1\};$
- $\mu = [\ ]_1;$
- $w_1 = l_0 a_1^{k_1} \dots a_m^{k_m};$
- $i_0 = 1.$

Initially the membrane contains the object l_0 and the input objects $a_1^{k_1} \dots a_m^{k_m}$. The vector $(k_1, \dots, k_m)$ represents the vector that needs to be accepted by our adaptive P system. The content of register r is represented by the number of copies of the object a_r, where $1 \le r \le m$. The instructions of M are simulated by the following rules in R_1:

▶ $l_1 : (ADD(r), l_2, l_3)$, with $l_1 \in B \setminus \{l_h\}$, $l_2, l_3 \in B$, $1 \le j \le m$
is simulated by the rules

$$r_{11} : l_1 \rightarrow \{a_r\} a_r l_2; a_r l_2,$$

$$r_{12} : l_1 \rightarrow \{a_r\} a_r l_3; a_r l_3.$$

The adaptive P system starts the computation by simulating the first instruction l_0 of the machine program. Let us assume that the current instruction to be executed is of type $(ADD(r), l_2, l_3)$. Then in membrane 1 any of the rules r_{11} and r_{12} is applied non-deterministically and, regardless of the number of a_r objects present, it creates a new object a_r and move to the next instruction l_2 or l_3, depending which of the rules r_{11} and r_{12} was applied. The evolution is depicted in Fig. 2.

▶ $l_1 : (SUB(r), l_2, l_3)$, with $l_1 \in B \setminus \{l_h\}$, $l_2, l_3 \in B$, $1 \le r \le m$
is simulated by the rules

$$r_{21} : l_1 \rightarrow \{a_r\} l'_2; l_3$$

$$r_{22} : a_r \rightarrow \{l'_2\} a'_{rl_2}; a_r$$

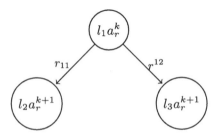

Fig. 2. Simulating ADD instruction.

$$r_{23} : l_2'' \rightarrow \{a_r\}l_2''; \varepsilon$$

$$r_{24} : a_{rl_2}' \rightarrow \{a_r\}a_{rl_2}'; a_{rl_2}''$$

$$r_{25} : a_{rl_2}'' \rightarrow \{a_{rl_2}''\}a_r; l_2.$$

If a subtraction instruction $l_1 : (SUB(r), l_2, l_3)$ is simulated, then in membrane 1 it is executed the rule $r_{21} : l_1 \rightarrow \{a_r\}l_2'; l_3$. Due to the form of the rule in adaptive P systems, this rule is a zero-test. If there is no object a_r present in membrane 1, then the right branch of the rule is executed and the object l_1 is replaced by l_3. If there exists at least one a_r object in membrane 1, then the guard is satisfied and the left part of the rule is executed by replacing object l_1 by object l_2'. Object l_2' will be used in the following steps to remove an object a_r and to create object l_2. In the next step, by using the rule $r_{22} : a_r \rightarrow \{l_2'\}a_{rl_2}'; a_r$, all objects a_r are rewritten to a_{rl_2}'. In parallel, depending on whether rule r_{23} is used or not, either object l_2' remains the same if still are objects a_r in membrane 1 to which rule r_{22} can be applied, or object l_2' is removed if all these objects where rewritten using r_{22} rules. As regardless when rule r_{23} is applied, all the objects a_r are changed to a_{rl_2}', and then object l_2' will be removed (in this step). For this, objects a_{rl_2}' are

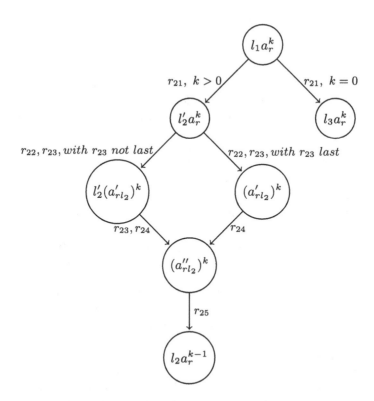

Fig. 3. Simulating SUB instruction.

rewritten to a''_{rl_2} regardless of the content of membrane 1. This allows that after this step, we reach the same configuration $(a''_{rl_2})^k$ regardless if l'_2 was or not present in the previous configuration. As a last step, by applying rule r_{25}, all the objects a''_{rl_2} (excepting one) are rewritten to a_r, while the excepting one is rewritten to l_2. Thus, the final configuration is $a_r^{k-1}l_2$ which marks a correct simulation. The evolution is depicted in Fig. 3.

▶ $l_h : HALT$ is simulated by $r_h : l_h \rightarrow \{\varepsilon\}\varepsilon; \varepsilon$.

When the computation stops in M, the object l_h is removed and no further rules can be applied. The remaining objects in the system represent the result computed by M.   □

5   Conclusion

Inspired by the biological context-sensitivity, we introduced and studied the *adaptive P systems* that are able to adjust dynamically their behaviours according to the available resources. The main ingredient is the *guard* used on the right side of the rules; such a guard allows to define an adaptive behaviour in the evolution of this new class. The generality of the guards, their power and flexibility make the new class of adaptive P systems useful in modelling various biological systems and in solving hard problems in the framework of membrane computing.

A variant of adaptive P systems was presented previously in [5]; this paper is an improved and extended version of the work presented in [5]. The main difference is related to the key ingredient of these systems: the guards. In this paper the guards are used in rules of the form $r : u \rightarrow \{g\}v; w$ to define adaptive branching during the evolution of the system. A rule $r : u \rightarrow \{g\}v; w$ is applicable to a multiset x if $u \leq x$. The guard is satisfied if $g \leq x - u$, and so u is rewritten to v; otherwise, u is rewritten to w. This means that a guard is used to 'promote' one of the branches and 'inhibit' the other at the same time. This is different from [5], where the guards g have the values *true* and *false*, and a rule is applicable only when the guard is *true*. The guards in [5] are similar to those used in kernel P systems [16], where the rules having a guard are in the generic form $r\{g\}$, and a guard g could have the values *true*, *false*, $\neg g$, $g \wedge g$, $g \vee g$ and γa^n, where γa^n is true with respect to a multiset w if the relation $|w|_a \gamma n$ is true (where $\gamma \in \{<, \leq, =, \neq, \geq, >\}$). In kernel P systems, a rule r is applicable only when the guard g is true, in contrast with the situation we have in adaptive P systems where a rule is applicable regardless of the truth value of the guard inside it. More exactly, in adaptive P system the truth value of the guard is used to establish which branch is executed. The multiset u is always consumed, and the result depends on the value of the guard (it is a multiset v whenever the guard returns *true*, or it is a multiset w whenever the guard returns *false*).

We illustrated the expressive power of the new adaptive P systems by showing how the AND gates could be modelled. Then we provided a uniform linear solution for an NP-complete problem by employing a linear number of objects and evolution steps. This simple and rather elegant solution to Subset Sum problem requires a smaller working space than other previous approaches used in the framework of membrane computing.

We showed that the computational completeness of the adaptive P systems can be obtained by using only non-cooperative rules (with guards) working in the accepting case. Regarding this aspect of computation power, it is worth noting that we do not use any catalyst to obtain the Turing completeness, as it happens in [20].

References

1. Aman, B., Ciobanu, G.: Describing the immune system using enhanced mobile membranes. Electron. Notes Theor. Comput. Sci. **194**(3), 5–18 (2008)
2. Aman, B., Ciobanu, G.: Turing completeness using three mobile membranes. In: Calude, C.S., Costa, J.F., Dershowitz, N., Freire, E., Rozenberg, G. (eds.) UC 2009. LNCS, vol. 5715, pp. 42–55. Springer, Heidelberg (2009). https://doi.org/10.1007/978-3-642-03745-0_12
3. Aman, B., Ciobanu, G.: Mobility in Process Calculi and Natural Computing. Springer, Heidelberg (2011). https://doi.org/10.1007/978-3-642-24867-2
4. Aman, B., Ciobanu, G.: Solving a weak NP-complete problem in polynomial time by using mutual mobile membrane systems. Acta Informatica **48**(7–8), 409–415 (2011). https://doi.org/10.1007/s00236-011-0144-9
5. Aman, B., Ciobanu, G.: Adaptability in membrane computing. Analele Universității București Informatică **LXII**(3), 5–15 (2015)
6. Aman, B., Ciobanu, G.: Efficiently solving the bin packing problem through bio-inspired mobility. Acta Informatica **54**(4), 435–445 (2017). https://doi.org/10.1007/s00236-016-0264-3
7. Bottoni, P., Martín-Vide, C., Păun, G., Rozenberg, G.: Membrane systems with promoters/inhibitors. Acta Informatica **38**(10), 695–720 (2002)
8. Ciobanu, G.: Membrane computing and biologically inspired process calculi. "A.I. Cuza" University Press, Iași (2010)
9. Ciobanu, G.: Semantics of P systems. In: The Oxford Handbook of Membrane Computing, pp. 413–436. Oxford University Press, Oxford (2010)
10. Ciobanu, G., Todoran, E.N.: Denotational semantics of membrane systems by using complete metric spaces. Theor. Comput. Sci. **701**, 85–108 (2017)
11. Ciobanu, G., Păun, G., Pérez-Jiménez, M.J.: Applications of Membrane Computing. Natural Computing Series. Springer, Heidelberg (2006). https://doi.org/10.1007/3-540-29937-8
12. Dassow, J., Păun, G.: Regulated Rewriting in Formal Language Theory. Springer, Heidelberg (1989)
13. Dragomir, C., Ipate, F., Konur, S., Lefticaru, R., Mierla, L.: Model checking kernel P systems. In: Alhazov, A., Cojocaru, S., Gheorghe, M., Rogozhin, Y., Rozenberg, G., Salomaa, A. (eds.) CMC 2013. LNCS, vol. 8340, pp. 151–172. Springer, Heidelberg (2014). https://doi.org/10.1007/978-3-642-54239-8_12
14. Frisco, P., Gheorghe, M., Pérez-Jiménez, M.J. (eds.): Applications of Membrane Computing in Systems and Synthetic Biology. ECC, vol. 7. Springer, Cham (2014). https://doi.org/10.1007/978-3-319-03191-0
15. Garey, M., Johnson, D.: Computers and Intractability: A Guide to the Theory of NP-Completeness. Freeman, New York (1979)

16. Gheorghe, M., Ipate, F.: A kernel P systems survey. In: Alhazov, A., Cojocaru, S., Gheorghe, M., Rogozhin, Y., Rozenberg, G., Salomaa, A. (eds.) CMC 2013. LNCS, vol. 8340, pp. 1–9. Springer, Heidelberg (2014). https://doi.org/10.1007/978-3-642-54239-8_1
17. Gutiérrez-Naranjo, M.A., Pérez-Jiménez, M.J., Romero-Campero, F.J.: A uniform solution to SAT using membrane creation. Theor. Comput. Sci. **371**, 54–61 (2007)
18. Hennighausen, L., Furth, P.A.: Prospects for directing temporal and spatial gene expression in transgenic animals. In: Transgenic Animals: Generation and Use, pp. 303–306. Harwood Academic Publishers (1997)
19. Ionescu, M., Păun, G., Yokomori, T.: Spiking neural P systems. Fundam. Inform. **71**, 279–308 (2006)
20. Ionescu, M., Sburlan, D.: On P systems with promoters/inhibitors. J. Univers. Comput. Sci. **10**(5), 581–599 (2004)
21. Ipate, F., et al.: Kernel P Systems: Applications and Implementations. In: Yin, Z., Pan, L., Fang, X. (eds.) Proceedings of The Eighth International Conference on Bio-Inspired Computing: Theories and Applications (BIC-TA). Advances in Intelligent Systems and Computing, vol. 212, pp. 1081–1089. Springer, Berlin (2013). https://doi.org/10.1007/978-3-642-37502-6_126
22. Kimmel, M., Axelrod, D.: Branching Processes in Biology. Springer, Heidelberg (2015). https://doi.org/10.1007/978-1-4939-1559-0
23. Leporati, A., Mauri, G., Zandron, C., Păun, G., Pérez-Jiménez, M.J.: Uniform solutions to SAT and subset sum by spiking neural P systems. Nat. Comput. **8**, 681–702 (2009)
24. Lewontin, R.C.: The Triple Helix: Gene, Organism, and Environment. Harvard University Press, Cambridge (2000)
25. Manca, V.: Infobiotics: Information in Biotic Systems. Springer, Heidelberg (2013). https://doi.org/10.1007/978-3-642-36223-1
26. Martín-Vide, C., Păun, G., Pazos, J., Rodríguez-Patón, A.: Tissue P systems. Theor. Comput. Sci. **296**, 295–326 (2003)
27. Păun, G.: Membrane Computing: An Introduction. Springer, Heidelberg (2002). https://doi.org/10.1007/978-3-642-56196-2
28. Păun, G., Rozenberg, G., Salomaa, A. (Eds.): The Oxford Handbook of Membrane Computing. Oxford University Press, Oxford (2010)
29. Peng, H., Wang, J., Shi, P., Pérez-Jiménez, M.J., Riscos-Núñez, A.: Fault diagnosis of power systems using fuzzy tissue-like P systems. Integr. Comput.-Aided Eng. **24**(4), 401–411 (2017)
30. Pérez-Jiménez, M.J., Riscos-Núñez, A.: A linear-time solution to the knapsack problem using P systems with active membranes. In: Martín-Vide, C., Mauri, G., Păun, G., Rozenberg, G., Salomaa, A. (eds.) WMC 2003. LNCS, vol. 2933, pp. 250–268. Springer, Heidelberg (2004). https://doi.org/10.1007/978-3-540-24619-0_19
31. Pérez-Jiménez, M.J., Riscos-Núñez, A.: Solving the subset-sum problem by P systems with active membranes. New Generat. Comput. **23**(4), 339–356 (2005)
32. Rozenberg, G., Salomaa, A. (eds.): Handbook of Formal Languages. Springer, Heidelberg (1997). https://doi.org/10.1007/978-3-642-59126-6
33. Song, B., Song, T., Pan, L.: A time-free uniform solution to subset sum problem by tissue P systems with cell division. Math. Struct. Comput. Sci. **27**, 17–32 (2017)
34. Suri, N., Cabri, G. (eds.): Adaptive, Dynamic, and Resilient Systems. CRC Press, Boca Raton (2014)
35. Zhang, G., Cheng, J., Wang, T., Wang, X., Zhu, J.: Membrane Computing: Theory and Applications. Science Press, Beijing (2015)
36. Zhang, G., Pérez-Jiménez, M.J., Gheorghe, M.: Real-life Applications with Membrane Computing. ECC, vol. 25. Springer, Cham (2017). https://doi.org/10.1007/978-3-319-55989-6

Chain Code P System Generating a Variant of the Peano Space-Filling Curve

Rodica Ceterchi[1(✉)], Atulya K. Nagar[2], and K. G. Subramanian[2]

[1] Faculty of Mathematics and Computer Science, University of Bucharest,
14 Academiei Street, 010014 Bucharest, Romania
rceterchi@gmail.com
[2] Faculty of Science, Liverpool Hope University, Hope Park,
Liverpool L16 9JD, UK

Abstract. Generation of the finite approximations of the well-known Hilbert and Peano space-filling curves, represented as chain-code words has been studied in an earlier work. The generation was done with parallel chain code P systems with objects as chain code words and rewriting with context-free rules in parallel. Continuing this line of work, finite approximations of a variant of the Peano curve considered by Wunderlich are generated here with parallel chain code P system. We also generate approximating polygons corresponding to the Peano curve with parallel chain code P system.

1 Introduction

In the area of membrane computing, the computing model with the generic name of P system was introduced by Păun [9] taking inspiration from biological features of cell structure and functioning. This model has developed into a fascinating framework for handling different kinds of problems [6] in several areas of computing, including picture generation and analysis. On the other hand, a grammatical model for describing chain code pictures introduced in [8] is a robust model which has been investigated subsequently in various studies (see, for example, [4,5]). Basically, a chain code picture is composed of unit lines in the two-dimensional plane and is represented by a word over the alphabet $\{l, r, u, d\}$ where l, r, u, d are respectively interpreted as standing for a drawn horizontal or vertical line of unit length to the left, right, up or down directions from the current position in the chain code picture. With a view of incorporating the chain code grammar features in the P system model, a context-free rewriting chain code P system was introduced in [15] on the lines of the string rewriting P system [9]. This P system [15] involves sequential rewriting of words with context-free string grammar rules in the regions with the terminal alphabet $\{l, r, u, d\}$ interpreted as mentioned earlier. Recently, incorporating

K. G. Subramanian—Honorary Visiting Professor.

© Springer Nature Switzerland AG 2019
T. Hinze et al. (Eds.): CMC 2018, LNCS 11399, pp. 73–83, 2019.
https://doi.org/10.1007/978-3-030-12797-8_6

the parallel mode of rewriting in the application of the rules in the regions of a chain code P system, Parallel chain code P system was introduced in [3] and, as an application, parallel chain code P systems were constructed to generate the patterns of approximations of space-filling Hilbert and Peano curves [7,13]. We continue here this line of investigation and construct a parallel chain code P system for generating the approximation patterns of a variant of the Peano curve due to Wunderlich ([11], Page 44 : Fig. 3.7.1), which we call here as Wunderlich space-filling curve. We also consider the approximating polygons ([11], Page 43: Fig. 3.6.2) of the Peano curve and construct a parallel chain code P system for generating the approximating polygons of the Peano curve.

2   Basic Definitions and Results

We briefly recall notions related to chain code pictures [5,8]. For notions on grammars and languages as well as P systems, unexplained here, we refer to [1,9,10,14].

The points in the two-dimensional plane one unit above or below, on the left or right of a given point s with integer coordinates (i, j) are respectively denoted by $l(s), r(s), u(s), d(s)$. A move along a unit line from s to $l(s)$ is simply denoted by l. The symbols r, u, d are interpreted in a similar manner. A connected chain code picture P is composed of connected unit lines in the plane. A chain code picture in the shape of a "double stair-case" is shown in Fig. 1 and can be described by a chain code word $w = rururrdrdrdr$. Note that this word describing the picture is not unique. For example, the word $w' = rurururrllrrdrdrdr$ describes also the same picture in Fig. 1.

Fig. 1. Double "stair-case" shaped chain code picture of equal height

2.1   Context-Free Parallel Chain Code P System

We now recall context-free parallel chain code P system introduced in [3].

A context-free parallel chain code P system of degree $n, n \geq 1$, is a construct

$$\Pi = (N, \Sigma, \mu, L_1, \cdots, L_n, R_1, \cdots, R_n, i_0)$$

where: $\Sigma = \{l, r, u, d\}$ is the terminal alphabet; N is a finite set of nonterminal symbols disjoint from Σ; $V = N \cup \Sigma$; μ is a membrane structure with n membranes labelled in a one-to-one way with $1, 2, \ldots, n$; $L_1, \ldots, L_n$ are finite sets of strings over V and $R_1, \ldots, R_n$ are finite sets of context-free rewriting rules associated with the n regions of μ; the rules are of the form $A \rightarrow \alpha(tar)$, where

$A \rightarrow \alpha$ is a context-free (CF) rule, $A \in N$, $\alpha \in V^*$ the rules have attached targets *here, out, in* (in general, we do not mention *here*) with the target specifying the region where the result of the rewriting should be placed in the next step: *here* means that the result remains in the same region where the rule was applied, *out* means that the string has to be sent to the region immediately surrounding the region where it has been produced, and *in* means that the string should go to one of the directly inner membranes, if any exists.

During a computation, all the nonterminals (if any) in a string object in a region are rewritten in parallel at the same time by available and applicable context-free rules in the region with the same target indication. The words over the terminal alphabet Σ are collected in the output membrane at the end of a successful halting computation and form the chain code picture language generated by the P system.

The set of all chain code picture languages generated by context-free parallel chain code P systems with n membranes is denoted by $PCCP_n(CF)$.

We give an example of parallel chain code P system. Let L_{st} be the set of chain code words describing double stair-case shaped chain code pictures (Fig. 1). We now construct a context-free parallel chain code P system with two membranes generating L_{st}. Let

$$\Pi = (\{A, B\}, \{l, r, u, d\}, [_1 [_2]_2]_1, \{ArrB\}, \emptyset, R_1, R_2, 2).$$

The rule sets are

$$R_1 = \{A \rightarrow ruA, B \rightarrow drB, A \rightarrow ru(in), B \rightarrow dr(in)\}, R_2 = \emptyset.$$

Initially, the string $ArrB$ is in region 1 and the region 2 has no string object. The rules $A \rightarrow ruA, B \rightarrow drB$ are applicable in parallel and can be applied as many times as we need. The generated string of the form $(ru)^{(n-1)} Arr(dr)^{(n-1)} B$ remains in the same region. If the rules $A \rightarrow ru, B \rightarrow dr$ with the same target indication *in* are applied in region 1, the resulting string $(ru)^n rr(dr)^n$ is sent to the output region 2. Thus Π generates L_{st}. Interpreting the symbols $\{l, r, u, d\}$ in the manner described earlier, the words $w = (ru)^n rr(dr)^n$ yield the corresponding chain code pictures.

2.2   The Peano Curve

Peano proposed the first space-filling curve, which is called the Peano curve. This curve is a continuous but nowhere differentiable function from the unit interval $[0, 1]$ to the unit square $[0, 1] \times [0, 1]$. Generation of the geometric patterns that are iterations of the Peano curve has been of interest and has been well-investigated (See for example [7,13]). Parallel chain code P system generating the geometric patterns of the Peano curve represented as chain code words over $\Sigma = \{l, r, u, d\}$ has been constructed in [3]. The first two members of the Peano curve patterns are shown in Fig. 2.

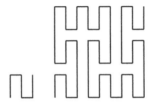

Fig. 2. The first two Peano curve patterns

3   Approximation Patterns of a Space-Filling Curve Due to Wunderlich

Following the Peano curve, several other space-filling curves have been proposed subsequently. A good account of these space-filling curves is dealt with by Sagan [11]. Walter Wunderlich [16], ([11], Page 44) gave three variations of the space-filling curve with two of these falling into one type which he called as Peano curve of the switch-back type and the third curve of a second type which was called by him as the meander type. Note that the original Peano curve [11] is of the switch-back type. Different methods of generating approximation patterns of space-filling curves have been considered [12,13]. Here we consider one of the switch-back type space-filling curves due to Wunderlich, which we call as Wunderlich curve and construct a parallel chain code P system generating the language of chain code words encoding the geometric patterns of the approximations of the Wunderlich curve.

In terms of the chain code symbols l, r, u, d, the words corresponding to the first two approximations of the Wunderlich curve are

$$W_{1,1} = uurddruu,$$

$$W_{1,2} = uurddruuullurrulluuurddruurrrdlldrrdddluuldd$$
$$drrdlldrrruurddruuullurrulluuurddruu,$$

The corresponding geometric patterns are shown in Fig. 3.

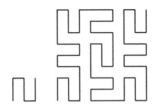

Fig. 3. The first two patterns of the Wunderlich curve

With the first approximation $W_1 = uurddruu$, and for $n > 1$, the subsequent approximations are given by $W_{1,n+1}$

$$= W_{1,n}ug_1(W_{1,n})uW_{1,n}rg_2(W_{1,n})dg_3(W_{1,n})dg_2(W_{1,n})rW_{1,n}ug_1(W_{1,n})uW_{1,n}$$

where g_1, g_2, g_3 are homomorphisms on Σ as given below:
$g_1(u) = l, g_1(d) = r, g_1(l) = d, g_1(r) = u;$
$g_2(u) = r, g_2(d) = l, g_2(l) = u, g_2(r) = d;$
$g_3(u) = d, g_3(d) = u, g_3(l) = r, g_3(r) = l.$

Let us consider the context-free parallel chain code P system Π_{W_1} given by

$$\Pi_{W_1} = (\{A, B, C, D\}, \{l, r, d, u\}, [_1[_2]_2]_1, \{A\}, \emptyset, R_1, R_2, 2)$$

where $R_2 = \emptyset$ and R_1 contains the following four rules with target indication *here*:

$$A \rightarrow AuBuArCdDdCrAuBuA, B \rightarrow BlDlBuArCrAuBlDlB,$$

$$C \rightarrow CrArCdDlBlDdCrArC, D \rightarrow DdCdDlBuAuBlDdCdD,$$

and the following four rules with target indication *in*:

$$A \rightarrow \lambda, B \rightarrow \lambda, C \rightarrow \lambda, D \rightarrow \lambda.$$

We note that the main idea in the construction of the rules involved in the P system is that each nonterminal "captures" a sub-pattern of an approximation pattern. This informally expressed notion is the basis of the following lemmas that lead to the main Theorem.

Theorem 1. *The P system Π_{W_1} above produces in membrane 2 the words $W_{1,n}$, where $W_{1,n}$ is the n-th Wunderlich word of type 1.*

Let us denote by γ the morphism given by the four rewriting rules with target *here*, and by f the morphism given by the four rewriting rules with target *in*. We will prove by induction that $f(\gamma^n(A))) = W_{1,n}$.

First, some technical lemmas.

Lemma 1. *The following hold:*

$g_1 \circ g_2 = g_2 \circ g_1 = (g_3)^2 = 1_\Sigma$
$(g_1)^2 = g_3 = (g_2)^2$
$g_2 \circ g_3 = g_3 \circ g_2 = g_1$
$g_1 \circ g_3 = g_3 \circ g_1 = g_2$

Proof. Note that g_1 is the rotation left by $90°$, that g_2 is the rotation right by $90°$, and that g_3 is the symmetry with respect to the origin. This and/or straightforward computations. □

Lemma 2. *The following hold:*

$f(\gamma(A)) = uurddruu = W_{1,1}$
$f(\gamma(B)) = llurrull = g_1(W_{1,1}) = g_1(f(\gamma(A)))$
$f(\gamma(C)) = rrdlldrr = g_2(W_{1,1}) = g_2(f(\gamma(A)))$
$f(\gamma(D)) = ddluuldd = g_3(W_{1,1}) = g_3(f(\gamma(A)))$

Proof. By straightforward computations. □

Lemma 3. *The following hold:*

$$f(\gamma(A)) = g_2(f(\gamma(B))) = g_1(f(\gamma(C))) = g_3(f(\gamma(D)))$$
$$f(\gamma(B)) = g_1(f(\gamma(A))) = g_3(f(\gamma(C))) = g_2(f(\gamma(D)))$$
$$f(\gamma(C)) = g_2(f(\gamma(A))) = g_3(f(\gamma(B))) = g_1(f(\gamma(D)))$$
$$f(\gamma(D)) = g_3(f(\gamma(A1))) = g_1(f(\gamma(B))) = g_2(f(\gamma(C)))$$

Proof. By applying the preceding two Lemmas combined.   □

Lemma 4. *The following relations hold:*

$$f(\gamma^n(A)) = g_2(f(\gamma^n(B))) = g_1(f(\gamma^n(C))) = g_3(f(\gamma^n(D)))$$
$$f(\gamma^n(B)) = g_1(f(\gamma^n(A))) = g_3(f(\gamma^n(C))) = g_2(f(\gamma^n(D)))$$
$$f(\gamma^n(C)) = g_2(f(\gamma^n(A))) = g_3(f(\gamma^n(B))) = g_1(f(\gamma^n(D)))$$
$$f(\gamma^n(D)) = g_3(f(\gamma^n(A))) = g_1(f(\gamma^n(B))) = g_2(f(\gamma^n(C)))$$

Proof. By induction. The case $n = 1$ is covered by Lemma 3.

Suppose now that all 12 relations hold for n. We compute for $n + 1$ the first relation.

$$f(\gamma^{n+1}(A)) = f(\gamma^n(AuBuArCdDdCrAuBuA))$$
$$= f(\gamma^n(A))uf(\gamma^n(B))uf(\gamma^n(A))rf(\gamma^n(C))df(\gamma^n(D))df(\gamma^n(C))r\cdot$$
$$\cdot f(\gamma^n(A))uf(\gamma^n(B))uf(\gamma^n(A))$$
$$= g_2(f(\gamma^n(B)))g_2(l)g_2(f(\gamma^n(D)))g_2(l)g_2(f(\gamma^n(B)))g_2(u)\cdot$$
$$\cdot g_2(f(\gamma^n(A)))g_2(r)g_2(f(\gamma^n(C)))g_2(r)g_2(f(\gamma^n(A)))g_2(u)\cdot$$
$$\cdot g_2(f(\gamma^n(B)))g_2(l)g_2(f(\gamma^n(D)))g_2(l)g_2(f(\gamma^n(B)))$$
$$= g_2(f(\gamma^n(BlDlBuArCrAuBlDlB))) = g_2(f(\gamma^{n+1}(B))).$$

The other 11 relations follow by similar computations.   □

Proof. We complete the proof of the Theorem 1. We will show that $f(\gamma^n(A)) = W_{1,n}$. Again by induction on n. For $n = 1$ we have the relation from Lemma 2. We will suppose the relation holds for n. For $n + 1$ we compute:

$$f(\gamma^{n+1}(A)) = f(\gamma^n(AuBuArCdDdCrAuBuA))$$
$$= f(\gamma^n(A))uf(\gamma^n(B))uf(\gamma^n(A))rf(\gamma^n(C))df(\gamma^n(D))df(\gamma^n(C))r\cdot$$
$$\cdot f(\gamma^n(A))uf(\gamma^n(B))uf(\gamma^n(A))$$
$$= f(\gamma^n(A))ug_1(f(\gamma^n(A)))uf(\gamma^n(A))r\cdot$$
$$\cdot g_2(f(\gamma^n(A)))dg_3(f(\gamma^n(A)))dg_2(f(\gamma^n(A)))r\cdot$$
$$\cdot f(\gamma^n(A))ug_1(f(\gamma^n(A)))uf(\gamma^n(A))$$
$$= W_{1,n}ug_1(W_{1,n})uW_{1,n}rg_2(W_{1,n})dg_3(W_{1,n})dg_2(W_{1,n})rW_{1,n}ug_1(W_{1,n})uW_{1,n}$$
$$= W_{1,n+1}.$$

     □

We note that no more than two membranes are needed but one membrane is not enough as then all the rules can have only target here and so the intended combination of the rules cannot be applied in parallel, thereby not yielding only the approximation patterns of Wunderlich curve.

By similar computations, we can change the starting symbol in membrane 1, and we obtain:

Theorem 2. *The following relations hold:*

$$f(\gamma^n(A)) = W_{1,n}$$
$$f(\gamma^n(B)) = g_1(W_{1,n})$$
$$f(\gamma^n(C)) = g_2(W_{1,n})$$
$$f(\gamma^n(D)) = g_3(W_{1,n})$$

4   Approximating Polygons for the Peano Curve

Approximating polygons of the Peano curve form a sequence of continuous curves converging to the Peano curve. Instead of the chain code symbols, we consider the symbols $f_{ne}, f_{nw}, f_{se}, f_{sw}$ respectively corresponding to moves along the diagonals of a unit square from the lower left corner, lower right corner, upper left corner or upper right corner to the opposite corner. Expressed formally, for a unit square $PQRS$ in the plane with the corners P, Q, R, S having integer coordinates $(i, j), (i + 1, j), (i + 1, j + 1), (i, j + 1)$ respectively, we denote by the symbols $f_{ne}, f_{nw}, f_{se}, f_{sw}$ moves along the diagonals P to R, S to Q, Q to S, and R to P respectively. In terms of these symbols, we can represent by words, the approximating polygons of the Peano curve ([11], Page 35: Fig. 3.3.2). The first two members of these approximating polygons are shown in ([11], Page 43: Fig. 3.6.2). The corresponding words are

$$P_1 = f_{ne} f_{nw} f_{ne} f_{se} f_{sw} f_{se} f_{ne} f_{nw} f_{ne}$$

$$P_2 = f_{ne} f_{nw} f_{ne} f_{se} f_{sw} f_{se} f_{ne} f_{nw} f_{ne} f_{nw} f_{ne} f_{nw} f_{sw} f_{se} f_{sw} f_{nw} f_{ne} f_{nw} f_{ne} f_{nw} f_{ne}$$

$$f_{se} f_{sw} f_{se} f_{ne} f_{nw} f_{ne} f_{se} f_{sw} f_{se} f_{ne} f_{nw} f_{ne} f_{se} f_{sw} f_{se} f_{sw} f_{se} f_{sw} f_{nw} f_{ne} f_{nw}$$

$$f_{sw} f_{se} f_{sw} f_{se} f_{sw} f_{se} f_{ne} f_{nw} f_{ne} f_{se} f_{sw} f_{se}$$

and for $n > 1$,

$$P_{n+1} = P_n \sigma_1(P_n) P_n \sigma_2(P_n) \sigma_3(P_n) \sigma_2(P_n) P_n \sigma_1(P_n) P_n$$

where $\sigma_1, \sigma_2, \sigma_3$ are given by

$$\sigma_1(f_{ne}) = f_{nw}, \sigma_1(f_{nw}) = f_{ne}, \sigma_1(f_{se}) = f_{sw}, \sigma_1(f_{sw}) = f_{se}$$

$$\sigma_2(f_{ne}) = f_{se}, \sigma_2(f_{nw}) = f_{sw}, \sigma_2(f_{se}) = f_{ne}, \sigma_2(f_{sw}) = f_{nw}$$

$$\sigma_3(f_{ne}) = f_{sw}, \sigma_3(f_{nw}) = f_{se}, \sigma_3(f_{se}) = f_{nw}, \sigma_3(f_{sw}) = f_{ne}$$

We consider a modified context-free parallel chain code system and call it context-free parallel chain code type P system. The modification is that the set of terminal symbols is $\{f_{ne}, f_{nw}, f_{se}, f_{sw}\}$. We have shown in Figs. 4 and 5 the

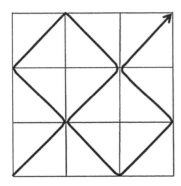

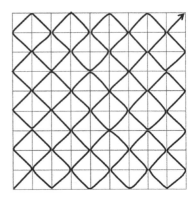

Fig. 4. The first approximating polygon ([11], Page 43: Fig. 3.6.2) of the Peano curve

Fig. 5. The second approximating polygon ([11], Page 43: Fig. 3.6.2) of the Peano curve

first and the second approximating polygons of the Peano curve. The context-free parallel chain code type P system Π_{AP} generating the words P_n, $n \geq 1$ corresponding to the approximating polygons of the Peano curve is given by

$$\Pi_{AP} = (\{X, Y, Z, U\}, \{f_{ne}, f_{nw}, f_{se}, f_{sw}\}, [_1[_2]_2]_1, \{X\}, \emptyset, R_1, R_2, 2)$$

where $R_2 = \emptyset$ and R_1 contains the following four rules with target indication *here*:

$$X \rightarrow XYXZUZXYX, \quad Y \rightarrow YXYUZUYXY,$$

$$Z \rightarrow ZUZXYXZUZ, \quad U \rightarrow UZUYXYUZU,$$

and the following four rules with target indication *in*:

$$X \rightarrow f_{ne}, Y \rightarrow f_{nw}, Z \rightarrow f_{se}, U \rightarrow f_{sw}.$$

Theorem 3. *The P system Π_{AP} above produces in membrane 2 the words P_n, where P_n is the n−th approximating polygon of the Peano Curve.*

Let us denote by γ the morphism given by the four rewriting rules with target *here*, and by f the morphism given by the four rewriting rules with target *in*. We will prove by induction that $f(\gamma^n(X)) = P_n$. As usual, first, some technical lemmas.

Lemma 5. *The following hold:*

$$\sigma_1^2 = \sigma_2^2 = \sigma_3^2 = 1_\Sigma$$
$$\sigma_1 \circ \sigma_2 = \sigma_2 \circ \sigma_1 = \sigma_3$$
$$\sigma_1 \circ \sigma_3 = \sigma_3 \circ \sigma_1 = \sigma_2$$
$$\sigma_2 \circ \sigma_3 = \sigma_3 \circ \sigma_2 = \sigma_1$$

Proof. Note that σ_1 is the symmetry with respect to the Oy axis, exchanging e and w, and leaving n and s unchanged; that σ_2 is the symmetry with respect to the Ox axis, exchanging n and s, and leaving e and w unchanged, and that σ_3 is the symmetry with respect to the origin. Also straightforward computations. □

Lemma 6. *The following hold:*

$$f(\gamma(X)) = f(XYXZUZXYX) = f_{ne}f_{nw}f_{ne}f_{se}f_{sw}f_{se}f_{ne}f_{nw}f_{ne} = P_1$$
$$f(\gamma(Y)) = f(YXYUZUYXY) = f_{nw}f_{ne}f_{nw}f_{sw}f_{se}f_{sw}f_{nw}f_{ne}f_{nw} = \sigma_1(P_1)$$
$$f(\gamma(Z)) = f(ZUZXYXZUZ) = f_{se}f_{sw}f_{se}f_{ne}f_{nw}f_{ne}f_{se}f_{sw}f_{se} = \sigma_2(P_1)$$
$$f(\gamma(U)) = f(UZUYXYUZU) = f_{sw}f_{se}f_{sw}f_{nw}f_{ne}f_{nw}f_{sw}f_{se}f_{sw} = \sigma_3(P_1)$$

Proof. By straightforward computations. □

Lemma 7. *The following hold:*

$$f(\gamma(X)) = \sigma_1(f(\gamma(Y))) = \sigma_2(f(\gamma(Z))) = \sigma_3(f(\gamma(U)))$$
$$f(\gamma(Y)) = \sigma_1(f(\gamma(X))) = \sigma_3(f(\gamma(Z))) = \sigma_2(f(\gamma(U)))$$
$$f(\gamma(Z)) = \sigma_2(f(\gamma(X))) = \sigma_3(f(\gamma(Y))) = \sigma_1(f(\gamma(U)))$$
$$f(\gamma(U)) = \sigma_3(f(\gamma(X))) = \sigma_2(f(\gamma(Y))) = \sigma_1(f(\gamma(Z)))$$

Proof. By applying the preceding two Lemmas combined. For instance, we note that the first column of equalities is precisely Lemma 6. We also use the fact that each σ_i is its own inverse. □

Lemma 8. *The following relations hold for every natural n:*

$$f(\gamma^n(X)) = \sigma_1(f(\gamma^n(Y))) = \sigma_2(f(\gamma^n(Z))) = \sigma_3(f(\gamma^n(U)))$$
$$f(\gamma^n(Y)) = \sigma_1(f(\gamma^n(X))) = \sigma_3(f(\gamma^n(Z))) = \sigma_2(f(\gamma^n(U)))$$
$$f(\gamma^n(Z)) = \sigma_2(f(\gamma^n(X))) = \sigma_3(f(\gamma^n(Y))) = \sigma_1(f(\gamma^n(U)))$$
$$f(\gamma^n(U)) = \sigma_3(f(\gamma^n(X))) = \sigma_2(f(\gamma^n(Y))) = \sigma_1(f(\gamma^n(Z)))$$

Proof. By induction. The case $n = 1$ is covered by Lemma 7.

Suppose now that all 12 relations hold for n. We compute for $n+1$ the first relation.

$$f(\gamma^{n+1}(X)) = f(\gamma^n(XYXZUZXYX))$$
$$= f(\gamma^n(X))f(\gamma^n(Y))f(\gamma^n(X))f(\gamma^n(Z))f(\gamma^n(U))f(\gamma^n(Z))\cdot$$
$$\cdot f(\gamma^n(X))f(\gamma^n(Y))f(\gamma^n(X))$$
$$= \sigma_1(f(\gamma^n(Y)))\sigma_1(f(\gamma^n(X)))\sigma_1(f(\gamma^n(Y)))\cdot$$
$$\cdot\sigma_1(f(\gamma^n(U)))\sigma_1(f(\gamma^n(Z)))\sigma_1(f(\gamma^n(U)))\cdot$$
$$\cdot\sigma_1(f(\gamma^n(Y)))\sigma_1(f(\gamma^n(X)))\sigma_1(f(\gamma^n(Y)))$$
$$= \sigma_1(f(\gamma^n(YXYUZUYXY))) = \sigma_1(f(\gamma^{n+1}(Y))).$$

□

Proof. We now complete the proof of the Theorem 3.

We show by induction that $f(\gamma^n(X)) = P_n$. Suppose the relation is true for n, and we show for $n + 1$.

$$f(\gamma^{n+1}(X)) = f(\gamma^n(XYXZUZXYX))$$
$$= f(\gamma^n(X))f(\gamma^n(Y))f(\gamma^n(X))f(\gamma^n(Z))f(\gamma^n(U))f(\gamma^n(Z))\cdot$$
$$\cdot f(\gamma^n(X))f(\gamma^n(Y))f(\gamma^n(X))$$
$$=$$
$$f(\gamma^n(X))\sigma_1(f(\gamma^n(X)))f(\gamma^n(X))\sigma_2(f(\gamma^n(X)))\sigma_3(f(\gamma^n(X)))\sigma_2(f(\gamma^n(X)))\cdot$$
$$\cdot f(\gamma^n(X))\sigma_1(f(\gamma^n(X)))f(\gamma^n(X))$$
$$= P_n\sigma_1(P_n)P_n\sigma_2(P_n)\sigma_3(P_n)\sigma_2(P_n)P_n\sigma_1(P_n)P_n = P_{n+1} \qquad \square$$

By similar computations, we can change the starting symbol in membrane 1, and we obtain the more complete result:

Theorem 4. *The following relations hold:*

$$f(\gamma^n(X)) = P_n$$
$$f(\gamma^n(Y)) = \sigma_1(P_n)$$
$$f(\gamma^n(Z)) = \sigma_2(P_n)$$
$$f(\gamma^n(U)) = \sigma_3(P_n)$$

5   Conclusions

Parallel chain code P systems are constructed for the generation of the approximation patterns of the Wumderlich space-filling curve [16]. Using modified chain code symbols, approximating polygons of the Peano curve are also generated with P systems involving rewriting in parallel. Also in [2], we have considered the problem of generation of approximating polygons of Hilbert curve [12] and another space-filling curve, called Lebesgue's curve [11] with P systems. One can explore the problem of constructing P systems of a similar kind to generate the sequence of geometric approximation patterns that define each of the other two Wunderlich curves. The first two members of these two sequences are given in [11] in Fig. 3.7.2 (Page 44) and Fig. 3.7.3 (Page 45).

Acknowledgements. We thank the anonymous referees for their valuable suggestions and comments which greatly helped to improve the paper.

References

1. Ceterchi, R., Mutyam, M., Păun, G., Subramanian, K.G.: Array - rewriting P systems. Nat. Comput. **2**, 229–249 (2003)
2. Ceterchi, R., Nagar, A.K., Subramanian, K.G.: Approximating polygons for space-filling curves generated with P systems. In: Graciani, C., Riscos-Núñez, A., Păun, G., Rozenberg, G., Salomaa, A. (eds.) Enjoying Natural Computing. LNCS, vol. 11270, pp. 57–65. Springer, Cham (2018). https://doi.org/10.1007/978-3-030-00265-7_5

3. Ceterchi, R., Subramanian, K.G., Venkat, I.: P systems with parallel rewriting for chain code picture languages. In: Beckmann, A., Mitrana, V., Soskova, M. (eds.) CiE 2015. LNCS, vol. 9136, pp. 145–155. Springer, Cham (2015). https://doi.org/10.1007/978-3-319-20028-6_15

4. Dassow, J., Habel, A., Taubenberger, S.: Chain-code pictures and collages generated by hyperedge replacement. In: Cuny, J., Ehrig, H., Engels, G., Rozenberg, G. (eds.) Graph Grammars 1994. LNCS, vol. 1073, pp. 412–427. Springer, Heidelberg (1996). https://doi.org/10.1007/3-540-61228-9_102

5. Drewes, F.: Some remarks on the generative power of collage grammars and chain-code grammars. In: Ehrig, H., Engels, G., Kreowski, H.-J., Rozenberg, G. (eds.) TAGT 1998. LNCS, vol. 1764, pp. 1–14. Springer, Heidelberg (2000). https://doi.org/10.1007/978-3-540-46464-8_1

6. Gheorghe, M., Păun, Gh., Pérez Jiménez, M.J., Rozenberg, G.: Research frontiers of membrane computing: open problems and research topics. Int. J. Found. Comput. Sci. 24(5), 547–624 (2013)

7. Kitaev, S., Mansour, T., Seebold, P.: The Peano curve and counting occurrences of some patterns. J. Autom. Lang. Combin. 9(4), 439–455 (2004)

8. Maurer, H.A., Rozenberg, G., Welzl, E.: Using string languages to describe picture languages. Inf. Control 54, 155–185 (1982)

9. Păun, Gh.: Computing with membranes. J. Comput. Syst. Sci. 61, 108–143 (2000)

10. Salomaa, A.: Formal Languages. Academic Press, London (1973)

11. Sagan, H.: Space-Filling Curves. Springer, New York (1994). https://doi.org/10.1007/978-1-4612-0871-6

12. Seebold, P.: Tag system for the Hilbert curve. Discrete Math. Theor. Comput. Sci. 9, 213–226 (2007)

13. Siromoney, R., Subramanian, K.G.: Space-filling curves and infinite graphs. In: Ehrig, H., Nagl, M., Rozenberg, G. (eds.) Graph Grammars 1982. LNCS, vol. 153, pp. 380–391. Springer, Heidelberg (1983). https://doi.org/10.1007/BFb0000120

14. Subramanian, K.G.: P systems and picture languages. In: Durand-Lose, J., Margenstern, M. (eds.) MCU 2007. LNCS, vol. 4664, pp. 99–109. Springer, Heidelberg (2007). https://doi.org/10.1007/978-3-540-74593-8_9

15. Subramanian, K.G., Venkat, I., Pan, L.: P systems generating chain code picture languages. In: Proceedings of Asian Conference on Membrane Computing, pp. 115–123 (2012)

16. Wunderlich, W.: Über Peano-Kurven. Elem. Math. 28, 1–10 (1973)

APCol Systems with Agent Creation

Lucie Ciencialová[(⊠)]

Institute of Computer Science and Research Institute of the IT4Innovations
Centre of Excellence, Silesian University in Opava, Opava, Czech Republic
lucie.ciencialova@fpf.slu.cz

Abstract. We introduce a specific type of rules for APCol systems
(Automaton-like P colonies), variants of P colonies where the environment of the agents is given by a string and during functioning the agents
change their own states and process the string similarly to automata.
These rules enrich the actioning of APCol systems by agent creation.
Finally, we show that even APCol systems with agent creation, systems
without inner structure, can solve 3SAT in linear time.

Keywords: P colony · Membrane systems · String processing · SAT

1 Introduction

APCol systems are variants of P colonies (introduced in [5]) – very simple membrane systems inspired by colonies of formal grammars. The APCol systems were
introduce in 2014 in [1]. The interested reader is referred to [9] for detailed information on P systems (membrane systems) and to [6] and [3] for more information
on grammar systems theory; for more details on P colonies consult [4] and [2].

An APCol system consists of a finite number of agents – finite collections
of objects in a cell – and a shared environment. The agents have programs
consisting of rules. These rules are of two types: they may change the objects of
the agents and they can be used for interacting with the joint shared environment
– a string.

The computation in APCol systems starts with an input string, representing
the environment, and with each agent in its initial state.

Every computational step means a maximally parallel action of the active
agents: an agent is active if it is able to perform at least one of its programs,
and the joint action of the agents is maximally parallel if no more active agent
can be added to the synchronously acting agents.

The computation ends if there are no more applicable programs in the system.

We equip the agents with agent creation programs. They are applicable when
a special object appears inside the agent. An agent with the special object can
make one copy of itself containing objects specified by the program.

In membrane computing, the notion of creation is not new in P systems. It
was introduced in [7] and in [8]. The membrane creation by membrane division
is the frequently investigated way for obtaining an exponential working space in

© Springer Nature Switzerland AG 2019
T. Hinze et al. (Eds.): CMC 2018, LNCS 11399, pp. 84–94, 2019.
https://doi.org/10.1007/978-3-030-12797-8_7

a linear time, and on this basis solving hard problems, typically NP-complete problems, in polynomial (often, linear) time. Details can be found in [8,10]. Recently, PSPACE- complete problems were also attacked in this way (see [12]).

In this paper, we recall the definition of APCol systems and the notion of accepting, generating and verifying mode of computation and we introduce the computing mode. Then we define agent creation actions and show that APCol system with agent creation can solve 3SAT in polynomial time.

2 Preliminaries and Basic Notions

Throughout the paper we assume the reader to be familiar with the basics of the formal language theory and membrane computing [9,11].

For an alphabet Σ, the set of all words over Σ, including the empty word, ε, is denoted by Σ^*. We denote the length of a word $w \in \Sigma^*$ by $|w|$ and the number of occurrences of the symbol $a \in \Sigma$ in w by $|w|_a$.

For every string $x \in \Sigma^*$, $perm(x)$ denotes the set of all permutations of x and $pref(x)$ denotes the set of prefixes of x.

A multiset of objects M is a pair $M = (O, f)$, where O is an arbitrary (not necessarily finite) set of objects and f is a mapping $f : O \rightarrow N$; f assigns to each object in O its multiplicity in M. Any multiset of objects M with the set of objects $O = \{x_1, \dots x_n\}$ can be represented as a string w over alphabet O with $|w|_{x_i} = f(x_i)$; $1 \leq i \leq n$. Obviously, all words obtained from w by permuting the letters can also represent the same multiset M, and ε represents the empty multiset.

2.1 SAT

A SAT problem is represented using n propositional variables $x_1, x_2, \dots, x_n$, which can be assigned truth values 0 (false) or 1 (true). A literal l is either a variable x_i (i.e., a positive literal) or its complement $\neg x_i$ (i.e., a negative literal). A clause α is a disjunction of literals and a CNF formula φ is a conjunction of clauses. A literal l_j of a clause α that is assigned truth value 1 satisfies the clause, and the clause is said to be satisfied. If the literal is assigned truth value 0 then it can be removed from the clause. A clause with a single literal is said to be a unit and its literal has to be assigned value 1 for the clause to be satisfied. The derivation of an empty clause indicates that the formula is unsatisfied for the given assignment. The formula is satisfied if all its clauses are satisfied. The SAT problem consists of deciding whether there exists a truth assignment to the variables such that the formula becomes satisfied. Determining the satisfiability of a formula in the conjunctive normal form where each clause is limited to at most three literals is NP-complete, too; this problem is called 3-SAT.

2.2 APCol System

APCol system is a kind of P colonies. It is formed from agents with capacity 2 processing the string. They act according to programs as it is usual in P colonies.

Each program is formed from two rules of two types. The first type called rewriting is of the form $a \rightarrow b$ and by execution of this rule, the object a inside the agent is rewritten to the object b. The second type of rules is called replacing. The rewriting rules are of the form $c \leftrightarrow d$ and by use of them, the agent replaces the symbol d in the string by object c initially placed inside the agent. If $c = e$ ($e \leftrightarrow d$) it means that agent erases symbol d from the string. If $d = e$ ($c \leftrightarrow e$) it means that agent inserts symbol d to the string.

Let us make a few comments about the application of the programs.

1. Agent can act in only one place in the string in one step of computation.
2. $\langle a \leftrightarrow b; c \leftrightarrow e \rangle$ $\Rightarrow$ $b \rightarrow ac$ in the string,
   $\langle c \leftrightarrow e; a \leftrightarrow b \rangle$ $\Rightarrow$ $b \rightarrow ca$ in the string,
   $\langle a \rightarrow b; c \leftrightarrow e \rangle$ $\Rightarrow$ $\varepsilon \rightarrow c$ in the string, insert c anywhere to the string,
   and rewrite a to b inside agent
   $\langle a \leftrightarrow b; e \leftrightarrow d \rangle$ $\Rightarrow$ $d \rightarrow \varepsilon$ in the string, delete one d from the string, and
   rewrite a to b inside agent

Definition 1. *An APCol system is a construct* $\Pi = (O, e, A_1, \ldots, A_n)$, *where*

- O *is an alphabet, its elements are called the objects;*
- $e \in O$, *called the basic object;*
- A_i, $1 \leq i \leq n$, *are agents; each agent is a triplet* $A_i = (\omega_i, P_i, F_i)$, *where*
  - ω_i *is a multiset over* O, *describing the initial state (contents) of the agent,* $|\omega_i| = 2$,
  - $P_i = \{p_{i,1}, \ldots, p_{i,k_i}\}$ *is a finite set of programs associated with the agent, where each program is a pair of rules. Each rule is in one of the following forms:*
    - $*$ $a \rightarrow b$, *where* $a, b \in O$, *called a rewriting rule,*
    - $*$ $c \leftrightarrow d$, *where* $c, d \in O$, *called a communication rule;*
  - $F_i \subseteq O^*$ *is a finite set of final states (contents) of agent* A_i.

The APCol system is called restricted if its programs consist of one evolution rule $(a \rightarrow b)$ *and one communication rule* $(a \leftrightarrow b)$.

The computation starts in the initial configuration where all agents contain their initial multiset of objects and there is an input string over the alphabet T on the APCol system. Consequently, an initial configuration of the APCol system is an $(n + 1)$-tuple $c = (\omega; \omega_1, \ldots, \omega_n)$ where ω is the initial state of the environment and the other n components are multisets of strings of objects, given in the form of strings, the initial states of the agents.

A configuration of an APCol system Π is given by $(w; w_1, \ldots, w_n)$, where $|w_i| = 2$, $1 \leq i \leq n$, w_i represents all the objects inside the ith agent and $w \in (O - \{e\})^*$ is the string to be processed.

At each step of the computation every agent attempts to find one of its programs to use. If the number of applicable programs is higher than one, then the agent non-deterministically chooses one of them. At one step of computation, the maximal possible number of agents have to be active, i.e., have to perform a program.

By executing programs, the APCol system passes from one configuration to another configuration. A sequence of configurations started from the initial configuration is called a computation.

The computation halts when no agent has an applicable program.

Accepting Mode. In the accepting mode a halting computation is called accepting if and only if at least one agent is in final state and the string to be processed is ε. Hence, the string ω is accepted by the APCol system Π if there exists a computation by Π such that it starts in the initial configuration $(\omega; \omega_1, \ldots, \omega_n)$ and the computation ends by halting in the configuration $(\varepsilon; w_1, \ldots, w_n)$, where at least one of $w_i \in F_i$ for $1 \leq i \leq n$.

Generating Mode. The situation is slightly different when the APCol system works in the generating mode. A halting computation is called successful only if it starts with empty environmental string and at the end at least one agent is in a final state. The string w_F is generated by Π if and only if there exists computation starting in the initial configuration $(\varepsilon; \omega_1, \ldots, \omega_n)$ and the computation ends by halting in the configuration $(w_F; w_1, \ldots, w_n)$, where at least one of $w_i \in F_i$ for $1 \leq i \leq n$.

Verifying Mode. An input string is verified by the APCol system if the computation process is halting, and moreover, for every i, $1 \leq i \leq m$ - supposed that the length of the input string is m -, each agent rewrites some symbol at position i in some of the environmental strings occurring in the computation process. This means that the agents "visit" every position (of the input string or that of its descendants), i.e., they verify the environment.

Computing Mode. Inspired by computation of a Turing machine we introduce the computing mode. In the computing mode, a computation starts in an initial configuration with an input string possibly different from ε. An input string is accepted if and only if there exists a halting computation starting in a corresponding initial configuration and at least one agent is in a final state. We can also say that an APCol system computes a string that can be found in the environment after a computation halts and at least one agent is in a final state.

3   APCol Systems with Agent Creation

In this section, we introduce the programs for agent creation. For this purpose, we define a new special object @. If an agent contains such an object, the agent makes a copy of itself. This action is done by executing a program formed from two rewriting rules. Let $a@$ be a contents of agent A_1 with program $p_1 = \langle @ \to b; a \to c \rangle$. After execution of the program p_1 there is one new child-agent in the APCol system with the same label and the same set of programs as the parent-agent A_1 has. The contents of the parent-agent after the execution of the program is bc while the contents of the child-agent is ba.

If the parent-agent has a program $p_2 = \langle a \rightarrow c; @ \rightarrow b \rangle$, then after the execution of the program p_2 the contents of parent-agent after the execution of the program is bc and the contents of the child-agent is bc, too.

The order of rules determines whether the rewriting rule without @ is used before or after the creation of the child-agent.

Definition 2. *An APCol system with agent creation is a construct*

$$\Pi = (O, e, @, A_1, \ldots, A_n),$$

where

- *O is an alphabet, its elements are called the objects;*
- *$e \in O$, called the basic object;*
- *$@ \in O$, called the agent creation object;*
- *A_i, $1 \leq i \leq n$, are agents. Each agent is a triplet $A_i = (\omega_i, P_i, F_i)$, where*
  - *ω_i is a multiset over O, describing the initial state (contents) of the agent, $|\omega_i| = 2$,*
  - *$P_i = \{p_{i,1}, \ldots, p_{i,k_i}\}$ is a finite set of programs associated with the agent, where each program is a pair of rules. Each rule is in one of the following forms:*
    - *$a \rightarrow b$, where $a, b \in O$, called an rewriting rule,*
    - *$c \leftrightarrow d$, where $c, d \in O$, called a communication rule;*
    If @ appears on the left side of the rule in the program, both rules of this program must be rewriting;
  - *$F_i \subseteq O^*$ is a finite set of final states (contents) of agent A_i.*

When an agent obtains the object @ by the execution of a rewriting or a communication rule in the program, the agent must create a new agent in the next step of the computation in the way described within the above definition.

4   Solving 3-SAT

Let φ be a formula in CNF such that every clause α_j in it has at most 3 literals. Let n be a number of its variables and m be the number of its clauses.

As it is usual for APCol systems we add the special symbol \$ to the environmental string as a prefix of the formula.

Lemma 1. *Let φ be formula in CNF as mentioned above. Then there exists an APCol system that encodes the string $\$\varphi$ into a string of the form*

$$\wedge_1 \boxed{x_{1_1} x_{1_2} x_{1_3}} \wedge_2 \boxed{x_{2_1} x_{2_2} x_{2_3}} \cdots \wedge_m \boxed{x_{m_1} x_{m_2} x_{m_3}},$$

where x_{i_j} is l_{i_j} for a positive literal, $\overline{l_{i_j}}$ for a negative literal or ε, in linear time.

The idea of the proof is that there are two agents in APCol system. They cooperate in replacing triplets of literals by one complex symbol, they erase parentheses and add indices to $\wedge$-symbols.

We construct APCol system $\Pi_e = (O, e, A_1, A_2)$ such that:

- $O = \{e, \$, A, B, C, C', D, E, R, \vee, \neg\} \cup$
  $\cup \{i, \bar{i}, \wedge_i \mid 1 \leq i \leq m\} \cup \{L, \overline{L} \mid \forall \text{ literals } l \text{ in } \varphi\} \cup$
  $\cup \left\{\boxed{Y_{i1}Y_{i2}Y_{i3}} \mid Y_{ij} \in \{\text{literals, negative literals}, e\}, 1 \leq i \leq m\right\}$
- $A_1 = (ee, P_1)$
- $A_2 = (ee, P_2)$

The sets of programs are described below.

The agent A_1 has programs for reading the first symbols ($\$()$) and replacing them by $\vee_1 \bar{1}$. The agent prepares itself for computation – generates A.

A_1 1 $\langle e \to \bar{i}; \ e \to \wedge_i \rangle$ A_2 A $\langle e \to A; \ e \to e \rangle$
     2 $\langle \wedge_i \leftrightarrow \$; \ \bar{i} \leftrightarrow () \rangle$ for $1 \leq i \leq m$
     3 $\langle \$ \to e; \ (\leftrightarrow C) \rangle$

In the next phase the agent A_1 replaces a literal or a negative literal by its capitalized version or capitalized over-lined version.

A_1 4 $\langle C \leftrightarrow \bar{i}; \ e \leftrightarrow l_{1,i} \rangle$ 7 $\langle C \leftrightarrow \bar{1}; \ e \leftrightarrow \neg \rangle$
     5 $\langle \bar{i} \leftrightarrow C; \ l_{1,i} \to L_{1,i} \rangle$ 8 $\langle \bar{i} \to i; \ \neg \to e \rangle$
     6 $\langle C \to e; \ L_{1,i} \leftrightarrow \bar{i} \rangle$ 9 $\langle i \leftrightarrow C; \ e \to e \rangle$
                                       10 $\langle C \leftrightarrow i; \ e \leftrightarrow l_{1,i} \rangle$
                                       11 $\langle i \to \bar{i}; \ l_{1,i} \to \overline{L_{1,i}} \rangle$
                                       12 $\langle \bar{i} \leftrightarrow C; \ \overline{L_{1,i}} \to \overline{L_{1,i}} \rangle$
                                       13 $\langle C \to e; \ \overline{L_{1,i}} \leftrightarrow \bar{i} \rangle$

The agent A_2 consumes capitalized literal and remakes it into a special object – boxed triplet $\boxed{Y_{1,i}ee}$ – box with capitalized literal and two es inside the box.

A_2 B $\langle e \to e; \ A \leftrightarrow Y_{1,i} \rangle$ $Y_{1,i} \in \{L_{1,i}; \overline{L_{1,i}}; F\}$
     C $\left\langle e \to \boxed{Y_{1,i}ee}; \ Y_{1,i} \to B \right\rangle$
     D $\left\langle \boxed{Z_{1,i}Z_{2,i}Z_{3,i}} \leftrightarrow \boxed{Z_{1,i}Z_{2,i}Z_{3,i}}; \ B \leftrightarrow A \right\rangle$
                               $Z_{j,i} \in \{l_{j,i}; \overline{L_{j,i}}; F; e \mid 1 \leq j \leq 3, 1 \leq i \leq m\}$

When B appears in the environment it is time for the agent A_1 to consume $\vee$ (programs $14, 15$) and a following literal or a negative literal will be processed by executing programs $4 - 6$ or $6 - 13$.

A_1 14 $\langle \bar{1} \leftrightarrow B; \ e \leftrightarrow \vee \rangle$
     15 $\langle B \leftrightarrow C; \ \vee \to e \rangle$

The agent A_2 consumes capitalized literal again and replaces the first occurrence of e in boxed triplet by this capitalized literal. the situation is similar for the third processed literal from a clause.

A_2 E $\left\langle \boxed{Z_{1,i}Z_{2,i}Z_{3,i}} \to \boxed{Z_{1,i}Z_{2,i}Z_{3,i}}; \ A \leftrightarrow Y_{2,i} \right\rangle$ $Y_{2,i} \in \{L_{2,i}; \overline{L_{2,i}}; F\}$
     F $\left\langle \boxed{Z_{1,i}ee} \to \boxed{Z_{1,i}Y_{2,i}e}; \ Y_{2,i} \to B \right\rangle$
     G $\left\langle \boxed{Z_{1,i}Z_{2,i}Z_{3,i}} \to \boxed{Z_{1,i}Z_{2,i}Z_{3,i}}; \ A \leftrightarrow Y_{3,i} \right\rangle$ $Y_{3,i} \in \{L_{3,i}; \overline{L_{3,i}}; F\}$
     H $\left\langle \boxed{Z_{1,i}Z_{2,i}e} \to \boxed{Z_{1,i}Z_{2,i}Y_{3,i}}; \ Y_{3,i} \to B \right\rangle$

When a whole clause is processed the agent A_1 consumes) instead of $\vee$. The agent generates $\wedge_2$ and continues by processing the next clause.

$$A_1 \; 16 \; \langle \overline{1} \leftrightarrow B; \; e \leftrightarrow) \rangle$$
$$17 \; \langle B \rightarrow D; \;) \rightarrow R \rangle$$
$$18 \; \langle R \leftrightarrow \overline{1}; \; D \leftrightarrow e \rangle$$
$$19 \; \langle \overline{1} \leftrightarrow D; \; e \leftrightarrow \wedge \rangle$$
$$20 \; \langle D \rightarrow E; \; \wedge \leftrightarrow \wedge \rangle$$
$$21 \; \langle E \leftrightarrow \overline{i}; \; \wedge \rightarrow \wedge_{i+1} \rangle$$
$$22 \; \langle \overline{i} \rightarrow \overline{i+1}; \; \overline{i+1} \rightarrow \overline{i+1} \rangle$$
$$23 \; \langle \overline{i+1} \leftrightarrow E; \; \overline{i+1} \leftrightarrow (\rangle$$

The agent A_2 writes the boxed triplet into the string (programs I, J).

$$A_2 \; I \; \left\langle \boxed{Z_{1,i}Z_{2,i}Z_{3,i}} \rightarrow \boxed{Z_{1,i}Z_{2,i}Z_{3,i}}; \; A \leftrightarrow R \right\rangle$$
$$J \; \left\langle \boxed{Z_{1,i}Z_{2,i}Z_{3,i}} \leftrightarrow A; \; R \rightarrow e \right\rangle$$
$$K \; \langle A \rightarrow A; \; e \rightarrow D \rangle$$

If the currently processed clause is the last one, there is no object for the agent A_1 to consume after). The agent A_1 is in the state $\overline{m}e$ and has no program to be executed. Object D stays in the environment unprocessed by the agent A_1. Then agent A_2 consumes it and has no applicable program in the state AD.

The agent A_1 consumes one unread symbol in at most 7 steps of the computation; hence, the number of steps of each computation is at most $7 \cdot (8 \cdot m - 1)$.

Theorem 1. *To every string corresponding to a formula in CNF with at most three literals in each clause (encoded by an APCol system from Lemma 1), there exists an APCol system with agent creation that can determine if it is satisfiable or not.*

The idea of the proof: We construct an APCol system with agent creation with three agents. Let n be the number of variables in a formula and m be the number of clauses in a formula, $3m \geq n$ the length of the encoded input string is $2m$.

The first agent will generate agents with an object corresponding to the combination of values of variables inside agents. This object is in the form ordered variables ordered values . $x_i, 1 \leq i \leq n$ is variable and $j_i \in \{0; 1\}$.

$$A_1 \; 1 \; \left\langle e \rightarrow @; \; e \rightarrow \overset{x_1}{0} \right\rangle$$
$$2 \; \left\langle @ \rightarrow a; \; \overset{x_1}{0} \rightarrow \overset{x_1}{1} \right\rangle$$
$$3 \; \left\langle @ \rightarrow a; \; \overset{x_1 x_2}{j \; 0} \rightarrow \overset{x_1 x_2}{j \; 1} \right\rangle$$
$$\vdots$$
$$n+1 \; \left\langle @ \rightarrow e; \; \overset{x_1 x_2}{j_1 j_2} \cdots \overset{x_{n-1} x_n}{j_{n-1} \; 0} \rightarrow \overset{x_1 x_2}{j_1 j_2} \cdots \overset{x_{n-1} x_n}{j_{n-1} \; 1} \right\rangle$$

$$A_1 \; n+2 \; \left\langle @ \to a; \; \overset{x_1}{j_1} \to \overset{x_1 x_2}{j_1} \, 0 \right\rangle$$

$$n+3 \; \left\langle @ \to a; \; \overset{x_1 x_2}{j_1 j_2} \to \overset{x_1 x_2 x_3}{j_1 j_2} \, 0 \right\rangle$$

$$\vdots$$

$$n+n \; \left\langle @ \to a; \; \overset{x_1 x_2}{j_1 j_2} \cdots \overset{x_{n-1}}{j_{n-1}} \to \overset{x_1 x_2}{j_1 j_2} \cdots \overset{x_{n-1} x_n}{j_{n-1} j_0} \right\rangle$$

The first group of programs is to create new agent with different value of the last variable in the ordered set of variables. The second group of programs is to add new variable to the ordered set of variables.

After $2 \cdot n$ steps there is 2^n agents with label A_1 containing

$$e \; \overset{x_1 x_2}{j_1 j_2} \cdots \overset{x_{n-1} x_n}{j_{n-1}} \, 0 \to \overset{x_1 x_2}{j_1 j_2} \cdots \overset{x_{n-1} x_n}{j_{n-1} j_n}$$

The agent A_2 will generate agents containing an object corresponding to some triplet-object in a string. $Z_{j,k}$ is literal or negative literal or F, $1 \leq j \leq 3$; $1 \leq k \leq m$. The agent puts object F (false) to the string.

$A_2 \; 1 \; \langle e \to \$; \; e \to F \rangle$

$\quad 2 \; \left\langle F \leftrightarrow \wedge_1; \; \$ \leftrightarrow \boxed{Z_{1,k} Z_{2,k} Z_{3,k}} \right\rangle$

$\quad 3 \; \left\langle \wedge_1 \to @; \; \boxed{Z_{1,k} Z_{2,k} Z_{3,k}} \to \boxed{Z_{1,k} Z_{2,k} Z_{3,k}}_1 \right\rangle$

$\quad 4 \; \left\langle @ \to 1; \; \boxed{Z_{1,k} Z_{2,k} Z_{3,k}}_1 \to e \right\rangle$

$\quad 5 \; \langle 1 \to 1'; \; e \leftrightarrow \$ \rangle$

$\quad 5' \; \langle i \to i'; \; e \leftrightarrow \$ \rangle$

$\quad 6 \; \langle 1' \to 1'; \; \$ \to e \rangle$

$\quad 6' \; \langle i' \to i'; \; \$ \to e \rangle$

$\quad 7 \; \left\langle 1' \leftrightarrow \wedge_2; \; e \leftrightarrow \boxed{Z_{1,k} Z_{2,k} Z_{3,k}} \right\rangle$

$\quad 7' \; \left\langle i' \leftrightarrow \wedge_{i+1}; \; e \leftrightarrow \boxed{Z_{1,k} Z_{2,k} Z_{3,k}} \right\rangle$

$\quad 8 \; \left\langle \wedge_2 \to @; \; \boxed{Z_{1,k} Z_{2,k} Z_{3,k}} \to \boxed{Z_{1,k} Z_{2,k} Z_{3,k}}_2 \right\rangle$

$\quad 8' \; \left\langle \wedge_{i+1} \to @; \; \boxed{Z_{1,k} Z_{2,k} Z_{3,k}} \to \boxed{Z_{1,k} Z_{2,k} Z_{3,k}}_{i+1} \right\rangle$

$\quad 9 \; \left\langle @ \to 2; \; \boxed{Z_{1,k} Z_{2,k} Z_{3,k}}_2 \to e \right\rangle$

$\quad 9' \; \left\langle @ \to i+1; \; \boxed{Z_{1,k} Z_{2,k} Z_{3,k}}_{i+1} \to e \right\rangle$

Child-agents of A_2 that contain $_i\boxed{Z_{1,k} Z_{2,k} Z_{3,k}}_i$ have to wait until the agent with ie inside processes whole sting.

$A_2 \; 10 \; \left\langle i \to i_1; \; \boxed{Z_{1,k} Z_{2,k} Z_{3,k}}_i \to \boxed{Z_{1,k} Z_{2,k} Z_{3,k}}_{i'} \right\rangle$

$\quad 11 \; \left\langle i_p \to i_{p+1}; \; \boxed{Z_{1,k} Z_{2,k} Z_{3,k}}_i \to \boxed{Z_{1,k} Z_{2,k} Z_{3,k}}_{i'} \right\rangle \quad 1 \leq p \leq 3$

$\quad 12 \; \left\langle i_4 \to i+1; \; \boxed{Z_{1,k} Z_{2,k} Z_{3,k}}_i \to \boxed{Z_{1,k} Z_{2,k} Z_{3,k}}_{i'} \right\rangle \quad 1 \leq i \leq m-1$

$\quad 13 \; \left\langle m \to @; \; \boxed{Z_{1,k} Z_{2,k} Z_{3,k}}_i \to \boxed{Z_{1,k} Z_{2,k} Z_{3,k}}_i^0 \right\rangle$

In the next phase agents with label A_2 create 2^n copies of themselves.

$$A_2 \ 14 \ \left\langle \ \boxed{Z_{1,k}Z_{2,k}Z_{3,k}}_i^{\ 0} \ \rightarrow \ \boxed{Z_{1,k}Z_{2,k}Z_{3,k}}_i^{\ 1} \ ; \ @ \rightarrow @ \right\rangle$$

$$15 \ \left\langle \ \boxed{Z_{1,k}Z_{2,k}Z_{3,k}}_i^{\ q} \ \rightarrow \ \boxed{Z_{1,k}Z_{2,k}Z_{3,k}}_i^{\ q+1} \ ; \ @ \rightarrow @ \right\rangle \quad 1 \leq q \leq n-2$$

$$16 \ \left\langle \ \boxed{Z_{1,k}Z_{2,k}Z_{3,k}}_i^{\ n-1} \ \rightarrow \ \boxed{Z_{1,k}Z_{2,k}Z_{3,k}}_i^{\ n} \ ; \ @ \rightarrow a \right\rangle$$

$$17 \ \left\langle \ \boxed{Z_{1,k}Z_{2,k}Z_{3,k}}_i^{\ n} \ \rightarrow \ \boxed{Z_{1,k}Z_{2,k}Z_{3,k}}_i^{\ q+1} \ ; \ a \rightarrow a_1 \right\rangle$$

The contents of every agent labelled A_2 is in a form $a_1 \boxed{Z_{1,k}Z_{2,k}Z_{3,k}}_i^{\ q+1}$. In every second step the agents put 2^n copies of $\boxed{Z_{1,k}Z_{2,k}Z_{3,k}}$.

$$A_2 \ 18 \ \left\langle a_1 \rightarrow a_1'; \ \boxed{Z_{1,k}Z_{2,k}Z_{3,k}}_1 \ \rightarrow \ \boxed{Z_{1,k}Z_{2,k}Z_{3,k}} \right\rangle$$

$$19 \ \left\langle a_1' \rightarrow a_2; \ \boxed{Z_{1,k}Z_{2,k}Z_{3,k}} \leftrightarrow e \right\rangle \qquad\qquad 1 \leq q \leq n-2$$

$$20 \ \left\langle a_i \rightarrow a_i'; \ \boxed{Z_{1,k}Z_{2,k}Z_{3,k}}_j \ \rightarrow \ \boxed{Z_{1,k}Z_{2,k}Z_{3,k}}_j \right\rangle \qquad \text{if } i > j$$

$$21 \ \left\langle a_i' \rightarrow a_{i+1}; \ \boxed{Z_{1,k}Z_{2,k}Z_{3,k}}_j \ \rightarrow \ \boxed{Z_{1,k}Z_{2,k}Z_{3,k}}_j \right\rangle \qquad \text{if } i > j$$

$$22 \ \left\langle a_i \rightarrow a_i'; \ \boxed{Z_{1,k}Z_{2,k}Z_{3,k}}_j \ \rightarrow \ \boxed{Z_{1,k}Z_{2,k}Z_{3,k}} \right\rangle \qquad \text{if } i = j < m$$

$$23 \ \left\langle a_i' \rightarrow a_{i+1}; \ \boxed{Z_{1,k}Z_{2,k}Z_{3,k}} \leftrightarrow e \right\rangle \qquad\qquad \text{if } i = j < m$$

$$24 \ \left\langle a_m \rightarrow a_m'; \ \boxed{Z_{1,k}Z_{2,k}Z_{3,k}}_m \ \rightarrow \ \boxed{Z_{1,k}Z_{2,k}Z_{3,k}} \right\rangle$$

$$25 \ \left\langle a_m' \rightarrow q; \ \boxed{Z_{1,k}Z_{2,k}Z_{3,k}} \leftrightarrow e \right\rangle$$

$$26 \ \langle q \rightarrow q'; \ e \rightarrow q \rangle$$

$$27 \ \langle q' \rightarrow q'; \ q \leftrightarrow e \rangle$$

After the agents from both groups have been created, the agents from the first group put their contents into the string. Then the second group starts to consume them in such a way that they consume at one moment the triplet-symbols corresponding to the first clause. If the value of the clause is false, the agent rewrites the symbol of the combination of the values of variables into false and continues in consuming of triplet-objects. After all triplet-objects have been consumed (this takes m steps) the agents that have no object false inside generate object true and send it to the string.

$$A_1 \ A \ \left\langle e \leftrightarrow \boxed{Z_{1,k}Z_{2,k}Z_{3,k}}; \ j_1j_2 \overset{x_1x_2}{\cdots} \overset{x_n}{j_n} \rightarrow j_1j_2 \overset{x_1x_2}{\cdots} \overset{x_n}{j_n} \right\rangle$$

$$B \ \left\langle \boxed{Z_{1,k}Z_{2,k}Z_{3,k}} \rightarrow e; \ j_1j_2 \overset{x_1x_2}{\cdots} \overset{x_n}{j_n} \rightarrow j_1j_2 \overset{x_1x_2}{\cdots} \overset{x_n}{j_n} \right\rangle$$

if interpretation of $Z_{1,k}Z_{2,k}Z_{3,k}$ for values $j_1, \ldots j_n$ of variables $x_1, \ldots, x_n$ is T (true)

$$C \ \left\langle \boxed{Z_{1,k}Z_{2,k}Z_{3,k}} \rightarrow e; \ j_1j_2 \overset{x_1x_2}{\cdots} \overset{x_n}{j_n} \rightarrow F \right\rangle$$

if interpretation of $Z_{1,k}Z_{2,k}Z_{3,k}$ for values $j_1, \ldots j_n$ of variables $x_1, \ldots, x_n$ is F (false)

$$D \left\langle e \leftrightarrow \boxed{Z_{1,k} Z_{2,k} Z_{3,k}}; \ F \to F \right\rangle$$
$$E \left\langle \boxed{Z_{1,k} Z_{2,k} Z_{3,k}} \to e; \ F \to F \right\rangle$$
$$F \left\langle e \leftrightarrow q; \ \overset{x_1 x_2}{j_1 j_2} \cdots \overset{x_n}{j_n} \to T \right\rangle$$
$$G \left\langle q \to q; \ T \leftrightarrow e \right\rangle$$
$$H \left\langle e \leftrightarrow q; \ F \to F \right\rangle$$

If there is any T in the environmental string the agent A_3 can consume a false and a true symbol and replace them by one true symbol.

A_3 1 $\langle e \leftrightarrow T; \ e \to e \rangle$
    2 $\langle T \leftrightarrow F; \ e \to e \rangle$

Every computation with correct input string is halting. The environmental string in a halting configuration is formed from one symbol false or from at least one symbol true. No other symbols are present in a string at the end of a successful computation.

5 Conclusions

We have introduced the new type of APCol systems that contain programs for agent creation. We have shown that such APCol systems can solve the 3-SAT problem in linear time.

In future research, we will focus on the use of agent creation programs in 2D P colonies – P colonies where agents are placed in an environment having the form of a 2D grid of cells. We will investigate the capability of such a kind of P colonies to simulate, for example, a spread of an infection.

Acknowledgments. This work was supported by The Ministry of Education, Youth and Sports from the National Programme of Sustainability (NPU II) project IT4Innovations excellence in science - LQ1602, by SGS/13/2016.

References

1. Cienciala, L., Ciencialová, L., Csuhaj-Varjú, E.: Towards on P colonies processing strings. In: Proceedings of BWMC 2014, Sevilla, pp. 102–118. Fénix Editora, Sevilla (2014)
2. Ciencialová, L., Csuhaj-Varjú, E., Cienciala, L., Sosík, P.: P colonies. Bull. Int. Membr. Comput. Soc. **1**(2), 119–156 (2016)
3. Csuhaj-Varjú, E., Kelemen, J., Păun, G., Dassow, J. (eds.): Grammar Systems: A Grammatical Approach to Distribution and Cooperation. Gordon and Breach Science Publishers Inc., Newark (1994)
4. Kelemenová, A.: P colonies, chap. 23.1. In: Păun, Gh., Rozenberg, G., Salomaa, A. (eds.) The Oxford Handbook of Membrane Computing, pp. 584–593. Oxford University Press, Oxford (2010)
5. Kelemen, J., Kelemenová, A., Păun, G.: Preview of P colonies: a biochemically inspired computing model. In: Workshop and Tutorial Proceedings. Ninth International Conference on the Simulation and Synthesis of Living Systems (ALIFE IX), Boston, MA, pp. 82–86 (2004)

6. Kelemen, J., Kelemenová, A.: A grammar-theoretic treatment of multiagent systems. Cybern. Syst. **23**(6), 621–633 (1992)
7. Krishna, S.N., Rama, R.: A variant of P systems with active membranes: solving NP-complete problems. Rom. J. Inf. Sci. Technol. **2**(4), 357–367 (1999)
8. Mutyam, M., Krithivasan, K.: P systems with membrane creation: universality and efficiency. In: Margenstern, M., Rogozhin, Y. (eds.) MCU 2001. LNCS, vol. 2055, pp. 276–287. Springer, Heidelberg (2001). https://doi.org/10.1007/3-540-45132-3_19
9. Păun, Gh., Rozenberg, G., Salomaa, A. (eds.): The Oxford Handbook of Membrane Computing. Oxford University Press Inc., New York (2010)
10. Păun, Gh.: P systems with active membranes: attacking NP-complete problems. J. Autom. Lang. Comb. **6**(1), 75–90 (2001)
11. Rozenberg, G., Salomaa, A. (eds.): Handbook of Formal Languages I-III. Springer, Heidelberg (1997)
12. Sosík, P.: Solving a PSPACE-complete problem by P systems with active membranes. In: Cavaliere, M., Martín-Vide, C., Păun, Gh. (eds.) Proceedings of the Brainstorming Week on Membrane Computing, Report GRLMC 26/03, pp. 305–312 (2012)

APCol Systems with Verifier Agents

Lucie Ciencialová[1], Erzsébet Csuhaj-Varjú[2(✉)], György Vaszil[3],
and Ludek Cienciala[1]

[1] Institute of Computer Science, Silesian University in Opava, Opava, Czech Republic
{lucie.ciencialova,ludek.cienciala}@fpf.slu.cz
[2] Faculty of Informatics, ELTE Eötvös Loránd University, Budapest, Hungary
csuhaj@inf.elte.hu
[3] Faculty of Informatics, University of Debrecen, Debrecen, Hungary
vaszil.gyorgy@inf.unideb.hu

Abstract. APCol systems (Automaton-like P colonies) are variants
of P colonies where the environment is given by a string and the
agents change their own states and the environmental string similarly
to automata. By the original definition, the input (initial environmental) string is accepted if it can be reduced to the empty word. In this
paper, we continue the examination of a variant of APCol systems where
the agents explore and verify their common environment (the notion was
introduced as verifying APCol systems). In this case, an input string of
length n is accepted if there is a halting computation c such that the
length of the environmental strings remains unchanged during the computation and for every agent and for each position each i, $1 \leq i \leq n$,
there is an environmental string obtained by c such that the agent applies
a rule to position i. Improving a previous result, we show that APCol systems with verifier agents simulate nondeterministic two-way multihead
automata. The result implies that any language in NSPACE($\log n$)can
be accepted by an APCol system with verifier agents.

1   Introduction

Automaton-like P colonies (APCol systems, for short), introduced in [1], are
variants of P colonies (introduced in [10]) that are very simple membrane systems
inspired by certain types of grammar systems called colonies. We refer to [13]
for detailed information on P systems (membrane systems) and to [11] and [6]
for more information to grammar systems theory. For more details on P colonies
consult [9] and [4].

An APCol system consists of a finite set of agents (also called cells). Each
agent is represented by a finite multiset of objects and these multisets are placed
in a shared environment. The agents have programs consisting of rules. These
programs serve for changing the objects inside the cells (inside the agents) and
the objects in the environment. The rules are of two types: they may change the
objects of the agents and they can be used for interaction between the agent and
the environment. While in the case of standard P colonies the environment is

© Springer Nature Switzerland AG 2019
T. Hinze et al. (Eds.): CMC 2018, LNCS 11399, pp. 95–107, 2019.
https://doi.org/10.1007/978-3-030-12797-8_8

represented by a multiset of objects, in case of APCol systems it is represented by a string. The number of objects inside each agent is set by definition and it remains constant during the functioning of the system. Usually, it is a very small number: 1, 2 or 3. The environmental string is processed by the agents and it serves as an indirect communication channel for the agents as well, since through the string, the agents are able to affect the behaviour of other agents. We may easily observe that APCol systems resemble automata: the current configuration of the system (the objects inside the agents) and the current environmental string corresponds to the current state of an automaton and the currently processed input string, respectively.

In case of standard P colonies the agents may perform rewriting, communication or checking rules [10]. APCol systems use only rewriting and communication rules. A rewriting rule $a \rightarrow b$ allows the agent to rewrite (evolve) one object a to object b. Both objects are located inside the agent. Communication rule $c \leftrightarrow d$ makes possible to exchange object c placed inside the agent with object d in the environmental string. The rules are combined into programs. A program is a multiset of rules and the number of rules in the program is the same as the number of objects inside the agent. Whenever a program of the agent is performed, its rules are is applied in parallel to the object inside the agent.

The computation in APCol systems starts with an input string, representing the initial state of the environment and with each agents having its initial multiset of objects (initial state). In the literature, very often the initial state of the agents is given as a finite multiset of symbols e, which is a so-called basic object or "background" object being available in the environmental multiset in an arbitrary number of copies.

A computational step means a maximally parallel action of the active agents, i.e., agents that can apply at least one of their programs. The computation ends if the input string is reduced to the empty word, there are no more applicable programs in the system, and meantime at least one of the agents is in so-called final state. For more detailed information on APCol systems we refer to [2,3].

In this paper, we continue our previous investigations on a variant of APCol systems, called verifying APCol systems, introduced in [1,5]. This model, where the agents verify their environment, resembles nondeterministic multihead finite automata. In this case, a string of length n is accepted if during some halting computation the length of the environmental string in the configurations does not change and in the course of this computation for each agent and for each position i, $1 \leq i \leq n$ there is a computational step when the agent applies a rule to the symbol occupying position i in the string. In [5], we proved that any nondeterministic one-way multihead finite automaton can be simulated by a verifying APCol system. Improving this result, in this paper we show that APCol systems with verifier agents simulate nondeterministic two-way multihead finite automata as well. Thus, any language in NSPACE($\log n$) can be accepted by an APCol system with verifier agents. We also provide problems and topics for further study.

2   Preliminaries

Throughout the paper we assume the reader to be familiar with the basics of formal language theory and membrane computing [13,14].

For an alphabet Σ, the set of all words over Σ (including the empty word, ε), is denoted by Σ^*. We denote the length of a word $w \in \Sigma^*$ by $|w|$ and the number of occurrences of the symbol $a \in \Sigma$ in w by $|w|_a$.

For a string $x \in \Sigma^*$, $x[i]$ denotes the symbol at the ith position of x, i.e., if $x = x_1 \ldots x_n$, $x_i \in \Sigma$, $1 \leq i \leq n$, then $x[i] = x_i$. For every string $x \in \Sigma^*$, $x[0] = \varepsilon$.

For every string $x \in \Sigma^*$, $perm(x)$ denotes the set of all permutations of x and $pref(x)$ denotes the set of prefixes of x.

A multiset of objects M is a pair $M = (O, f)$, where O is an arbitrary (not necessarily finite) set of objects and f is a mapping $f : O \rightarrow N$; f assigns to each object in O its multiplicity in M. Any multiset of objects M with the set of objects $O = \{x_1, \ldots x_n\}$ can be represented as a string w over alphabet O with $|w|_{x_i} = f(x_i)$; $1 \leq i \leq n$. Obviously, all words obtained from w by permuting the letters can also represent the same multiset M, and ε represents the empty multiset.

2.1   Multihead Finite Automata

We first recall some basic notions concerning nondeterministic multihead finite automata; the terms and notations we use are based on [8].

A nondeterministic two-way k-head finite automaton (a 2NFA(k), for short) is a construct $M = (Q, \Sigma, k, \delta, \triangleright, \triangleleft, q_0, F)$, where Q is the finite set of states, Σ is the set of input symbols, $k \geq 1$ is the number of heads, $\triangleright \notin \Sigma$ and $\triangleleft \notin \Sigma$ are the left and the right endmarkers, respectively, $q_0 \in Q$ is the initial state, $F \subseteq Q$ is the set of accepting states, and δ is the partial transition function which maps $Q \times (\Sigma \cup \{\triangleright, \triangleleft\})^k$ into subsets of $Q \times \{-1, 0, 1\}^k$, where 1 or -1 means that the head moves one tape cell to the right or to the left, respectively, and 0 means that it remains at the same position.

Note that according to the definition, the heads of a 2NFA(k) do not need to move away from the scanned tape cell after reading the input symbol. Moreover, if the scanned symbol is the left (or right) endmarker $\triangleright$ (or $\triangleleft$), then any transition of the automaton is such, that the corresponding head does not make a left-move (right-move).

A configuration of a 2NFA(k) $M = (Q, \Sigma, k, \delta, \triangleright, \triangleleft, q_0, F)$ is a triplet $c = (w, q, p)$, where $w \in \Sigma^*$ is the input, $q \in Q$ is the current state, and $p = (p_1, \ldots, p_k) \in \{0, 1, \ldots, |w| + 1\}^k$ gives the head positions. If a position p_i is 0, then head i is scanning the symbol $\triangleright$, if $1 \leq p_i \leq |w|$, then head i scans the p_ith letter of w, and if $p_i = |w| + 1$, then the ith head is scanning the symbol $\triangleleft$.

The initial configuration for an input $w \in \Sigma^*$ is $(w, q_0, (1, \ldots, 1))$, that is, a 2NFA(k) starts processing an input word with all of its heads positioned on the first symbol of the input word.

In the course of the computation, M performs direct changes of its configurations. Let $w = a_1 \ldots a_n$, be the input, $a_0 = \triangleright$, $a_{n+1} = \triangleleft$. For two configurations, $c_1 = (w, q, (p_1, \ldots, p_k))$ and $c_2 = (w, q', (p_1', \ldots, p_k'))$, we say that c_2 directly follows c_1, denoted by $c_1 \vdash c_2$, if $(q', (d_1, \ldots, d_k)) \in \delta(q, (a_{p_1}, \ldots, a_{p_k}))$ and $p_i' = p_i + d_i$, $1 \leq i \leq k$. The reflexive transitive closure of $\vdash$ is denoted by $\vdash^*$. Note that due to the restriction of the transition function, the heads cannot move beyond the endmarkers.

The language $L(M)$ accepted by a 2NFA(k) $M = (Q, \Sigma, k, \delta, \triangleright, \triangleleft, q_0, F)$ is the set of words w such that there is a computation which starts with $\triangleright w \triangleleft$ on the input tape and ends when M reaches an accepting state, i.e.,

$$L(M) = \{w \in \Sigma^* \mid (w, q_0, (1, \ldots, 1)) \vdash^* (w, q_f, (p_1, \ldots, p_k)), \; q_f \in F\}.$$

For technical reasons, we assume that the automaton has a single accepting state, $F = \{q_f\}$, and it enters this state only when all heads scan the right endmarker, that is, for all transitions $(q_f, (d_1, \ldots, d_k)) \in \delta(q, (a_{p_1}, \ldots, a_{p_k}))$, we have $a_{p_i} = \triangleleft$ and $d_i = 0$ for all $1 \leq i \leq k$.

Without loss of generality, we also assume that the automaton starts in initial configuration $(w, q_0, (0, \ldots, 0))$, i.e. all heads are placed on the left endmarker at the beginning of the computation.

The class of languages accepted by 2NFA(k), for $k \geq 1$, is denoted by $\mathcal{L}(2\text{NFA}(k))$.

If δ is a partial transition function which maps $Q \times (\Sigma \cup \{\triangleright, \triangleleft\})^k$ into subsets of $Q \times \{0, 1\}^k$, i.e., if the heads never move to the left, then M is said to be a non-deterministic one-way k-head finite automaton, a 1NFA(k), for short. The class of languages accepted by 1NFA(k), for $k \geq 1$, is denoted by $\mathcal{L}(1\text{NFA}(k))$.

It is known that $\text{NSPACE}(\log n) = \bigcup_{k \geq 1} \mathcal{L}(2\text{NFA}(k))$ [7]. $\text{NSPACE}(\log n)$, denoted also NL, is an interesting complexity class: $\text{NL} \subseteq \text{P}$, but it is not known whether the inclusion is proper or not. Further important results related to nondeterministic multihead finite automata are that the emptiness, finiteness, infiniteness, universality, inclusion, equivalence, regularity and context-freeness are not semidecidable for $\mathcal{L}(1\text{NFA}(k))$ and $\mathcal{L}(2\text{NFA}(k))$, $k \geq 2$ (for details, see [8] and the papers cited in the article).

2.2 APCol Systems

In this subsection we recall the notion of an APCol system following [1].

As standard P colonies, agents of the APCol systems contain objects, each of them is an element of a finite alphabet. Every agent is associated with a set of programs, every program consists of two rules that can be one of the following two types. The first one, called an evolution rule, is of the form $a \rightarrow b$. In this case object a inside of the agent is rewritten to object b. The second type, called a communication rule, is of the form $c \leftrightarrow d$. When this rule is applied, if objects c and d are different from e, object c inside the agent and a symbol d in the string representing the environment are exchanged. If $c = e$, then the agent erases d from the string and if $d = e$, symbol c is inserted into the string.

The computation in APCol systems starts with an input string, representing the environment, and with each agent having its initial multiset of objects.

A computational step means a maximally parallel action of the active agents, i.e., agents that can apply their rules. Every symbol can be object of the action of only one agent. The computation ends when the input string is reduced to the empty word, there are no more applicable programs in the system, and meantime at least one of the agents is in so-called final state.

An APCol system is a construct $\Pi = (O, e, A_1, \ldots, A_n)$, where

- O is an alphabet; its elements are called the objects,
- $e \in O$, called the basic object,
- A_i, $1 \le i \le n$, are agents. Each agent is a triplet $A_i = (\omega_i, P_i, F_i)$, where
  - ω_i is a multiset over O, describing the initial state (content) of the agent, $|\omega_i| = 2$,
  - $P_i = \{p_{i,1}, \ldots, p_{i,k_i}\}$ is a finite set of programs associated with the agent, where each program is a pair of rules. Each rule is in one of the following forms:
    * $a \to b$, where $a, b \in O$, called an evolution rule,
    * $c \leftrightarrow d$, where $c, d \in O$, called a communication rule,
  - $F_i \subseteq O^*$ is a finite set of final states (contents) of agent A_i.

The APCol system is called restricted if each one of its program consist of one evolution rule $(a \to b)$ and one communication rule $(a \leftrightarrow b)$.

During the work of the APCol system, the agents perform programs. Since both rules in a program can be communication rules, an agent can work with two objects in the string in one step of the computation. In the case of program $\langle a \leftrightarrow b; c \leftrightarrow d \rangle$, a substring bd of the input string is replaced by string ac. Notice that although the order of rules in the programs is usually irrelevant, here it is significant, since it expresses context-dependence. If the program is of the form $\langle c \leftrightarrow d; a \leftrightarrow b \rangle$, then a substring db of the input string is replaced by string ca. Thus, the agent is allowed to act only at one position of the string in the one step of the computation and the result of its action to the string depends both on the order of the rules in the program and on the interacting objects. In particular, we have the following types of programs with two communication rules:

1. $\langle a \leftrightarrow b; c \leftrightarrow e \rangle$ - b in the string is replaced by ac,
2. $\langle c \leftrightarrow e; a \leftrightarrow b \rangle$ - b in the string is replaced by ca,
3. $\langle a \leftrightarrow e; c \leftrightarrow e \rangle$ - ac is inserted in a non-deterministically chosen place in the string,
4. $\langle e \leftrightarrow b; e \leftrightarrow d \rangle$ - bd is erased from the string,
5. $\langle e \leftrightarrow b; c \leftrightarrow d \rangle$ - bd is replaced by c,
6. $\langle a \leftrightarrow b; c \leftrightarrow d \rangle$ - bd is replaced by ac,
7. $\langle e \leftrightarrow e; e \leftrightarrow d \rangle$; $\langle e \leftrightarrow e; c \leftrightarrow d \rangle$, $\ldots$ - these programs can be replaced by programs of type $\langle e \to e; e \leftrightarrow d \rangle$, $\langle e \to e; c \leftrightarrow d \rangle$, and so on.

If a program deletes or inserts symbols from the environmental string, it is called a deleting or inserting program, respectively. (Programs of type 1–3 above are inserting, programs of type 4–5 are deleting).

At the beginning of the work of the APCol system (at the beginning of the computation), the environment is given by a string ω of objects which are different from e. This string represents the initial state of the environment. Consequently, an initial configuration of the APCol system is an $(n + 1)$-tuple $c = (\omega; \omega_1, \ldots, \omega_n)$ where ω is the initial state of the environment and the other n components are multisets of objects, given in the form of strings, the initial states the of agents.

A configuration of an APCol system Π is given by $(w; w_1, \ldots, w_n)$, where $|w_i| = 2$, $1 \leq i \leq n$, w_i represents all the objects inside the ith agent and $w \in (O - \{e\})^*$ is the string being processed.

At each step of the computation every agent attempts to find one of its programs to use. If the number of applicable programs is higher than one, then the agent nondeterministically chooses one of them. At each step of the computation, the maximal possible number of agents has to be active, i.e., has to perform programs in parallel.

By applying programs, the APCol system passes from one configuration to some other (not necessarily different) configuration. A sequence of configurations starting from the initial configuration is called a computation. A configuration is halting if the APCol system has no applicable program.

The result of a computation depends on the mode in which the APCol system works. In the case of accepting mode, the string ω is accepted by the APCol system Π if there exists a computation by Π such that it starts in the initial configuration $(\omega; \omega_1, \ldots, \omega_n)$ and the computation ends by halting in the configuration $(\varepsilon; w_1, \ldots, w_n)$, where at least one of $w_i \in F_i$ for $1 \leq i \leq n$.

In [1] it was shown that the family of languages accepted by jumping finite automata (introduced in [12]) is properly included in the family of languages accepted by APCol systems with one agent, and it was proved that any recursively enumerable language can be obtained as a projection of a language accepted by an APCol system with two agents.

A jumping finite automaton (a JFA) is a construct $M = (Q, \Sigma, R, s, F)$ where Q is the finite set of states, Σ is the finite alphabet of input symbols, R is a finite set of productions of the form $py \rightarrow q$, where $p, q \in Q$, $y \in \Sigma$, $s \in Q$ is the initial state and $F \subseteq$ is the set of final states. M performs a transition as follows: If $x, z, x', z' \in \Sigma^*$ such that $xz = x'z'$ and $py \rightarrow q \in R$, then M makes a jump (a transition) from $xpyz$ to $x'qz'$.

3   APCol Systems with Verifier Agents

In this section we continue studying variants of APCol system where the agents verify their environment [5]. The notion, called verifying APCol system, was inspired both by the behaviour of agents exploring their environment and by the behaviour of the reading heads of multi-head finite automata. In case of standard APCol systems, the agents make efforts to erase symbols (objects) present in their current environmental string. In the case of APCol systems with verifier agents, the agent indicates that it has "explored and visited" a certain position in the current environmental string, usually by rewriting the symbol at that position to some symbol that refers to this event.

Definition 1. *Let $\Pi = (O, e, A_1, \ldots, A_n)$, $n \geq 1$, be an APCol system working in the maximally parallel mode. We say that Π verifies input string w if there exists a halting computation c in Π with $w = w_0$, $s \geq 1$,*

$$c = (w_0; w_1, \ldots, w_n) \Longrightarrow (w_{0,1}; w_{1,1}, \ldots, w_{n,1}) \Longrightarrow \ldots (w_{0,s}; w_{1,s}, \ldots, w_{n,s}),$$

such that the following properties are satisfied:

- *$|w_0| = |w_{0,j}|$ for $1 \leq j \leq s$, and*
- *for every agent A_i, $1 \leq i \leq n$ and for every j, $1 \leq j \leq m$ where $|w| = m$, there exists k, $1 \leq k \leq s$ such that the symbol at the jth position of $w_{0,(k-1)}$ is symbol b and A_i applies a rule $a \leftrightarrow b$ to position j of $w_{0,(k-1)}$.*

Computation c is called a verifying computation. The set of all words that can be verified by Π is called the language verified by Π and is denoted by $L_{ver}(\Pi)$.

We shortly discuss the definition. Suppose that the environment is given by a string w of length m at the beginning. During a verifying computation, every agent visits each position j, where $1 \leq j \leq m$ at least once. Every letter which occurs in position j is rewritten (it may be rewritten to itself) by some of the agents and there is no agent which does not check this position. In some sense, while exploring, the agents agree on accepting this part of the environment. By definition, the length of the environmental string remains unchanged but this constraint does not imply that during the computation the agents are not allowed to use rules that delete symbols from or insert symbols into the string. However, if some agent erases a symbol (which is possible due to the rules of the APCol system), some other one should insert a new one in the same computational step in order to ensure the unchanged length of the string. This fact needs clarification of the term "the agent applies a rule to a symbol at position i". For non-inserting rules the position is obvious, the ith letter of the string is affected. In case of inserting rules, the rule is applied to the ith position if the inserted symbol, say a, is not e and there are $i - 1$ symbols in the string preceding the inserted letter.

If an APCol system with verifier agents does not use inserting or deleting rules at all, we call it an APCol system with only replacement.

Since verifying computations are halting, in the following we do not specify the final contents F of the agents of APCol systems $A = (w, P, F)$, as introduced in the original definition. The agents will be given as $A = (w, P)$, pairs of initial contents and rule sets.

We present an example for a language accepted by a nondeterministic one-way finite automaton that can be verified by an APCol system.

Example 1. Let $\Pi = (O, e, A_1, A_2)$ be an APCol system where the object alphabet is $O = \{a, a', b, b', \$, \bar{\$}, \$', \$'', T\}$, and $A_i = (\omega_i, P_i)$, $1 \leq i \leq 2$, with

$\omega_1 = \bar{\$}\bar{\$}$,

$P_1 = \{\langle \bar{\$} \leftrightarrow a; \bar{\$} \leftrightarrow b \rangle, \langle a \rightarrow a'; b \rightarrow b' \rangle, \langle a' \rightarrow \$'; b' \rightarrow \$' \rangle, \langle \$' \leftrightarrow a; \$' \leftrightarrow \$ \rangle,$
$\quad\quad \langle a \rightarrow \$'', \$ \rightarrow \$'' \rangle, \langle \$'' \leftrightarrow \$''; \$'' \leftrightarrow b \rangle, \langle \$'' \rightarrow \$'; b \rightarrow \$' \rangle,$
$\quad\quad \langle \$' \leftrightarrow a; \$' \leftrightarrow \$' \rangle, \langle a \rightarrow \$'', \$' \rightarrow \$'' \rangle, \langle \$' \leftrightarrow \$', \$' \rightarrow T \rangle,$
$\quad\quad \langle \$'' \leftrightarrow \$'', \$'' \rightarrow T \rangle \}$,

$\omega_2 = ee$,

$P_2 = \{\langle e \rightarrow \$; e \rightarrow \$ \rangle, \langle \$ \leftrightarrow \bar{\$}; \$ \leftrightarrow \bar{\$} \rangle, \langle \bar{\$} \rightarrow \$''; \bar{\$} \rightarrow \$'' \rangle, \langle \$'' \leftrightarrow \$; \$'' \leftrightarrow b \rangle,$
$\quad\quad \langle \$ \rightarrow \$'; b \rightarrow \$' \rangle, \langle \$' \leftrightarrow a; \$' \leftrightarrow \$' \rangle, \langle a \rightarrow \$''; \$' \rightarrow \$'' \rangle,$
$\quad\quad \langle \$'' \leftrightarrow \$'', \$'' \leftrightarrow b \rangle, \langle \$'' \rightarrow \$'; b \rightarrow \$' \rangle, \langle \$' \leftrightarrow \$'; \$' \rightarrow T \rangle,$
$\quad\quad \langle \$'' \leftrightarrow \$'', \$'' \rightarrow T \rangle \}$.

This system is able to verify strings of the form $a^n b^n$, $n \geq 1$. We note that the example shows cooperation of agents to validate input and that not every halting computation is validating.

To see how this system works, consider the following. In the first step, the string $a^n b^n$, $n \geq 1$ is changed to $a^{n-1}\bar{\$}\bar{\$}b^{n-1}$ by the first agent, and this is the only possible replacement, as the only occurrence of the substring ab is in the middle of the input. Next, the second agent produces $a^{n-1}\$\$b^{n-1}$, then both agents work in parallel providing $a^{n-2}\$'\$'\$''\$''b^{n-2}$. Now the agents exchange roles, and we get $a^{n-3}\$'\$'\$'\$''\$''\$''b^{n-3}$, then similarly $a^{n-4}\$'\$'\$'\$'\$''\$''\$''\$''b^{n-4}$, and so on, until $\$'^n\$''^n$ is produced in the environment, and the object T appears inside both of the agents. As no program can be applied to T, and all positions in the environmental string have been visited by both of the agents, the computation described above is a verifying computation. Note that only strings with an equal number of as and bs can be verified, this is the only case when both agents are able to visit all positions of the input.

In the following we show that verifying APCol systems simulate nondeterministic two-way multihead finite automata, even if they don't use inserting or deleting programs.

Theorem 1. *Let $M = (Q, \Sigma, n, \delta, \triangleright, \triangleleft, q_0, F)$, $n \geq 1$, be a nondeterministic two-way n-head finite automaton. Then we can construct an APCol system Π of $n+1$ agents with only replacement, such that $L_{ver}(\Pi) = L(M)$.*

Proof. We construct an APCol system $\Pi = (O, e, A_{ini}, A_1, \ldots, A_n)$ such that each agent A_j, $1 \leq j \leq n$ simulates the work of the jth reading head of M, while A_{ini} serves the initializing of the simulation. The verifying process in Π corresponds to an accepting process in M: If a symbol a in the environmental string was scanned by reading heads $\{i_1, \ldots, i_r\} \subseteq \{1, \ldots, n\}$, then this fact will be indicated by having symbol $a^{(x)}$ instead of a, where $(x) = (i_1 \ldots i_r)$ is a sequence of numbers representing a permutation of $\{i_1, \ldots, i_r\}$, the numbers of reading heads that scanned symbol a.

In the following, Perm$(\leq n)$ will denote the set of the sequences of numbers $i_1 i_2 \ldots i_k$, for all $\{i_1, \ldots, i_k\} \subseteq \{1, 2, \ldots, n\}$, $1 \leq k \leq n$. For $x = i_1 i_2 \ldots i_k \in$ Perm$(\leq n)$, we will write $l \in x$, if $l = i_j$ for some i_j, $1 \leq j \leq k$, otherwise $l \notin x$. Moreover, we will also write $y = x + l$ for some $x, y \in$ Perm$(\leq n)$, $l \leq n$, if x represents a permutation of $\{i_1, \ldots, i_k\}$, $l \notin x$, and y represents a permutation of $\{i_1, \ldots, i_k, l\}$.

Every computation step in M is simulated by a sequence of computation steps performed by agents $A_1, \ldots A_n$, the input word for Π is of the form $\triangleright w \triangleleft$.

Let

$$O = \{a, a^{()}, a^{(x)} \mid \text{ for } a \in \Sigma \cup \{\triangleleft\} \text{ and } x \in \text{Perm}(\leq n)\} \cup$$
$$\{q_{t,i}, q'_{t,i}, q_{t,i}^{(12\ldots n)} \mid \text{ for all } q \in Q \cup \{\triangleright\}, \ 1 \leq i \leq n, \text{ and}$$
$$\text{transitions } t : (p, (d_1, \ldots, d_n)) \in \delta(q, (\alpha_1, \ldots, \alpha_n))\} \cup$$
$$\{\bar{\triangleright}, T\}.$$

The agents and their programs are defined as follows. We have $A_{ini} = (ee, P_{ini})$ where

$$P_{ini} = \{\langle e \to \bar{\triangleright}; e \to a^{()}\rangle, \langle \bar{\triangleright} \leftrightarrow \triangleright; a^{()} \leftrightarrow a\rangle, \langle \triangleright \to b^{()}; a \to a^{()}\rangle,$$
$$\langle a^{()} \leftrightarrow a^{()}; b^{()} \leftrightarrow b\rangle, \langle a^{()} \to b^{()}; c \to d^{()}\rangle, \langle a^{()} \to b^{()}; c \to \triangleleft^{()}\rangle,$$
$$\langle a^{()} \leftrightarrow a^{()}; \triangleleft^{()} \leftrightarrow \triangleleft\rangle, \langle \triangleleft \to q_{0,t,1}^{(12\ldots n)}; a^{()} \to b^{()}\rangle,$$
$$\langle q_{0,t,1}^{(12\ldots n)} \leftrightarrow \bar{\triangleright}; a^{()} \leftrightarrow a^{()}\rangle \mid \text{ for all } a, b, c, d \in \Sigma, \text{ and for all}$$
$$\text{transitions } t : (p, (d_1, \ldots, d_n)) \in \delta(q_0, (\triangleright, \ldots, \triangleright))\}.$$

This agent transfers the input string $\triangleright a_1 a_2 \ldots a_m \triangleleft$ initially in the environment to the string

$$q_{0,t,1}^{(12\ldots n)} a_1^{()} a_2^{()} \ldots a_m^{()} \triangleleft^{()}$$

indicating that all the n the heads are scanning the left endmarker, that M is in state $q_0 \in Q$ and the simulation of the computation of M will start by simulating a transition t where $t : (p, (d_1, \ldots, d_n)) \in \delta(q_0, (\triangleright, \ldots, \triangleright))$ (a transition from the initial configuration where the internal state is q_0 and all heads scan the left endmarker). The index 1 in $q_{0,t,1}^{(12\ldots n)}$ can be interpreted as the index of the reading head whose movement will be simulated first.

The system Π also has an agent for the ith head of M for each i, $1 \leq i \leq n$, $A_i = (ee, P_i)$ where

$P_i = \bigcup_{t \text{ is a transition of } M} P_{t,i}$ with

$P_{t,i} = \{\langle e \to \rhd_{t,i}; e \to e\rangle, \langle \rhd_{t,i} \leftrightarrow q_{t,i}^{(12\ldots n)}; e \to e\rangle, \langle q_{t,i}^{(12\ldots n)} \to q'_{t,i}; e \to e\rangle\}\cup$

$\{\langle q'_{t,i} \leftrightarrow \rhd_{t,i}; e \to b^{(yi)}\rangle, \langle \rhd_{t,i} \leftrightarrow q'_{t,i}; b^{(yi)} \leftrightarrow b^{(y)}\rangle \mid$ where $t : (p, (d_1, \ldots, d_n)) \in \delta(q, (\alpha_1, \ldots, \alpha_n))$ with $\alpha_i = \rhd$, $d_i = 1$, and $y \in \mathrm{Perm}(\leq n), 1 \notin y\}\cup$

$\{\langle q'_{t,i} \leftrightarrow \rhd_{t,i}; e \to b^{(y)}\rangle, \langle \rhd_{t,i} \leftrightarrow q'_{t,i}; b^{(y)} \leftrightarrow b^{(y)}\rangle \mid$ where $t : (p, (d_1, \ldots, d_n)) \in \delta(q, (\alpha_1, \ldots, \alpha_n))$ with $\alpha_i = \rhd$, $d_i = 0$, and $y \in \mathrm{Perm}(\leq n),\ i \notin y\}\cup$

$\{\langle q'_{t,i} \leftrightarrow a^{(x)}; e \to b^{(yi)}\rangle, \langle a^{(x)} \leftrightarrow q'_{t,i}; b^{(yi)} \leftrightarrow b^{(y)}\rangle \mid$ where $t : (p, (d_1, \ldots, d_n)) \in \delta(q, (\alpha_1, \ldots, \alpha_n))$ with $\alpha_i = a$, $d_i = 1$, and $x, y \in \mathrm{Perm}(\leq n),\ i \in x, i \notin y\}\cup$

$\{\langle q'_{t,i} \leftrightarrow a^{(x)}; e \to b^{(y)}\rangle, \langle a^{(x)} \leftrightarrow q'_{t,i}; b^{(y)} \leftrightarrow b^{(y)}\rangle \mid$ where $t : (p, (d_1, \ldots, d_n)) \in \delta(q, (\alpha_1, \ldots, \alpha_n))$ with $\alpha_i = a \neq \lhd$, $d_i = 0$, and $x, y \in \mathrm{Perm}(\leq n),\ i \in x, i \notin y\}\cup$

$\{\langle q'_{t,i} \leftrightarrow a^{(x)}; e \to q_{t,i}\rangle, \langle a^{(x)} \to a^{(x')}; q_{t,i} \to b^{(y)}\rangle,$
$\langle a^{(x')} \leftrightarrow q'_{t,i}; b^{(y)} \leftrightarrow b^{(y)}\rangle \mid$ where $t : (p, (d_1, \ldots, d_n)) \in \delta(q, (\alpha_1, \ldots, \alpha_n))$ with $\alpha_i = a \neq \lhd$, $d_i = -1$, and $i \in x, i \notin y, x = x' + i\}\cup$

$\{\langle q'_{t,i} \leftrightarrow \lhd^{(x)}; e \to q_{t,i}\rangle, \langle \lhd^{(x)} \leftrightarrow q'_{t,i}; q_{t,i} \to b^{(y)}\rangle \mid b \in \Sigma, y \in \mathrm{Perm}(\leq n)$ and $t : (p, (d_1, \ldots, d_n)) \in \delta(q, (\alpha_1, \ldots, \alpha_n))$ with $\alpha_i = \lhd$, $d_i = 0$, $i \in x\}\cup$

$\{\langle q'_{t,i} \leftrightarrow \lhd^{(x)}; e \to q_{t,i}\rangle, \langle \lhd^{(x)} \to \lhd^{(x')}; q_{t,i} \to b^{(y)}\rangle, \langle \lhd^{(x')} \leftrightarrow q'_{t,i}; b^{(y)} \to b^{(y)}\rangle \mid$
$b \in \Sigma, y \in \mathrm{Perm}(\leq n)$ and $t : (p, (d_1, \ldots, d_n)) \in \delta(q, (\alpha_1, \ldots, \alpha_n))$ with $\alpha_i = \lhd$, $d_i = -1$, and $i \in x,\ x = x' + i\}\cup$

$\{\langle q'_{t,i} \to q_{t,i+1}^{(12\ldots n)}; b^{(y)} \to e\rangle, \langle q_{t,i+1}^{(12\ldots n)} \leftrightarrow \rhd_{t,i}; e \to e\rangle \mid$ if $i < n$, where $q \in Q, b \in \Sigma \cup \{\lhd\}$, and t is a transition of $M\}\cup$

$\{\langle q'_{t,n} \to p_{r,1}^{(12\ldots n)}; b^{(y)} \to e\rangle, \langle p_{r,1}^{(12\ldots n)} \leftrightarrow \rhd_{t,n}; e \to e\rangle \mid$ where $b \in \Sigma$, $y \in \mathrm{Perm}(\leq n)$, and $t : (p, (d_1, \ldots, d_n)) \in \delta(q, (\alpha_1, \ldots, \alpha_n))$, $r : (s, (d'_1, \ldots, d'_n)) \in \delta(p, (\alpha'_1, \ldots, \alpha'_n))\}\cup$

$\{\langle q'_{t,n} \to q_f^{(12\ldots n)}; b^{(y)} \to e\rangle, \langle q_f^{(12\ldots n)} \leftrightarrow \rhd_{t,n}; e \to T\rangle \mid$ where $b \in \Sigma$, $y \in \mathrm{Perm}(\leq n)$, $t : (q_f, (0, \ldots, 0)) \in \delta(q, (\lhd, \ldots, \lhd))$, and q_f is the final state$\}\cup$

$\{\langle \rhd_{t,i} \to q_f^{(12\ldots n)}; e \to e\rangle, \langle q_f^{(12\ldots n)} \leftrightarrow \rhd_{t,i}; e \to T\rangle \mid$ where t is a transition, q_f is the final state, $0 < i < n\}\cup$

$\{\langle \rhd_{t,i} \to e; e \to e\rangle\}.$

To see how these agents work, consider an environmental string of the form

$$q_{t,i}^{(12...n)} a_1^{(x_1)} a_2^{(x_2)} \ldots a_m^{(x_m)} \triangleleft^{(x_{m+1})} .$$

This string is of the same form as the one produced by the initial component, it can be interpreted in the same way: The state of the environmental string corresponds to a configuration of M where it is in state q, and the position of the reading heads can be extracted from the information contained in x_j, $1 \leq j \leq m+1$: The ith head is scanning the jth position, if x_j is the rightmost sequence with $i \in x_j$. The subscript t also indicates that Π will attempt to simulate a transition of M which can be written as $t : (p, (d_1, \ldots, d_n)) \in \delta(q, (\alpha_1, \ldots, \alpha_n))$. The simulation of the transition t starts by checking if the heads read the symbols required by t, and then by executing the head movements for each head, one by one, currently for head i, as indicated by the subscript i of $q_{t,i}^{(12...n)}$. This will be achieved by the programs in $P_{t,i} \subseteq P_i$ (these are dedicated to simulate the action of the ith head during transition t).

If $d_i = 1$, then the programs produce the environmental string

$$q_{t,i}^{(12...n)} a_1^{(x_1)} a_2^{(x_2)} \ldots a_j^{(x_j i)} \ldots a_m^{(x_m)} \triangleleft^{(x_{m+1})}$$

where the $(j-1)$th position is the one that has been scanned by the ith head (thus, $i \in x_{j-1}$, but $i \notin x_j$), and it is also made sure by the system that $\alpha_i = a_{j-1}$, thus, the ith head has been reading the symbol required by the transition t.

If $d_i = 0$, the string

$$q_{t,i}^{(12...n)} a_1^{(x_1)} a_2^{(x_2)} \ldots a_j^{(x_j)} \ldots a_m^{(x_m)} \triangleleft^{(x_{m+1})}$$

is produced because the ith head does not move during this transition.

If $d_i = -1$, then the programs produce the environmental string

$$q_{t,i}^{(12...n)} a_1^{(x_1)} a_2^{(x_2)} \ldots a_j^{(x_j')} \ldots a_m^{(x_m)} \triangleleft^{(x_{m+1})}$$

where the jth position is the one that has been scanned by the ith head (thus, $i \in x_j$, but $i \notin x_{j+1}$). The head moves to the left, so the head positions are modified to x_j', such that $x_j = x_j' + i$.

After checking the read symbol and updating the information on the position of the ith head, the string

$$q_{t,i+1}^{(12...n)} a_1^{(x_1')} a_2^{(x_2')} \ldots a_m^{(x_m')} \triangleleft^{(x_{m+1}')}$$

is produced, indicating that a similar procedure can be started for the $(i+1)$th reading head of M.

If $i = n$, that is, if the movements of all heads had been simulated, then the environmental string becomes

$$p_{r,1}^{(12...n)} a_1^{(x_1)} a_2^{(x_2)} \ldots a_m^{(x_m)} \triangleleft^{(x_{m+1})}$$

where $p \in Q$ is the next internal state of M, as indicated by the transition that was simulated, $t : (p, (d_1, \ldots, d_n)) \in \delta(q, (\alpha_1, \ldots, \alpha_n))$, and r is a possible next transition, $r : (s, (d'_1, \ldots, d'_n)) \in \delta(p, (\alpha'_1, \ldots, \alpha'_n))$ which the system will attempt to simulate next.

If the new state is the final state q_f, then the simulation of the work of M was successful, and since the transition t was of the form $t : (q_f, (0, \ldots, 0)) \in \delta(q, (\triangleleft, \ldots, \triangleleft))$, we also see that all positions of the environmental string have been visited by all components of Π. Moreover, after $q_f^{(12\ldots n)}$ is present in an environmental string agents $A_1, \ldots A_{n-1}$ consume it one by one, generate terminating symbol T and put $q_f^{(12\ldots n)}$ back into the string, and then the computation halts. Thus, the successful simulation implies a successful verification of the input string and $L(M) \subseteq L_{ver}(\Pi)$. By the construction of the agents, their programs and rules it can be seen that any verifying computation corresponds to an accepting computation of M, which implies that $L(M) = L_{ver}(\Pi)$.

Corollary 1. *Any language in NL can be verified by an APCol system with only replacement.*

4   Final Remarks

In this paper we demonstrated a further connection between APCol systems and automata, as we proved that verifying APCol systems simulate nondeterministic two-way multihead finite automata. This implies that any language in NL can be accepted by an APCol system with verifier agents. It is an interesting open question how much accepting power verifying APCol systems have? We guess that they are (almost) Turing complete. Some other research direction is to relate them to jumping multihead finite automata. We plan investigations in these topics in the future.

Acknowledgments. The work of L. Ciencialová and L. Cienciala was supported by The Ministry of Education, Youth and Sports from the National Programme of Sustainability (NPU II) project IT4Innovations excellence in science - LQ1602, by SGS/13/2016. The work of E. Csuhaj-Varjú and Gy. Vaszil was supported by Grant No. 120558 of the National Research, Development, and Innovation Office, Hungary.

References

1. Cienciala, L., Ciencialová, L., Csuhaj-Varjú, E.: Towards on P colonies processing strings. In: Proceedings of BWMC 2014, Sevilla, pp. 102–118 (2014). Fénix Editora, Sevilla (2014)
2. Cienciala, L., Ciencialová, L., Csuhaj-Varjú, E.: P colonies processing strings. Fundam. Inform. **134**(1–2), 51–65 (2014)
3. Cienciala, L., Ciencialová, L., Csuhaj-Varjú, E.: A class of restricted P colonies with string environment. Nat. Comput. **15**(4), 541–549 (2016)
4. Ciencialová, L., Csuhaj-Varjú, E., Cienciala, L., Sosík, P.: P colonies. Bull. Int. Membr. Comput. Soc. **1**(2), 119–156 (2016)

5. Cienciala, L., Ciencialová, L., Csuhaj-Varjú, E., Vaszil, Gy.: Verifying APCol systems. In: Hinze, T., Behre, J. (eds.) Proceedings of the 19th International Conference on Membrane Computing (CMC19), pp. 247–258. Verlag ProBusiness, Berlin (2018)
6. Csuhaj-Varjú, E., Kelemen, J., Păun, G., Dassow, J. (eds.): Grammar Systems: A Grammatical Approach to Distribution and Cooperation. Gordon and Breach Science Publishers Inc., Newark (1994)
7. Hartmanis, J.: On non-determinacy in simple computing devices. Acta Informatica **1**, 336–344 (1972)
8. Holzer, M., Kutrib, M., Malcher, A.: Complexity of multi-head finite automata: origins and directions. Theor. Comput. Sci. **412**, 83–96 (2011)
9. Kelemenová, A.: P colonies, chap. 23.1. In: Păun, Gh., Rozenberg, G., Salomaa, A. (eds.) The Oxford Handbook of Membrane Computing, pp. 584–593. Oxford University Press, Oxford (2010)
10. Kelemen, J., Kelemenová, A., Păun, G.: Preview of P colonies: a biochemically inspired computing model. In: Workshop and Tutorial Proceedings. Ninth International Conference on the Simulation and Synthesis of Living Systems (ALIFE IX), Boston, MA, pp. 82–86 (2004)
11. Kelemen, J., Kelemenová, A.: A grammar-theoretic treatment of multiagent systems. Cybern. Syst. **23**(6), 621–633 (1992)
12. Meduna, A., Zemek, P.: Jumping finite automata. Int. J. Found. Comput. Sci. **23**(7), 1555–1578 (2012)
13. Păun, G., Rozenberg, G., Salomaa, A. (eds.): The Oxford Handbook of Membrane Computing. Oxford University Press Inc., New York (2010)
14. Rozenberg, G., Salomaa, A. (eds.): Handbook of Formal Languages I-III. Springer, Heidelberg (1997). https://doi.org/10.1007/978-3-642-59126-6

A Semantic Investigation of Spiking Neural P Systems

Gabriel Ciobanu[1,2] and Eneia Nicolae Todoran[3(✉)]

[1] Romanian Academy, Institute of Computer Science,
Iaşi, Romania
[2] A.I. Cuza University of Iaşi, Iaşi, Romania
gabriel@info.uaic.ro
[3] Technical University, Department of Computer Science,
400027 Cluj-Napoca, Romania
eneia.todoran@cs.utcluj.ro

Abstract. We present a metric denotational semantics for an experimental concurrent language inspired by the spiking neural P systems. At syntactic level, the language provides constructions for specifying the neurons, synapses and rules with time delays defining a spiking neural P system. The denotational semantics presented in this paper is designed by using continuations. We employ metric spaces, including a metric powerdomain to describe the nondeterministic behaviour. Our denotational semantics describes accurately the time delays between firings and spikings, the nondeterministic behaviour and the synchronized functioning that are specific of a spiking neural P system. An implementation in the functional language Haskell is also provided; it can be tested and evaluated, being available for software experiments.

1 Introduction

Spiking neural P systems (shortly, SN P systems) were introduced in [14] as a class of distributed parallel computing models inspired from the way neurons communicate with each other by means of electrical impulses, where there exists a synapse between each pair of connected neurons. A spiking neural P system consists of a set of neurons placed in the nodes of a directed graph, where neurons send signals (spikes) along synapses (arcs of the graph). These systems were proven to be computationally equivalent in power with Turing machines [18], and able to solve NP-complete problems in polynomial time [16].

In this paper we present a semantic investigation of spiking neural P systems by using a concurrent programming language named $\mathcal{L}_{SNP}$, and developing an interpreter based on a mathematical semantics provided for $\mathcal{L}_{SNP}$.

The language $\mathcal{L}_{SNP}$ has constructions for neurons, synapses and rules with time delays that define a spiking neural P system. The execution of a program starts with its statement in the first neuron specified in the declaration list. Intuitively, each statement is 'executed' by a neuron whose behaviour is specified by a declaration mentioning the set of neurons that are involved in such an execution. Each neuron stores a multiset of spikes which are used during the

© Springer Nature Switzerland AG 2019
T. Hinze et al. (Eds.): CMC 2018, LNCS 11399, pp. 108–130, 2019.
https://doi.org/10.1007/978-3-030-12797-8_9

execution for the selection of rules; a spiking rule is applied when the neuron contains a specified number of spikes and all these spikes are consumed. A spike is an elementary process; a parallel composition of several spikes represents a multiset of processes which are executed concurrently.

A neuron can be open or closed. An open neuron accepts spikes, while a closed neuron cannot receive spikes (initially, all neurons are open). All neurons act concurrently and communicate by means of spikes, but each neuron works in a sequential and nondeterministic manner with at most one rule used in each step covering all spikes present in the neuron. A global clock is assumed (measuring the time delays associated with spiking rules) and the system operates synchronously.

For the language $\mathcal{L}_{SNP}$ we present a formal semantics designed by using continuations and metric spaces [6]. It is a denotational semantics, meaning that it is compositional: the semantics of a compound construction is given solely by the semantics of its constituents. This denotational semantics describes faithfully the time delays between firings and spikings, the nondeterministic behaviour and the synchronization specific to spiking neural systems.

By using the functional programming language Haskell [20] (as a metalanguage for the denotational semantics), we developed a prototype semantic interpreter for $\mathcal{L}_{SNP}$; it is an accurate implementation of the mathematical semantics presented in the paper. Using this implementation, various spiking neural P systems can be simulated, tested and evaluated (including the $\mathcal{L}_{SNP}$ programs discussed in this paper). The semantic interpreter is available at [24].

2   Mathematical Preliminaries

We present a denotational semantics designed with continuations [5,23] and higher-order functions. We assume the reader is familiar with the λ-calculus notation [7] and the basic set theory [17]. The notation $(x \in)X$ introduces the set X with typical element x ranging over X. The powerset $\mathcal{P}(X)$ denotes the set of all subsets of X, while $\mathcal{P}_\pi(X)$ denotes the set of all subsets of X with property π. Let $f \in X \to Y$ be a function. The function $(f \mid x \mapsto y) : X \to Y$, is defined (for $x, x' \in X, y \in Y$) by: $(f \mid x \mapsto y)(x') = $ if $x' = x$ then y else $f(x')$. Instead of $((f \mid x_1 \mapsto y_1) \cdots \mid x_n \mapsto y_n)$, we often write $(f \mid x_1 \mapsto y_1 \mid \cdots \mid x_n \mapsto y_n)$.

Let $f : X \to Y$ be a function with domain X and range Y; we denote by $\mathsf{dom}(f)$ and $\mathsf{ran}(f)$ the domain and the range of f, respectively. Let $f : X \to Y$ and $g : Y \to Z$ be functions. We denote by $g \circ f$ the function $g \circ f : X \to Z$ defined by $(g \circ f)(x) = g(f(x))$ for any $x \in X$. Strictly speaking, f and g can be composed if $\mathsf{ran}(f) \subseteq \mathsf{dom}(g)$. Function composition is associative; if h, g and f are functions with suitable domains and ranges, then $h \circ (g \circ f) = (h \circ g) \circ f$.

2.1   Metric Spaces

The denotational semantics given in this paper is built within the mathematical framework of *complete metric spaces*. We work with the following notions which we assume known: *metric* and *ultrametric* spaces, *isometry* (distance preserving bijections between metric spaces, denoted by '$\cong$'), *complete* metric spaces, and *compact* sets. For details the reader can consult [6]. We recall that if (M_1, d_1) and (M_2, d_2) are metric spaces, a function $f : M_1 \to M_2$ is a *contraction* if there exists $c \in \mathbb{R}$ with $0 \le c < 1$ such that $d_2(f(x), f(y)) \le c \cdot d_1(x, y)$ for all $x, y \in M_1$. In metric semantics, it is customary to attach a contracting factor $c = \frac{1}{2}$ to each computation step; when $c = 1$, the function f is called *non-expansive*; by $M_1 \xrightarrow{1} M_2$ we denote the set of all non-expansive functions from M_1 to M_2. Let $f : X \to X$ be a function; if $f(x) = x$, then x is a *fixed point* of f. When this fixed point is unique, we write $x = \text{fix}(f)$. The following theorem is at the core of metric semantics.

Theorem 1 (Banach). *Let (M, d) be a non-empty complete metric space.*

Each contraction $f : M \to M$ has a unique fixed point.

If $(x, y \in) M$ is any non-empty set, one can define the *discrete metric* on M $(d : M \times M \to [0, 1])$ as follows: $d(x, y) = 0$ if $x = y$, and $d(x, y) = 1$ otherwise. (M, d) is a complete ultrametric space.

Definition 2. *Let $(M, d_M), (M_1, d_{M_1}), (M_2, d_{M_2})$ be (ultra) metric spaces. On $(x \in) M$, $(f \in) M_1 \to M_2$ (the function space), $(x_1, x_2) \in M_1 \times M_2$ (the Cartesian product), $u, v \in M_1 + M_2$ (the disjoint union of M_1 and M_2, which can be defined by $M_1 + M_2 = (\{1\} \times M_1) \cup (\{2\} \times M_2)$), and $U, V, W \in \mathcal{P}(M)$ (the powerset of M), we can define the following metrics:*

(a) $d_{\frac{1}{2} \cdot M} : M \times M \to [0, 1]$, $\quad d_{\frac{1}{2} \cdot M}(x, x') = \frac{1}{2} \cdot d_M(x, x')$,

(b) $d_{M_1 \to M_2} : (M_1 \to M_2) \times (M_1 \to M_2) \to [0, 1]$,
$\quad d_{M_1 \to M_2}(f, f') = \sup_{x_1 \in M_1} d_{M_2}(f(x_1), f'(x_1))$,

(c) $d_{M_1 \times M_2} : (M_1 \times M_2) \times (M_1 \times M_2) \to [0, 1]$,
$\quad d_{M_1 \times M_2}((x_1, x_2), (x_1', x_2')) = max\{d_{M_1}(x_1, x_1'), d_{M_2}(x_2, x_2')\}$,

(d) $d_{M_1 + M_2} : (M_1 + M_2) \times (M_1 + M_2) \to [0, 1]$,
$\quad d_{M_1 + M_2}(u, v) = $ if $(u, v \in M_1)$ then $d_{M_1}(u, v)$
$\quad\quad\quad\quad\quad\quad\quad$ else if $(u, v \in M_2)$ then $d_{M_2}(u, v)$ else 1,

(e) $d_H : \mathcal{P}(M) \times \mathcal{P}(M) \to [0, 1]$ $\quad$ (d_H is the so-called Hausdorff metric),
$\quad d_H(U, V) = max\{\sup_{x \in U} d(x, V), \sup_{x' \in V} d(x', U)\}$
$\quad$ where $d(x, W) = \inf_{x' \in W} d_M(x, x')$ and by convention $\sup \emptyset = 0, \inf \emptyset = 1$.

We often suppress the metrics in domain definitions, and write, e.g., $\frac{1}{2} \cdot M$ instead of $(M, d_{\frac{1}{2} \cdot M})$. We denote by $\mathcal{P}_{co}(M)$ and $\mathcal{P}_{nco}(M)$ the powersets of *compact* and *non-empty and compact* subsets of M, respectively.

Remark 3. *Let (M, d_M), (M_1, d_{M_1}), (M_2, d_{M_2}), $d_{\frac{1}{2} \cdot M}$, $d_{M_1 \to M_2}$, $d_{M_1 \times M_2}$, $d_{M_1 + M_2}$ and d_H be as in Definition 2. In case d_M, d_{M_1}, d_{M_2} are ultrametrics, so are $d_{\frac{1}{2} \cdot M}, d_{M_1 \to M_2}, d_{M_1 \times M_2}, d_{M_1 + M_2}$ and d_H. Moreover, if (M, d_M), (M_1, d_{M_1}), (M_2, d_{M_2}) are complete then $\frac{1}{2} \cdot M$, $M_1 \to M_2$, $M_1 \xrightarrow{1} M_2$, $M_1 \times M_2$, $M_1 + M_2$, $\mathcal{P}_{co}(M)$ and $\mathcal{P}_{nco}(M)$ (with the metrics defined above) are also complete metric spaces [6].*

By $\mathcal{P}_{fin}(\cdot)$ we denote the powerset of all *finite* subsets of '$\cdot$', and by $\mathcal{P}_{nfin}(\cdot)$ we denote the power set of all *non-empty and finite* subsets of '$\cdot$'. In general, constructions $\mathcal{P}_{fin}(\cdot)$ and $\mathcal{P}_{nfin}(\cdot)$ are not complete spaces. We use these constructions to create structures endowed with discrete metrics. Any set endowed with a discrete metric is a complete ultrametric space.

2.2 Multisets

A *multiset* is a generalization of a set. Intuitively, a multiset is a collection in which an element may occur more than once; formally, a multiset of elements of type X is a function $X \to \mathbb{N}$, or a partial function $X \to \mathbb{N}^+$, where $\mathbb{N}^+ = \mathbb{N} \setminus \{0\}$. Let $(x \in) X$ be a countable set. We use the notation $[X] = \{m : A \to \mathbb{N}^+ \mid A \in \mathcal{P}_{fin}(X)\}$, where $\mathcal{P}_{fin}(X)$ is the powerset of all finite subsets of X. Since X is countable, then $\mathcal{P}_{fin}(X)$ is countable, and $[X]$ is also countable [17]. $[X]$ is the set of all finite multisets of elements of type X. An element $m \in [X]$ is a finite multiset of elements of type X, namely a function $m : A \to \mathbb{N}^+$ for a finite subset $A \subseteq X$ such that $m(x) > 0$ for all $x \in A$. The number $m(x)$ of occurrences of x in m is called its multiplicity.

It is possible to represent a multiset $m \in [X]$ by enumerating its elements between square brackets [and]. For example, [ ] is the empty multiset, and $[x_1, x_2, x_2]$ is the multiset with one occurrence of x_1 and two occurrences of x_2, i.e. $m : \{x_1, x_2\} \to \mathbb{N}^+$ with $m(x_1) = 1$ and $m(x_2) = 2$. The elements of a multiset are *not* ordered; this means that $m = [x_1, x_2, x_2] = [x_2, x_1, x_2] = [x_2, x_2, x_1]$. Let $m : A \in [X]$ be a multiset, with $\mathsf{dom}(m) = \{x_1, \ldots, x_n\}$. We can also represent m as $[x_1^{m(x_1)}, \ldots, x_n^{m(x_n)}]$. For example, if $m : \{x_1, x_2, x_3\} \to \mathbb{N}^+$ with $m(x_1) = 2$, $m(x_2) = 1$ and $m(x_3) = 3$, then $m = [x_1, x_1, x_2, x_3, x_3, x_3] = [x_1^2, x_2^1, x_3^3]$. We can define various operations on multisets $m_1, m_2 \in [X]$.

- *Multiset sum* $m_1 \uplus m_2$; $\uplus : ([X] \times [X]) \to [X]$

$$\mathsf{dom}(m_1 \uplus m_2) = \mathsf{dom}(m_1) \cup \mathsf{dom}(m_2)$$

$$(m_1 \uplus m_2)(x) = \begin{cases} m_1(x) + m_2(x) & \text{if } x \in \mathsf{dom}(m_1) \cap \mathsf{dom}(m_2) \\ m_1(x) & \text{if } x \in \mathsf{dom}(m_1) \setminus \mathsf{dom}(m_2) \\ m_2(x) & \text{if } x \in \mathsf{dom}(m_2) \setminus \mathsf{dom}(m_1) \end{cases}$$

- *Multiset difference* $m_1 \setminus m_2$; $\setminus : ([X] \times [X]) \to [X]$

$$\mathsf{dom}(m_1 \setminus m_2) = (\mathsf{dom}(m_1) \setminus \mathsf{dom}(m_2)) \cup$$
$$\{x \mid x \in \mathsf{dom}(m_1) \cap \mathsf{dom}(m_2), m_1(x) > m_2(x)\}$$

$$(m_1 \setminus m_2)(x) = \begin{cases} m_1(x) & \text{if } x \in \mathsf{dom}(m_1) \setminus \mathsf{dom}(m_2) \\ m_1(x) - m_2(x) & \text{if } x \in \mathsf{dom}(m_1) \cap \mathsf{dom}(m_2) \\ & \text{and } m_1(x) > m_2(x) \end{cases}$$

Let $x \in X$ and $m \in [X]$. We write $x \in m$ to express that $x \in \mathsf{dom}(m)$, and write $m_1 = m_2$ to express that the multisets m_1 and m_2 are equal: $m_1 = m_2$ iff $\mathsf{dom}(m_1) = \mathsf{dom}(m_2)$ and $m_1(x) = m_2(x)$ for all $x \in \mathsf{dom}(m_1)$. More about the mathematics of multisets can be found in [1].

2.3   Strings, Regular Expressions and Multisets

Let $(a \in)O$ be an alphabet. $(u, v \in)O^*$ is the free monoid generated by O with respect to the concatenation operation and the identity λ (the empty string); O^* is the set of all finite, possibly empty, strings over O. The concatenation of two strings $u, v \in O^*$ is denoted by $u \cdot v$, or shorter by uv. Regular expressions are patterns used to specify sets of strings. We assume the reader is familiar with the notion of a regular expression (including the way a regular expression can be constructed by using the operations of union, concatenation and Kleene $+$) and the way a regular expression E describes a corresponding regular language $L(E)$. For example, the regular expression $a_1^+ a_2$ (defined over the alphabet O) matches the strings $a_1 a_2, a_1 a_1 a_2, a_1 a_1 a_1 a_2$ and so on. For a comprehensive presentation of formal languages theory the reader may consult [22].

In membrane computing a multiset is often represented by (the permutations of) a string. We define a function $ms : O^* \to [O]$ as follows: $ms(\lambda) = [\ ]$ and $ms(av) = [a] \uplus ms(v)$, for any $a \in O$ and $v \in O^*$. The function ms maps any string $u \in O^*$ to a corresponding multiset $w \in [O]$; the notation $[\cdot]$ was introduced in Sect. 2.2. For example, $ms(a_1 a_2 a_2) = ms(a_2 a_1 a_2) = ms(a_2 a_2 a_1) = [a_1, a_2, a_2]$. In general, $ms(u) = ms(v)$, whenever u is a permutation of v. Let $(a \in)O$ be a given alphabet and E a regular expression over O. Let $L(E)$ be the language associated with the regular expression E. Let $w \in [O]$ be a multiset over O. We write $w \in L(E)$ to express that $\exists u \in L(E) : w = ms(u)$, i.e., there is a string $u \in L(E)$ such that $w = ms(u)$.

In the particular case when $O = \{a\}$ is a singleton, any string over O is either λ or of the form a^n, $n > 0$. Note that in this case all permutations of a string a^n (seen as a sequence of a's) are identical, hence there is a one-to-one correspondence between strings and multisets. The multiset corresponding to string a^n is $m = ms(a^n) = [a^n] \in [O]$, i.e., the function $m : \{a\} \to \mathbb{N}^+$, $m(a) = n$. For example, $a^3 = a \cdot a \cdot a = aaa$, and the corresponding multiset $m = ms(a^3)$ is $m : \{a\} \to \mathbb{N}^+$, $m(a) = 3$ (or $ms(a^3) = [a, a, a] = [a^3]$).

We use the notation a^n to represent both a string (of length n) and the multiplicity of an element occurring in a multiset of the form $[\ldots, a^n, \ldots]$. However, there is no risk of confusion here because in the case of a multiset the expression a^n occurs always enclosed between square brackets.

3   Syntax of $\mathcal{L}_{SNP}$ and Informal Explanation

In this paper we present a semantic investigation of spiking neural P systems. For this purpose we use methods and tools well-known in the tradition of programming language semantics. In particular, the elements of the language $\mathcal{L}_{SNP}$ are syntactic constructions that we call *statements*, or *programs*. Also, when we describe the behaviour of an $\mathcal{L}_{SNP}$ program we use the term *execution*. As the *spikes* (also called *objects*) encountered in an SN P system are statements in our language, we speak sometimes of the 'execution of a spike'.

Let $(a \in)O$ be an alphabet of *spikes* (we also say *objects*). Let $(N \in)Nname$ be a set of *neuron names* or *neuron identifiers*. Let $(w \in)W = [O]$ be the set of all finite multisets over O; the notation $[\cdot]$ was introduced in Sect. 2.2. Let $(\xi \in)\varXi = \mathcal{P}_{fin}(Nname)$; an element $\xi \in \varXi$ is a finite set of neuron names or neuron identifiers. We describe the syntax of $\mathcal{L}_{SNP}$ by using a BNF specification.

Definition 4 *(Syntax of $\mathcal{L}_{SNP}$)*

(a) (Statements) $x(\in X)$ ::= $a \mid \mathsf{send}(y, \xi) \mid x \parallel x$
     where $y(\in Y)$ ::= $a \mid y \parallel y$ *(obviously, $Y \subseteq X$)*
(b) (Rules) $r(\in Rs)$ ::= $r_\epsilon \mid \varrho, r$
     where $\varrho(\in R)$ ::= $E/w \to x; t \mid w \to \lambda,$ $w \neq [\,]$
     with E a regular expression over O, and $t \geq 0, t \in \mathbb{N}$
(c) (Neuron declarations)
        $d(\in ND)$ ::= $\mathsf{neuron}\, N\, \{\, r \mid \xi \,\}$
        $D(\in NDs)$ ::= $d \mid d, D$
(d) (Programs) $\rho(\in \mathcal{L}_{SNP})$ ::= D, x

Notation 5. *We write $\langle a^n \rangle$ as an abbreviation for $(a \parallel (\cdots \parallel (a \parallel a) \cdots))$, where the spike a occurs n times, $n \geq 1$.[1] In this case we use angle brackets surrounding the expression a^n to avoid any confusion between the statement $\langle a^n \rangle$, the string a^n and a multiset of the form $[\ldots, a^n, \ldots]$; (the notations for strings a^n and multisets $[\ldots, a^n, \ldots]$ were introduced in Sect. 2.3).*

Let $\varrho \in R$ be a rule and $r \in Rs$. We use the notation $\varrho \in r$ to express that either $r = \varrho, r'$ or $r = \varrho_1, \ldots, \varrho_i, \varrho, r'$ for some $r' \in Rs, \varrho_1, \ldots, \varrho_i \in R$. We usually write a non-empty list of rules $r = \varrho_1, \ldots, \varrho_i, r_\epsilon$ without the terminating r_ϵ, i.e., we write r as $r = \varrho_1, \ldots, \varrho_i$. Also, as in [14], we write a (spiking or firing) rule of the form $E/[a^c] \to x; t$ with $L(E) = \{a^c\}$ (i.e., a spiking rule applied when the neuron contains exactly c spikes and all these spikes are consumed) in the simpler form $[a^c] \to x; t$.

The declaration of a neuron $\mathsf{neuron}\, N\, \{\, r \mid \xi \,\}$ comprises a neuron name (or neuron identifier) $N \in Nname$, a finite list of rules $r \in Rs$, and a set of neuron names $\xi \in \varXi$. An $\mathcal{L}_{SNP}$ program $\rho = D, x$ comprises a list of neuron declarations D followed by a statement x.

Remark 6. *To be valid, the neuron names $N_0, \ldots, N_m$ in a list of neuron declarations $D = \mathsf{neuron}\, N_0\, \{\, r_0 \mid \xi_0 \,\}, \ldots, \mathsf{neuron}\, N_m\, \{\, r_m \mid \xi_m \,\}$ must be pairwise distinct. There is a special (reserved) neuron name $N_0 \in Nname$ which must always occur as the name of the first neuron in a list of declarations $D = \mathsf{neuron}\, N_0\, \{\, r_0 \mid \xi_0 \,\}, \ldots, \mathsf{neuron}\, N_m\, \{\, r_m \mid \xi_m \,\} \in NDs$. In other words, for a list of neuron declarations $D \in NDs$ to be valid, the name of the first neuron in D must be N_0. As each neuron is uniquely identified by its name, we can speak of 'the neuron with name N', or simply 'the neuron N'. Also, a list of rules $r \in Rs$ is valid only if for each (firing) rule of the form $E/w \to x; t$ and for each (forgetting) rule of the form $w' \to \lambda$, we have $\neg(w' \in L(E))$ (the notation $w' \in L(E)$ was introduced in Sect. 2.3).*

---

[1] We will see later that in $\mathcal{L}_{SNP}$ the parallel composition operator $\parallel$ is commutative and associative; see Proposition 14. Hence the parentheses in the expression $(a \parallel (\cdots \parallel (a \parallel a) \cdots))$ are actually not needed.

The reader may wonder why we use the semantic notions of a set $\xi \in \Xi$ in the specification of a statement $\mathsf{send}(y, \xi)$ and in a neuron declaration $\mathsf{neuron}\, N\, \{\, r\, \mid \xi\,\}$, as well as a multiset $w \in W$ in the specification of a firing rule $E/w \to x; t$. Both sets and multisets could be defined as lists, by using appropriate syntax definitions. However, we use sets and multisets because the order in which the neuron names occur in the component ξ of a statement $\mathsf{send}(y, \xi)$ or in a neuron declaration $\mathsf{neuron}\, N\, \{\, r\, \mid\, \xi\,\}$, and the order in which the spikes occur in the component w of a rule $E/w \to x; t$ are irrelevant. In this way, we also avoid some obvious conversions between syntactic and semantic representations [12].

Intuitively, each statement $x \in X$ is 'executed' by a neuron whose behaviour is specified by a declaration $\mathsf{neuron}\, N\, \{\, r_N\, \mid\, \xi_N\,\}$, where ξ_N is the set of (names of) neurons that are adjacent (neighbouring) to the neuron N. In the sequel we often say that 'a neuron N executes a statement x'. Typically, a statement x is executed by a neuron N declared as $\mathsf{neuron}\, N\, \{\, r_N\, \mid\, \xi_N\,\}$ if x occurs in the right-hand side of a rule occurring in r_N. There is just one exception which is described in the following paragraph.

By convention, the execution of an $\mathcal{L}_{SNP}$ program $\rho = D, x$ starts with the execution of statement x in the first neuron $\mathsf{neuron}\, N_0\, \{\, r_0\, \mid\, \xi_0\,\}$ specified in the list of declarations $D = \mathsf{neuron}\, N_0\, \{\, r_0\, \mid\, \xi_0\,\}, \ldots, \mathsf{neuron}\, N_m\, \{\, r_m\, \mid\, \xi_m\,\}$. The statement x is executed immediately (no delay is imposed upon the execution of x). A neuron can be *open* or *closed* [14]. A closed neuron cannot receive (new) spikes. An open neuron accepts spikes. Initially, all neurons are open and empty (i.e., contain no spikes). The statement x can be used to create an arbitrary initial configuration in a single initial step. At 'execution time', each neuron can store a multiset of objects (spikes), and its behaviour is described both by the current number of spikes present in it and by the number of steps (time units) to count down until it becomes open [14].

An $\mathcal{L}_{SNP}$ statement may be either a spike (an object) $a \in O$, a send statement $\mathsf{send}(y, \xi)$ where y is a statement of type Y and $\xi \in \Xi$ is a set of neuron names, or a parallel composition of two $\mathcal{L}_{SNP}$ statements $x_1 \parallel x_2$.

$E/w \to x; t$ is a *firing* (or a *spiking*) *rule*, where E is a regular expression, $w \in W$ is a non-empty multiset of spikes (or objects), $x \in X$ is an $\mathcal{L}_{SNP}$ statement and $t \geq 0$ is a natural number specifying a time interval. A firing rule $\varrho = E/w \to x; t$ can be executed (applied or fired) by a neuron N declared as $\mathsf{neuron}\, N\, \{\, r_N\, \mid\, \xi_N\,\}$ if $\varrho \in r_N$, the neuron N (currently) contains a multiset of spikes w_N such that $w_N \in L(E)$ and $w \subseteq w_N$. In this situation the rule is fired, meaning that the multiset w is consumed (only $w_N \setminus w$ spikes remain in the neuron), and the statement x becomes ready for execution. However, the statement x is suspended for t time units if $t > 0$. The statement x is executed after exactly t time units, and has the effect of producing spikes. A statement x of the form $y \parallel \mathsf{send}(y_1, \xi_1) \parallel \cdots \parallel \mathsf{send}(y_i, \xi_i)$ transmits the spikes in y (i.e., the spikes in $ms_Y(y)$, see Remark 7) to all neurons with names in the set ξ_N, and the spikes in $y_1, \ldots, y_i$ to the neurons with names in the sets $\xi_1 \cap \xi_N, \ldots, \xi_i \cap \xi_N$, respectively. According to Proposition 14, the parallel composition operator $\parallel$

is commutative and associative, hence any $\mathcal{L}_{SNP}$ statement x is semantically equivalent to a statement of the form $y \parallel \mathsf{send}(y_1, \xi_1) \parallel \cdots \parallel \mathsf{send}(y_i, \xi_i)$.

The fact that a neuron can be *open* or *closed* is related to the execution of a firing (spiking) rule $E/w \rightarrow x; t$. In the time interval between firing (when the statement x becomes ready for execution) and spiking (when the statement x is actually executed) the neuron is *closed* (this corresponds to the refractory period from neurobiology). A closed neuron cannot receive (new) spikes. The time interval between firing and spiking takes t time units. After t time units, the neuron becomes open, and an open neuron accepts spikes.

$w \rightarrow \lambda$ (where w is a non-empty multiset of spikes) is a *forgetting rule*; such a rule is executed by a neuron N only if N currently contains exactly the multiset of spikes w. In this case the multiset of spikes w is removed from neuron N, meaning that all spikes are removed from N.

The links between the $\mathcal{L}_{SNP}$ rules and the SN P system rules [9,14,15] is discussed in Sect. 3.1 by means of an example.

Remark 7. *Concurrent processes naturally form multisets, in the sense that multiple copies of a process can be executed concurrently. If we see a spike in $\mathcal{L}_{SNP}$ as kind of elementary 'process', then a parallel composition of several spikes is a multiset of 'processes' that are 'executed' concurrently. Thus, we can see an $\mathcal{L}_{SNP}$ statement of type Y (recall that $y(\in Y) ::= a \mid y \parallel y$) as the specification of a multiset of spikes. We can define a function $ms_Y : Y \rightarrow [O]$ computing the multiset of spikes corresponding to a statement of type Y as follows: $ms_Y(a) = [a]$ and $ms_Y(y_1 \parallel y_2) = ms_Y(y_1) \uplus ms_Y(y_2)$. For example, $ms_Y((a_1 \parallel a_2) \parallel a_1) = [a_1, a_1, a_2]$.*

A statement $x = y \in Y$ executed by a neuron N behaves as follows: the spikes contained in y (i.e., the spikes contained in the multiset $ms_Y(y)$) can be transmitted to all neurons with names in ξ_N according to the rules r_N. $\mathsf{send}(y, \xi)$ is a selective send operation (or an operation with target indication [2,19]); such a statement $\mathsf{send}(y, \xi)$ executed by a neuron N declared as neuron $N \{ r_N \mid \xi_N \}$ behaves almost like y, but with the restriction that the spikes in y (i.e., the spikes in $ms_Y(y)$) can only be transmitted to the neurons with names in the set $\xi \cap \xi_N$.

According to Proposition 14, any $\mathcal{L}_{SNP}$ statement x is semantically equivalent to a statement of the form $y \parallel \mathsf{send}(y_1, \xi_1) \parallel \cdots \mathsf{send}(y_i, \xi_i)$. More generally, every statement $x \in X$ executed by a neuron declared as neuron $N \{ r_N \mid \xi_N \}$ can be seen as a multiset of spikes that are executed concurrently. The destination of the objects contained in y is given by ξ_N.[2] The destinations of the objects contained in $y_1, \ldots, y_i$ are given by $\xi_1 \cap \xi_N, \ldots, \xi_i \cap \xi_N$, respectively.

When an $\mathcal{L}_{SNP}$ program (D, x) starts up, the execution of the initial statement x is started automatically (as explained above). However, this is a special case. In all other cases the execution of a statement x is triggered by the application of a firing rule of the form $E/w \rightarrow x; t$.

---

[2] More precisely, we can say that the destination of the objects contained in $ms_Y(y)$ is given by ξ_N.

All neurons act concurrently, but each neuron works in a sequential and nondeterministic manner, with at most one rule used in each step covering all spikes present in the neuron. A global clock is assumed (measuring the time delays associated with spiking rules), and the system works synchronously. The synchronized functioning is specific of SN P systems [14]; it is also expressed in the denotational semantics of the language $\mathcal{L}_{SNP}$ presented in this paper and in the Haskell implementation available from [24].

3.1 An Example of $\mathcal{L}_{SNP}$ Program

To illustrate the concepts embodied in $\mathcal{L}_{SNP}$, we present an example. The $\mathcal{L}_{SNP}$ program ρ_1 presented below implements the SN P system Π_1 given in [14], Sect. 5, Fig. 2. By using the notation employed in [14], the SN P system Π_1 is defined formally as a tuple $\Pi_1 = (\{a\}, \sigma_1, \sigma_2, \sigma_3, syn, 3)$, where $\{a\}$ is (in this example) the singleton *alphabet of spikes*, σ_1, σ_2 and σ_3 are *neurons* represented as pairs (n_i, R_i), where n_i is the initial number of spikes contained in neuron σ_i and R_i is a set of rules, $syn \subseteq \{1, 2, 3\} \times \{1, 2, 3\}$ describes (the directed graph representing) the *synapses* between neurons, and 3 indicates the *output neuron*. The three neurons behave as follows:

$$\sigma_1 = (2k - 1, \{a^+/a \rightarrow a; 2\}),$$
$$\sigma_2 = (0, \{a^k \rightarrow a; 1\}),$$
$$\sigma_3 = (1, \{a \rightarrow a; 0\})$$

Initially, the three neurons contain $2k - 1, 0$ and 1 spikes, respectively, for some $k \in \mathbb{N}^+$. In this example, each neuron contains exactly one firing (or spiking) rule of the form $E/a^r \rightarrow a; t$, where E is a regular expression over the alphabet $\{a\}$, a^r is a string (multiset) containing $r \geq 1$ spikes, and $t \geq 0$ is the time delay between firing and spiking specified by this rule. The following notation is used as in [14]: a spiking rule of the form $E/a^r \rightarrow a; t$ with $L(E) = \{a^r\}$ is written in the simpler form $a^r \rightarrow a; t$.

By convention, it is required that the output neuron spikes at least twice during the computation and the result of the computation is the number of steps elapsed between the first spike and the second spike produced by the output neuron (no matter if the computation subsequently halts or not). We assume the reader is familiar with the meaning of SN P (firing and forgetting) rules. The behaviour of the above SN P system Π_1 is described in detail in [14]. Here, we only explain how the SN P system Π_1 is implemented by the $\mathcal{L}_{SNP}$ program ρ_1 presented below, and we describe accurately the behaviour of Π_1. The program $\rho_1 \in \mathcal{L}_{SNP}$ is defined by $\rho_1 = (D_1, x_1)$, where the statement $x_1 \in X$ is

$$x_1 = \mathsf{send}((\langle a^{2k-1} \rangle, \{N_1\}) \parallel \mathsf{send}(a, \{N_3\})$$

and the declaration $D_1 \in NDs$ is given by:

$$
\begin{aligned}
D_1 = \quad &\text{neuron } N_0 \,\{\, r_\epsilon \mid \{N_1, N_2, N_3\} \,\}, \\
&\text{neuron } N_1 \,\{\, a^+/[a] \rightarrow a; 2 \mid \{N_2\} \,\}, \\
&\text{neuron } N_2 \,\{\, [a^k] \rightarrow a; 1 \mid \{N_3\} \,\}, \\
&\text{neuron } N_3 \,\{\, [a] \rightarrow a; 0 \mid \{N_0\} \,\}
\end{aligned}
$$

In what concerns the representation of rules, we believe that the analogy between the two formal systems is clear. A rule of an SN P system of the form $E/a^r \rightarrow a; t$ is implemented by a corresponding $\mathcal{L}_{SNP}$ (ρ_1) rule $E/[a^r] \rightarrow a; t$ as follows: the *string* a^r is implemented by the *multiset* $[a^r]$, and the (spike) *symbol* a is implemented by the corresponding *statement* a. In the above example, the $\varPi_1$ rule $a^+/a \rightarrow a; 2$ is implemented by the corresponding ρ_1 rule $a^+/[a] \rightarrow a; 2$. In general, the statement x occurring in the right-hand side of an $\mathcal{L}_{SNP}$ firing rule $E/w \rightarrow x; t$ may be more complex (according to Definition 4(a)). The three neurons specified in $\varPi_1$ are also declared in ρ_1.

The SN P system $\varPi_1$ specifies the initial content of each neuron. In the initial state, σ_1 contains $2k - 1$ spikes, σ_2 contains no spikes (i.e., 0 spikes), and σ_3 contains 1 spike. By contrast, any $\mathcal{L}_{SNP}$ program starts its execution with all neurons empty: in the initial state of an $\mathcal{L}_{SNP}$ program each neuron contains an empty multiset of spikes. However, an $\mathcal{L}_{SNP}$ program can produce an arbitrary initial configuration in a single execution step. The program ρ_1 consumes one step for initialization. Apart from this initial step, the $\mathcal{L}_{SNP}$ program ρ_1 behaves the same as the SN P system $\varPi_1$. In general, an $\mathcal{L}_{SNP}$ program can describe faithfully the behaviour of an SN P system. Each neuron stores a (possibly empty) multiset of spikes, which are used during execution for the selection of rules. Each firing rule can start the execution of an $\mathcal{L}_{SNP}$ statement (occurring in the right-hand side of the rule). In the example program ρ_1 all spikes are identical. Hence, in this example we can describe each multiset w_N stored in a neuron N by the number of spikes contained in w_N.

The $\mathcal{L}_{SNP}$ program ρ_1 starts up by executing the statement x_1 in neuron N_0. In the initial state, all neurons are empty. The statement x_1 transmits $2k - 1$ spikes to neuron N_1 (by executing $\mathsf{send}(\langle a^{2k-1}\rangle, \{N_1\})$), and 1 spike to neuron N_3 (by executing $\mathsf{send}(a, \{N_3\})$). Thus, after this initialization step, neuron N_1 contains (a multiset of) $2k - 1$ spikes, neuron N_3 contains 1 spike, neuron N_2 contains 0 spikes (N_2 remains empty), and neuron N_0 remains empty. We see that after this initialization phase the state of the $\mathcal{L}_{SNP}$ program ρ_1 coincides with the initial state of the SN P system $\varPi_1$ described in [14].

Remark 8. *The main objective of this work is to design a denotational semantics describing accurately the behaviour of SN P systems. The execution strategy based on an initialization step and the introduction of the selective send operation* $\mathsf{send}(y, \xi)$ *in* $\mathcal{L}_{SNP}$ *were motivated by the aim to describe the behaviour of SN P systems in a compositional manner. By using the primitive* $\mathsf{send}(y, \xi)$, *a whole SN P system can be initialized in a single step. A similar solution was investigated in [13] for a representative class of membrane systems. An operational semantics for membrane systems is presented in [10].*

We offer a compositional approach to the semantics of SN P systems. The denotational semantics is designed in continuation-passing style, a technique providing sufficient flexibility for handling the complex interactions and the synchronized functioning that are specific to an SN P system. The semantics of each $\mathcal{L}_{SNP}$ *statement is defined compositionally with respect to a corresponding continuation which encapsulates the behaviour of the rest of the SN P system.*

The $\mathcal{L}_{SNP}$ program ρ_1 declares four neurons, while the system Π_1 includes only three neurons. The neurons N_1, N_2 and N_3 declared in the $\mathcal{L}_{SNP}$ program ρ_1 implement the neurons σ_1, σ_2 and σ_3 from the SN P system Π_1, respectively. However, the neuron N_0 has no counterpart in the SN P system Π_1. The neuron N_0 is used in $\mathcal{L}_{SNP}$ to initialize the execution of the program ρ_1. In this example, neuron N_0 is also used to capture the spikes emitted by the output neuron N_3 for an easier visualization of results, occurring in the set of neighbours in the declaration of neuron N_3: neuron $N_3 \{ [a] \rightarrow a; 0 \mid \{N_0\} \}$. In the example presented in [14], the output neuron σ_3 has an exit arrow (synapses linking the neurons are represented by arrows in [14]) pointing to the environment. In our implementation neuron N_0 also plays the role of the environment capturing the spikes produced by the output neuron N_3.

In the present version, the language $\mathcal{L}_{SNP}$ provides no special meaning to the output neuron because the denotational semantics function (and the corresponding Haskell implementation) produces all the execution traces, and each execution trace shows the history of states for each neuron. Hence, the behaviour of the output neuron can be extracted from the yield of the denotational semantics (and from the yield of the Haskell semantic prototype). The yield of the denotational semantics describing the behaviour of the $\mathcal{L}_{SNP}$ program ρ_1 is presented in Example 19 for the particular case when $k = 2$.

As explained in [14], the number computed by the SN P system Π_1 is $3k+2$. Our denotational semantics gives the same result. The $\mathcal{L}_{SNP}$ program captures accurately the behaviour of a corresponding SN P system. Apart from the supplementary initialization step, the $\mathcal{L}_{SNP}$ program ρ_1 presented above behaves exactly like the SN P system Π_1 presented in [14]. In our denotational semantics (and in our Haskell implementation), the neuron N_3 (representing the output neuron) spikes firstly in the second step (the first step is used for initialization). Next, neuron N_3 spikes for the second time in the step $(3k + 3) + 1 = 3k + 4$. Hence, the number computed by ρ_1 is $(3k+4) - 2 = 3k+2$, exactly as in [14]. In Example 19 we put $k = 2$; the computed number is $3k + 2 = 8$ (i.e., the number of steps between the two spikes produced by the output neuron N_3 is 8).

The following $\mathcal{L}_{SNP}$ program ρ'_1 behaves the same as ρ_1; the two programs ρ_1 and ρ'_1 are similar in some aspects and different in others. The program ρ'_1 is defined as (D'_1, x'_1), where the statement $x'_1 \in X$ is identical to the statement x_1 occurring in the definition of the program ρ_1, namely

$$x'_1 = \mathsf{send}((\langle a^{2k-1} \rangle, \{N_1\}) \parallel \mathsf{send}(a, \{N_3\}),$$

and the declaration $D'_1 \in NDs$ is given by:

$$
\begin{aligned}
D'_1 = \quad &\mathsf{neuron}\ N_0 \{ r_\epsilon \mid \{N_1, N_2, N_3\} \}, \\
&\mathsf{neuron}\ N_1 \{ a^+/[a] \rightarrow \mathsf{send}(a, \{N_2\}); 2 \mid \{N_1, N_2, N_3\} \}, \\
&\mathsf{neuron}\ N_2 \{ [a^k] \rightarrow \mathsf{send}(a, \{N_3\}); 1 \mid \{N_1, N_2, N_3\} \}, \\
&\mathsf{neuron}\ N_3 \{ [a] \rightarrow a; 0 \mid \{N_0\} \}.
\end{aligned}
$$

The initialization statements x_1 and x'_1 are identical. The rules are similar, but not identical. Note that the rules declared by the neurons of program ρ'_1 use selective send statements, rather than simple spikes. Also, the interconnections (implementing synapse links) between neurons are different in ρ_1 and ρ_1'. Following the definition of the SN P system Π_1 presented in [14], in ρ_1 the neurons N_1 and N_2 are only connected (by synapse links) to neurons N_2 and N_3, respectively. On the other hand, in the $\mathcal{L}_{SNP}$ program ρ_1' the neurons N_1 and N_2 are connected by links to all neurons with names in the set $\{N_1, N_2, N_3\}$. However, by using selective send statements in the right-hand sides of the rules declared by the neurons of program ρ_1', the spikes are always transmitted to the same destinations as in program ρ_1. Our denotational semantics yields the same meanings for both programs ρ_1 and ρ_1' (see Example 19). The reader can also verify this automatically, by running the Haskell implementation of the denotational semantics available at [24].

4   Denotational Semantics of $\mathcal{L}_{SNP}$

We present a denotational semantics designed with metric spaces and continuations for the language $\mathcal{L}_{SNP}$. The denotational semantics of statements is a function $[\![\cdot]\!] : X \to \mathbf{D}$, where the semantic domain $(\varphi \in)\mathbf{D}$ is defined by a recursive domain equation $\mathbf{D} \cong \mathbf{K} \xrightarrow{1} \mathbf{K}$. The domain $(\kappa \in)\mathbf{K} = \mathbf{\Gamma} \xrightarrow{1} \mathbf{P}$ is the domain of continuations, where $(\gamma \in)\mathbf{\Gamma}$ is a domain of (neural) configurations presented in Sect. 4.2, and $(p \in)\mathbf{P}$ is the final semantic domain presented in Sect. 4.1. Note that, the domain variable $\mathbf{D}$ occurs (recursively) in the definition of $\mathbf{\Gamma}$ (see Sect. 4.2). We recall that we use the symbol $\cong$ to describe an isometry between metric spaces [6].

4.1   Final Semantic Domain

We define a set $(\omega \in)\Omega$ of observables for our denotational semantics as follows:

$$\Omega = \{\omega \mid \omega \in \mathcal{P}_{nfin}(Nname \times W), \ \nu(\omega)\}$$

The predicate $\nu : \mathcal{P}_{nfin}(Nname \times W) \to Bool$ is given by:

$$\nu(\{(N_0, w_0), \ldots, (N_m, w_m)\}) = \begin{cases} \text{true} & \text{if } N_i \neq N_j, \forall 0 \leq i, j \leq m, i \neq j \\ \text{false} & \text{otherwise} \end{cases}$$

An element $\omega \in \Omega$ is a non-empty and finite set of pairs $\{(N_0, w_0), \ldots, (N_m, w_m)\}$ such that $N_i \neq N_j$ whenever $i \neq j$; thus, each pair $(N_i, w_i) \in \omega$ is uniquely identified by the neuron name N_i.

The final domain of our denotational semantics is a standard linear time domain [6] defined as follows:

$$(p \in)\mathbf{P} = \mathcal{P}_{nco}(\mathbf{Q})$$

$$(q \in)\mathbf{Q} \cong \{\epsilon\} + (\Omega \times \frac{1}{2} \cdot \mathbf{Q})$$

In the above domain equation, the set Ω is endowed with the discrete metric (every set endowed with the discrete metric is a complete ultrametric space). An element of Ω is a collection of pairs (N, w), where N is a neuron name and $w \in W = [O]$ is a finite multiset of spikes (objects) of type $(a \in)O$.

An element of the domain $\mathbf{P}$ is a non-empty and compact collection of sequences of type $\mathbf{Q}$. $\mathbf{Q}$ is a domain of finite and infinite sequences over Ω; ϵ is the empty sequence. Instead of $(w_1, (w_2, \ldots (w_n, \epsilon) \ldots))$ and $(w_1, (w_2, \ldots))$, we write $w_1 w_2 \ldots w_n$ and $w_1 w_2 \ldots$, respectively. In particular, instead of (w, ϵ) (a sequence of length 1) we write just w.

We express the nondeterministic behaviour in $\mathcal{L}_{SNP}$ by using the operator $\oplus : (\mathbf{P} \times \mathbf{P}) \to \mathbf{P}$ given by:

$$p_1 \oplus p_2 = \{q \mid q \in p_1 \cup p_2, q \neq \epsilon\} \cup \{\epsilon \mid \epsilon \in p_1 \cap p_2\}$$

We use the notations: $w \cdot q = (w, q)$ and $w \cdot p = \{w \cdot q \mid q \in p\}$, for any $w \in \Omega$, $q \in \mathbf{Q}$, $p \in \mathbf{P}$. Note that $d(w \cdot p_1, w \cdot p_2) = \frac{1}{2} \cdot d(p_1, p_2)$, for any $w \in \Omega$, $p_1, p_2 \in \mathbf{P}$ [6].

Remark 9. *The operator $\oplus$ is well-defined, non-expansive, idempotent, associative and commutative* [6].

4.2   Computations and Continuations

For the language $\mathcal{L}_{SNP}$ we define the domain of *computations* (*denotations*) $\mathbf{D}$, the domain of *continuations* $\mathbf{K}$ and a domain Γ of (neural) *configurations* defined by using a domain Σ of (neuron) *states* by the following equations:

$$(\varphi \in)\mathbf{D} \cong \mathbf{K} \xrightarrow{1} \mathbf{K} \qquad\qquad (\phi \in)\mathbf{Den} = \{d_0\} + \mathbf{D}$$

$$(\kappa \in)\mathbf{K} = \Gamma \xrightarrow{1} \mathbf{P} \qquad (\gamma \in)\Gamma = \{\!|\Sigma|\!\} \qquad (\sigma \in)\Sigma = \mathbf{Open} + \mathbf{Closed}$$

$$\mathbf{Open} = \Xi \times W \qquad\qquad \mathbf{Closed} = \Xi \times W \times \mathbb{N} \times W \times \frac{1}{2} \cdot \mathbf{D}$$

where we use the notation:

$$\{\!|\Sigma|\!\} \stackrel{not.}{=} \Xi \times (Nname \to \Sigma).$$

In the above domain equation, the sets $Nname, \Xi, \mathbb{N}$ and W are endowed with the discrete metric (the sets $Nname, \Xi$ and W were introduced in Sect. 3, and $\mathbb{N}$ is the set of natural numbers). The composed metric spaces are built up using the composite metrics given in Definition 2. Note that in the above domain equation the domain variable $\mathbf{D}$ occurs in the left-hand side of a function space construction. To conclude that such a domain equation has a unique solution up to isometry $\cong$, we rely on the general method of solving reflexive domain equations in a category of complete metric spaces presented in [4]. The solution for the domain $\mathbf{D}$ is obtained as a complete ultrametric space. The domains $\mathbf{Den}, \mathbf{K}, \boldsymbol{\Gamma}$ and $\boldsymbol{\Sigma}$ (are expressed in terms of $\mathbf{D}$ and the final domain $\mathbf{P}$ defined in Sect. 4.1) are also complete ultrametric spaces. $\mathbf{Den}$ is an auxiliary domain that is used in the definition of a scheduler mapping presented in Sect. 4.4.

The definitions of the domain $\boldsymbol{\Sigma}$ of (neuron) states and the construction $\{\!|\boldsymbol{\Sigma}|\!\}$ that we use to represent (neural) configurations require some further explanations. An element of type $\{\!|\boldsymbol{\Sigma}|\!\}$ is a pair (ξ, ϖ) with $\xi \in \Xi$ and $\varpi \in Nname \to \boldsymbol{\Sigma}$. On $\boldsymbol{\Gamma} = \{\!|\boldsymbol{\Sigma}|\!\}$ we define operators $id(\cdot) : \{\!|\boldsymbol{\Sigma}|\!\} \to \Xi, (\cdot)(\cdot) : \{\!|\boldsymbol{\Sigma}|\!\} \times Nname \to \boldsymbol{\Sigma}$ and $[\cdot \mid \cdot \mapsto \cdot] : (\{\!|\boldsymbol{\Sigma}|\!\} \times Nname \times \boldsymbol{\Sigma}) \to \{\!|\boldsymbol{\Sigma}|\!\}$ as follows:

$$id(\xi, \varpi) = \xi,$$

$$(\xi, \varpi)(N) = \varpi(N),$$

$$[(\xi, \varpi) \mid N \mapsto \sigma] = (\xi, (\varpi \mid N \mapsto \sigma)).$$

The construction $\{\!|\cdot|\!\}$ was used in [11,13] to design continuation structures for concurrency semantics. In this work, the construction $\{\!|\boldsymbol{\Sigma}|\!\}$ is used to represent (finite) neural configurations. The basic idea is that we treat a pair $(\xi, \varpi) \in \{\!|\boldsymbol{\Sigma}|\!\}$ as a 'function' with finite graph $\{(N, \varpi(N)) \mid N \in \xi\}$, thus ignoring the behaviour of ϖ for any $N \notin \xi$ (ξ is the 'domain' of (ξ, ϖ)). We expect that the number of neurons in a configuration (ξ, ϖ) is fixed, hence the component ξ (representing the 'domain' of the 'function') never changes. Only the states of the neurons contained in such a configuration may change.

We consider $(\gamma \in)\boldsymbol{\Gamma} = \{\!|\boldsymbol{\Sigma}|\!\}$. Let $\gamma = (\xi, \varpi) \in \boldsymbol{\Gamma} = \{\!|\boldsymbol{\Sigma}|\!\}$. The operators behave as follows: $id(\gamma) = id(\xi, \varpi)$ returns the set ξ of neuron names (or neuron identifiers) contained in the configuration γ; $\gamma(N) = (\xi, \varpi)(N)$ returns the state of the neuron with name (identifier) N; $[\gamma \mid N \mapsto \sigma] = [(\xi, \varpi) \mid N \mapsto \sigma]$ updates the state of neuron N (the notation $(\varpi \mid N \mapsto \sigma)$ was introduced in Sect. 2).

Instead of $[[\gamma \mid N_1 \mapsto \sigma_1] \cdots \mid N_i \mapsto \sigma_i]$ we write $[\gamma \mid N_1 \mapsto \sigma_1 \mid \cdots \mid N_i \mapsto \sigma_i]$.

Let $\gamma \in \boldsymbol{\Gamma} = \{\!|\boldsymbol{\Sigma}|\!\}$ be a configuration. If $N \in id(\gamma)$ then $\gamma(N) = \sigma$, where $\sigma \in \boldsymbol{\Sigma} = \mathbf{Open} + \mathbf{Closed}$ represents the state of the neuron with name N. If $\sigma = (\xi, w) \in \mathbf{Open}$ then the neuron is *open*, which means that it accepts spikes; ξ is the set of neuron names adjacent to neuron N in the configuration γ, and w is the multiset of spikes (objects) currently contained by neuron N. If $\sigma = (\xi, w, t, w_r, \varphi) \in \mathbf{Closed}$, then the neuron is *closed*, which means that it does not accept spikes in the next t time units; ξ is the set of neuron names adjacent to neuron N in the configuration γ, w is the multisets of spikes (objects) currently contained by neuron N, w_r is the multiset of objects that remain in the neuron after t time units (when the neuron will produce spikes by executing the computation φ), and φ is a computation that will be executed after t time units.

Definition 10 *(Semantics of parallel composition in continuation semantics).*
We define a semantic operator for parallel composition $\| : (\mathbf{D} \times \mathbf{D}) \xrightarrow{1} \mathbf{D}$ *as follows:*

$$\varphi_1 \parallel \varphi_2 = \lambda\kappa . \lambda\gamma . ((\varphi_1 \, \lfloor \, \varphi_2)(\kappa)(\gamma) \oplus (\varphi_2 \, \lfloor \, \varphi_1)(\kappa)(\gamma)).$$

The operator $\lfloor : (\mathbf{D} \times \mathbf{D}) \overset{1}{\to} \mathbf{D}$ *is defined by*

$$\varphi_1 \lfloor \varphi_2 = \varphi_1 \circ \varphi_2,$$

where $\circ$ *is the function composition operator presented in Sect. 2.*

Remark 11. *It is easy to show that the semantic operator* $\parallel$ *is well-defined and non-expansive in both arguments. Since the function composition is associative, the semantic operator* $\lfloor$ *is also associative. Also, the semantic operators for parallel composition* $\parallel$ *is commutative. Commutativity of* $\parallel$ *follows easily from the symmetry in the definition of* $\parallel$ *(Definition 10) and the fact that the operator for nondeterministic choice* $\oplus$ *is commutative (see Remark 9).*

4.3   Semantics of the $\mathcal{L}_{SNP}$ Statements

Let $(\theta \in)\Theta = \{\mathsf{all}\} \cup \Xi$, and let $(\alpha \in)Alpha = Nname \times \Theta$.
We define an operator $\mathbb{m} : (\Xi \times Alpha) \to Alpha$ as follows:

$$\xi \mathbb{m} (N, \mathsf{all}) = (N, \xi),$$
$$\xi \mathbb{m} (N, \xi') = (N, \xi \cap \xi'),$$

where $\xi \cap \xi'$ is the set theoretic intersection of ξ and ξ'.

Definition 12. *The denotational semantics* $[\![\cdot]\!] : X \to Alpha \to \mathbf{D}$ *of* $\mathcal{L}_{SNP}$ *statements is defined as follows:*

$$[\![a]\!](\alpha) = \lambda\kappa \,.\, \lambda\gamma \,.\, \kappa(send(a, \alpha, \gamma)),$$
$$[\![\,send(y, \xi)\,]\!](\alpha) = [\![y]\!](\xi \mathbb{m} \alpha),$$
$$[\![x_1 \parallel x_2]\!](\alpha) = [\![x_1]\!](\alpha) \parallel [\![x_2]\!](\alpha).$$

The semantic operator for parallel composition $\parallel$ *was presented in Definition 10.*

The auxiliary operator $send : (O \times Alpha \times \Gamma) \to \Gamma$ behaves as follows:

$$
\begin{aligned}
send(a, (N, \mathsf{all}), \gamma) =\ & \text{let } \{N_1, \ldots, N_i\} = nbs(N, \gamma) \\
& \text{in } [\gamma \mid N_1 \mapsto add(a, \gamma(N_1)) \mid \cdots \mid N_i \mapsto add(a, \gamma(N_i))], \\
send(a, (N, \xi), \gamma) =\ & \text{let } \{N_1, \ldots, N_i\} = nbs(N, \gamma) \cap \xi \\
& \text{in } [\gamma \mid N_1 \mapsto add(a, \gamma(N_1)) \mid \cdots \mid N_i \mapsto add(a, \gamma(N_i))].
\end{aligned}
$$

The mappings $nbs : (Nname \times \Gamma) \to \Xi$ and $add : (O \times \Sigma) \to \Sigma$ are given by:

$$
\begin{aligned}
nbs(N, \gamma) =\ & \text{if } \gamma(N) = (\xi, w) \in \mathbf{Open} \text{ then } \xi \\
& \text{else if } \gamma(N) = (\xi, w, t, w_r, \varphi) \in \mathbf{Closed} \text{ then } \xi,
\end{aligned}
$$

$$add(a, (\xi, w)) = (\xi, w \uplus [a]);$$
$$add(a, (\xi, w, t, w_r, \varphi)) = (\xi, w, t, w_r, \varphi).$$

The operator $send(a, (N, \text{all}), \gamma)$ transmits the spike a to all neurons that are adjacent to N. The operator $send(a, (N, \xi), \gamma)$ transmits the spike a to all neurons that are adjacent to N and also have their names in the set ξ. The mapping $nbs(N, \gamma)$ computes the set of neuron names that are adjacent (neighbours) to neuron N in the configuration γ. The mapping $add(a, \sigma)$ adds the spike a to the multiset of spikes contained by a neuron σ (only) if the neuron is open, i.e., if $\sigma \in$ **Open**.

In Proposition 14 we show that continuations can be used to reason in a compositional manner upon the behaviour of SN P systems specified by using the language $\mathcal{L}_{SNP}$. Proposition 14 states that the operator for parallel composition $\|$ is associative and commutative in the language $\mathcal{L}_{SNP}$. In the proof of Proposition 14 we use Lemma 13. We omit here a detailed proof of Lemma 13. It is easy to see that Lemma 13(a) follows from the definition of the operator $send$. The proof of Lemma 13(b) can proceed by structural induction on x in two steps: first for all statements y of type Y, then for all statements x of type X. Lemma 13(c) can be established by induction on the sum of the sizes[3] of the two terms x_1 and x_2 by using Lemmas 13(a) and (b).

Lemma 13. *For any* $a_1, a_2 \in O$, $\alpha, \alpha_1, \alpha_2 \in Alpha$, $\gamma \in \Gamma$, $\kappa_1, \kappa_2 \in \mathbf{K}$ *and* $x, x_1, x_2 \in X$ *we have:*

(a) $send(a_1, \alpha_1, send(a_2, \alpha_2, \gamma)) = send(a_2, \alpha_2, send(a_1, \alpha_1, \gamma));$
(b) $[\![x]\!](\alpha)(\lambda\gamma' . \kappa_1(\gamma') \oplus \kappa_2(\gamma'))(\gamma) = [\![x]\!](\alpha)(\kappa_1)(\gamma) \oplus [\![x]\!](\alpha)(\kappa_1)(\gamma);$
(c) $[\![x_1]\!](\alpha_1) \lfloor [\![x_2]\!](\alpha_2) = [\![x_2]\!](\alpha_2) \lfloor [\![x_1]\!](\alpha_1).$

Proposition 14. *For any* $x_1, x_2, x_3 \in X$ *and* $\alpha_1, \alpha_2 \in Alpha$ *we have:*

(a) $[\![x_1]\!](\alpha_1) \| [\![x_2]\!](\alpha_2) = [\![x_1]\!](\alpha_1) \lfloor [\![x_2]\!](\alpha_2) = [\![x_2]\!](\alpha_2) \lfloor [\![x_1]\!](\alpha_1);$
(b) $[\![x_1 \| x_2]\!] = [\![x_2 \| x_1]\!];$
(c) $[\![x_1 \| (x_2 \| x_3)]\!] = [\![(x_1 \| x_2) \| x_3]\!].$

Proof. Proposition 14(a) is an easy consequence of Lemma 13(c) combined with Remark 9 which states that the semantic operator $\oplus$ for nondeterministic choice is idempotent. Proposition 14(b) follows immediately from Remark 11. For Proposition 14(c) it is enough to show that $[\![x_1 \| (x_2 \| x_3)]\!](\alpha) = [\![(x_1 \| x_2) \| x_3]\!](\alpha)$ for any $\alpha \in Alpha$. Indeed:

---

[3] The size of a term is given by the number of nodes in its abstract syntax tree [21].

$$\llbracket x_1 \parallel (x_2 \parallel x_3) \rrbracket(\alpha)$$
$$= \llbracket x_1 \rrbracket(\alpha) \parallel \llbracket x_2 \parallel x_3 \rrbracket(\alpha) \qquad \text{[Proposition 14(a)]}$$
$$= \llbracket x_1 \rrbracket(\alpha) \lfloor \llbracket x_2 \parallel x_3 \rrbracket(\alpha)$$
$$= \llbracket x_1 \rrbracket(\alpha) \lfloor (\llbracket x_2 \rrbracket(\alpha) \parallel \llbracket x_3 \rrbracket(\alpha)) \qquad \text{[Proposition 14(a)]}$$
$$= \llbracket x_1 \rrbracket(\alpha) \lfloor (\llbracket x_2 \rrbracket(\alpha) \lfloor \llbracket x_3 \rrbracket(\alpha)) \qquad \text{[Remark 11]}$$
$$= (\llbracket x_1 \rrbracket(\alpha) \lfloor \llbracket x_2 \rrbracket(\alpha)) \lfloor \llbracket x_3 \rrbracket(\alpha) \qquad \text{[Proposition 14(a)]}$$
$$= (\llbracket x_1 \rrbracket(\alpha) \parallel \llbracket x_2 \rrbracket(\alpha)) \lfloor \llbracket x_3 \rrbracket(\alpha)$$
$$= \llbracket x_1 \parallel x_2 \rrbracket(\alpha) \lfloor \llbracket x_3 \rrbracket(\alpha) \qquad \text{[Proposition 14(a)]}$$
$$= \llbracket x_1 \parallel x_2 \rrbracket(\alpha) \parallel \llbracket x_3 \rrbracket(\alpha)$$
$$= \llbracket (x_1 \parallel x_2) \parallel x_3 \rrbracket(\alpha).$$

$\square$

4.4 Auxiliary Functions

We define the semantics of $\mathcal{L}_{SNP}$ programs in Sect. 4.5 with the aid of an *initial continuation* κ_0 which is defined as the fixed point of a higher-order mapping $\Psi_{\mathbf{K}}$ [12]. In the definition of $\Psi_{\mathbf{K}}$ we use a scheduler mapping *sched*, and a predicate $halt_{NS}$ which decides whether an execution has reached a halting configuration. The scheduler mapping $sched : (\mathbf{\Gamma} \times NDs) \rightarrow \mathcal{P}_{co}(\mathbf{Den} \times \mathbf{\Gamma})$ takes as arguments a configuration and a list of neuron declarations and yields a compact set of pairs, where each pair consists of a computation ϕ of the type $\mathbf{Den}$ and a corresponding configuration γ of type $\mathbf{\Gamma}$. We recall that $\mathbf{Den} = \{d_0\} + \mathbf{D}$. On $\mathbf{Den}$ we define a parallel composition operator $\parallel : (\mathbf{Den} \times \mathbf{Den}) \xrightarrow{1} \mathbf{Den}$ based on the operator $\parallel$ introduced in Definition 10 as follows:

$$d_0 \parallel d_0 = d_0,$$
$$d_0 \parallel \varphi = \varphi,$$
$$\varphi \parallel d_0 = \varphi,$$
$$\varphi_1 \parallel \varphi_2 = \varphi_1 \parallel \varphi_2.$$

for any $\varphi, \varphi_1, \varphi_2 \in \mathbf{D}$. It is easy to see that the operator $\parallel$ is well-defined and non-expansive. For any $m, n \in \mathbb{N}$, we use the notation $\parallel_{i=n}^{m} \phi_i = d_0$ if $n > m$, and $\parallel_{i=n}^{m} \phi_i = \phi_n \parallel (\parallel_{i=n+1}^{m} \phi_i)$, if $n \leq m$.
  We define the scheduler mapping $sched : (\mathbf{\Gamma} \times NDs) \rightarrow \mathcal{P}_{co}(\mathbf{Den} \times \mathbf{\Gamma})$ by:

$$sched(\gamma, D) = \text{let } \{N_0, \ldots, N_m\} = id(\gamma)$$
$$\text{in } \{(\parallel_{i=0}^{m} \phi_i, [\gamma \mid N_0 \mapsto \sigma_0 \mid \cdots \mid N_m \mapsto \sigma_m])$$
$$\mid (\phi_0, \sigma_0) \in schedN(N_0, \gamma(N_0), D), \ldots,$$
$$(\phi_m, \sigma_m) \in schedN(N_m, \gamma(N_m), D)\}.$$

The mapping *sched* defines the behaviour of a configuration of neurons assuming a global clock which measures the delays associated to spiking rules. It models an SN P system of (concurrent) neurons which work synchronously.

The behaviour at the level of each neuron is defined with the aid of the function $schedN : (Nname \times \Sigma \times NDs) \rightarrow \mathcal{P}_{co}(\mathbf{Den} \times \Sigma)$. The predicate $halt_N$ used in the definition of $schedN$ is introduced below.

$$
\begin{aligned}
schedN&(N, (\xi, w), D) = \\
&\text{if } halt_N(N, (\xi, w), D) \text{ then } \{(d_0, (\xi, w))\} \\
&\text{else} \ \ \text{let } r = rules(D, N) \\
&\quad \text{in } \{(\llbracket x \rrbracket(N, \mathsf{all}), (\xi, w \setminus w_r)) \\
&\qquad \mid (E/w_r \rightarrow x; t) \in r, w \in L(E), w_r \subseteq w, t = 0\} \cup \\
&\qquad \{(d_0, (\xi, w, t - 1, w \setminus w_r, \llbracket x \rrbracket(N, \mathsf{all}))) \\
&\qquad \mid (E/w_r \rightarrow x; t) \in r, w \in L(E), w_r \subseteq w, t > 0\} \cup \\
&\qquad \{(d_0, (\xi, [\,])) \mid (w_r \rightarrow \lambda) \in r, w_r = w\}; \\
schedN&(N, (\xi, w, t, w_r, \varphi), D) = \\
&\text{if } t = 0 \text{ then } \{(\varphi, (\xi, w_r))\} \text{ else } \{(d_0, (\xi, w, t - 1, w_r, \varphi))\}.
\end{aligned}
$$

Remark 15. *The mapping schedN always yields a finite (hence a compact) set, because any list of rules $r \in Rs$ is finite. As $schedN(N, \sigma, D)$ yields a finite set for any $N \in Nname, \sigma \in \Sigma$ and $D \in NDs$ and the set $id(\gamma)$ is always finite, it follows that the mapping $sched(\gamma, D)$ also yields a finite set for any configuration $\gamma \in \Gamma$ and list of neuron declarations D. Since any finite set is compact [6], the scheduler mapping sched is well-defined.*

The predicate $halt_{NS} : (\Gamma \times NDs) \rightarrow Bool$ decides whether an execution has reached a halting configuration; the decision is taken for a configuration $\gamma \in \Gamma$ with respect to a list of neuron declarations $D \in NDs$. We recall that a configuration $\gamma \in \Gamma$ contains a collection of neurons.

$$
\begin{aligned}
halt_{NS}(\gamma, D) = halt_N(N_0, \gamma(N_0), D) \wedge \cdots \wedge halt_N(N_m, \gamma(N_m), D) \\
\text{where } \{N_0, \ldots, N_m\} = id(\gamma).
\end{aligned}
$$

The predicate $halt_N : (Nname \times \Sigma \times NDs) \rightarrow Bool$ verifies the halting condition for a single neuron:

$$
\begin{aligned}
halt_N(N, (\xi, w), D) = (\neg (appR(\varrho_1, w))) \wedge \cdots \wedge (\neg (appR(\varrho_i, w))) \\
\text{where } \varrho_1, \ldots, \varrho_i = rules(D, N); \\
halt_N(N, (\xi, w, t, w_r, \varphi), D) = \mathsf{false}.
\end{aligned}
$$

The predicate $appR : (R \times W) \rightarrow Bool$ verifies whether a rule $\varrho \in R$ can be applied upon a multiset of spikes (objects) $w \in W$:

$$
\begin{aligned}
appR(E/w_r \rightarrow x; t, w) = (w \in L(E)); \\
appR(w_r \rightarrow \lambda, w) = (w = w_r).
\end{aligned}
$$

The mapping $rules : (NDs, Nname) \rightarrow Rs$ returns the list of rules corresponding to a neuron name N in a list of neuron declarations:

$$rules(\ldots, \text{ neuron } N \{ r \mid \xi \}, \ldots, N) = r.$$

4.5   Semantics of the $\mathcal{L}_{SNP}$ Programs

We define the semantics of an $\mathcal{L}_{SNP}$ program with respect to an initial continuation $\kappa_0 \in \mathbf{K}$ by using an appropriate fixed point construction. Definition 16 is justified by Lemma 17 and Banach's Theorem. The mappings $halt_{NS}$ and $sched$ were presented in Sect. 4.4.

The set Ω of observables does not contain time information. Time is implicit in our model. The functioning of an SN P system is synchronized. A global clock is assumed. The value of the clock is given by the number of steps in each execution trace. Each execution trace is a sequence of observables of type $\mathbf{Q}$ ($\mathbf{Q}$ is defined in Sect. 4.1). The mapping $to_\Omega : \Gamma \rightarrow \Omega$ extracts from a configuration $\gamma \in \Gamma$ the information that is produced as an observable value of type Ω.

$$to_\Omega(\gamma) = \{(N, aux(\gamma(N))) \mid N \in id(\gamma)\}$$
$$\text{where } \quad aux : \Sigma \rightarrow W$$
$$aux(\xi, w) = w$$
$$aux(\xi, w, t, w_r, \varphi) = w$$

Definition 16. *Let* $\Psi_{\mathbf{K}} : NDs \rightarrow \mathbf{K} \rightarrow \mathbf{K}$ *be given by*

$$\Psi_{\mathbf{K}}(D)(\kappa)(\gamma) =$$
$$to_\Omega(\gamma) \cdot (\text{ if } halt_{NS}(\gamma, D) \text{ then } \{\epsilon\}$$
$$\text{else } \bigoplus\{\varphi(\kappa)(\gamma') \mid (\varphi, \gamma') \in sched(\gamma, D)\} \oplus$$
$$\bigoplus\{\kappa(\gamma') \mid (d_0, \gamma') \in sched(\gamma, D)\}).$$

For any $D \in NDs$, *we define the* initial continuation $\kappa_0 \in \mathbf{K}$ *by* $\kappa_0 = $ fix$(\Psi_{\mathbf{K}}(D))$. *Also, we define the* initial configuration $\gamma_0 \in \Gamma$ *by* $\gamma_0 = init_\Gamma(D)$, *where* $init_\Gamma : NDs \rightarrow \Gamma$ *is given by:*

$$init_\Gamma(\text{ neuron } N_0 \{ r_0 \mid \xi_0 \}, \ldots, \text{ neuron } N_m \{ r_m \mid \xi_m \}) =$$
$$(\{N_0, \ldots, N_m\}, [\lambda N . (\emptyset, [\ ]) \mid N_0 \mapsto (\xi_0, [\ ]) \mid \cdots \mid N_m \mapsto (\xi_m, [\ ])]).$$

The scheduler function $sched$ yields a finite set of computations (Remark 15). Thus, $\Psi_{\mathbf{K}}$ is defined as a finite union of $\mathbf{P}$ compact sets[4]. A finite union of compact sets is always compact. More generally, a compact union of compact sets is also a compact set [6], hence $\Psi_{\mathbf{K}}$ is well-defined. Lemma 17 states that the higher-order mapping $\Psi_{\mathbf{K}}(D)$ is a contraction for any $D \in NDs$; in particular, $\Psi_{\mathbf{K}}(D)$ is a contraction due to the "$to_\Omega(\gamma)$"-step in its definition.

---

[4] $\oplus$ is defined based on the set union operator $\cup$.

Lemma 17. $\Psi_{\mathbf{K}}(D) \in \mathbf{K} \xrightarrow{\frac{1}{2}} \mathbf{K}$ *for any $D \in MDs$.*

Definition 18 *(Semantics of $\mathcal{L}_{SNP}$ programs). We define $\mathcal{D}[\![\cdot]\!] : \mathcal{L}_{SNP} \to \mathbf{P}$ for any $\rho = (D, x) \in \mathcal{L}_{SNP}$ by*

$$\mathcal{D}[\![\rho]\!] = \mathcal{D}[\![D, x]\!] = [\![x]\!](\alpha_0)(\kappa_0)(\gamma_0),$$

where $\alpha_0 = (N_0, \mathsf{all})$, $\gamma_o = init_{\Gamma}(D)$, $\kappa_0 = fix(\Psi_{\mathbf{K}}(D))$, and $\Psi_{\mathbf{K}}$ is as in Definition 16.

Example 19. *Let $\rho_1 = (D_1, x_1)$ and $\rho_1' = (D_1', x_1')$ be the $\mathcal{L}_{SNP}$ programs presented in Sect. 3.1. The statements $x_1, x_1' \in X$ are identical:*

$$x_1 = x_1' = \mathsf{send}(\langle a^{2k-1} \rangle, \{N_1\}) \parallel \mathsf{send}(a, \{N_3\})$$

and the declarations $D_1, D_1' \in NDs$ are given by:

$$
\begin{aligned}
D_1 \;=\; & \mathsf{neuron}\, N_0 \,\{\, r_\epsilon \mid \{N_1, N_2, N_3\} \,\}, \\
& \mathsf{neuron}\, N_1 \,\{\, a^+/[a] \to a; 2 \mid \{N_2\} \,\}, \\
& \mathsf{neuron}\, N_2 \,\{\, [a^k] \to a; 1 \mid \{N_3\} \,\}, \\
& \mathsf{neuron}\, N_3 \,\{\, [a] \to a; 0 \mid \{N_0\} \,\} \\
D_1' \;=\; & \mathsf{neuron}\, N_0 \,\{\, r_\epsilon \mid \{N_1, N_2, N_3\} \,\}, \\
& \mathsf{neuron}\, N_1 \,\{\, a^+/[a] \to \mathsf{send}(a, \{N_2\}); 2 \mid \{N_1, N_2, N_3\} \,\}, \\
& \mathsf{neuron}\, N_2 \,\{\, [a^k] \to \mathsf{send}(a, \{N_3\}); 1 \mid \{N_1, N_2, N_3\} \,\}, \\
& \mathsf{neuron}\, N_3 \,\{\, [a] \to a; 0 \mid \{N_0\} \,\}
\end{aligned}
$$

In the executions of ρ_1 and ρ_1' given below, we take $k = 2$. We put:

$$
\begin{aligned}
\omega_1 &= (N_0, [\,]), (N_1, [a, a, a]), (N_2, [\,]), (N_3, [a]), \\
\omega_2 &= (N_0, [a]), (N_1, [a, a, a]), (N_2, [\,]), (N_3, [\,]), \\
\omega_3 &= (N_0, [a]), (N_1, [a, a, a]), (N_2, [\,]), (N_3, [\,]), \\
\omega_4 &= (N_0, [a]), (N_1, [a, a]), (N_2, [a]), (N_3, [\,]), \\
\omega_5 &= (N_0, [a]), (N_1, [a, a]), (N_2, [a]), (N_3, [\,]), \\
\omega_6 &= (N_0, [a]), (N_1, [a, a]), (N_2, [a]), (N_3, [\,]), \\
\omega_7 &= (N_0, [a]), (N_1, [a]), (N_2, [a, a]), (N_3, [\,]), \\
\omega_8 &= (N_0, [a]), (N_1, [a]), (N_2, [a, a]), (N_3, [\,]), \\
\omega_9 &= (N_0, [a, a]), (N_1, [a]), (N_2, [\,]), (N_3, [a]), \\
\omega_{10} &= (N_0, [\,]), (N_1, [\,]), (N_2, [a]), (N_3, [\,]).
\end{aligned}
$$

Let $\alpha_0 = (N_0, \mathsf{all})$, $\kappa_0 = \mathsf{fix}(\Psi_{\mathbf{K}}(D_1))$ and $\gamma_0 = init_{\Gamma}(D_1)$. One can check that

$$\mathcal{D}[\![\rho_1]\!] = [\![x_1]\!](\alpha_0)(\kappa_0)(\gamma_0) = \{\omega_1 \omega_2 \omega_3 \omega_4 \omega_5 \omega_6 \omega_7 \omega_8 \omega_9 \omega_{10}\}.$$

As it can be seen from this execution of $\mathcal{L}_{SNP}$ program ρ_1, the number of steps elapsed between the first spike and the second spike produced by neuron N_3 is $8 = 3k+2$ (when $k = 2$). This number $(3k+2)$ is the result of the computation, which coincides with the result produced by the SN P system Π_1 described in [14].

Since $\mathcal{D}[\![\rho_1']\!] = [\![x_1']\!](\alpha_0)(\kappa_0')(\gamma_0')$, where $\kappa_0' = \mathsf{fix}(\Psi_{\mathbf{K}}(D_1'))$ and $\gamma_0' = \mathsf{init}_{\boldsymbol{\Gamma}}(D_1')$, one can check that

$$\mathcal{D}[\![\rho_1']\!] = \{\omega_1\omega_2\omega_3\omega_4\omega_5\omega_6\omega_7\omega_8\omega_9\omega_{10}\},$$

and so $\mathcal{D}[\![\rho_1]\!] = \mathcal{D}[\![\rho_1']\!]$, as expected.

In Example 19 the results of the denotational semantics are (singleton) sets containing exactly one (finite) execution trace. The programs ρ_1 and ρ_1' are deterministic. This is a particular case. In general, the yield of the denotational semantics is a non-empty and compact collection of execution traces.

The calculations required in Example 19 and other $\mathcal{L}_{SNP}$ examples could be laborious. However, the results can be verified by using the Haskell implementation available at [24]. The semantic interpreter can be used to run various $\mathcal{L}_{SNP}$ programs, including (Haskell implementations of) the $\mathcal{L}_{SNP}$ programs ρ_1 and ρ_1' presented in Sect. 3 and Example 19. In addition, the semantic interpreter includes a Haskell implementation of the SN P system Π_3 presented in [14] on p. 11 (Fig. 4). This SN P system Π_3 is nondeterministic; in this case our denotational semantics yields a non-empty and compact collection of execution traces.

The Haskell semantic interpreter of $\mathcal{L}_{SNP}$ is available at [24] in two variants: `Lsnp.hs` and `Lsnp-fin.hs`. The semantic interpreter available in the file `Lsnp.hs` implements accurately the denotational (mathematical) semantics presented in this paper, but can only be used to run toy $\mathcal{L}_{SNP}$ programs like ρ_1 and ρ_1'. For a nondeterministic program, our semantic interpreters try to produce all possible execution traces (even if the number of execution traces is infinite). The semantic interpreter available in the file `Lsnp-fin.hs` stops the execution of $\mathcal{L}_{SNP}$ programs after a given number of steps (accepted as an argument by the semantic interpreter), hence it can be used to simulate and analyze the execution of arbitrary $\mathcal{L}_{SNP}$ programs, including nondeterministic and nonterminating programs. The semantic interpreter `Lsnp-fin.hs` prunes the collection of execution traces, preserving only a finite prefix for each execution trace. The semantic interpreter `Lsnp-fin.hs` can be used to simulate and analyze the execution of the SN P system Π_3 presented in [14] (p. 11, Fig. 4), which is designed to generate all natural numbers greater than 1 in a nondeterministic manner.

5   Conclusion

This article presents a metric denotational semantics for an experimental concurrent language $\mathcal{L}_{SNP}$ inspired by the spiking neural P systems. The language $\mathcal{L}_{SNP}$ provides constructions for specifying the neurons, the synapses and the rules that define a spiking neural P system. The denotational semantics is designed by using continuations and metric spaces. It describes faithfully the time delays, the nondeterministic behaviour and the synchronized functioning that are specific to the spiking neural P system.

Based on this semantics, an implementation in the functional language Haskell is derived. The implementation is useful to simulate, test and evaluate various spiking neural P systems, and this is illustrated by examples.

A stochastic version of the spiking neural P systems is presented in [3], where these stochastic systems are also translated into a network of timed automata. This translation allows the verification of several (qualitative and quantitative) properties of stochastic spiking neural P systems by using the statistical model checking UPPAAL. A different attempt of describing complex neural systems by using stochastic spiking neural P systems is given in [8].

References

1. Alexandru, A., Ciobanu, G.: Mathematics of multisets in the Fraenkel-Mostowski framework. Bull. Math. Soc. Sci. Math. Roumanie **58**(106), 3–18 (2015)
2. Alhazov, A., Freund, R., Oswald, M., Slavkovik, M.: Extended spiking neural P systems. In: Hoogeboom, H.J., Păun, G., Rozenberg, G., Salomaa, A. (eds.) WMC 2006. LNCS, vol. 4361, pp. 123–134. Springer, Heidelberg (2006). https://doi.org/10.1007/11963516_8
3. Aman, B., Ciobanu, G.: Automated verification of stochastic spiking neural P systems. In: Rozenberg, G., Salomaa, A., Sempere, J.M., Zandron, C. (eds.) CMC 2015. LNCS, vol. 9504, pp. 77–91. Springer, Cham (2015). https://doi.org/10.1007/978-3-319-28475-0_6
4. America, P., Rutten, J.J.M.M.: Solving reflexive domain equations in a category of complete metric spaces. J. Comput. Syst. Sci. **39**, 343–375 (1989)
5. Appel, A.W.: Compiling with Continuations. Cambridge University Press, Cambridge (2007)
6. de Bakker, J.W., de Vink, E.P.: Control Flow Semantics. MIT Press, Cambridge (1996)
7. Barendregt, H.P.: The Lambda Calculus, Its Syntax and Semantics. Elsevier, Amsterdam (1984)
8. Cavaliere, M., Mura, I.: Experiments on the reliability of stochastic spiking neural P systems. Nat. Comput. **7**, 453–470 (2008)
9. Chen, H., Ionescu, M., Isidorj, T.O., Păun, A., Păun, Gh., Pérez-Jiménez, M.J.: Spiking neural P systems with extended rules: universality and languages. Nat. Comput. **7**, 147–166 (2008)
10. Ciobanu, G.: Semantics of the P systems. In: Handbook of Membrane Computing, pp. 413–436. Oxford University Press (2010)
11. Ciobanu, G., Todoran, E.N.: Continuation semantics for asynchronous concurrency. Fundam. Inform. **131**(3–4), 373–388 (2014)
12. Ciobanu, G., Todoran, E.N.: Continuation passing semantics for membrane systems. In: Leporati, A., Rozenberg, G., Salomaa, A., Zandron, C. (eds.) CMC 2016. LNCS, vol. 10105, pp. 165–176. Springer, Cham (2017). https://doi.org/10.1007/978-3-319-54072-6_11
13. Ciobanu, G., Todoran, E.N.: Denotational semantics of membrane systems by using complete metric spaces. Theor. Comput. Sci. **701**, 85–108 (2017)
14. Ionescu, M., Păun, Gh., Yokomori, T.: Spiking neural P systems. Fundam. Inform. **71**, 279–308 (2006)

15. Ionescu, M., Păun, Gh., Pérez-Jiménez, M.J., Rodriguez-Patón, A.: Spiking neural P systems with several types of spikes. Int. J. Comput. Commun. Control **6**, 647–655 (2011)

16. Ishdorj, T.O., Leporati, A.: Uniform solutions to SAT and 3-SAT by spiking neural P systems with pre-computed resources. Nat. Comput. **7**, 519–534 (2008)

17. Jech, T.: Set Theory. Springer, Heidelberg (2002)

18. Leporati, A., Zandron, C., Ferretti, C., Mauri, G.: On the computational power of spiking neural P systems. Int. J. Unconv. Comput. **5**, 459–473 (2009)

19. Păun, Gh.: Membrane Computing: An Introduction. Springer, Heidelberg (2002). https://doi.org/10.1007/3-540-44761-X

20. Jones, S.P., Hughes, J. (eds.): Report on the Programming Language Haskell 98: A Non-Strict Purely Functional Language (1999). http://www.haskell.org

21. Pierce, B.: Types and Programming Languages. MIT Press, Cambridge (2002)

22. Rozenberg, G., Salomaa, A. (eds.): Handbook of Formal Languages, vol. 3. Springer, Heidelberg (1998)

23. Todoran, E.N.: Metric semantics for synchronous and asynchronous communication: a continuation-based approach. Electron. Notes Theor. Comput. Sci. **28**, 101–127 (2000)

24. WWW: Haskell implementation of the denotational semantics presented in this paper (2018). http://ftp.utcluj.ro/pub/users/gc/eneia/cmc19

Towards Automated Analysis of Belousov-Zhabotinsky Reactions in a Petri Dish by Membrane Computing Using Optic Flow

Benjamin Förster[1] and Thomas Hinze[2]([⊠])

[1] Institute of Computer Science, Brandenburg University of Technology,
Cottbus, Germany
benjamin.foerster@b-tu.de
[2] Department of Bioinformatics, Friedrich Schiller University Jena, Jena, Germany
thomas.hinze@uni-jena.de

Abstract. Belousov-Zhabotinsky (BZ) reactions exhibit spiking oscillations over time and in space. Treated as an *in-vitro* model system for chemical transmission of information via frequency encoding, they came into the focus of systems biology. Conducted in a Petri dish, monitoring of BZ reactions induces comprehensive video material and image sequences that need to be analysed in order to understand the reaction scheme and its parameters including side effects in detail. Aimed by the objective to relieve the biologist from this dreary task, we present a method to automate the identification and localisation of BZ oscillatory spots in a Petri dish by means of *optic flow*. As defined by Horn and Schunck, optic flow is the distribution of apparent movement velocities of brightness patterns in an image sequence. We extend the standard algorithm and adjust its parameters to make it applicable for automated analysis of BZ reactions in terms of membrane computing as molecular information processing units in space. Our approach introduces methods to cope with perturbations like different kinds of noise typically occurring by undesired alterations within brightness patterns caused by environmental influences and interference of different oscillatory spots. Current work in progress addresses estimation of propagation velocities for expanding concentric rings of each spot.

1 Relevance of BZ-Like Reactions in Cells and Organisms

Spiking oscillations turn out to be a highly energy-efficient medium of biological signal transduction by frequency encoding. Here, the information is expressed by the number and periodicity of spikes which assures an outstanding robustness against environmental perturbations and weakening of the signal when spreading out in space. *Calcium oscillations* for intracellular signal propagation, *ion channels* as sensors, and the function of *neurotransmitters* for information exchange across neurons represent three prominent examples for utilisation of spiking oscillations responsible for a multiplicity of signalling processes in living organisms

© Springer Nature Switzerland AG 2019
T. Hinze et al. (Eds.): CMC 2018, LNCS 11399, pp. 131–141, 2019.
https://doi.org/10.1007/978-3-030-12797-8_10

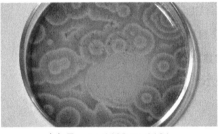
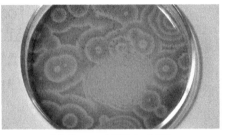

(a) Frame 1100 to 1101   (b) Frame 1200 to 1201

Fig. 1. Images of the frames 1100 and 1200 recording the BZ reactions obtained from Petri dish out of a video sequence from https://www.youtube.com/watch? v=jRQAndvF4sM. All further images provided in this paper refer to these frames and their follow-ups 1101 and 1201.

[1,7]. Chemical reaction systems for generation of spiking oscillations have in common a positive feedback loop by autocatalysis. The *Brusselator* emerged as an abstract metamodel for corresponding systems [8]. Its *in-vitro* implementation can be done by the dissipative Belousov-Zhabotinsky scheme within a Petri dish in which a ferroin indicator makes visible expanding concentric rings surrounding an oscillatory spot [15].

Treated as an experimental model system for spiking oscillations in space, a huge amount of video data and image sequences exist monitoring the spatiotemporal behaviour of BZ systems in practice. In order to learn about fine tuning of the reactions and adjustment of parameters for obtaining a certain oscillation period and for achievement of a uniform propagation of the waves into the environmental space out of a spot, underlying image data have to be analysed. This is an application of membrane computing since coloured pixels in an image sequence act as particles moving inside regions of a two-dimensional space and able to interfere with each other. Following this line, we make accessible the methodology of *optic flow* for membrane computing by automated identification and localisation of BZ oscillatory spots and further analysis techniques based on image sequences explained and demonstrated throughout the next sections.

2   Introduction to Motion Segmentation

The goal of motion segmentation is to separate different motions in an image sequence and assign them to a source or an object. Depending on the method used we are able to achieve different results. The simplest method to determine motion in a scene is to take the difference between brightness intensities of two subsequent images of a sequence. Everything not equal zero will then be interpreted as motion. Methods of this kind are often very sensitive to noise, camera movements (which creates motion everywhere in a scene) and different kinds of rotations. Exclusively by consideration of differences between brightness intensities throughout the underlying images, it is only possible to determine motion of rigid bodies. In case we try to compute a motion vector field representing the motion of objects composed of pixels we can expect very erroneous results, so these methods are often only used to receive a yes-or-no answer to the overall presence of motion and its localisation within a scene. For example, this can be employed for compression of movies by saving motionless areas of scenes just once.

For motion segmentation, there exist also methods that need a prepared fore-ground and background distinction. They can determine rotations and deforma-tions until some degree but these methods are still not able to handle scenes without a background or with motion everywhere. In this paper, we will focus on optic flow which is another approach to motion segmentation. This app-roach was first observed and analysed by the psychologist Gibson in the 1940s [3]. In 1981 the first mathematical approaches in optic flow appeared by Horn and Schunck [5] and Lucas and Kanade [9] which still enjoy great relevance in research nowadays.

The proposed methods result in a *vector field* determining the motion for every pixel in an image sequence separately by considering a motion pattern. Both methods are robust to noise up to a certain degree, able to handle a mobile scene and capable of coping with rotations. They expect the brightness inten-sities and therefore the resulting brightness patterns in each scene to be nearly constant from one frame to a follow up frame. This leads to difficulties when using optic flow in an open environment which undergoes changes of brightness intensities or incorporates reflecting surfaces. The property of optic flow com-putation separately for each pixel is a great advantage because it allows to deal with non-rigid body motions.

3   Brightness Constancy Equation

Optic flow methods [5,9] map the location of each pixel in one frame to a pixel in a successor frame by comparing their brightness intensities E expressed by real-valued numbers and considering a surrounding intensity pattern. As the brightness constancy assumption proposes, for small enough motions there is a pixel in the frame under study which matches exactly with a pixel from the predecessor frame. Coloured pixels need to be mapped into their grey scale value relatively to each other. Formally, the brightness constancy assumption reads:

$$E(x(t), y(t), t) = E(x(t) + \Delta x, y(t) + \Delta y, t + \Delta t) \tag{1}$$

The brightness constancy assumption implies that brightness intensities do not significantly change within a small environment of an arbitrary pixel during a short period of time whereas the shifts in space Δx, Δy as well as the shift in time Δt might be chosen infinitesimally small. Due to the limits of real discrete data, the computation will be done by using numerical approximations.

There are also experiments using different colour channels which represent brightness intensities instead of grey scaled images but they could not justify

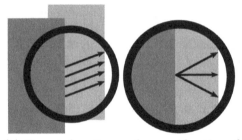

(a) Expected motion when considering the brightness intensities of pixels separately.

(b) Expected motion under consideration of intensities of neighbouring pixels. First observed by Hans Wallach as barberpole illusion.

Fig. 2. An example for the aperture problem which was first observed by Wallach [12] in 1935 as barberpole illusion. The circle points out your local vision. The underlying motion might follow different directions as exemplified in part (b).

the much higher computation effort by marginally better results or even no improvements.

Because we expect each point in a pattern to have constant brightness intensity it follows with the total derivation dE

$$E_x \frac{\delta x}{\delta t} + E_y \frac{\delta y}{\delta t} + E_t = E_x \cdot v_x + E_y \cdot v_y + E_t = 0 \tag{2}$$

The velocities v_x and v_y in x and y direction are two unknowns. There are different methods to solve this equation. One simple method was proposed by several researchers nearly simultaneously. One of the earliest practicable proposals was made by Horn et al. [6] and improved shortly afterwards by Silva et al. [11]. These proposals based on normal flow to compute the motion vector field take into account only the brightness constancy equation. These methods do not utilise a brightness pattern or neighbouring pixels for motion estimation and are therefore called egomotion methods.

To get more precise results it is necessary to analyse the motion of the neighbouring pixels which will lead to optic flow methods. Therefore let us first incorporate a motion analysis of neighbouring pixels to determine the optic flow more precisely.

4   Smoothness Constraint

The problem which occurs by using only the brightness constancy equation once per observed pixel motion was already observed by Wallach [12] in 1935. It was called barberpole illusion by him and it is nowadays known as the aperture problem. Figure 2a and b give an example.

To solve the aperture problem, there have been a lot of attempts since 1981. Horn and Schunck [5] and Lucas and Kanade [9] proposed almost simultaneously a method in 1981. Horn and Schunck computed the optic flow globally by trying to minimise the variations of the velocities of the surrounding brightness intensities whereas Lucas and Kanade suggested a local approach in which the optic flow will be computed by solving an overdetermined equation system of the brightness constancy equations of the neighbouring points. The overdetermined linear equation system will be solved using the least square method. Nowadays exist a lot of promising approaches. Examples are improvements to the weighting of the constraints, the addition of edge detection, neural networks, and deep learning or the use of complex weighting matrices as well as further specific methods mostly applied to small groups of motion problems.

One constraint introduced by Horn and Schunck in 1981, is called the smoothness constraint and it penalises the variation of velocities in a surrounding pattern of a pixel. It is expected that the variation between two frames is extremely small.

$$\mathcal{E}^2_{smooth} = (\nabla^2 v_x)^2 + (\nabla^2 v_y)^2 = (\frac{\delta^2 v_x}{\delta x} + \frac{\delta^2 v_x}{\delta y})^2 + (\frac{\delta^2 v_y}{\delta x} + \frac{\delta^2 v_y}{\delta y})^2 \quad (3)$$

5 Minimisation of the Error

Having constraint (3) at hand, we are able to estimate the total error which is the sum of the squares of the error of the brightness constancy Eq. (2) and smoothness constraint (3) combined with a factor α to adjust the weighting of both constraints.

$$\mathcal{E}^2 = (E_x \cdot v_x + E_y \cdot v_y + E_t)^2 + \alpha^2 \mathcal{E}^2_{smooth} \quad (4)$$

This error can be minimised using the Euler-Lagrange equation.

$$\mathcal{E}_{HS} = \int \int (E_x \cdot v_x + E_y \cdot v_y + E_t)^2 + \alpha^2 \mathcal{E}^2_{smooth} \, dx \, dy \quad (5)$$

Along with suitable numerical approximations for constraints (3) and (5) and by means of further simplifications, we end up in a linear equation system which can be solved using fixed-point iterations like Gauss-Seidel or using the Jacobi method. In order to obtain one or more vector fields representing the motion of a given video sequence, we have to determine the velocities v_x and v_y of each pixel in a pair of two or more consecutive frames by solving the Euler-Lagrange Eq. (5). Then, velocities in x and y direction yield the resulting vector at this point in the frame. Let us assume that each frame is composed of m pixels in x direction and n pixels in y direction, respectively. For each coordinate (x_i, y_j) with $i = 1, \ldots, m$ and $j = 1, \ldots, n$, we obtain corresponding velocities subsumed by matrices $\vec{V}_x$ and $\vec{V}_y$ representing the vector field $\vec{V}_{m,n} = (\vec{V}_x, \vec{V}_y)$ of optic flow.

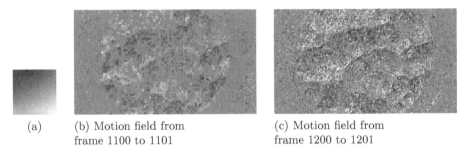

| (a) | (b) Motion field from frame 1100 to 1101 | (c) Motion field from frame 1200 to 1201 |

Fig. 3. Resulting optic flow vector fields have been computed using Horn and Schunck's approach [5]. Magnitudes of the vectors were scaled by a factor of 100 and motions greater than five pixels have been cropped. The motion vectors are encoded using colours represented in part (a) where the centre is grey (RGB hex value #808080) which represents a vector with magnitude of zero. Any colour different from grey represents a relative motion in the direction of this colour. (Color figure online)

Nowadays, the constraints for optic flow computation with Horn and Schunck have been weighted in an alternative way in order to achieve slightly better results. In [13,14] and additional recent papers, the constraints are not weighted quadratically like in Eq. (5) but instead, a certain function called TV-L1 is applied. TV is the total variation regularisation of the flow field and L1 (also called Manhattan norm) is the norm that replaces the quadratic weighting of the terms. These changes preserve discontinuities and add robustness against noise, illumination changes, and occlusions.

The optic flow approach by Horn and Schunck is well suited for BZ-like reactions because of smooth transitions between concentric rings caused by different oscillatory spots. It is able to correct errors of the brightness constancy equation by considering the surrounding motion pattern and due to the weighting factor α able to be determined. The method is robust against a certain degree of noise which also holds for reflections.

6   Optic Flow Results

We used several optic flow methods to determine the motion field of the recorded BZ reaction: Two aforementioned methods by Horn and Schunck [5] (global method) and Lucas and Kanade [9] (local method) as well as an approach by Nagel [10] to improve Horn and Schunck's method by using a weighting matrix. The only optic flow results we succeeded in reliable gaining and for which we were able to determine a decent result with some post processing were the ones computed with the algorithm by Horn and Schunck. Two results are depicted in Fig. 3. As mentioned in its caption, it was only possible to visualise the vector fields accepting a tremendous loss of information. So, the images are sufficient for demonstration but improper for direct identification and localisation of oscillatory spots. The results are still erroneous and we were unable to detect motion at

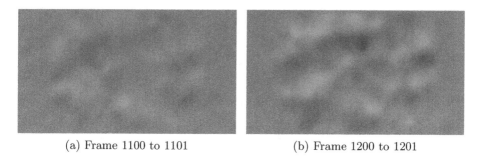

(a) Frame 1100 to 1101   (b) Frame 1200 to 1201

Fig. 4. Optic flow field after 1000 applications of our smoothing filter defined in Sect. 8. For better visibility, the optic flow is again scaled by a factor of 100 and motions larger than 5 pixels are cropped.

some points inside the frames. In the next two sections, we introduce an attempt to fix these problems and to precisely determine vector fields yielding the exact motion (Fig. 4).

7   The Prerequisite of Noise Reduction

Optic flow facilitates detection of pixel motion across an image sequence by measurement of the direction and magnitude of motion based on the intensity of pixels. Since we have to cope with significant variations in that, we first convert the image sequences of BZ reactions in a Petri dish into a grey scaled format. In addition, sequences might contain homogeneous areas which are equally coloured and contain much noise which is caused by interferences of expanding concentric rings that are in superposition and create differing specular artifacts. Another obstacle towards reliable identification of sources consists in some vectors pointing into inappropriate directions. This error emerges since the area covered by a ring increases during expansion. Most optic flow methods are unable to map the increased number of pixels to their origin. Our evaluations have shown that Horn and Schunck is best-suited to determine the motion vector field. The algorithm takes into account the complete surrounding instead of just a small neighbourhood when evaluating the motion in a point and its smoothed transitions between motions into various directions. Due to the nature of BZ reactions, there is no clear spatial separation of intersecting oscillatory spots. In case of this scenario, the oscillatory spots get delimited in a way that they remain disjoint to each other. This strategy coincides with the characteristics of the Horn and Schunck algorithm. Noise caused by interferences is also partially reduced. Although sufficient in most case studies, there is still a need to eliminate further forms of unusual noise and improperly aligned vectors before sinks and sources can be detected without any errors. In Fig. 5, the leftmost images are divergence fields computed directly on the optic flow without applying any post-processing to the images. Therefore, we introduce in the next section a smoothing method improving the quality of the vector field. This allows us to identify the true motions by means of a dense motion field. Based on that, the positions of oscillatory spots can be reliably and precisely localised.

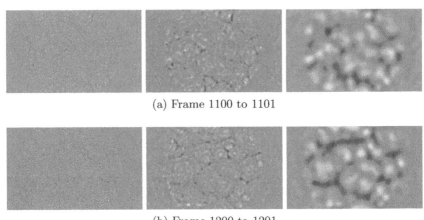

(a) Frame 1100 to 1101

(b) Frame 1200 to 1201

Fig. 5. The two leftmost images represent a divergence field computed on the raw optic flow results. The two images in the central part show the divergence field after 100 applications of our smoothing filter and the two rightmost images represent optic flow after 1000 applications of the filter. The bright yellow spots in the images indicate sources (positive scalars) whereas the blueish spots show sinks (negative scalars). The sources coincide with the locations of the oscillatory spots in the video. (Color figure online)

8   Determining the Oscillatory Spots

The *divergence* of a vector field reveals whether it contains sinks or sources and the position of those spots. A positive divergence in a point represents a source and a negative value a sink. Points in which the scalar field is zero are neither source nor sink. A source stands for an oscillatory spot because the expanding concentric rings imply a vector field directed outwards from its initial spot. Sinks can appear between oscillatory spots due to clashing concentric rings from different spots. Sinks are helpful to separate various sources since they are localised between sources. The divergence of a two-dimensional vector field

$$\vec{V}_{m,n} = (\vec{V}_x, \vec{V}_y) \tag{6}$$

with the components given as follows

$$\vec{V}_x \colon \mathbb{R}^{m \times n} \mapsto \mathbb{R} \text{ and } \vec{V}_y \colon \mathbb{R}^{m \times n} \mapsto \mathbb{R}. \tag{7}$$

The divergence of a vector field is defined as

$$div \ \vec{V}_{m,n} \colon (\mathbb{R}^{m \times n} \mapsto \mathbb{R}, \mathbb{R}^{m \times n} \mapsto \mathbb{R}) \mapsto (\mathbb{R}^{m \times n} \mapsto \mathbb{R}) \tag{8}$$

with

$$div \ \vec{V}_{m,n} = \nabla \cdot \vec{V}_{m,n} = \frac{\delta}{\delta x} \vec{V}_x + \frac{\delta}{\delta y} \vec{V}_y \tag{9}$$

which is a scalar field that yields how sourcish or sinkish a certain pixel is. A positive scalar represents a point that tends to be a source whereas a negative value tends to be a sink. Values close to zero are neither of both.

To compute the partial derivatives, we employ a suitable numeric approximation. Due to noise effects mentioned in the previous section, we fail in computing the divergence directly on the vector field. To overcome this obstacle, we firstly need to *smooth* the elements of the vector field to reduce the influence of noise prior to identification of sources. Smoothing harmonises the intensities of brightness among adjacent pixels throughout a vector field belonging to at least two consecutive frames of a sequence. Technically, it is organised like a moving average unit. We introduce a smoothing method or filter for the vector field that computes a *mean* taking into consideration surrounding pixels from the spatial neighbourship. Therefore, we utilise a matrix S with an analogical kernel to those of Horn and Schunck [5] for approximation of the Laplacian. In our approach, the modified value for a vector component at a certain position exclusively results from a weighted mean of the pixels in its surrounding area. Our empirically chosen weight matrix S reads as follows:

$$S = \begin{pmatrix} s_{1,1} & s_{2,1} & s_{3,1} \\ s_{1,2} & s_{2,2} & s_{3,2} \\ s_{1,3} & s_{2,3} & s_{3,3} \end{pmatrix} = \begin{pmatrix} \frac{1}{12} & \frac{1}{6} & \frac{1}{12} \\ \frac{1}{6} & 0 & \frac{1}{6} \\ \frac{1}{12} & \frac{1}{6} & \frac{1}{12} \end{pmatrix}. \tag{10}$$

Let $\vec{V}_{m,n} = (\vec{V}_{\tau,x}, \vec{V}_{\tau,y})$ be a *vector field* whose $m \times n$ matrices are composed from elements $V_{\tau,x}(p,q)$ and $V_{\tau,y}(p,q)$ with $p = 1, \ldots, m$ and $q = 1, \ldots, n$.

Now, we can formalise the *iterative smoothing* using weight matrix S to successively update our vector field $\vec{V}_{m,n}$ for all non-zero elements:

$$V_{\tau+1,x}(p,q) = \sum_i \sum_j s_{i+2,j+2} \cdot V_{\tau,x}(p+i, q+j) \quad \text{with} \quad i,j \in \{-1,0,1\} \tag{11}$$

The same holds for $V_{\tau+1,y}(p,q)$, respectively. The initial vector field $(\vec{V}_{0,x}, \vec{V}_{0,y})$ is the original optic flow and hence the outcome of the used optic flow algorithm. Our smoothing method was tested with a varying number of iterations (increments of τ) in total to figure out the best intensity of smoothing since too little and too much portions will diminish the quality of spot identification. We found out that a number of around $1,000$ iterations gives the best results of the scalar field representing the divergences of the vector field whose sources mark the positions of oscillatory spots. Figure 5 shows our results. In order to get a sense of accuracy of the method, its results might be compared with Fig. 1 of the BZ reaction recordings.

9   Conclusions

By extension of the standard algorithm from Horn and Schunck by grey scaling and iterated smoothing, we succeeded in development of an automated method to localise the oscillatory spots from BZ reactions in a Petri dish by computing a smooth divergence field. For identification of the centre inside an oscillatory spot, we have to employ a method that further smoothes our divergence field. Afterwards, we are in a position to determine local maxima and minima using mathematical morphology and image dilation [2,4]. By means of suitable relative thresholds, we are able to distinct different oscillatory spots. By repeating the complete process of optic flow and divergence field computation for certain areas, we can raise the precision and optimise the results even further. Based on that, we are going to obtain the number of active oscillatory spots within an image sequence of a Petri dish. This indicates the area in which we determine the velocities of the expanding concentric rings for further study to estimate the oscillation frequency. Our toolbox for automated analysis of BZ reactions in a Petri dish using optic flow is available from the first author upon request opening a new field of applications within membrane computing.

References

1. Bernhardini, F., Manca, V.: Dynamical aspects of P systems. Biosystems **70**(2), 85–93 (2003)
2. van den Boomgaard, R., van Balen, R.: Methods for fast morphological image transforms using bitmapped binary images. CVGIP: Graph. Models Image Process. **54**, 252–258 (1992)
3. Gibson, J.J.: The Perception of the Visual World. Houghton Mifflin, Boston (1950)
4. Haralick, R.M., Shapiro, L.G.: Computer and Robot Vision. Addison-Wesley, Reading (1992)
5. Horn, B.K.P., Schunck, B.G.: Determining optical flow. Artif. Intell. **17**(1–3), 185–203 (1981)
6. Horn, B.K.P., Weldon, E.J.: Direct methods for recovering motion. Int. J. Comput. Vis. **2**(1), 51–76 (1988)
7. Karp, G.: Cell and Molecular Biology. Wiley VCH, New York (2009)
8. Lefever, R., Nicolis, G., Borckmans, P.: The brusselator: it does oscillate all the same. J. Chem. Soc. Faraday Trans. **84**, 1013–1023 (1988)
9. Lucas, B.D., Kanade, T.: An iterative image registration technique with an application to stereo vision. In: Proceedings of the 7th International Joint Conference on Artificial Intelligence, IJCAI 1981, vol. 2, pp. 674–679 (1981)
10. Nagel, H.H.: On the estimation of optical flow: relations between different approaches and some new results. Artif. Intell. **33**(3), 299–324 (1987)
11. Silva, C., Santos-Victor, J.: Direct egomotion estimation. In: 1996 Proceedings of the 13th International Conference Pattern Recognition, pp. 702–706. IEEE (1996)
12. Wallach, H.: Über visuell wahrgenommene Bewegungsrichtung. Psychologische Forschung **20**(1), 325–380 (1935)

13. Wedel, A., Pock, T., Zach, C., Bischof, H., Cremers, D.: An improved algorithm for TV-L^1 optical flow. In: Cremers, D., Rosenhahn, B., Yuille, A.L., Schmidt, F.R. (eds.) Statistical and Geometrical Approaches to Visual Motion Analysis. LNCS, vol. 5604, pp. 23–45. Springer, Heidelberg (2009). https://doi.org/10.1007/978-3-642-03061-1_2

14. Zach, C., Pock, T., Bischof, H.: A duality based approach for realtime TV-L^1 optical flow. In: Hamprecht, F.A., Schnörr, C., Jähne, B. (eds.) DAGM 2007. LNCS, vol. 4713, pp. 214–223. Springer, Heidelberg (2007). https://doi.org/10.1007/978-3-540-74936-3_22

15. Zhabotinsky, A.M.: Periodical process of oxidation of malonic acid solution. Biofisika **9**, 306–311 (1964)

Testing Identifiable Kernel P Systems Using an X-Machine Approach

Marian Gheorghe[1(✉)], Florentin Ipate[2], Raluca Lefticaru[1,2], and Ana Turlea[2]

[1] School of Electrical Engineering and Computer Science, University of Bradford, Bradford, West Yorkshire BD7 1DP, UK
{m.gheorghe,r.lefticaru}@bradford.ac.uk
[2] Department of Computer Science, Faculty of Mathematics and Computer Science and ICUB, University of Bucharest, Str. Academiei nr. 14, 010014 Bucharest, Romania
florentin.ipate@ifsoft.ro, ana.turlea@fmi.unibuc.com

Abstract. This paper presents a testing approach for kernel P systems (*kP systems*), based on the X-machine testing method and the concept of cover automaton. The testing methodology ensures that the implementation conforms the specifications, under certain conditions, such as the *identifiability* concept in the context of kernel P systems.

Keywords: Membrane computing · Kernel P systems · X-machines · Cover automata · Testing

1 Introduction

Membrane computing [20] is a research field initiated twenty years ago [18,19] by Gheorghe Păun. Initially inspired by the structure and functioning of the living cells, the field has been developed very fast, different types of membrane systems (or *P systems*) being investigated.

More recently a new type of P system, called *kernel P system* (*kP system*, for short), has been introduced [9]. These systems have a great expressive power, benefiting from a formal specification language and can be simulated with a software framework, called kPWORKBENCH [5] or some earlier variants (so called *simple kP systems*) using P-Lingua and the MeCoSim simulator [11].

Having so many computational models (cell-like, tissue-like P systems, P colonies, kP systems) and also different software implementations for these models associated with various applications, it is important to devise testing methodologies that ensure that the implementation conforms with the specification. The testing task is not trivial, given the fact that the models are parallel and non-deterministic. Previous works on P systems testing address problems specified using general classes of such systems and include testing cell-like P systems with methods like finite state-based inspired [13], stream X-machine based testing [14], mutation testing for evaluating the efficiency of the test sets [17], model-checking based testing [15].

© Springer Nature Switzerland AG 2019
T. Hinze et al. (Eds.): CMC 2018, LNCS 11399, pp. 142–159, 2019.
https://doi.org/10.1007/978-3-030-12797-8_11

In this paper we present a testing approach for *kP systems*, which is based on the X-machine method and has as core concept the *identifiability* of multisets of rules. In [10] the concept of identifiable P system has been introduced and studied for cell-like P systems and a testing strategy based on X-machines has been considered for this model. Here we extend this study to kP systems, looking at the associated testing method derived from this model. This extension is not trivial as these kP systems use rules more complex than those present in the models previously studied and various execution strategies may be involved.

This paper is structured as follows: Sect. 2 presents the preliminaries regarding kP systems and theoretical background regarding automata and X-machine based testing. Section 3 introduces the concept of *identifiable* kP systems, formulating the main results, while Sect. 4 illustrates our testing approach for identifiable kP systems. Finally, conclusions are presented in Sect. 5.

2   Preliminaries

This section briefly presents the notations used, then gives the basic definitions regarding kernel P systems [9] and presents the previous testing approaches for automata and X-machines, that have been applied also for testing simple cell-like P systems.

In the following we introduce the notations used in the paper. For a finite alphabet $A = \{a_1, \ldots, a_p\}$, A^* represents the set of all strings (sequences) over A. The empty string is denoted by λ and $A^+ = A^* \setminus \{\lambda\}$ denotes the set of non-empty strings. A^n denotes the set of all strings of length n, $n \geq 0$, with members in the alphabet A, and $A[n] = \bigcup_{0 \leq i \leq n} A^i$ denotes the set of all strings of length at most n.

For a string $u \in A^*$, $|u|_a$ denotes the number of occurrences of a in u, where $a \in A$. For a subset $S \subseteq A$, $|u|_S$ denotes the number of occurrences of the symbols from S in u. The length of a string u is given by $\sum_{a_i \in A} |u|_{a_i}$. The length of the empty string is 0, i.e. $|\lambda| = 0$.

A multiset over A is a mapping $f : A \to \mathbb{N}$. Considering only the elements from the support of f (where $f(a_{i_j}) > 0$, for some j, $1 \leq j \leq p$), the multiset is represented as a string $a_{i_1}^{f(a_{i_1})} \ldots a_{i_p}^{f(a_{i_p})}$, where the order is not important. In the sequel multisets will be represented by such strings.

2.1   Kernel P Systems

In the following we will give a formal definition of kernel P systems (or kP systems) [9]. We start by introducing the concept of a *compartment type* utilised later in defining the compartments of a kernel P system (kP system).

Definition 1. *T is a set of compartment types,* $T = \{t_1, \ldots, t_s\}$, *where* $t_i = (R_i, \sigma_i)$, $1 \leq i \leq s$, *consists of a set of rules,* R_i, *and an execution strategy,* σ_i, *defined over* $Lab(R_i)$, *the labels of the rules of* R_i.

Kernel P systems have features inspired by object-oriented programming, for example one *compartment type* can have one or more *instances*. These instances share the same set of rules and execution strategies (so will deliver the same functionality), but they may contain different multisets of objects and different neighbours according to the graph relation specified.

Definition 2. *A kP system of degree n is a tuple $k\Pi = (A, \mu, C_1, \ldots, C_n, i_0)$, where*

- *A is a finite set of elements called objects;*
- *μ defines the membrane structure, which is a graph, (V, E), where V is a set of vertices representing components (compartments), and E is a set of edges, i.e., links between components;*
- *$C_i = (t_i, w_{i,0})$, $1 \leq i \leq n$, is a compartment of the system consisting of a compartment type, t_i, from a set T and an initial multiset, $w_{i,0}$ over A; the type $t_i = (R_i, \sigma_i)$ consists of a set of evolution rules, R_i, and an execution strategy, σ_i;*
- *i_0 is the output compartment where the result is obtained.*

In this paper we will only deal with a simplified version of kP systems having *one single compartment* as this does not affect the general method introduced here and makes the presentation easier to follow. For details regarding the ways of flattening an arbitrary P system, including the kP system discussed in this paper, we refer to [1,7,21]. The kP system will be denoted $k\Pi = (A, \mu_1, C_1, 1)$, where μ_1 denotes the graph with one node.

Within the general kP systems framework, the following types of evolution rules have been considered so far:

- *rewriting and communication* rule: $x \to y\{g\}$, where g represents a **guard** (will be formally explained in Definition 4), $x \in A^+$ and $y \in A^*$, where y is a multiset with potential different compartment type targets (each symbol from the right side of the rule can be sent to a different compartment, specified by its type; if multiple compartments of the same type are linked to the current compartment, then one is randomly chosen to be the target). Unlike cell-like P systems, the targets in kP systems indicate only the types of compartments to which the objects will be sent, not particular instances (for example, $y = (a_1, t_1) \ldots (a_h, t_h)$, where $h \geq 0$, and for each $1 \leq j \leq h$, $a_j \in A$ and t_j indicates a compartment type from T).
- *structure changing* rules: membrane division, membrane dissolution, link creation and link destruction rules, which all may also incorporate complex guards and that are covered in detail in [9]. However, this type of rules will not be considered in the following discussion.

Remark 1. In the context of *one compartment kP systems*, there will be no need to specify the target compartment, so the rules will be simple communication rules, which in addition can have *guards*. Each rule occurring in the following discussion has the form $r : x \to y\{g\}$, where r identifies the rule and is called

label, $x \rightarrow y$ is the rule itself and g is its **guard**. The part $x \rightarrow y$ is also called the **body** of the rule, denoted also $b(r)$. The guards are constructed using multisets over A, as operands, and relational or Boolean operators. The definition of the guards is now introduced. We start with some notations.

For a multiset w over A and an element $a \in A$, we denote by $|w|_a$ the number of objects a occurring in w. Let us denote $Rel = \{<, \leq, =, \neq, \geq, >\}$, the set of relational operators, $\gamma \in Rel$, a relational operator, and a^n a multiset, consisting of n copies of a. We first introduce an *abstract relational expression*.

Definition 3. *If g is the* abstract relational expression *denoting* γa^n *and w a multiset, then the guard g applied to w denotes the* relational expression $|w|_a \gamma n$.

The abstract relational expression g is true for the multiset w, if $|w|_a \gamma n$ is true.

We consider now the following Boolean operators $\neg$ (negation), $\wedge$ (conjunction) and $\vee$ (disjunction). An *abstract Boolean expression* is defined by one of the following conditions:

- any abstract relational expression is an abstract Boolean expression;
- if g and h are abstract Boolean expressions then $\neg g$, $g \wedge h$ and $g \vee h$ are abstract Boolean expressions.

The concept of a guard, introduced for kP systems, is a generalisation of the promoter and inhibitor concepts utilised by some variants of P systems.

Definition 4. *If g is an* abstract Boolean expression *containing* g_i, $1 \leq i \leq q$, *abstract relational expressions and w a multiset, then g applied to w means the* Boolean expression *obtained from g by applying g_i to w for any $i, 1 \leq i \leq q$.*

As in the case of an abstract relational expression, the guard g is true with respect to the multiset w, if the abstract Boolean expression g applied to w is true.

Example 1. If g is the guard defined by the abstract Boolean expression $\geq a^4 \wedge < b^2 \vee \neg > c$ and w a multiset, then g applied to w is true if it has at least 4 a's and less than 2 b's or no more than one c.

In addition to its evolution rules, each compartment type in a kP system has an associated *execution strategy*. The rules corresponding to a compartment can be grouped in blocks, each having one of the following strategies:

In kP systems the way in which rules are executed is defined for each compartment type t from T – see Definition 1. As in Definition 1, $Lab(R)$ is the set of labels of the rules R.

Definition 5. *For a compartment type $t = (R, \sigma)$ from T and $r \in Lab(R)$, $r_1, \ldots, r_s \in Lab(R)$, the execution strategy, σ, is defined by the following*

- $\sigma = \lambda$, *means no rule from the current compartment will be executed;*

- $\sigma = \{r\}$ – the rule r is executed;
- $\sigma = \{r_1, \ldots, r_s\}$ – one of the rules labelled $r_1, \ldots, r_s$ will be non-deterministically chosen and executed; if none is applicable then nothing is executed; this is called alternative or choice;
- $\sigma = \{r_1, \ldots, r_s\}^*$ – the rules are applied an arbitrary number of times (arbitrary parallelism);
- $\sigma = \{r_1, \ldots, r_s\}^\top$ – the rules are executed according to the maximal parallelism strategy;
- $\sigma = \sigma_1 \& \ldots \& \sigma_s$, means executing sequentially $\sigma_1, \ldots, \sigma_s$, where $\sigma_i, 1 \leq i \leq s$, describes any of the above cases; if one of σ_i fails to be executed then the rest is no longer executed.

These execution strategies and the fact that in any compartment several blocks with different strategies can be composed and executed offer a lot of flexibility to the kP system designer, similarly to procedural programming.

Definition 6. *A* configuration *of a kP system, $k\Pi$, with n compartments, is a tuple $c = (c_1, \ldots, c_n)$, where $c_i \in A^*$, $1 \leq i \leq n$, is the multiset from compartment i. The* initial configuration *is $(w_1, \ldots, w_n)$, where $w_i \in A^*$ is the initial multiset of the compartment i, $1 \leq i \leq n$.*

A *transition* (or *computation step*), introduced by the next definition, is the process of passing from one configuration to another.

Definition 7. *Given two configurations $c = (c_1, \ldots, c_n)$ and $c' = (c'_1, \ldots, c'_n)$ of a kP system, $k\Pi$, with n compartments, where for any $i, 1 \leq i \leq n$, $u_i \in A^*$, and a multiset of rules $M_i = r_{1,i}^{n_{1,i}} \ldots r_{k_i,i}^{n_{k_i,i}}$, $n_{j,i} \geq 0$, $1 \leq j \leq k_i, k_i \geq 0$, a transition or a computation step is the process of obtaining c' from c by using the multisets of rules M_i, $1 \leq i \leq n$, denoted by $c \Longrightarrow^{(M_1, \ldots, M_n)} c'$, such that for each i, $1 \leq i \leq n$, c'_i is the multiset obtained from c_i by first extracting all the objects that are in the left-hand side of each rule of M_i from c_i and then adding all the objects a that are in the right-hand side of each rule of M_i represented as (a, t_i) and all the objects b that are in the right-hand side of each rule of M_j, $j \neq i$, such that b is represented as (b, t_i).*

In the theory of kP systems, each compartment might have its own execution strategy. In the sequel we focus on three such execution strategies, namely maximal parallelism, arbitrary parallelism (also called asynchronous execution) and sequential execution. These will be denoted by $max, async$ and seq, respectively. When in a transition from c to c' using $(M_1, \ldots, M_m)$, we intend to refer to a specific transition mode tm, $tm \in \{max, async, seq\}$, then this will be denoted by $c \Longrightarrow_{tm}^{(M_1, \ldots, M_m)} c'$.

A *computation* in a P system is a sequence of transitions (computation steps).

A configuration is called *final configuration*, if no rule can be applied to it. In a final configuration the computation stops.

As usual in P systems, we only consider terminal computations, i.e., those arriving in a final configuration and using one of the above mentioned transition modes. We are now ready to define the result of a computation.

Definition 8. *For a kP system $k\Pi$ using the transition mode tm, tm $\in$ {max, async, seq}, in each compartment, we denote by $N_{tm}(\Pi)$ the number of objects appearing in the output compartment of a final configuration.*

Two kP systems $k\Pi$ and $k\Pi'$ are called *equivalent* with respect to the transition mode tm, tm $\in$ {max, async, seq}, if $N_{tm}(k\Pi) = N_{tm}(k\Pi')$.

In this paper we will only deal with kP systems having *one single compartment* as this does not affect the general method introduced here and makes the presentation easier to follow.

2.2   The *W*-Method for Testing Finite Cover Automata

In the following subsection we introduce the basic finite cover automata concepts [3,12] and the *W*-method for generating test suites from finite cover automata [13]. We will consider only deterministic finite automata.

Finite Cover Automata

Definition 9. *A finite automaton (abbreviated FA) is a tuple $A = (V, Q, q_0, F, h)$, where: V is the finite input alphabet, Q is the finite set of states, $q_0 \in Q$ is the initial state, $F \subseteq Q$ is the set of final states, $h : Q \times V \to Q$ is the next-state function.*

The next-state (partial) function h can be extended to take sequences in the usual manner, i.e. $h : Q \times V^* \longrightarrow Q$ [6].

Given $q \in Q$, the set L_A^q is defined by $L_A^q = \{s \in V^* \mid h(q, s) \in F\}$. When q is the initial state of A, the set is called the *language accepted (defined) by A* and the simpler notation L_A is used.

A state $q \in Q$ is called *reachable* if there exists $s \in V^*$ such that $h(q_0, s) = q$. A is called *reachable* if all states of A are reachable.

Given $Y \subseteq V^*$, two states $q_1, q_2 \in Q$ are called *Y-equivalent* if $L_A^{q_1} \cap Y = L_A^{q_2} \cap Y$. Otherwise q_1 and q_2 are called *Y-distinguishable*. If $Y = V^*$ then q_1 and q_2 are simply called *equivalent* or *distinguishable*, respectively. Two FAs are called *($Y-$)equivalent* or *($Y-$)distinguishable* if their initial states are *($Y-$)equivalent* or *($Y-$)distinguishable*, respectively.

Definition 10. *Let $A = (V, Q, q_0, F, h)$ be a FA, $U \subseteq V^*$ a finite language and l the length of the longest sequence(s) in U. Then A is called a deterministic finite cover automaton (DFCA) of U if $L_A \cap V[l] = U$. A minimal DFCA for U is a DFCA for U having the least number of states.*

The concept of DFCA was introduced by Câmpeanu et al. [2,3]. A minimal DFCA have considerably fewer states than the minimal FA that accepts U.

In the following we provide the necessary concepts for characterising and constructing a minimal DFCA (largely from [2] and [16]).

Let $U \subseteq V^*$ be a finite language, l be the length of the longest sequence(s) in U and A be a FA; for simplicity, A is assumed to be reachable. For every state q

of A, we define $level(q)$ as the length of the shortest input sequences that reach q, i.e. $level(q) = min\{|s| \mid s \in V^*, h(q_0, s) = q\}$. Recall that a minimal FA that accepts U is a FA in which all states are reachable and pairwise distinguishable. In a DFCA only sequences of length at most l are considered; thus, every states q_1 and q_2 will have to be distinguished by some input sequence of length at most $l - max\{level(q_1), level(q_2)\}$. If this is the case, we say that q_1 and q_2 are l-dissimilar. Unlike state equivalence, similarity is not a transitive relation [2].

Definition 11. *Let* $A = (V, Q, q_0, F, h)$ *be a reachable FA. States* q_1 *and* q_2 *are said to be similar, written* $q_1 \sim q_2$ *if* q_1 *and* q_2 *are* $V[j]$-*equivalent whenever* $j = l - max\{level(q_1), level(q_2)\} \geq 0$. *Otherwise,* q_1 *and* q_2 *are said to be dissimilar, written* $q_1 \not\sim q_2$.

A minimal DFCA for U can be obtained by decomposing the state set of A based on the similarity criterion, obtaining a partition of Q, $(Q_i)_{1 \leq i \leq n}$, for which every two elements of the same class are similar and every two distinct classes have at least a pair of dissimilar elements.

Theorem 1. *[16] Let* $A = (V, Q, q_0, F, h)$ *be a reachable DFCA for U and let* $(Q_i)_{1 \leq i \leq n}$ *be a state similarity decomposition of Q. For every i, choose* $q_i \in Q_i$ *such that* $level(q_i) = min\{level(q) \mid q \in Q_i\}$. *Define* $A' = (V, Q', q_0', F', h')$ *by* $Q' = \{Q_1, \ldots, Q_n\}$, $q_0' = [q_0]$, $F' = \{[q] \mid q \in F\}$ *and* $h'(Q_i, a) = [h(q_i, a)]$ *for all i, $1 \leq i \leq n$, and $a \in V$. Then A' is a minimal DFCA for U.*

As similarity is not an equivalence relation, the state similarity decomposition may not be unique and, thus, there may be more than one DFCA for the same finite language U.

The W-Method

In *conformance testing* there is a formal specification of the system (for example a FA) and the aim is to generate a test suite such that whenever the implementation under test (IUT) passes all tests, it is guaranteed to conform to the specification. The IUT is unknown but it is assumed to behave like some element from a set of models, called *fault model*. In the case of the W-method, the fault model consists of all FAs A' with the same input alphabet V as the specification A, whose number of states m' does not exceed the number of states m of A by more than k ($m' - m \leq k$), where $k \geq 0$ is a predetermined integer that must be estimated by the tester.

The W-method was originally devised for when the conformance relation is automata equivalence [4], but in this paper we are interested in conformance for bounded sequences. This problem is described in [10] as follows: given an FA specification A and an integer $l \geq 1$ (the upper bound) such that L_A contains at least one sequence of length l, we want to construct a set of sequences of length less than or equal to l that can establish whether the implementation behaves as specified for all sequences in $V[l]$. Since L_A contains at least one sequence of length l, A is a $DFCA$ for $L_A \cap V[l]$ and so the test suite will check whether the IUT model A' is also a DFCA for $L_A \cap V[l]$.

A *test suite* will be a finite set $Y_k \subseteq V[l]$ of input sequences that, for every A' in the fault model that is not $V[l]$-equivalent to A, will produce at least one erroneous output. That is, A and A' are $V[l]$-equivalent whenever A and A' are Y_k-equivalent.

Suppose the specification A used for test generation is a minimal DFCA for $L_A \cap V[l]$. The W-method for bounded sequences, as developed in [12], involves the selection of two sets of input sequences, S and W, as follows:

Definition 12. *$S \subseteq V^*$ is called a proper state cover of A if for every state q of A there exists $s \in S$ such that $h(q_0, s) = q$ and $|s| = level(q)$.*

Definition 13. *$W \subseteq V^*$ is called a strong characterisation set of A if for every two states q_1 and q_2 of A and every $j \geq 0$, if q_1 and q_2 are $V[j]$-distinguishable then q_1 and q_2 are $(W \cap V[j])$-distinguishable.*

Naturally, in the above definition, it is sufficient for q_1 and q_2 to be $(W \cap V[j])$-distinguishable when j is the length of the shortest sequences that distinguish between q_1 and q_2.

Once S and W have been selected, the test suite is obtained using the formula: $Y_k = SV[k+1](W \cup \{\lambda\}) \cap V[l] \setminus \{\lambda\}$ [12].

2.3   X-Machine Based Testing

This subsection presents the X-machine based testing methodology, giving the formal definitions for X-machines, the test transformation of an X-machine and l-bounded conformance test suites. For more details and complete proofs [10] can be consulted, here only the main results are given.

An X-machine is a finite automaton in which transitions are labelled by partial functions on a data set X instead of mere symbols [6].

Definition 14. *An X-machine (XM) is a tuple $Z = (Q, X, \Phi, H, q_0, x_0)$ where:*

- *Q is a finite set of states;*
- *X is the (possible infinite) data set;*
- *Φ is a finite set of distinct processing functions; a processing function is a non-empty (partial) function of type $X \rightarrow X$;*
- *H is the (partial) next-state function, $H : Q \times \Phi \rightarrow Q$;*
- *$q_0 \in Q$ is the initial state;*
- *$x_0 \in X$ is the initial data value.*

We regard an X-machine as a finite automaton with the arcs labelled by functions from the set Φ, which is often called the *type* of Z. The automaton $A_Z = (\Phi, Q, H, q_0)$ over the alphabet Φ is called the *associated finite automaton* (FA) of Z. The language accepted by the automaton is denoted by L_{A_Z}.

Definition 15. *A computation of Z is a sequence $x_0, \ldots x_n$, with $x_i \in X, 1 \leq i \leq n$, such that there exist $\phi_1, \ldots, \phi_n \in \Phi$ with $\phi_i(x_{i-1}) = x_i, 1 \leq i \leq n$ and $\phi_1 \ldots \phi_n \in L_{A_Z}$. The set of computations of Z is denoted by $Comp(Z)$.*

A sequence of processing functions that can be applied in the initial data value x_0 is said to be controllable.

Definition 16. *A sequence $\phi_1, \ldots, \phi_n \in \Phi^*$, with $\phi_i \in \Phi, 1 \leq i \leq n$, is said to be controllable if there exist $x_1, \ldots x_n \in X$ such that $\phi_i(x_{i-1}) = x_i, 1 \leq i \leq n$. A set $P \subseteq \Phi^*$ is called controllable if for every $p \in P$, p is controllable.*

Let us assume we have an X-machine specification Z and an (unknown) IUT that behaves like an element Z' of a fault model. In this case, the fault model will be a set of X-machines with the same data set X, type Φ and initial data value x_0 as the specification. The idea of test generation from an X-machine is to reduce checking that the IUT Z' conforms to the specification Z to checking that the associated automaton of the IUT conforms to the associated automaton of the X-machine specification.

Definition 17. *The test transformation of Z is the (partial) function $t : \Phi^* \rightarrow X^*$ defined by:*

- $t(\lambda) = x_0$. (1)
- *Let $p \in \Phi^*$ and $\phi \in \Phi$.*
  - *Suppose $t(p)$ is defined. Let $t(p) = x_0 \ldots x_n$.*
    - *If $x_n \in dom\phi$ then:*
      - *If $p \in L_{A_Z}$ then $t(p\phi) = t(p)\phi(x_n)$. (2)*
      - *Else $t(p\phi) = t(p)$. (3)*
    - *Else $t(p\phi)$ is undefined. (4)*
  - *Otherwise, $t(p\phi)$ is undefined. (5)*

Lemma 1. *Let t be a test transformation of Z and $p = \phi_1 \ldots \phi_n$, with $\phi_1, \ldots, \phi_n \in \Phi$.*

- *Suppose p is controllable and let $x_1, \ldots, x_n \in X$ such that $\phi_i(x_{i-1}) = x_i, 1 \leq i \leq n$.*
  - *If $p \in L_{A_Z}$, then $t(p) = x_0 \ldots x_n$.*
  - *If $p \notin L_{A_Z}$, then $t(p) = x_0 \ldots x_{k+1}$, where $0 \leq k \leq n - 1$, is such that $\phi_1 \ldots \phi_k \in L_{A_Z}$ and $\phi_1 \ldots \phi_k \phi_{k+1} \notin L_{A_Z}$.*
- *If p is not controllable, then $t(p)$ is not defined.*

In order to establish that the associated automaton of the IUT Z' conforms to the associated automaton of the X-machine specification Z, we have to be able to identify the processing functions that are applied when the computations of Z and Z' are examined.

Definition 18. *Φ is called* identifiable *if for all $\phi_1, \phi_2 \in \Phi$, whenever there exists $x \in X$ such that $\phi_1(x) = \phi_2(x)$, $\phi_1 = \phi_2$.*

If Φ is identifiable, then we are able to establish if a controllable sequence of processing functions is correctly implemented by examining the computations of the specification Z and the implementation Z', as shown by the following lemma.

Lemma 2. *Let Z and Z' be XMs with type Φ. Suppose Φ is identifiable. Let $p = \phi_1 \ldots \phi_n \in \Phi^*$, with $\phi_i \in \Phi$, $1 \leq i \leq n$, be a controllable sequence. Suppose $t(p)$ is a computation of Z if and only if $t(p)$ is a computation of Z'. Then $p \in L_{A_Z}$ if and only if $p \in L_{A'_Z}$.*

Definition 19. *Let Z be an X-machine and C a fault model for Z. An l-bounded conformance test suite for Z w.r.t. C, $l > 0$, is a set $T \subseteq X[l+1]$ such that for every $Z' \in C$ the following holds: if $T \cap Comp(Z) = T \cap Comp(Z')$ then $Comp(Z) \cap X[l+1] = Comp(Z') \cap X[l+1]$.*

That is, whenever any element of T is a computation of Z if and only if it is a computation of Z', Z' conforms to Z for sequences of length up to l. The following theorem shows that the test transformation defined earlier provides a mechanism for converting test suites for finite automata into set suites for X-machines.

Theorem 2. *Let Z be an XM with type Φ, data set X and initial data value x_0. Suppose Φ is identifiable and $L_{A_Z} \cup \Phi[l]$ is controllable. Let C be a set of XMs such that for every $Z' \in C$, $L_{A'_Z} \cap \Phi[l]$ is controllable. Let $P \subseteq \Phi[l]$, such that, for every $Z' \in C$, whenever $P \cap L_{A_Z} = P \cap L_{A'_Z}$ we have $L_{A_Z} \cap \Phi[l] = L_{A'_Z} \cap \Phi[l]$. Then $t(P)$ is an l-bounded conformance test suite for Z w.r.t. C.*

Let $l > 0$ be a predefined upper bound. We assume that Φ is identifiable and $L_{A_Z} \cap \Phi[l]$ is controllable. We assume that A_Z, the associated automaton of Z, is a minimal DFCA for $L_{A_Z} \cup \Phi[l]$ (if not, this is minimised[1]). Suppose the fault model C is the set of X-machines Z' with the same data set X, type Φ and initial data value x_0 as Z such that $L_{A_{Z'}} \cap \Phi[l]$ is controllable, whose number of states m' does not exceed the number of states m of Z by more than k ($m' - m \leq k$), $k \leq 0$. Then an l-bounded conformance test suite for Z w.r.t. C is

$$T_k = t(S\Phi[k+1](W \cup \{\lambda\}) \cap \Phi[l] \setminus \{\lambda\}),$$

where S is a proper state cover of A_Z, W is a strong characterisation set of A_Z and t is a test transformation of Z.

3   Identifiable Transitions in Kernel P Systems

The concept of identifiable transitions in cell-like P systems was first introduced in [10] and then extended to kernel P systems in [8]. We now aim to present the *identifiability* concept in the context of kP systems and then illustrate how it is used as basis for kP systems testing. The identifiability concept is first introduced for simple rules and then is generalised for multisets of rules.

Definition 20. *Two rules $r_1 : x_1 \rightarrow y_1\{g_1\}$ and $r_2 : x_2 \rightarrow y_2\{g_2\}$ from R_1, are said to be* identifiable *if there is configuration c where they are applicable and if $c \Longrightarrow^{r_1} c'$ and $c \Longrightarrow^{r_2} c'$ then $b(r_1) = b(r_2)$.*

---

[1] The minimisation preserves the controlability requirements as the set $L_{A_Z} \cap \Phi[l]$ remains unchanged.

According to the above definition the rules r_1 and r_2 are identifiable in c if when the result of applying them to c is the same then their bodies, $x_1 \rightarrow y_1$ and $x_2 \rightarrow y_2$, are identical. The rules are not identifiable when the condition from Definition 20 is not satisfied.

A multiset or rules $M = r_1^{n_1} \ldots r_k^{n_k}$, $M \in R_1^*$, where $r_i : x_i \rightarrow y_i\{g_i\}$, $1 \leq i \leq k$, is applicable to the multiset c iff $x_1^{n_1} \ldots x_k^{n_k} \subseteq c$ and g_i is true in c for $1 \leq i \leq k$.

Definition 21. *The multisets of rules $M', M'' \in R_1^*$, are said to be identifiable, if there is a configuration c where M' and M'' are applicable and if $c \Longrightarrow^{M'} c'$ and $c \Longrightarrow^{M''} c'$ then $b(M') = b(M'')$.*

Example 2. Considering the rules $r_1 : a \rightarrow x\{\geq a\}$, $r_2 : b \rightarrow y\{\geq b\}$, $r_3 : a \rightarrow y\{\geq a\}$, $r_4 : b \rightarrow x\{\geq b\}$, and the configuration ab it is clear that the multisets of rules $M' = r_1 r_2$ and $M'' = r_3 r_4$ are not identifiable in the configuration $c = ab$, as $c = ab \Longrightarrow^{M'} c' = xy$ and $c = ab \Longrightarrow^{M''} c' = xy$, but $b(M') \neq b(M'')$.

A kP system $k\Pi$ has its *rules identifiable* if any two multisets of rules, $M', M'' \in R_1^*$, are identifiable.

Given a multiset of rules $M = r_1^{n_1} \ldots r_k^{n_k}$, where $r_i : x_i \rightarrow y_i\{g_i\}$, $1 \leq i \leq k$, we denote by r_M the rule $x_1^{n_1} \ldots x_k^{n_k} \rightarrow y_1^{n_1} \ldots y_k^{n_k}\{g_1 \wedge \cdots \wedge g_k\}$, i.e., the concatenation of all the rules in M. One can observe that the applicability of the multiset of rules M to a certain configuration is equivalent to the applicability of the rule r_M to that configuration. It follows that one can study first the usage of simple rules.

Remark 2. For any two rules $r_i : x_i \rightarrow y_i$, $1 \leq i \leq 2$, when we check whether they are identifiable or not one can write them as $r_i : uv_i \rightarrow wz_i\{g_i\}$, $1 \leq i \leq 2$, where for any $a \in V$, a appears in at most one of the v_1 or v_2, i.e., all the common symbols on the left-hand side of the rules are in u. Let us denote by c_{r_1,r_2}, the configuration uv_1v_2. Obviously this is the smallest configuration in which r_1 and r_2 are applicable, given that g_1 and g_2 are true in uv_1v_2.

Remark 3. If $r_i : x_i \rightarrow y_i$ $\{g_i\}$, $1 \leq i \leq 2$, are applicable in a configuration c and $c \subseteq c'$ then they are not always applicable to c'. They are applicable to c' when all g_i, $1 \leq i \leq 2$, are true in c'.

Remark 4. If the rules r_1, r_2 are not applicable to c_{r_1,r_2} then there must be minimal configurations c where the rules are applicable and they are minimal, i.e., there is no c_1, $c_1 \subset c$ where the rules are applicable. Such minimal configurations where r_1, r_2 are applicable are of the form tc_{r_1,r_2}, where $t \in A^*$, $t \neq \lambda$.

In the following we introduce some theoretical results, characterising the identifiability or non-identifiability or rules and multisets of rules under certain conditions. The complete proofs for these results are given in [8].

Lemma 3. *Two rules which are identifiable in a configuration c are identifiable in any configuration containing c in which they are applicable.*

Lemma 4. *Two rules which are identifiable in a minimal configuration c are identifiable in any other minimal configuration c' where they are applicable.*

Corollary 1. *Two rules r_1 and r_2 identifiable in a minimal configuration tc_{r_1,r_2}, $t \in A^*$, are identifiable in any configuration in which they are applicable.*

Corollary 2. *Two multisets of rules M_1 and M_2 identifiable in $tc_{r_{M_1},r_{M_2}}$, $t \in A^*$, are identifiable in any configuration in which they are applicable.*

From now on, we will always verify the identifiability (or non identifiability) only for the smallest configurations associated with rules or multisets of rules and will not mention these configurations anymore in the results to follow.

The applicability of two rules (multisets of rules) to a certain configuration depends not only on the fact that there left hand sides (the concatenation of the left hand sides) must be contained in the configuration and the guards must be true, but takes into account the execution strategy.

Remark 5. For the *async* transition mode two multisets of rules (and two rules) applicable in a configuration are also applicable in any other bigger configuration, when the corresponding guards are true. For the *seq* mode this is true only for multisets with one single element and obviously for simple rules. In the case of the *max* mode the applicability of the multisets of rules (or rules) to various configurations depends on the contents of the configurations and other available rules. For instance if we consider a P system containing the rules $r_1 : a \rightarrow a \ \{\geq a\}; r_2 : ab \rightarrow abb \ \{\leq b^{100}\}; r_3 : bb \rightarrow c \ \{\geq b^2\}$ and the configuration $c = ab$ then in c only the multisets r_1 and r_2 are applicable and identifiable, but in $c_1 = abb$, containing c, the multiset r_1 is no longer applicable, but instead we have the multisets r_2 and $r_1 r_3$ applicable. In ab^{101} r_2 and any multiset containing it are not applicable due to the guard being false; also the multiset r_1 is no longer applicable, but $r_1 r_3^{55}$ is now applicable, due to maximal parallelism.

4   Testing Identifiable Kernel P Systems

In this section we will present how we can apply the *W*-method on kP systems. First, a corresponding X-machine model needs to be constructed. As discussed in Sect. 2, multi-compartment P systems can be flattened into one membrane P systems and there are different ways to realise this [1,7,21]. Consequently, we will illustrate the testing approach using an one-membrane kP system model $k\Pi = (V, T, \mu_1, w_1, R_1, 1)$.

The main idea is to construct an X-machine $Z^t = (Q^t, X, \Phi, H^t, q_0^t, x_0)$, corresponding to the computation tree of $k\Pi$. As the computation tree of the kP system might be infinite, we will consider only computations of maximum l steps, where $l > 0$ is a predefined integer. Let $R_1 = \{r_1, \ldots, r_n\}$ be the set of rules of $k\Pi$. As only finite computations are considered, for every rule $r_i \in R_1$ there will be some N_i such that, in any step, r_i can be applied at most N_i times, $1 \leq i \leq n$. The X-machine $Z^t = (Q^t, X, \Phi, H^t, q_0^t, x_0)$ is defined as follows:

- Q^t is the set of nodes of the computation tree of maximum l steps;
- q_0^t is the root node;
- X is the set of multisets with elements in V;
- x_0 is the initial multiset w_1;
- Φ is the set of (partial) functions induced by the application of multisets of rules $r_1^{i_1} \dots r_n^{i_n}$, $0 \leq i_1 \leq N_1, \dots, 0 \leq i_n \leq N_n$, $i_1 + \dots i_n > 0$;
- H^t is the next-state function determined by the computation tree.

Remark 6. Note that, by definition, L_{A_Z} is controllable, i.e. any sequence of processing functions from the associated automaton A_Z can be applied in the initial data x_0 (corresponding to the initial multiset w_1). Intuitively a path in the DFCA corresponds to a path in the computation tree of the kP system.

Remark 7. The set of (partial) functions, Φ, from the above definition is identifiable (according to Definition 18) if and only if the corresponding multisets of rules are pairwise identifiable (according to Definition 21).

Example 3. Let us consider one compartment kP system $k\Pi_1 = (V, V, \mu_1, w_1, R_1, 1)$, where $V = \{a, b, c\}$, $w_1 = ab$, and

$$R_1 = \{r_1 : a \to b\{< a^4\}, r_2 : a \to aa\{\leq b^2\}\}$$

Let us build the computation tree considering that rules are applied in the maximally parallel mode.

The initial configuration $w_1 = aab$ is at the root of the tree (level 0 of the tree). Three computation steps are possible from the root: $a^2b \Longrightarrow^{r_1^2} b^3$, $a^2b \Longrightarrow^{r_1 r_2} a^2b^2$ and $a^2b \Longrightarrow^{r_2^2} a^4b$. These configurations are at the first level of the tree.

The second level of the tree contains the configurations generated by the following computation steps. No rule can be applied in b^3. From a^2b^2 we have he following computations: $a^2b^2 \Longrightarrow^{r_1^2} b^4$, $a^2b^2 \Longrightarrow^{r_1 r_2} a^2b^3$ and $a^2b^2 \Longrightarrow^{r_2^2} a^4b^2$. From a^4b, there are four computation steps: $a^4b \Longrightarrow^{r_1^3 r_2} a^2b^4$, $a^4b \Longrightarrow^{r_1^2 r_2^2} a^4b^3$, $a^4b \Longrightarrow^{r_1 r_2^3} a^6b^2$ and $a^4b \Longrightarrow^{r_2^4} a^8b$.

It can be easily checked that any two of the above multisets of rules are identifiable, and consequently they produce different results when applied to the same configuration, according to Definitions 20 and 21, and Corollaries 1 and 2.

Let the upper bound on the number of computation steps considered be $l = 2$. For this value of l, the rule r_1 has been applied at most three times and r_2 has been applied at most four times, so $N_1 = 3$ and $N_2 = 4$. Therefore the type Φ of the X-machine Z^t corresponding to the computation tree is the set of partial functions induced by the multisets $r_1^{i_1} r_2^{i_2}$, $0 \leq i_1 \leq 3, 0 \leq i_2 \leq 4$, $i_1 + i_2 > 0$. The associated automaton A_{Z^t} is as represented in Fig. 1, where the root is $q_0 = a^2b$, on the first level we have the following nodes: $q_1 = b^3$, $q_2 = a^2b^2$, $q_3 = a^4b$ and on the second level we have: $q_4 = b^4$, $q_5 = a^2b^3$, $q_6 = a^4b^2$, $q_7 = a^2b^4$, $q_8 = a^4b^3$, $q_9 = a^6b^2$ and $q_{10} = a^8b$.

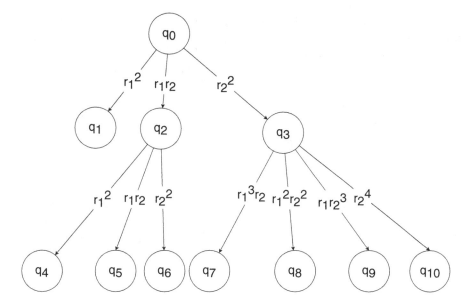

Fig. 1. The associated automaton A_{Z^t} corresponding to the computation tree for $k\Pi_1$ and $l = 2$

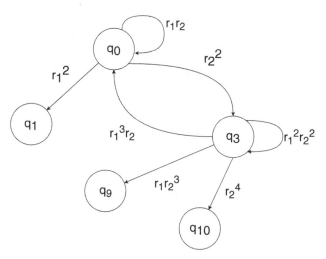

Fig. 2. The DFCA for $L_{A_{Z^t}}$

Let $L_{A_{Z^t}} \subseteq \Phi^*$ be the language accepted by the associated automaton A_{Z^t}. In order to apply the test generation method presented in Sect. 2.3, an X-machine Z whose associated automaton A_Z is a DFCA for $L_{A_{Z^t}}$ needs to be constructed first.

Let $\le$ be a total order on Q^t such that $q_1 \le q_2$ whenever $level(q_1) \le level(q_2)$ and denote $q_1 < q_2$ if $q_1 \le q_2$ and $q_1 \ne q_2$. In other words, the node at the superior level in the tree is before the node at the inferior level; if the nodes are at the same level then their order is arbitrarily chosen. Define $P^t = \{q \in Q^t \mid \neg\exists q' \in Q^t \cdot q' \sim q, q' < q\}$ and $[q] = \{q' \in Q^t \mid q' \sim q \wedge \neg\exists q'' \in P^t \cdot q'' \sim q', q'' < q\}$ for every $q \in P^t$ (i.e. $[q]$ denotes the set of all states q' for which q is the minimum state similar to q'). Then we have the following result (the proof is given in [10]).

Theorem 3. *Let $Z = (Q, X, \Phi, H, q_0, x_0)$, where $Q = \{[q] \mid q \in P^t\}$, $q_0 = [q_0^t]$, $H([q], \phi) = [H^t(q, \phi)]$ for all $q \in P^t$ and $\phi \in \Phi$. Then A_Z is a minimal DFCA for $L_{A_{Z^t}}$.*

Remark 8. Consider Z^t as in the previous example. $P^t = \{q_0, q_1, q_3, q_9, q_{10}\}$; $[q_0] = \{q_0, q_2, q_5, q_7\}$, $[q_1] = \{q_1, q_4\}$, $[q_3] = \{q_3, q_6, q_8\}$, $[q_9] = \{q_9\}$, $[q_{10}] = \{q_{10}\}$. Then $Z = (Q, X, \Phi, H, q_0, x_0)$, where $Q = \{[q_0], [q_1], [q_3 t], [q_9], [q_{10}]\}$ and $q_0 = [q_0]$. The associated automaton of Z is a minimal DFCA for $L_{A_{Z^t}}$ and is as represented in Fig. 2.

Once the X-machine Z has been constructed the test generation process entails the following steps:

1. **Construct the sets S and W (proper state cover and characterisation sets, respectively).**
   It can be easily remarked from Fig. 2 that λ, r_1^2, r_2^2, $r_2^2\ r_1 r_2^3$, $r_2^2\ r_2^4$ are the sequences of minimum length[2] that reach $[q_0], [q_1], [q_3], [q_9]$ and $[q_{10}]$, respectively. Consequently $S = \{r_1^2, r_2^2, r_2^2\ r_1 r_2^3, r_2^2\ r_2^4\}$ is a proper state cover of Z. Furthermore, since r_1^2 distinguishes $[q_0]$ from all remaining states and r_1^3 hold the same property for $[q_3]$, $W = \{r_1^2, r_1^3\}$ is a strong characterisation set of Z.
2. **Determine the fault model of the IUT.**
   This entails establishing the transitions that a (possibly faulty) implementation is capable to perform. For example, when the correct application of rules (in the P system specification) is in the maximally parallel mode *max*, one fault that we may consider is when the rules are applied in a less restrictive mode such that the asynchronous mode *async*. Hence the notion of controllability for P systems is defined by considering this, less restrictive, application mode.

Definition 22. *A sequence of multisets of rules $p = M_1 \ldots M_m$, with $M_i \in R_1^*$, $1 \le i \le m$, is said to be controllable if there exist configurations $u_0 = w_1, u_1, \ldots, u_m$, $u_i \in V^*$, $0 \le i \le m$, such that $u_{i-1} \Longrightarrow_{FM}^{M_i} u_i$, $1 \le i \le m$, where $u \Longrightarrow_{FM}^{M} u'$ denotes a computation step in the fault model from configuration u to configuration u' by applying the multiset of rules M.*

---

[2] Notation: for rules r and r', rr' denotes the application of rules r and r' in one single step, whereas $r\ r'$ (separated by space) denotes the application of rule r in one step followed by the application of rule r' in the following step; the second notation is also used for multisets of rules.

Consider again the P system $k\Pi_1$ as in Example 3. Then we have the computation step: $aab \Longrightarrow^{r_2^2} a^4b$ but we can't have this computation step: $a^4b \Longrightarrow^{r_2} a^5b$, since the rules of $k\Pi_1$ must be applied in the maximally parallel mode. However, if we consider that in the fault model of the IUT rules may be applied in the asynchronous mode, the sequence $r_2^2 r_2$ is controllable. The fault model is also determined by the maximum number of states $m + k$ that the IUT may have, where m is the number of states of the X-machine Z and $k \geq 0$ is a non-negative integer estimated by the tester.

3. **Construct an l-bounded conformance test suite.**
   This is $T_k = t(Y_k)$, where $Y_k = S\Phi[k+1](W \cup \{\lambda\}) \cap \Phi[l] \setminus \{\lambda\}$ and t is a test transformation of Z.
   According to [4], the upper bound for the number of sequences in $S\Phi[k+1]W$ is $m^2 \cdot r^{k+1}$ and the total length of all sequences is not greater that $m^2 \cdot (m+k) \cdot r^{k+1}$, where r is the number of elements of Φ. In particular, for $k = 0$, the respective bounds are $m^2 \cdot r$ and $m^3 \cdot r$. The increase in size produced by replacing W with $W \cup \{\lambda\}$ in the above formula is negligible. Note that these bounds refer to the worst case; in an average case, the size of Y_k is much lower. Furthermore, the size of $t(Y_k)$ is normally significantly lower than the size of Y_k since only the controllable sequences are in the domain of t.
   The construction of Y_k is straightforward, so we illustrate only the construction of the test transformation t with an example. Consider again rule application mode is maximal parallelism for $k\Phi$ and the asynchronous mode for the fault model. Consider the sequences $s_0 = \lambda$, $s_1 = r_2^2$, $s_2 = s_1 r_2$, $s_3 = s_2 r_2$, $s_4 = s_3 r_1$ and $r_5 = s_4 r_1$. By rule (1) of Definition 17, $t(s_0) = x_0 = aab$. As $aab \Longrightarrow^{r_2^2} a^4b$, by rule (2) $t(s_1) = aab\ a^4b$.
   In the maximally parallel mode, r_2 cannot be applied in configuration a^4b, but $a^4b \Longrightarrow^{r_2}_{FM} a^6b$ (in the asynchronous mode) and so, by rule (2), $t(s_2) = aab\ a^4b\ a^5b$. Furthermore, $a^5b \Longrightarrow^{r_2}_{FM} a^6b$ and so, by rule (3) of Definition 17, $t(s_3) = t(s_2) = aab\ a^4b\ a^5b$.
   As r_1 cannot be applied in a^6b, by rule (4) $t(s_4)$ is undefined. Furthermore, by rule (5), $t(s_5)$ is also undefined, so no test sequences will be generated for s_4 and s_5.

5   Conclusions

This paper presents a testing approach for kernel P systems that, under certain conditions, ensures that the implementation conforms to the specification. The methodology is based on the *identifiable kernel P systems* concept, which is essential for testing, and has been introduced for one-compartment kP systems with rewriting rules, but can be extended to kP systems with multiple compartments and general rules.

Acknowledgements. This work is supported by a grant of the Romanian National Authority for Scientific Research, CNCS-UEFISCDI, project number PN-III-P4-ID-PCE-2016-0210.

References

1. Agrigoroaiei, O., Ciobanu, G.: Flattening the transition P systems with dissolution. In: Gheorghe, M., Hinze, T., Păun, G., Rozenberg, G., Salomaa, A. (eds.) CMC 2010. LNCS, vol. 6501, pp. 53–64. Springer, Heidelberg (2010). https://doi.org/10.1007/978-3-642-18123-8_7

2. Câmpeanu, C., Sântean, N., Yu, S.: Minimal cover-automata for finite languages. In: Champarnaud, J.-M., Ziadi, D., Maurel, D. (eds.) WIA 1998. LNCS, vol. 1660, pp. 43–56. Springer, Heidelberg (1999). https://doi.org/10.1007/3-540-48057-9_4

3. Câmpeanu, C., Santean, N., Yu, S.: Minimal cover-automata for finite languages. Theor. Comput. Sci. **267**(1–2), 3–16 (2001). https://doi.org/10.1016/S0304-3975(00)00292-9

4. Chow, T.S.: Testing software design modeled by finite-state machines. IEEE Trans. Softw. Eng. **4**(3), 178–187 (1978). https://doi.org/10.1109/TSE.1978.231496

5. Dragomir, C., Ipate, F., Konur, S., Lefticaru, R., Mierla, L.: Model checking kernel P systems. In: Alhazov, A., Cojocaru, S., Gheorghe, M., Rogozhin, Y., Rozenberg, G., Salomaa, A. (eds.) CMC 2013. LNCS, vol. 8340, pp. 151–172. Springer, Heidelberg (2014). https://doi.org/10.1007/978-3-642-54239-8_12

6. Eilenberg, S.: Automata, Languages, and Machines. Academic Press, Cambridge (1974)

7. Freund, R., Leporati, A., Mauri, G., Porreca, A.E., Verlan, S., Zandron, C.: Flattening in (tissue) P systems. In: Alhazov, A., Cojocaru, S., Gheorghe, M., Rogozhin, Y., Rozenberg, G., Salomaa, A. (eds.) CMC 2013. LNCS, vol. 8340, pp. 173–188. Springer, Heidelberg (2014). https://doi.org/10.1007/978-3-642-54239-8_13

8. Gheorghe, M., Ipate, F.: Identifiable kernel P systems (2018, submitted)

9. Gheorghe, M., et al.: Kernel P systems - Version I. In: Eleventh Brainstorming Week on Membrane Computing (11BWMC), pp. 97–124 (2013). http://www.gcn.us.es/files/11bwmc/097_gheorghe_ipate.pdf

10. Gheorghe, M., Ipate, F., Konur, S.: Testing based on identifiable P systems using cover automata and X-machines. Inf. Sci. **372**, 565–578 (2016). https://doi.org/10.1016/j.ins.2016.08.028

11. Gheorghe, M., et al.: 3-Col problem modelling using simple kernel P systems. Int. J. Comput. Math. **90**(4), 816–830 (2013). https://doi.org/10.1080/00207160.2012.743712

12. Ipate, F.: Bounded sequence testing from deterministic finite state machines. Theor. Comput. Sci. **411**(16–18), 1770–1784 (2010). https://doi.org/10.1016/j.tcs.2010.01.030

13. Ipate, F., Gheorghe, M.: Finite state based testing of P systems. Nat. Comput. **8**(4), 833 (2009). https://doi.org/10.1007/s11047-008-9099-3

14. Ipate, F., Gheorghe, M.: Testing non-deterministic stream X-machine models and P systems. Electron. Notes Theor. Comput. Sci. **227**, 113–126 (2009). https://doi.org/10.1016/j.entcs.2008.12.107

15. Ipate, F., Gheorghe, M., Lefticaru, R.: Test generation from P systems using model checking. J. Log. Algebr. Program. **79**(6), 350–362 (2010). https://doi.org/10.1016/j.jlap.2010.03.007

16. Körner, H.: A time and space efficient algorithm for minimizing cover automata for finite languages. Int. J. Found. Comput. Sci. **14**(06), 1071–1086 (2003)

17. Lefticaru, R., Gheorghe, M., Ipate, F.: An empirical evaluation of P system testing techniques. Nat. Comput. **10**(1), 151–165 (2011). https://doi.org/10.1007/s11047-010-9188-y

18. Păun, G.: Computing with membranes. Technical report, Turku Centre for Computer Science (1998). http://tucs.fi/publications/view/?pub_id=tPaun98a
19. Păun, G.: Computing with membranes. J. Comput. Syst. Sci. **61**(1), 108–143 (2000). https://doi.org/10.1006/jcss.1999.1693
20. The P systems website. http://ppage.psystems.eu. Accessed 12 May 2018
21. Verlan, S.: Using the formal framework for P systems. In: Alhazov, A., Cojocaru, S., Gheorghe, M., Rogozhin, Y., Rozenberg, G., Salomaa, A. (eds.) CMC 2013. LNCS, vol. 8340, pp. 56–79. Springer, Heidelberg (2014). https://doi.org/10.1007/978-3-642-54239-8_6

Actor-Like cP Systems

Alec Henderson and Radu Nicolescu$^{(\boxtimes)}$

The University of Auckland, Auckland, New Zealand
ahen386@aucklanduni.ac.nz, r.nicolescu@auckland.ac.nz

Abstract. We propose a new version of our cP systems, extended to match the Actor model, thereby solving an earlier open problem. In the new version, top-cells have control upon the input message flow, to decide which message types are acceptable and at what time. We assess its capabilities by proposing a revised version of our previous best models for the Byzantine agreement problem – a famous problem in distributed algorithms, with non-trivial data structures and algorithms. The new actor-based solution uses a substantially shorter fixed sized alphabet and ruleset, independent of the problem size. Moreover, in contrast to our previous models, additional helper/firewall cells are not anymore needed to ensure protection against Sybil attacks. Also, as any standard distributed algorithm, the novel actor-based cP model uses exactly one top-level cell for each process in Byzantine agreement, thus solving another open problem.

Keywords: Distributed algorithms · Synchronous model ·
Actor model · Membrane computing · P systems · cP systems ·
Prolog terms and unification · Inter-cell parallelism ·
Intra-cell parallelism · Byzantine agreement · EIG trees

1 Introduction

As noted in Cooper and Nicolescu [4], cP systems share the fundamental features of the traditional cell-like (tree-based) and tissue (graph-based) P systems: top-cells are organised in graph/digraph networks, top-cells contain nested (and labelled) sub-cells, the evolution is governed by multiset rewriting rules, possibly running in maximal parallel modes. Top-cell represent nodes in a distributed computation, and interact by messages (aka inter-cell parallelism). Subcells represent local data that can be processed either sequentially or in the max-parallel mode (aka intra-cell parallelism). Although not strictly necessary – but also shared with other versions of the traditional P systems – our typical rulesets are state based and run in a weak priority mode.

The previous cP systems were based on two fundamental innovations. First, unlike in traditional cell-like P systems, sub-cells do NOT have their own rules. Basically, the sub-cells are just nested passive repositories of other sub-cells or atomic symbols; therefore, they can also be viewed as nested compound terms.

© Springer Nature Switzerland AG 2019
T. Hinze et al. (Eds.): CMC 2018, LNCS 11399, pp. 160–187, 2019.
https://doi.org/10.1007/978-3-030-12797-8_12

This seems a severe limitation. However, it is more than compensated by the provision of higher level rules, which extend the classical multiset rewriting rules with concepts borrowed from logic programming, namely Prolog unification. In other words, cP systems may be seen as evolving the classical Prolog unification from structured terms to multiset-based terms – which again is a novel feature.

However, unlike traditional Prolog, where rules are applied in a backward-chaining mode, with possible backtracks, cP rules work in a forward mode, like all known P system rules. This seems to allow better parallelism capabilities than the past and actual parallel versions of concurrent Prolog – but this topic will not be further followed here.

The net result was a powerful system that can crisply and efficiently solve many complex problems, with small fixed-size alphabets and small, fast fixed-size rulesets. In particular, cP systems enable a reasonably straightforward creation and manipulation of high-level data structures typical of high-level languages, such as: numbers, lists, trees, relations (graphs), associative arrays, strings.

In this sense, cP systems have been successfully used to develop parallel and distributed models in a large variety of domains, such as distributed algorithms, graph theory, image processing, NP complete problems.

However, the model was not totally adequate in some complex scenarios, which require tight control of the incoming message flow, such as Byzantine agreement – a famous problem in distributed algorithms, with non-trivial data structures and algorithms. To solve such cases, we had previously introduced additional "firewall" cells and rules.

In Actor models [8,9], each actor can control its incoming flow, by deciding when to accept incoming data and of what format. For example, to control their inbox queues, F# actors use `Receive` and `Scan` operations, while Akka actors use `receive` and `stash` operations.

We now propose a new version of our cP systems, further extended with a novel fundamental capability designated by a new '?' operator, which enables good control of the incoming message flow. This new operator is smooth-lessly integrated in the lhs of our high-level rewriting rules. Further, the new term grammar elevates numbers and list as top-level constructs, simplifying the expression of complex rulesets.

We assess these new capabilities by proposing a novel revised version of our previous best models for the Byzantine agreement problem, in the *synchronous* case. The new model follows quite closely the conceptual description of the algorithm, without any additional cells or rules.

The Byzantine agreement problem was first proposed by Pease *et al.* in 1980 [16] and further elaborated in Lamport *et al.*'s seminal paper [10]. This problem addresses a fundamental issue in complex systems: correctly functioning processes must be able to overcome their possible differences and achieve a consensus, despite arbitrarily faulty processes that can give conflicting information to different parts of the system.

The Byzantine agreement has become one of the most studied problems in distributed algorithms – some even consider it the "crown jewel" of distributed algorithms. Lynch covers several versions of this problem and their solutions, including a complete description of the classical algorithm, based on Exponential Information Gathering (EIG) trees as a data structure [11].

Recent years have seen revived interest in this problem and its solutions, to achieve higher performance or stronger resilience, in a wide variety of contexts [1–3,12], including solutions for a more robust Blockchain [7].

To the best of our knowledge, except our previous work on Byzantine agreement problem, e.g. [5,14], no other complete solutions for P systems has been published.

In this paper, we provide a novel Actor-based cP solution for the Byzantine agreement problem, based on EIG trees, for N processes connected in a complete graph. Each Byzantine process is modelled by exactly one cell, which is a considerable improvement over previous solutions: Dinneen et al. [5] uses $3N + 1$ cells per Byzantine process, and Nicolescu [14] still uses N cells per Byzantine process. In fact, our novel cP model is a substantial improvement on all other criteria, such as: vocabulary size, ruleset size, runtime performance.

Section 2 discusses the new actor-like feature that enables input message flow control. Sections 3 and 4 discuss the Byzantine algorithm and its classical implementation based on EIG trees; this material is reproduced or adapted from our earlier papers [5,6]. Section 5 gives a bird's eye view of the complex artefacts required for the previous P system solutions. Section 6 presents our new solution, based on our new actor-like input control. Section 7 evaluates the merits of the new version against the previous versions and presents conclusions. In the interests of self-containment, the Appendix presents a complete background on cP Systems, including the novel actor-like features.

2   Actor-Like cP Systems

In Actor-based systems, an actor can control its incoming flow, by deciding when to accept incoming data and of what format.

Simplifying the Actor semantics, messages which arrive at their target actors are first enqueued in *inbox* queues. Receiving actors have full control over the time and format of messages accepted from their inboxes, e.g. the F# Mailbox provides Receive and Scan methods, while Akka achieves the same goal via receive and stash methods. Messages not yet accepted remain in their inboxes.

Such facilities are very useful for some critical applications. For example, in the Byzantine agreement, non-faulty cells must protect themselves against faulty cells, which can flood them with ill-formed messages, or even messages pretending to come from other cells (so called Sybil attacks).

In our previous models, we have solved such problems by surrounding all main cells with "firewall" cells. These firewall cells allowed only well formed messages to pass through, and only at specific steps, thus protecting the main cells against any unexpected illegal messages (including Sybil attacks). This worked, but there were a few drawbacks: (i) the models were more complex than the conceptual problem model; (ii) more difficult to understand and prove; and (iii) performed more slowly, because the messages needed to pass through intermediate firewalls.

We propose here a revised version of cP systems, which includes an Actor-like facility for controlling the message flow. This considerably simplifies our Byzantine model, but is also very useful for other problems (not covered here). Essentially, we have now two communication primitives:

- '!': a *send* primitive, which can only appear on the *rhs* of the rules, and sends messages over *outgoing* arcs;

- '?': a *receive* primitive, which can only appear on the *lhs* of the rules, and receives (accepts) messages from *incoming* arcs.

Sent messages which arrive at the target cell are NOT immediately inserted among the target's contents; instead, these messages are conceptually "enqueued" and there is one message "queue" – in our case, read "multiset" – for each incoming arc. Then, these messages may be accepted by the receive primitive, '?', only at appropriate target steps. Moreover – like the send primitive '!' – the receive primitive '?' can also be associated with any term (including compound), which enables it to filter only queued messages meeting a specific pattern.

For example, consider two top-level cells, ι_1 and ι_2, connected by a communication channel symbolised by the (directed) arc (ι_1, ι_2), which is labelled by 2 at its source and 1 at its target, as in Fig. 1 – ignoring both ϕ_{12} and ϕ'_{12}, for the moment. Consider that cell ι_1 sends one a and then one b, via two steps, as shown by the following two rules:

S_0	$\rightarrow_1$	S_1	$!_2\{a\}$	ι_1 sends a to ι_2
S_1	$\rightarrow_1$	S_2	$!_2\{b\}$	ι_1 sends b to ι_2

The sent items, a and b, are not automatically inserted into the contents of ι_2. Consider that target cell ι_2 is in state S_0 and has the following rule:

S_0	$?_1\{b\}$	$\rightarrow_1$	S_1	$c\ c$	ι_2 expects b from ι_1

Then, cell ι_2 does not accept the first sent item, a, which remains in the inbox multiset (and may be accepted later). Thus, ι_2 idles one step, until it receives the second item, b, which is transformed by the rule into two c's. More complex (and interesting) scenarios can be designed using compound terms and variables.

We briefly suggest how this novel feature could be simulated, in the *synchronous* case, by explicit "firewall" cells on communication channels, without overly many ruleset changes. However, this may considerably obscure and slow down the system. Consider, like above, two connected main cells, ι_1 and ι_2, with an additional firewall cell, ϕ_{12}, standing on the communication channel, as in Fig. 1 – ignoring ϕ'_{12}, for the moment.

As before, cell ι_1 sends messages toward ι_2, without bothering that the sent messages are stored and filtered by firewall ϕ_{12}. Cell ϕ_{12} acts as a proxy for

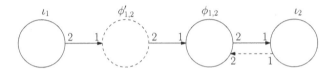

Fig. 1. Simulating an "inbox" multiset.

ι_2 and must be tightly synchronised with it, to ensure that only messages with required patterns are further relayed. But, these patterns may change over time. In some cases, ϕ_{12} may be able to automatically remain in sync with ι_1. However, in the general case, ϕ_{12} may need some feedback from ι_2, updating the format of the expected messages. This will work, except when ι_1 is Byzantine faulty and sends out a message, pretending to come from ι_2, and describing a pattern able to confuse ι_2.

In such cases, a more elaborate solution will be required, e.g. by inserting another firewall cell, ϕ'_{12}, on the same communication channel. The task of ϕ'_{12} is to slow down the traffic coming from ι_1, such that ϕ_{12} receives these messages at odd steps only. We can also ensure that ϕ_{12} receives feedback from ι_2 at even steps only. Thus, in the *synchronous* case, time could be used to differentiate between possible Sybil messages and genuine feedback. We do not further follow this issue here.

Our novel receive primitive, '?', does solve all such problems, without such artefacts, in both synchronous and asynchronous cases, while keeping the cP solution close to the conceptual model and its performance.

3   EIG Trees

We assume that the reader is familiar with the basic terminology and notations: functions, relations, graphs, nodes (vertices), arcs, directed graphs, dags, trees, alphabets, strings and multisets. Given two sets, A, B, a subset f of their Cartesian product, $f \subseteq A \times B$, is a *functional relation* if $\forall (x, y_1), (x, y_2) \in f \Rightarrow y_1 = y_2$. Obviously, any function $f : A \rightarrow B$ can be viewed a functional relation, $\{(x, f(x)) \mid x \in A\}$, and, vice-versa, any functional relation can be viewed as a function.

We now recall a few basic concepts from combinatorial enumerations. The *integer range* from m to n is denoted by $[m, n]$, i.e. $[m, n] = \{m, m+1, \ldots, n\}$, if $m \leq n$, and $[m, n] = \emptyset$, if $m > n$. The set of *permutations* of n of length m is denoted by $P(n, m)$, i.e. $P(n, m) = \{\pi : [1, m] \rightarrow [1, n] \mid \pi \text{ is injective}\}$. A permutation π is represented by the sequence of its values, i.e. $\pi = (\pi_1, \pi_2, \ldots, \pi_m)$, and we will often abbreviate this further as the sequence $\pi = \pi_1.\pi_2 \ldots \pi_m$. The sole element of $P(n, 0)$ is denoted by $()$, or by λ, if the context removes any possible ambiguity. Given a subrange $[p, q]$ of $[1, m]$, we define a *subpermutation* $\pi(p : q) \in P(n, q-p+1)$ by $\pi(p : q) = (\pi_p, \pi_{p+1}, \ldots, \pi_q)$. The *image* of a permutation π, denoted by $\mathrm{Im}(\pi)$, is the set of its values, i.e. $\mathrm{Im}(\pi) = \{\pi_1, \pi_2, \ldots, \pi_m\}$.

The *concatenation* of two permutations is denoted by $\odot$, i.e. given $\pi \in P(n, m)$ and $\tau \in P(n, k)$, such that $\text{Im}(\pi) \cap \text{Im}(\tau) = \emptyset$, $\pi \odot \tau = (\pi_1, \pi_2, \ldots, \pi_m, \tau_1, \tau_2, \ldots, \tau_k) \in P(n, m + k)$.

An *Exponential Information Gathering* (EIG) tree $T_{N,L}$, $N \geq L \geq 0$, is a labelled rooted tree of height L that is defined recursively as follows. The tree $T_{N,0}$ is a rooted tree with just one node, its root, labelled λ. For $L \geq 1$, $T_{N,L}$ is a rooted tree with $1 + N|T_{N-1,L-1}|$ nodes (where $|T|$ is the size of tree T), root λ, having N subtrees, where each subtree is isomorphic with $T_{N-1,L-1}$ and each node, except the root, is labelled by an element of $[1, N]$ that is *different* from any ancestor node (and also different from any left sibling node, if we want to display it like an ordered tree). Note that, $T_{N,L-1}$ is isomorphic and identically labelled with the tree obtained from $T_{N,L}$ by deleting all its leaves.

It is straightforward to see that there is a bijective correspondence between the permutations of $P(N, L)$ and the sequences (concatenations) of labels on all paths from root to the leaves of $T_{N,L}$. Thus, each node σ in an EIG tree $T_{N,L}$ is uniquely identified by a permutation $\pi_\sigma \in P(N, l)$, where $l \in [0, L]$ is also σ's depth, and, vice-versa, each such permutation π has a corresponding node σ_π. We will further use this node-permutation identification, while referring to nodes.

Given EIG tree $T_{N,L}$, an attribute is a function $\aleph : T_{N,L} \to V$, for some value set V; alternatively, $\aleph$ can be given as a functional subset of $\{\pi \in P(N, t) \mid t \in [0, L]\} \times V$. The classical EIG-based Byzantine algorithm uses two attributes: (i) a top-down attribute *val*, here called α; and (ii) a bottom-up attribute *newval*, here called β.

Figure 2 illustrates three isomorphic EIG trees, (a) $T_{4,2}^2$, (b) $T_{4,2}^3$, (c) $T_{4,2}^4$. As we will see next, theses are the EIG trees built by non-faulty processes 2, 3, 4 (respectively) in our sample scenario 1, where process 1 is Byzantine-faulty (so its own internal structure is irrelevant).

Consider EIG tree 2.b, for process 3, $T_{4,2}^3$. Level 0 corresponds to permutation set $\{\lambda\}$. Level 1 corresponds to permutation set $\{(1), (2), (3), (4)\}$. Level 2 corresponds to permutation set $\{(1, 2), (1, 3), (1, 4), (2, 1), (2, 3), (2, 4), (3, 1), (3, 2), (3, 4), (4, 1), (4, 2), (4, 3)\}$. This tree is decorated with two attributes, α and β. Using the alternate notation for permutations (to avoid embedded parentheses), attribute α corresponds to the functional relation $\{(\lambda, 1), (1, 0), (2, 0), (3, 1), (4, 1), (1.2, 0), (1.3, 0), (1.4, 1), (2.1, 0), (2.3, 0), (2.4, 0), (3.1, 0), (3.2, 1), (3.4, 1), (4.1, 1), (4.2, 1), (4.3, 1)\}$.

4   The EIG Algorithm

Each process starts with its *own* initial decision choice. At the end, all non-faulty processes must take the same final decision, even if the faulty processes attempt to disrupt the agreement, accidentally or intentionally.

A Byzantine faulty process is the most powerful consensus adversary. It can do anything, except changing or stopping messages sent by non-faulty processes: (*i*) it can read (but not change) other messages; (*ii*) it can stop sending its

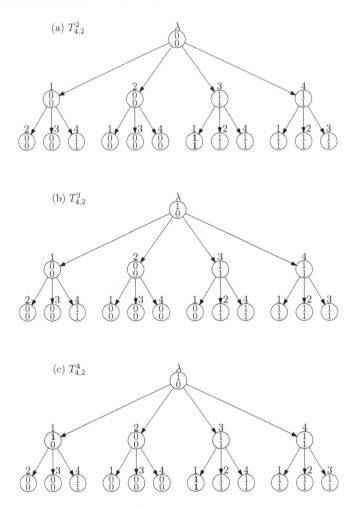

Fig. 2. Three sample EIG trees, $T_{4,2}^h$, $h \in \{2,3,4\}$, completed with two attributes, α and β. The node labels appear besides the node blob. Each node blob contains its two attribute values: the top-down α value at the top, and the bottom-up β value at the bottom.

own expected messages; (iii) it can send conflicting messages; (iv) it can send malformed messages (including unexpected, out-of-round); (v) it can send forged messages, pretending to come from other processes – aka Sybil attack.

The classical EIG-based algorithm solves the Byzantine agreement problem in the *binary decision* case (true $= 1$, false $= 0$), for N *processes*, connected in a *complete graph* (where edges indicate *reliable duplex communication lines*), provided that $N \geq 3F+1$, where F is the maximum number of faulty processes. This is a *synchronous* algorithm; celebrated results (see for example [11]) show that the Byzantine agreement is *not* possible if $N \leq 3F$, in the *asynchronous* case or when the communication links are *not* reliable.

Without providing a complete description, we provide a sketch of the classical algorithm, *reformulated* on the basis of the theoretical framework introduced in Sect. 3. For a more complete and verbose description of this algorithm, including correctness and complexity proofs, we refer the reader to Lynch [11].

Each non-faulty process, h, has its own copy of an EIG tree, $T_{N,L}^h$, where $L = F + 1$. This tree is decorated with two attributes, $\alpha^h, \beta^h : \{\pi \in P(N,t) \mid t \in [0,L]\} \to \{0,1,\text{null}\}$, where null designates undefined items (not yet evaluated). Attributes α^h and β^h are also known as val_h and $newval_h$ [11], or *top-down* and *bottom-up* [5]. As their alternative names suggest, α^h is first evaluated, in a top-down tree traversal, in increasing level order; next, β^h is evaluated, in a bottom-up traversal, in decreasing level order.

The algorithm works in two phases. Its *first phase* is a *messaging* phase which completes the evaluation of the top-down attribute α^h. Initially, $\alpha^h(\lambda) = v^h$, the initial choice of process h; all the other α^h and β^h values are still undefined. Next, there are L messaging rounds. At round $t \in [1,L]$, h broadcasts to all processes (including self), a reversibly encoded message which identifies its α^h values at level $t - 1$ and their EIG destinations. Here, we encode all these via the set $\{(\pi \odot h, \alpha^h(\pi)) \mid \pi \in P(N, t-1), h \notin \text{Im}(\pi)\}$. All other non-faulty processes broadcast messages, in a similar way. More compact encodings are possible, but we don't follow this issue here.

Process h decodes and processes the messages that it receives. From process f, $f \in [1,N]$, process h receives the set $\{(\pi \odot f, \alpha^f(\pi)) \mid \pi \in P(N, t-1)\}$. Each item $(\pi \odot f, \alpha^f(\pi))$ is used to assign further α^h values, to the next level down the EIG tree, by setting $\alpha^h(\pi \odot f) = \alpha^f(\pi)$.

As this formula suggests, it is indeed *critical* that h "knows" the origin f of each received message and that this origin mark cannot be faked by faulty processes that may use so-called Sybil attacks. Wrong or missing values are replaced by the value of a predefined default parameter, $v_0 \in \{0,1\}$. Thus, there are L messaging rounds and, after the last round, all nodes are decorated with values of attribute α. In fact, only the last level α values are actually needed, to start the next phase, a practical implementation can choose to discard the other α values.

Then, the algorithm switches to its *second phase*, the evaluation of the bottom-up attribute β^h. First, for leaves, $\beta^h(\pi) = \alpha^h(\pi), \pi \in P(N,L)$.

Next, given β^h values for level $t \in [1,L]$, each β^h value for the next level up, $\beta^h(\pi), \pi \in P(N, t-1)$, is evaluated on the basis of the β^h values of node π's children, i.e. on the multiset $\{\beta^h(\pi \odot f) \mid f \in [1,N] \setminus \text{Im}(\pi)\}$, using a local majority voting scheme: $\beta^h(\pi) = 0$, if a strict majority of the above multiset values are 0; or, $\beta^h(\pi) = 1$, if a strict majority of the above multiset values are 1; or, $\beta^h(\pi) = v_0$ (the same default parameter mentioned above), if there is a tie.

At the end, the β^h value for the EIG root, $\beta^h(\lambda)$, is process h's final decision. All non-faulty processes will simultaneously reach the same final decision; any decision taken by faulty nodes is not relevant.

Example 1. (Sample Byzantine scenario). Consider a Byzantine scenario with $N = 4$ and $F = 1$, thus $L = 2$. Assume that processes 1, 2, 3 and 4 start with initial choices 0, 0, 1, and 1, respectively. Further, assume that process 1 is faulty. Figure 3 shows sample messages which could be exchanged in this scenario and Fig. 2 shows the corresponding EIG trees, for non-faulty processes 2,3,4.

Each of the non-faulty processes, 1, 2 and 3, broadcasts identical messages to each of the four processes. The faulty process 1 sends conflicting messages. In our scenario, $x = 0$, in the message sent to 1, 2 and 3, but $x = 1$, in the message sent to 4. Also, $y = 1$, in the message sent to 1, 2 and 4, but $y = 0$, in the message sent to 3. White spaces are placeholders indicating potential messages which are not created, because they would have contained duplicated process numbers (1.1, 2.2, 3.3, 4.4). The second phase is not detailed here, except the common final decisions (the question mark indicates an irrelevant value).

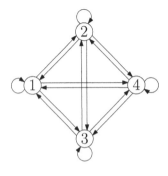

Process	1	2	3	4
Initial choice	0	0	1	1
Faulty	Yes	No	No	No
Round 1 messages	$(1, x)$	$(2, 0)$	$(3, 1)$	$(4, 1)$
Round 2 messages	$(2.1, 0)$ $(3.1, y)$ $(4.1, 1)$	$(1.2, 0)$ $(3.2, 1)$ $(4.2, 1)$	$(1.3, 0)$ $(2.3, 0)$ $(4.3, 1)$	$(1.4, 1)$ $(2.4, 0)$ $(3.4, 1)$
Final decision	?	0	0	0

Fig. 3. A sample Byzantine scenario, $N = 4$, $F = 1$, where process 1 is Byzantine faulty. Process 1 sends out syntactically correct but different messages to the non-faulty processes: $x = 0, y = 1$ to process 2; $x = 0, y = 0$ to process 3; $x = 1, y = 1$ to process 4. As shown in Fig. 2, non-faulty processes 2, 3, 4 build different EIG trees, but they still reach the same final decision.

The second phase is illustrated in Fig. 2, for all non-faulty processes 2, 3, 4. All three EIG tress are shown completed all attribute values. Consider the EIG tree (b) owned by process 3, $T^3_{4,2}$. The α^3 values are filled from messages received in the two messaging rounds, as indicated in Fig. 3.

The β^3 values are evaluated as required by the algorithm, by a local majority voting scheme. The evaluation of $\beta^3(\lambda)$ reaches a tie, on multiset $\{0, 0, 1, 1\}$, which has two 0's and two 1's; this tie is broken using the default value, here we assume $v_0 = 0$. Thus, $\beta^3(\lambda) = 0$ is the final decision of process 3, which is different from its initial choice, $\alpha^3(\lambda) = 1$.

A similar argument shows that all other non-faulty processes, 2 and 4, end with the same final decision, 0, thereby achieving the required agreement, despite starting with different initial choices and the conflicting messages sent by faulty process 1. Briefly, the Byzantine-faulty process may sometimes affect the outcome (between 0 and 1), but cannot affect the consensus: all non-faulty processes will take the same final decision.

5   Previous Models

Without going into details, in this section we take a bird's eye view on the previous best solutions, Dinneen et al. [5], and Nicolescu (2016/2017) [14], briefly highlighting their merits and problems.

Dinneen et al. [5] was the first P system solution to the Byzantine agreement. In fact, it is not one single solution, but (as usual in the classical model of P systems), it is a *family* of related solutions, each one with its own *variable number of symbols and rules*; in this case, $\mathcal{O}(N!)$ symbols and rules (factorial!), where N is the number of processes. Moreover, to ensure a correct solution, protected even against Sybil attacks, each process was modelled by a main cell surrounded by a constellation of $3N$ "firewall" cells, reduced to $2N$ in a subsequent version. Figures 4 and 5 highlights this network complexity, by illustrating the interconnections between processes #2 and #3 when $N = 4$.

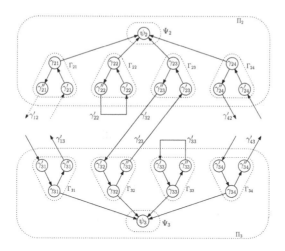

Fig. 4. Two main cells and their firewalls in Dinneen et al. [5].

Using the additional features offered by cP systems, Nicolescu (2016/2017) [14] was the first unitary solution (no family), with a *fixed number of symbols and rules*, not depending on N. However, without adequate control on the message input flow, it still needed Sybil protection by "firewall cells", this time only N per main top-cell. Figure 6 highlights this reduced network complexity, by illustrating all interconnections between all processes, for $N = 4$.

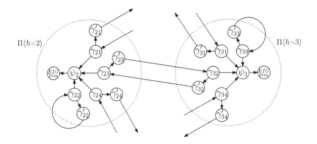

Fig. 5. Two main cells and their firewalls in an updated version of Dinneen et al. [5]

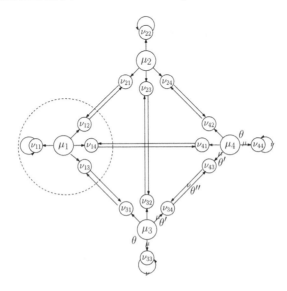

Fig. 6. Main cells and their firewalls in Nicolescu [14].

The novel solution proposed in this paper removes any need for such firewall artefacts and, in fact, improves the solution on all criteria. The new solution uses exactly N top-level cells, as in the conceptual model, illustrated in Fig. 3.

6   The Actor-Like Model

In this section we give a complete ruleset for a top-level cell which models a non-faulty process in the EIG-based Byzantine algorithm of Sect. 4. We illustrate this ruleset by traces for Byzantine process #2, used in Figs. 2 and 3.

6.1   Initial Top-Cell Configuration

Subcells $\bar{\delta}(v)$, $v \in \{0, 1\}$ define the two admissible decision values. Subcell $\bar{v}_0(v)$ contains $v = v_0 \in \{0, 1\}$, the default value known by all processors. Subcell

$\bar{\ell}(L)$ represents the maximum number of levels of the EIG tree, precomputed as $L = F + 1 = \lfloor (N + 2)/3 \rfloor$. Subcells $\bar{\pi}(i)$, $i \in \{1, 2, \ldots, N\}$, define the set of all process ID's.

Additionally, each cell $i \in \{1, 2, \ldots, N\}$, knows its own initial ID, given by subcell $\bar{\mu}(i)$. Subcell $\bar{\alpha}(v)$ contains $v = v_i \in \{0, 1\}$, the initial choice of process #i. Figure 7 shows the initial contents of top-level cell #2.

$$\bar{\delta}(0) \quad \bar{\delta}(1) \quad \bar{v_0}(0) \quad \bar{\ell}(2) \quad \bar{\pi}(1) \quad \bar{\pi}(2) \quad \bar{\pi}(3) \quad \bar{\pi}(4) \quad \bar{\mu}(2) \quad \bar{\alpha}(0)$$

Fig. 7. Initial configuration of top-cell #2, in state S_0.

6.2   Sending Messages

The rules for sending messages are given in Fig. 10. Rule (1) completes the initialisation, creating the root the EIG tree, where: (i) subcell ℓ represents the current level in the EIG tree; and (ii) subcell θ represents a node in the EIG tree, containing the following sub-subcells:

- ℓ: the node level;
- α: the node value (attribute), α in the top-down phase and then β in the bottom-up phase;
- π: the list of EIG node labels (Byzantine process IDs) *from this node to the root*;
- ρ: the set image of the above π list;

Note that the above order for π *reverses* the order used in Sect. 4, e.g. EIG node 3.2 is here represented via $\pi[2, 3]$. Also, ℓ and ρ are not strictly needed, but allows us to quickly check the node's level and if a given ID is or not in list π. Figure 8 shows the contents of top-level cell #2, after the EIG root is created.

$$\bar{\delta}(0) \quad \bar{\delta}(1) \quad \bar{v_0}(0) \quad \bar{\ell}(2) \quad \bar{\pi}(1) \quad \bar{\pi}(2) \quad \bar{\pi}(3) \quad \bar{\pi}(4) \quad \bar{\mu}(2) \quad \bar{\alpha}(0)$$
$$\ell(0) \quad \theta(\ell(0) \, \pi[] \, \rho() \, \alpha(\mathbf{0}))$$

Fig. 8. Top-cell #2 in S_1, after the initialisation of rule (1).

Rule (2) is the rule which stops the message sending rounds when the current level and the maximum number of levels are equal.

Rule (3) sends out messages to every cell (process), which is then stored in their corresponding input queues. The message contains an already incremented level, meaning the message contains the level that it should be stored on. Each message is a θ' term, containing only the essential parts of the corresponding θ term, i.e. without the redundant ρ subterm. The branch has also been indicated and the α value computed, based on its source tree branch. The final part of the rule is an inhibitor, which requires that the current process ID must not be present in the set of process ID's.

Rule (4) creates the templates for next level of EIG nodes. The nodes are initialised with the default value, v_0. Rule (5) increments the level, so we are now at the next level. Figure 9 shows the contents of top-level cell #2, after sending round #1 messages; note the prepared templates for receiving round #1 messages, initialised with $v_0 = 0$.

$\bar{\delta}(0)$ $\bar{\delta}(1)$ $\bar{v_0}(0)$ $\bar{\ell}(2)$ $\bar{\pi}(1)$ $\bar{\pi}(2)$ $\bar{\pi}(3)$ $\bar{\pi}(4)$ $\bar{\mu}(2)$ $\bar{\alpha}(0)$
$\ell(1)$ $\theta(\ell(0) \pi[] \rho() \alpha(0))$
$\theta(\ell(1) \pi[1] \rho(1) \alpha(0))$ $\theta(\ell(1) \pi[2] \rho(2) \alpha(0))$
$\theta(\ell(1) \pi[3] \rho(3) \alpha(0))$ $\theta(\ell(1) \pi[4] \rho(4) \alpha(0))$

Fig. 9. Top-cell #2 in S_2, after sending round #1 messages, i.e. broadcasting copies of $\theta'(\ell(1) \pi[2] \alpha(0))$.

6.3   Receiving Messages

Rule (6) receives well-formed messages. This rule will "consume" the next level template EIG node that was created in rule (4). Thus, the current templates match the well-formed messages received; non well-formed messages are not accepted and the template remains with the default value, v_0, created by rule (4).

Rule (7) makes the level above the current level take the default value. This means that all levels above the current level will contain the default value. Figure 11 shows the contents of top-level cell #2, after receiving round #1 messages.

The previous send and receive steps are repeated L times, where L is given by the contents of $\bar{\ell}(L)$. Figure 13 shows the contents of top-level cell #2, after sending round #2 messages. Figure 14 shows the contents of top-level cell #2, after receiving round #2 messages.

6.4   Second Phase

The second phase corresponds to the bottom-up evaluation of the EIG tree. Rule(8) corresponds to when the bottom up evaluation has finished in which case the final value (which is shared by all non faulty processors) will be stored in ω.

$$S_0 \quad \rightarrow_1 \quad S_1 \; \ell(0) \; \theta(\ell(0) \; \pi[] \; \rho() \; \alpha(V)) \qquad\qquad (1)$$
$$\| \; \bar{\alpha}(V)$$

$$S_1 \quad \rightarrow_1 \quad S_3 \qquad\qquad\qquad\qquad\qquad\qquad\qquad (2)$$
$$\| \; \bar{\ell}(L)$$
$$\| \; \ell(L)$$

$$S_1 \quad \rightarrow_+ \quad S_2 \; !_\forall \{\theta'(\ell(L1) \; \pi[X|P] \; \alpha(V))\} \qquad (3)$$
$$\| \; \bar{\mu}(X)$$
$$\| \; \ell(L)$$
$$\| \; \theta(\ell(L) \; \pi[P] \; \alpha(V) \; \rho(Z))$$
$$\neg \, (Z = XQ')$$

$$S_1 \quad \rightarrow_+ \quad S_2 \; \theta(\ell(L1) \; \pi[X|P] \; \alpha(V)) \qquad\quad (4)$$
$$\| \; \ell(L)$$
$$\| \; \bar{\pi}[X]$$
$$\| \; \bar{v_0}(V)$$
$$\| \; \theta(\ell(L) \; \pi[P] \; \alpha(\_) \; \rho(Z))$$
$$\neg \, (Z = XQ')$$

$$S_1 \; \ell(L) \rightarrow_1 \quad S_2 \; \ell(L1) \qquad\qquad\qquad\qquad (5)$$

Fig. 10. Ruleset for sending messages.

$$\bar{\delta}(0) \quad \bar{\delta}(1) \quad \bar{v_0}(0) \quad \bar{\ell}(2) \quad \bar{\pi}(1) \quad \bar{\pi}(2) \quad \bar{\pi}(3) \quad \bar{\pi}(4) \quad \bar{\mu}(2) \quad \bar{\alpha}(0)$$
$$\ell(1) \quad \theta(\ell(0) \; \pi[] \; \rho() \; \alpha(\mathbf{0}))$$
$$\theta(\ell(1) \; \pi[1] \; \rho(1) \; \alpha(\mathbf{0})) \quad \theta(\ell(1) \; \pi[2] \; \rho(2) \; \alpha(\mathbf{0}))$$
$$\theta(\ell(1) \; \pi[3] \; \rho(3) \; \alpha(\mathbf{1})) \quad \theta(\ell(1) \; \pi[4] \; \rho(4) \; \alpha(\mathbf{1}))$$

Fig. 11. Top-cell #2 in S_1, after receiving round #1 messages: here $\theta'(\ell(1) \; \pi[1] \; \alpha(0))$ from #1, $\theta'(\ell(1) \; \pi[2] \; \alpha(0))$ from #2 (self), $\theta'(\ell(1) \; \pi[3] \; \alpha(1))$ from #3, $\theta'(\ell(1) \; \pi[4] \; \alpha(1))$ from #4.

$$S_2 \; ?_Y\{\theta'(\ell(L1) \; \pi[Y|P] \; \alpha(V))\} \quad \rightarrow_+ \quad S_1 \; \theta(\ell(L1) \; \pi[Y|P] \; \rho(YQ) \; \alpha(V)) \quad (6)$$
$$\theta(\ell(L1) \; \pi[Y|P] \; \alpha(\_)) \qquad\qquad\qquad \| \; \theta(\ell(L) \; \pi[P] \; \rho(Q) \; \alpha(\_))$$
$$\| \; (Q \neq YQ')$$
$$\| \; \bar{\delta}(V)$$

$$S_2 \; \theta(\ell(L) \; \pi[X|P] \; \alpha(\_)) \qquad\quad \rightarrow_+ \quad S_1 \; \theta(\ell(L) \; \pi[X|P] \; \alpha(V)) \qquad (7)$$
$$\| \; \ell(L1)$$
$$\| \; \bar{v_0}(V)$$

Fig. 12. Ruleset for receiving messages.

$\bar{\delta}(0)$ $\bar{\delta}(1)$ $\bar{v}_0(0)$ $\bar{\ell}(2)$ $\bar{\pi}(1)$ $\bar{\pi}(2)$ $\bar{\pi}(3)$ $\bar{\pi}(4)$ $\bar{\mu}(2)$ $\bar{\alpha}(0)$

$\ell(2)$ $\theta(\ell(0)\ \pi[\,]\ \rho()\ \alpha(0))$

$\theta(\ell(1)\ \pi[1]\ \rho(1)\ \alpha(0))$ $\theta(\ell(1)\ \pi[2]\ \rho(2)\ \alpha(0))$

$\theta(\ell(1)\ \pi[3]\ \rho(3)\ \alpha(1))$ $\theta(\ell(1)\ \pi[4]\ \rho(4)\ \alpha(1))$

$\theta(\ell(2)\ \pi[2,1]\ \rho(2,1)\ \alpha(0))$ $\theta(\ell(2)\ \pi[3,1]\ \rho(3,1)\ \alpha(0))$

$\theta(\ell(2)\ \pi[4,1]\ \rho(4,1)\ \alpha(0))$

$\theta(\ell(2)\ \pi[1,2]\ \rho(1,2)\ \alpha(0))$ $\theta(\ell(2)\ \pi[3,2]\ \rho(3,2)\ \alpha(0))$

$\theta(\ell(2)\ \pi[4,2]\ \rho(4,2)\ \alpha(0))$

$\theta(\ell(2)\ \pi[1,3]\ \rho(1,3)\ \alpha(0))$ $\theta(\ell(2)\ \pi[2,3]\ \rho(2,3)\ \alpha(0))$

$\theta(\ell(2)\ \pi[4,3]\ \rho(4,3)\ \alpha(0))$

$\theta(\ell(2)\ \pi[1,4]\ \rho(1,4)\ \alpha(0))$ $\theta(\ell(2)\ \pi[2,4]\ \rho(2,4)\ \alpha(0))$

$\theta(\ell(2)\ \pi[3,4]\ \rho(3,4)\ \alpha(0))$

Fig. 13. Top-cell #2 in S_2, after sending round #2 messages, i.e. broadcasting copies of $\theta(\ell(2)\ \pi[2,1]\ \alpha(0))$, $\theta(\ell(2)\ \pi[2,3]\ \alpha(1))$, $\theta(\ell(2)\ \pi[2,4]\ \alpha(1))$.

$\bar{\delta}(0)$ $\bar{\delta}(1)$ $\bar{v}_0(0)$ $\bar{\ell}(2)$ $\bar{\pi}(1)$ $\bar{\pi}(2)$ $\bar{\pi}(3)$ $\bar{\pi}(4)$ $\bar{\mu}(2)$ $\bar{\alpha}(0)$

$\ell(2)$ $\theta(\ell(0)\ \pi[\,]\ \rho()\ \alpha(0))$

$\theta(\ell(1)\ \pi[1]\ \rho(1)\ \alpha(\mathbf{0}))$ $\theta(\ell(1)\ \pi[2]\ \rho(2)\ \alpha(\mathbf{0}))$

$\theta(\ell(1)\ \pi[3]\ \rho(3)\ \alpha(\mathbf{0}))$ $\theta(\ell(1)\ \pi[4]\ \rho(4)\ \alpha(\mathbf{0}))$

$\theta(\ell(2)\ \pi[2,1]\ \rho(2,1)\ \alpha(\mathbf{0}))$ $\theta(\ell(2)\ \pi[3,1]\ \rho(3,1)\ \alpha(\mathbf{0}))$

$\theta(\ell(2)\ \pi[4,1]\ \rho(4,1)\ \alpha(\mathbf{1}))$

$\theta(\ell(2)\ \pi[1,2]\ \rho(1,2)\ \alpha(\mathbf{0}))$ $\theta(\ell(2)\ \pi[3,2]\ \rho(3,2)\ \alpha(\mathbf{0}))$

$\theta(\ell(2)\ \pi[4,2]\ \rho(4,2)\ \alpha(\mathbf{0}))$

$\theta(\ell(2)\ \pi[1,3]\ \rho(1,3)\ \alpha(\mathbf{1}))$ $\theta(\ell(2)\ \pi[2,3]\ \rho(2,3)\ \alpha(\mathbf{1}))$

$\theta(\ell(2)\ \pi[4,3]\ \rho(4,3)\ \alpha(\mathbf{1}))$

$\theta(\ell(2)\ \pi[1,4]\ \rho(1,4)\ \alpha(\mathbf{1}))$ $\theta(\ell(2)\ \pi[2,4]\ \rho(2,4)\ \alpha(\mathbf{1}))$

$\theta(\ell(2)\ \pi[3,4]\ \rho(3,4)\ \alpha(\mathbf{1}))$

Fig. 14. Top-cell #2 in S_1, after receiving round #2 messages.

Rule(9) decrements the level so moves up the evaluation tree. Rule(9) removes all pairs of opposite values at the leaves. Rule (10) takes the value of the remaining leaves "after" (actually done in parallel, but can be simply viewed in this way, due to the weak priority order.) Rule (9). Rule (11) Removes the leaves of the bottom up evaluation. Rule (12) decrements the current level corresponding to moving up the evaluation tree. Figures 16 and 17 show the contents of top-level cell #2, after the first, respectively the second, bottom-up evaluation. Figure 18 shows the final contents of top-level cell #2, with its final decision in ω.

$$S_3 \, \ell() \, \theta(\ell() \, \pi[] \, \alpha(V)) \qquad \rightarrow_1 \; S_4 \, \omega(V) \tag{8}$$

$$\begin{aligned} &S_3 \, \theta(\ell(L1) \, \pi[\_|P] \, \alpha(1)) \quad \rightarrow_+ \; S_3 \\ &\theta(\ell(L1) \, \pi[\_|P] \, \alpha(0)) \qquad\qquad \| \, \ell(L1) \end{aligned} \tag{9}$$

$$\begin{aligned} &S_3 \, \theta(\ell(L1) \, \pi[\_|P] \, \alpha(X)) \quad \rightarrow_+ \; S_3 \, \theta(\ell(L) \, \pi[P] \, \alpha(X)) \\ &\theta(\ell(L) \, \pi[P] \, \alpha(\_)) \qquad\qquad\quad \| \, \ell(L1) \end{aligned} \tag{10}$$

$$\begin{aligned} &S_3 \, \theta(\ell(L1)\_) \qquad\qquad\quad \rightarrow_+ \; S_3 \\ &\qquad\qquad\qquad\qquad\qquad\quad \| \, \ell(L1) \end{aligned} \tag{11}$$

$$S_3 \, \ell(L1) \qquad\qquad\qquad \rightarrow_1 \; S_3 \, \ell(L) \tag{12}$$

Fig. 15. Ruleset for evaluating the EIG tree.

$$\begin{aligned} &\bar{\delta}(0) \quad \bar{\delta}(1) \quad \bar{v}_0(0) \quad \bar{\ell}(2) \quad \bar{\pi}(1) \quad \bar{\pi}(2) \quad \bar{\pi}(3) \quad \bar{\pi}(4) \quad \bar{\mu}(2) \quad \bar{\alpha}(0) \\ &\ell(1) \quad \theta(\ell(0) \, \pi[] \, \rho() \, \alpha(0)) \\ &\theta(\ell(1) \, \pi[1] \, \rho(1) \, \alpha(\mathbf{0})) \quad \theta(\ell(1) \, \pi[2] \, \rho(2) \, \alpha(\mathbf{0})) \\ &\theta(\ell(1) \, \pi[3] \, \rho(3) \, \alpha(\mathbf{1})) \quad \theta(\ell(1) \, \pi[4] \, \rho(4) \, \alpha(\mathbf{1})) \end{aligned}$$

Fig. 16. Top-cell #2 in S_3, after first bottom up evaluation.

7 Evaluations and Conclusions

To the best of our knowledge, the current model is the first P system model that maps each Byzantine process to exactly one cell, thus solving the open problem mentioned in [5,14]. As Figs. 4, 5 and 6 show, all our previous models required additional helper/firewall cells around the main cells, as protection against Sybil attacks. The new Actor-based model is much more robust and does not require such additional external protection.

$$\begin{aligned} &\bar{\delta}(0) \quad \bar{\delta}(1) \quad \bar{v}_0(0) \quad \bar{\ell}(2) \quad \bar{\pi}(1) \quad \bar{\pi}(2) \quad \bar{\pi}(3) \quad \bar{\pi}(4) \quad \bar{\mu}(2) \quad \bar{\alpha}(0) \\ &\ell(0) \quad \theta(\ell(0) \, \pi[] \, \rho() \, \alpha(\mathbf{0})) \end{aligned}$$

Fig. 17. Top-cell #2 in S_3, after second bottom up evaluation.

$$\begin{aligned} &\bar{\delta}(0) \quad \bar{\delta}(1) \quad \bar{v}_0(0) \quad \bar{\ell}(2) \quad \bar{\pi}(\iota_1) \quad \bar{\pi}(\iota_2) \quad \bar{\pi}(\iota_3) \quad \bar{\pi}(\iota_4) \quad \bar{\mu}(\iota_2) \quad \bar{\alpha}(0) \\ &\omega(\mathbf{0}) \end{aligned}$$

Fig. 18. Top-cell #2 in S_4, with final value in ω.

Table 1 compares the previous models [5,14], and the current model (2018), on several complexity measures: (i) several static complexity measures (first rows); and (ii) the runtime steps (the last two rows).

Table 1. Summary of complexity measures (where $L = \lfloor (N+2)/3 \rfloor$).

Measure	[5] (2010)	[14] (2016)	This model (2018)
Cells per process	$3N + 1^a$	$N + 1$	1
Atomic symbols	$\mathcal{O}(N!)$	18	14
States	$\mathcal{O}(L)$	14	5
Rules	$\mathcal{O}(N!)$	23	12^b
Ruleset size – raw	2338	2218	1481
Ruleset size – compressed	624	591	526
Raw/Compressed ratio	3.75	3.75	2.81
Steps per top-down level	5	4	2
Steps per bottom-up level	1	3^c	1

[a]$2N + 1$ in later versions.
[b]Cf. Figs. 10, 12, and 15.
[c]Can be reduced to 1.

As Table 1 highlights, the new Actor-based model substantially improves all considered measures. The raw size is the size of an ASCII text files containing the ruleset, described in LaTeX, but without any layout indications. The compressed size is the size of the raw file after compression with 7-Zip, with the LZMA2 compression method and Ultra compression level. The rulesets for firewalls have been included only once, without considering the code replication, $3N$ or N firewall cells per main Byzantine cell. As the files are relatively small, the compressed size is biased by the included compression dictionary, but nevertheless the results could be interesting.

The size of the compressed ruleset is intuitively related to the information content of the ruleset. Interestingly, all considered models have not very different information contents, which is understandable, as they all model the same problem. The raw sizes are however more different. The raw/compressed ratio is intuitively a measure of the ruleset expressivity: the lower the ratio, the better: less noise/redundancy and higher information density. The new Actor-based model seems the most expressive: it has the highest information density with the least noise.

To the best of our knowledge, the new model also compares favourably with any extant description – whether informal, pseudodocode, or code – of the classical EIG tree and algorithm: (i) it is fully formal; (ii) it directly executable; and (iii) it is crisper (without relying on any previously developed library). The reader is invited to compare our formal description to other, even informal descriptions, such as given in classical textbooks, e.g. Lynch [11], pages 108, 109, 120.

As still open problems, we are looking at modelling more sophisticated consensus algorithms (non EIG based), which offer better messaging performance and are actually used in large scale critical applications, such as Blockchains.

Acknowledgments. We are deeply indebted to the co-authors of our former studies on the Byzantine agreement, for their earlier contributions.

Appendix: P Systems with Compound Terms

In the interests of self-containment, we present here new and improved material describing the background of cP Systems, for the benefit of readers as yet unfamiliar with the topic. Much of this appeared in a similar form, most recently in [4], though it has now undergone several significant changes.

Besides some minor terminology and notation changes, here we start with an extended grammar, that includes three notable additions: (i) numbers; (ii) lists; and (iii) actor-like control on receiving messages. The first two items, numbers and lists, that were already possible as constructs derivable from the earlier basic grammar, have been now included, because these seem needed in almost any non trivial application. The last item, however, is a critical new addition, that would have previously been possible only by interfering with the internal cell logic and adding channel-like intermediary cells; the net effect would been loss in clarity, productivity, and efficiency.

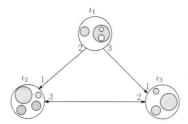

Fig. 19. Bird's eye view of a sample cP system, with top-level cells and subcells.

7.1   cP Systems

As seen in Fig. 19, *cP systems* share and extend some of the fundamental features of both traditional cell-like (tree-based) and tissue (graph-based) P systems:

- Top-level cells are organised in digraph networks and are usually differentiated by unique IDs. Top-level cells represent nodes in a distributed computation (aka inter-cell parallelism).

- Each arc represents a unidirectional communication channel and has two labels: one label at the source cell and another at the target cell (these two labels may, but need not, be different). Where graphs are used, each edge is considered a pair of opposite arcs.
- Top-level cells contain nested (and labelled) sub-cells. Subcells represent local data that can be processed either sequentially or in the max-parallel mode (aka intra-cell parallelism).
- The evolution is governed by multiset rewriting+communication rules, running in exactly-once or max-parallel modes.
- Only top-level cells have evolution rules – nested subcells are just passive data repositories. This seems a severe limitation; however, it is more than compensated by the provision of powerful higher-level rules.
- In a synchronous evolution, each internal step takes zero time units (sic!), and each message takes exactly one time unit to transit from source to target. This model is equivalent to the traditional model, where internal steps take one time unit and messages are instantaneous.
- In an asynchronous evolution, each message may take any finite real time (in $\mathcal{R}_{\geq 0}$) to transit from source to target. This model closely matches the standard runtime model of asynchronous distributed algorithms, and includes the synchronous model as a particular case.
- Top-level cells send messages – via rhs of rewriting rules, using symbol '!' – over outgoing arcs, to their structural neighbours.
- Top-level cells receive messages – via lhs of rewriting rules, using symbol '?' – over incoming arcs, from their structural neighbours.
- Messages which arrive at the target cell are not immediately inserted among the target's contents; instead, these messages are conceptually "enqueued" and there is one message "queue" – read "multiset" – for each incoming arc.
- Receiving cells have full control over the time and format of messages accepted from the message "queues". This model matches similar facilities of Actor models [8,9], such as Receive/Scan (F#) and receive/stash (Akka).
- Messages not yet accepted remain in their message "queues".

The last four items of the above list are brand new extensions, designed to match the capabilities of Actor models.

Note: although not strictly necessary – but also shared with other versions of the traditional P systems – our typical rulesets are state based and run in a weak priority mode.

Note: *subcells* – aka *compound terms* – play the roles of cellular micro-compartments or substructures, such as organelles, vesicles or cytoophidium assemblies ("snakes"), which are embedded in cells or travel between cells, but without having the full processing power of a complete cell. In our proposal, *subcells* represent nested labelled data compartments which have no own processing power: they are acted upon by the rules of their enclosing cells.

7.2   Extended Grammars for Terms and Rules

Our basic vocabulary consists of *atoms* and *variables*, collectively known as *simple terms*, plus a dedicated symbol, '*1*', and a few delimiters: '(', ')', '[', ']', '|'.

Compound terms are similar to Prolog-like *first-order terms*, but recursively built from *multisets* of atoms and variables. Roughly, our compound terms play the role of hierarchically nested subcells in traditional P systems. *Numbers* and *lists* are now explicit in this new extended grammar, although they are ad-hoc derivable as compound terms, by the other rules (as also shown below).

Together, simple terms, compound terms, numbers, and lists are collectively called *terms* and can be defined by the formal grammar in Fig. 20, where '...' denote arbitrary *multiset* repetitions, including zero times.

```
<term> ::= <simple−term> | <compound−term>
         | <number> | <list>
<simple−term> ::= <atom> | <variable>
<compound−term> ::= <functor> '(' <argument> ')'
<functor> ::= <atom>
<argument> ::= <term>...
<number> ::= 1...
<list> ::= '[]' | '[' <head> '|' <list> ']'
<head> ::= <term>...
```

Fig. 20. Term grammar

Symbol λ is an emphatic designation of the empty multiset. *Numbers* are represented in base 1, with *1* as unity symbol. *Atoms* are typically denoted by lower case letters, such as a, b, c. *Variables* are typically denoted by uppercase letters, such as X, Y, Z. If useful, atoms and variables may include subscripts or primes. *Functors* are subcell *labels*, not necessarily distinct; here functors can only be atoms (not variables).

For improved readability, we also consider *anonymous variables*, which are denoted by underscores ('_'). Each underscore occurrence represents a *new* unnamed variable and indicates that something, in which we are not interested, must fill that slot.

Terms that do *not* contain variables are called *ground*, e.g.:

- Ground terms: a, $a() = a(\lambda)$, $a(b)$, $a(bc)$, $a(b^2c)$, $a(b(c))$, $a(bc(\lambda))$, $a(b(c)d(e))$, $a(b(c)d(e))$, $a(b(c)d(e(\lambda)))$, $a(bc^2d)$.
- Terms which are not ground: X, $a(X)$, $a(bX)$, $a(b(X))$, $a(XY)$, $a(X^2)$, $a(XdY)$, $a(Xc())$, $a(b(X)d(e))$, $a(b(c)d(Y))$, $a(b(X^2)d(e(Xf^2)))$; also, using anonymous variables: $\_$, $a(b\_)$, $a(X\_)$, $a(b(X)d(e(\_)))$.

- This term-like construct which starts with a variable is not a term (this grammar defines first-order terms only): $X(aY)$.

In *concrete* models, *cells* may contain *ground* terms only (no variables). Rules may however contain *any* kind of terms, atoms, variables and terms (whether ground and not).

Unification. All terms which appear in rules (ground or not) can be (asymmetrically) *matched* against *ground* terms, using an ad-hoc version of *pattern matching*, more precisely, a *one-way first-order syntactic unification* (one-way, because cells may not contain variables). An atom can only match another copy of itself, but a variable can match any multiset of ground terms (including λ). This may create a combinatorial *non-determinism*, when a combination of two or more variables are matched against the same multiset, in which case an arbitrary matching is chosen. For example:

- Matching $a(b(X)fY) = a(b(cd(e))f^2g)$ deterministically creates a single set of unifiers: $X, Y = cd(e), fg$.
- Matching $a(XY^2) = a(de^2f)$ deterministically creates a single set of unifiers: $X, Y = df, e$.
- Matching $a(b(X)c(1X)) = a(b(1^2)c(1^3))$ deterministically creates one single unifier: $X = 1^2$.
- Matching $a(b(X)c(1X)) = a(b(1^2)c(1^2))$ fails.
- Matching $a(XY) = a(df)$ non-deterministically creates one of the following four sets of unifiers: $X, Y = \lambda, df$; $X, Y = df, \lambda$; $X, Y = d, f$; $X, Y = f, d$.

Performance Note. If the rules avoid any matching non-determinism, then this proposal should not affect the performance of P simulators running on existing machines. Assuming that multisets are efficiently represented, e.g. via hash-tables, our proposed unification probably adds an almost linear factor. Let us recall that, in similar contexts (no occurs check needed), Prolog unification algorithms can run in $O(ng(n))$ steps, where g is the inverse Ackermann function. Our conjecture must be proven though, as the novel presence of multisets may affect the performance.

7.3   High-Level or Generic Rewriting Rules

Typically, our rewriting rules use *states* and are applied top-down, in the so-called *weak priority* order.

Pattern Matching. Rewriting rules are matched against cell contents using the above discussed *pattern matching*, which involves the rule's left-hand side, promoters and inhibitors. Generally, variables have *global rule scope*; these are assumed to be introduced by *existential* quantifiers preceding the rule – with the exception of inhibitors, which may introduce *local variables*, as further discussed below.

Intuitively, the matching is *valid* only if, after substituting variables by their values, the rule's right-hand side contains ground terms only (so *no* free variables are injected in the cell or sent to its neighbours), as illustrated by the following sample scenario:

- The cell's *current content* includes the *ground term*:
  $n(a\,\phi(b\,\phi(c)\,\psi(d))\,\psi(e))$
- The following (state-less) *rewriting rule fragment* is considered:
  $n(X\,\phi(Y\,\phi(Y_1)\,\psi(Y_2))\,\psi(Z))\ \rightarrow\ v(X)\,n(Y\,\phi(Y_2)\,\psi(Y_1))\,v(Z)$
- Our pattern matching determines the following *unifiers*:
  $X = a,\,Y = b,\,Y_1 = c,\,Y_2 = d,\,Z = e.$
- This is a *valid* matching and, after *substitutions*, the rule's *right-hand* side gives the *new content*:
  $v(a)\,n(b\,\phi(d)\,\psi(c))\,v(e)$

Generic Rules Format. More precisely, the rewriting rules are defined by the formal grammar in Fig. 21, where '...' denote arbitrary repetitions (including zero times). We call this format generic, because it actually defines templates involving variables.

```
<rule>  ::= <lhs> →_α <rhs> <promoters> <inhibitors>
<lhs>   ::= <state> (<loc-term> | {<in-term>}?_δ)...
<rhs>   ::= <state> (<loc-term> | {<out-term>}!_δ)...
<state> ::= <compound-term>
<promoters>  ::= (| <term-or-eq>)...
<inhibitors> ::= (¬ <term-or-eq>)...
<state> ::= <atom> | <compound-term>
<loc-term> ::= <term>      // local term
<in-term>  ::= <term>      // input term
<out-term> ::= <term>      // output term
<term-or-eq> ::= <loc-term>
             | '('<loc-term> '=' <loc-term>')'
```

Fig. 21. Rule grammar

The rewriting rule is unified according to the following rules; ensuring that all states and cell contents are ground:

- Lhs local terms must be unifiable to the cell's ground contents.

- Promoter local terms must be unifiable to the cell's ground contents; but inhibitors must *not* be unifiable to the cell's ground contents; see also note below.
- Lhs local terms are consumed as in traditional P systems.
- Lhs input terms designated by the receive symbol, '$?_\delta$', are received over incoming arcs (from cell's structural neighbours):
  - δ is the label of an incoming arc, a set of such labels, or a variable (including the '_' wildcard).
  - $(a)?_i$ indicates that a is received over incoming arc i;
  - $(a)?_{i,j}$ indicates that a is received over incoming arc i *or* j;
  - $(a)!_X$ indicates that a is received over an arbitrary incoming arc, whose label will be unified with X;
  - Any queued messages that do not match the template 'a' are not accepted in the cell, but kept in the corresponding queue.
- Rhs must contain only ground terms!
- Rhs local terms become available after the end of the current step only, as in traditional P systems (we can also imagine that these are sent via an ad-hoc fast *loopback* arc).
- Rhs output terms designated by the send symbol, '$!_\delta$', are sent over outgoing arcs (to cell's structural neighbours):
  - δ is the label of an outgoing arc, a set of such labels, a variable, or the special symbol $\forall$.
  - $(a)!_i$ indicates that a is sent over outgoing arc i (unicast);
  - $(a)!_{i,j}$ indicates that a is sent over outgoing arcs i and j (multicast);
  - $(a)!_\forall$ indicates that a is sent over all outgoing arcs (broadcast).
- Application mode $\alpha \in \{1, +\}$, indicates the *exactly-once* (aka *min*) or *max-parallel* mode, as further discussed below.
- All terms sent out to the same destination and in the same step form one single *message* and travel together as one single block (regardless of the application modes used).

Application Modes: Exactly-Once and Max-Parallel. To explain our two rule application modes, *exactly-once* and *max-parallel*, let us consider a cell, σ, containing three counter-like compound terms, $c(1^2)$, $c(1^2)$, $c(1^3)$, and the two possible application modes of the following high-level "decrementing" rule:

$$S_1\ c(1\ X) \to_\alpha S_2\ c(X), \text{where } \alpha \in \{1, +\}. \tag{ρ_α}$$

The left-hand side of rule ρ_α, $c(1\ X)$, can be unified in three different ways, to each one of the three c terms extant in cell σ. Conceptually, we instantiate this rule in three different ways, each one tied and applicable to a distinct term:

$$
\begin{aligned}
S_1\ c(1^2) &\to S_2\ c(1), &\quad (\rho_1)\\
S_1\ c(1^2) &\to S_2\ c(1), &\quad (\rho_2)\\
S_1\ c(1^3) &\to S_2\ c(1^2). &\quad (\rho_3)
\end{aligned}
$$

1. If $\alpha = 1$, rule ρ_1 non-deterministically selects and applies *exactly one* of these virtual rules ρ_1, ρ_2, ρ_3. Using ρ_1 or ρ_2, cell σ ends with counters $c(1)$, $c(1^2)$, $c(1^3)$. Using ρ_3, cell σ ends with counters $c(1^2)$, $c(1^2)$, $c(1^2)$.

2. If $\alpha = +$, rule ρ_+ applies all these virtual rules ρ_1, ρ_2, ρ_3, in *max-parallel* mode. Cell σ ends with counters $c(1)$, $c(1)$, $c(1^2)$.

Semantically, the max-parallel mode is equivalent to a virtual sequential "while" loop around the same rule in the exactly-once mode, which would be then repeated until it is no more applicable.

Special Cases. Simple scenarios involving generic rules are sometimes semantically equivalent to sets of non-generic rules defined via bounded loops. For example, consider the rule

$$S_1 \; a(x(I) \; y(J)) \;\rightarrow_+\; S_2 \; b(I) \; c(J),$$

where the cell's contents guarantee that I and J only match integers in ranges $[1, n]$ and $[1, m]$, respectively. Under these assumptions, this rule is essentially equivalent to the following set of $n \times m$ non-generic rules:

$$S_1 \; a_{i,j} \;\rightarrow\; S_2 \; b_i \; c_j, \; \forall i \in [1, n], j \in [1, m].$$

However, unification is a much more powerful concept, which cannot be generally reduced to simple bounded loops.

Promoters and Inhibitors. To expressively define additional useful matchings, our promoters and inhibitors may also use virtual "equality" terms, written in infix format, with the '=' operator. For example, including the term $(ab = XY)$ indicates the following additional matching constraints on variables X and Y: either $X, Y = ab, \lambda$; or $X, Y = a, b$; or $X, Y = b, a$; or $X, Y = \lambda, ab$.

To usefully define inhibitors as full logical negations, variables which only appear in the scope of an inhibitor are assumed to have *local scope*. These variables are assumed to be defined by *existential* quantifiers, immediately after the negation. Semantically, this is equivalent as introducing these variables at the global rule level, but by *universal* quantifiers, after all other global variables, which are introduced by *existential* quantifiers.

As an illustration, consider a cell containing two terms, $a(1) \; a(111)$, and contrast the following two sample rule fragments (for brevity, other rule details are here omitted).

$\ldots \mid a(1XY) \;\neg\; a(X)$	(1)
$\ldots \mid a(1Z) \;\neg\; (Z = XY) \mid a(X)$	(2)

These two rules appear quite similar and their inhibitor tests seem to model the same intuitive expression: *no* $a(X)$ must be present in the cell. In fact, these rule fragments could be explicit with the following quantifiers:

$$
\begin{array}{lll}
\exists X, Y: & \ldots \mid & a(1XY), \; \neg a(X) & (1) \\
\exists Z: & \ldots \mid & a(1Z), \; \neg(\exists X,Y, \; (Z = XY), \; a(X)) & (2) \\
\exists Z, \forall X, Y: \ldots \mid & a(1Z), \; (Z = XY) \implies \neg a(X) & (2')
\end{array}
$$

Rule (1) uses two global variables, X and Y, that can be matched in four different ways: (i) $X, Y = \lambda, \lambda$; (ii) $X, Y = 11, \lambda$; (iii) $X, Y = \lambda, 11$; (iv) $X, Y = 1, 1$. The first three unifications, (i-iii), pass the inhibitor test, as there are *no* terms $a()$, $a(11)$, $a()$, respectively. However, unification (iv) fails the inhibitor test, because there *is* one cell term $a(1)$.

Rules (2, 2') use one global variable, Z, and two local inhibitor variables, X and Y. Variable Z can be matched in two different ways: (i) $Z = \lambda$; (ii) $Z = 11$. Unification (i) passes the inhibitor test, because it only checks one unification, $X, Y = \lambda, \lambda$, and there is *no* cell term $a()$. However, unification (ii) fails the inhibitor test, because it checks three local unifications: $X, Y = 11, \lambda$; $X, Y = \lambda, 11$; $X, Y = 1, 1$; and the last check fails, because of extant term $a(1)$.

The pattern of rule (2) has been further used, in [4], to define a one-step minimum finding ruleset.

Benefits. This type of generic rules allow algorithm descriptions with *fixed-size alphabets* and *fixed-sized rulesets*, independent of the size of the problem and number of cells in the system (often *impossible* with only atomic terms).

Synchronous vs Asynchronous. In our models, we do not make any *syntactic* difference between the synchronous and asynchronous scenarios; this is strictly a *runtime* assumption [13]. Any model is able to run on both the synchronous and asynchronous runtime "engines", albeit the results may differ. Our asynchronous model matches closely the standard definition for asynchronicity used in distributed algorithms; however, this is not needed in this paper so we don't follow this topic here.

7.4   Data Structures in cP Systems

In this section we discuss a few basic operations with our new extended structures, numbers and lists.

Natural Numbers. Natural numbers can be represented via *multisets* containing repeated occurrences of the *same* atom. The new extended cP terms grammar has a built-in symbol, 1, for the unary digit. Thus, the following compound terms can be used to describe the contents of an integer container a: (i) $a() = a(\lambda) \equiv$ the value of a is 0; (ii) $a(1^3) \equiv$ the value of a is 3.

For concise expressions, we may alias multisets of 1 by their corresponding multiplicity, e.g. $a() \equiv a(0), b(1^3) \equiv b(3)$. Nicolescu et al. [15] show how the basic arithmetic operations can be efficiently modelled by P systems with compound terms.

Figure 22 shows a few simple arithmetic assignments, expressions, and comparisons. Note that "strictly less than" $(<)$ requires the extra 1, because Y can match on λ.

$$
\begin{aligned}
x = 0 &\equiv x(\lambda) \\
x = 1 &\equiv x(1) \\
x = 2 &\equiv x(11) \\
x = n &\equiv x(1^n)
\end{aligned}
$$

$x := y + z \equiv y(Y)\, z(Z) \ \rightarrow_1 \ x(YZ)$ *destructive add*

$x := y + z \equiv \ \rightarrow_1 \ x(YZ) \mid y(Y)\, z(Z)$ *preserving add*
$x := y - z \equiv \ \rightarrow_1 \ x(X) \mid y(XZ)\, z(Z)$ *preserving subtract,* **if** $y \geq z$

$x = y \equiv x(X)\, y(X)$ *equality*
$x \leq y \equiv x(X)\, y(XY)$ *less than or equal to*
$x < y \equiv x(X)\, y(XY1)$ *strictly less than*

$x\%2 = 0 \equiv x(XX)$ *even*
$x\%2 = 1 \equiv x(XX1)$ *odd*

$x := \max(0, y - z) \equiv$ *preserving subtract (two rules)*
$ \rightarrow_1 \ x(X) \mid y(XZ)\, z(Z)$
$ \rightarrow_1 \ x() \mid y(Y)\, z(YZ)$

Fig. 22. Numbers: simple assignments, expressions, and comparisons

Lists. Consider the *list* y, containing the following sequence of values: $[u, v, w]$ (using a standard programming notation). List $[u, v, w]$ can be represented as a compound term: $.(u\ .(v\ .(w\ .())))$, where the ad-hoc functor '.' represents the standard list constructor *cons* and '.()' the empty list. However, to avoid ambiguities, different lists may need to use different *cons* functors.

To simplify list processing, the new extended grammar has an unambiguous built-in list, starting with the empty list '[]', and using operator | to separate the head and the tail of a non-empty list.

Thus, list $.(u\ .(v\ .(w\ .())))$ can now be represented as $[u \mid [v \mid [w \mid []]]]$. As a notational convenience, we can also use the standard list notation, $[u, v, w]$. Our named list y can be now represented as a compound term, $y([u, v, w])$, and, as the round parentheses are now redundant, directly as $y[u, v, w]$.

Our lists work as lists in functional programming, i.e. essentially as *stacks*. Figure 23 shows rule fragments for a few simple list/stack operations.

$$\begin{array}{ll}
\rightarrow_1 \; y[\,] & \textit{creating empty list } y \\
a \; y[Y] \;\rightarrow_1\; y[a \,|\, Y] & \textit{pushing } a \textit{ on list } y \\
a(X) \; y[Y] \;\rightarrow_1\; y[X \,|\, Y] & \textit{pushing contents of } a \textit{ on list } y \\
y[X \,|\, Y] \;\rightarrow_1\; b(X) \; y[Y] & \textit{popping the top of list } y \textit{ to contents of } b
\end{array}$$

Fig. 23. Lists: stack operations

References

1. Abd-El-Malek, M., Ganger, G.R., Goodson, G.R., Reiter, M.K., Wylie, J.J.: Fault-scalable Byzantine fault-tolerant services. In: Herbert, A., Birman, K.P. (eds.) SOSP, pp. 59–74. ACM (2005)

2. Cachin, C., Kursawe, K., Shoup, V.: Random oracles in Constantinople: practical asynchronous Byzantine agreement using cryptography. J. Cryptol. **18**(3), 219–246 (2005)

3. Castro, M., Liskov, B.: Practical Byzantine fault tolerance and proactive recovery. ACM Trans. Comput. Syst. **20**(4), 398–461 (2002)

4. Cooper, J., Nicolescu, R.: The travelling salesman problem in cP systems. In: Zhang, G., Wang, J., Pan, L., Qiang, Zeng, Y. (eds.) Asian Conference on Membrane Computing, pp. 9–21 (2017)

5. Dinneen, M.J., Kim, Y.-B., Nicolescu, R.: A faster P solution for the Byzantine agreement problem. In: Gheorghe, M., Hinze, T., Păun, G., Rozenberg, G., Salomaa, A. (eds.) CMC 2010. LNCS, vol. 6501, pp. 175–197. Springer, Heidelberg (2010). https://doi.org/10.1007/978-3-642-18123-8_15

6. Dinneen, M.J., Kim, Y.B., Nicolescu, R.: A faster P solution for the Byzantine agreement problem. Report CDMTCS-388, Centre for Discrete Mathematics and Theoretical Computer Science, The University of Auckland, Auckland, New Zealand, July 2010. http://www.cs.auckland.ac.nz/CDMTCS/researchreports/388-DKN.pdf

7. Gilad, Y., Hemo, R., Micali, S., Vlachos, G., Zeldovich, N.: Algorand: Scaling Byzantine agreements for cryptocurrencies. In: Proceedings of the 26th Symposium on Operating Systems Principles, pp. 51–68. ACM, New York (2017)

8. Hewitt, C.: What is computation? Actor model versus Turing's model. In: A Computable Universe: Understanding and Exploring Nature as Computation, pp. 159–185. World Scientific (2013)

9. Hewitt, C., Bishop, P., Steiger, R.: A universal modular actor formalism for artificial intelligence. In: Proceedings of the 3rd International Joint Conference on Artificial Intelligence, IJCAI 1973, pp. 235–245. Morgan Kaufmann Publishers Inc., San Francisco (1973). http://dl.acm.org/citation.cfm?id=1624775.1624804

10. Lamport, L., Shostak, R.E., Pease, M.C.: The Byzantine generals problem. ACM Trans. Program. Lang. Syst. **4**(3), 382–401 (1982)

11. Lynch, N.A.: Distributed Algorithms. Morgan Kaufmann Publishers Inc., San Francisco (1996)

12. Martin, J.P., Alvisi, L.: Fast Byzantine consensus. IEEE Trans. Dependable Sec. Comput. **3**(3), 202–215 (2006)

13. Nicolescu, R.: Parallel and distributed algorithms in P systems. In: Gheorghe, M., Păun, G., Rozenberg, G., Salomaa, A., Verlan, S. (eds.) CMC 2011. LNCS, vol. 7184, pp. 35–50. Springer, Heidelberg (2012). https://doi.org/10.1007/978-3-642-28024-5_4

14. Nicolescu, R.: Revising the membrane computing model for Byzantine agreement. In: Leporati, A., Rozenberg, G., Salomaa, A., Zandron, C. (eds.) CMC 2016. LNCS, vol. 10105, pp. 317–339. Springer, Cham (2017). https://doi.org/10.1007/978-3-319-54072-6_20

15. Nicolescu, R., Wu, H.: Complex objects for complex applications. Roman. J. Inf. Sci. Technol. **17**(1), 46–62 (2014)

16. Pease, M.C., Shostak, R.E., Lamport, L.: Reaching agreement in the presence of faults. J. ACM **27**(2), 228–234 (1980)

Solving QSAT in Sublinear Depth

Alberto Leporati[1(✉)], Luca Manzoni[1], Giancarlo Mauri[1],
Antonio E. Porreca[1,2], and Claudio Zandron[1]

[1] Dipartimento di Informatica, Sistemistica e Comunicazione,
Università degli Studi di Milano-Bicocca, Viale Sarca 336/14, 20126 Milano, Italy
{leporati,luca.manzoni,mauri,porreca,zandron}@disco.unimib.it
[2] Aix Marseille Université, Université de Toulon, CNRS, LIS, Marseille, France
antonio.porreca@lis-lab.fr

Abstract. Among **PSPACE**-complete problems, QSAT, or *quantified SAT*, is one of the most used to show that the class of problems solvable in polynomial time by families of a given variant of P systems includes the whole **PSPACE**. However, most solutions require a membrane nesting depth that is *linear* with respect to the number of variables of the QSAT instance under consideration. While a system of a certain depth is needed, since depth 1 systems only allows to solve problems in $\mathbf{P}^{\#\mathbf{P}}$, it was until now unclear if a linear depth was, in fact, necessary. Here we use P systems with active membranes with charges, and we provide a construction that proves that QSAT can be solved with a *sublinear* nesting depth of order $\frac{n}{\log n}$, where n is the number of variables in the quantified formula given as input.

1 Introduction

The solution of the quantified SAT problem (QSAT) by means of P Systems with a "deep" membrane structure is a common way to prove that uniform families of P systems are able to solve all the problems in **PSPACE** [1,12]. Most of these approaches exploit the fact that, to verify the validity of a quantified formula φ, it is sufficient to "dedicate" a level of the membrane structure to a single quantifier, with each membrane acting either as an *or* gate (for existential quantifiers) or as an *and* gate (for universal quantifiers). The result is a membrane structure whose depth is, in the case of uniform families, linear with respect to the number of variables in φ.

We already know that part of the power of P systems with active membranes with charges is given by the depth of the membrane structure, that allows them to generate finely partitioned structures otherwise impossible to attain with depth 1 systems. In fact, depth 1 systems have been proved [2] to be limited to solve in polynomial time the problems in $\mathbf{P}^{\#\mathbf{P}}$, a class which is conjecturally smaller than **PSPACE**. Furthermore, even with constant depth the currently known problems that can be solved all reside inside the counting hierarchy [3] and we conjecture this inclusion to actually be an upper bound on the computational power of constant depth P systems. Even in other models of P systems, like

© Springer Nature Switzerland AG 2019
T. Hinze et al. (Eds.): CMC 2018, LNCS 11399, pp. 188–201, 2019.
https://doi.org/10.1007/978-3-030-12797-8_13

tissue P systems or depth 1 P systems with antimatter, the class $\mathbf{P}^{\#\mathbf{P}}$ provides a strict upper bound on the computational power [4,5].

Since the nesting depth of the membrane structure in the presence of division is such an important factor, it is somewhat surprising that there is a very large gap in our knowledge: the computational power endowed to P systems by a sublinear (but more than constant) depth is currently unknown. Existing characterisations show that those kinds of systems contain at least the whole counting hierarchy **CH** and are limited above by **PSPACE**. Their exact characterisation is, however, currently unknown. Also in traditional complexity theory the landscape of classes inhabiting the space between **CH** and **PSPACE** is surprisingly empty: does that mean that everything will collapse to **CH** or will reach **PSPACE** or that there are new, unknown, complexity classes that are naturally characterised by uniform families of P systems?

Here we start our investigation by proving that the linear depth (with respect to the number of variables) usually employed to solve QSAT is actually unnecessary and that, in fact a sublinear depth of $O(\frac{n}{\log n})$ is sufficient. We prove this result by "compressing" the usual membrane structure and delegating part of its duties to the internal membranes. Each one of them is, in fact, able to simulate a membrane sub-structure that is traditionally of logarithmic depth. While this first result seems, at a first glance, to suggest that even smaller depths might be sufficient to solve QSAT, we notice that it is unlikely that this same technique can be employed to further reduce the nesting depth: to obtain further results, different techniques might be needed.

2   Basic Notions

For an introduction to membrane computing and the related notions of formal language theory and multiset processing, we refer the reader to *The Oxford Handbook of Membrane Computing* [10]. Here we recall the formal definition of P systems with active membranes using weak non-elementary division rules [9,13].

Definition 1. *A P system with active membranes with weak non-elementary division rules of initial degree $d \geq 1$ is a tuple*

$$\Pi = (\Gamma, \Lambda, \mu, w_{h_1}, \ldots, w_{h_d}, R)$$

where:

- *Γ is an alphabet, i.e., a finite non-empty set of symbols, usually called objects;*
- *Λ is a finite set of labels;*
- *μ is a membrane structure (i.e., a rooted unordered tree, usually represented by nested brackets) consisting of d membranes labelled by elements of Λ in a one-to-one way;*
- *$w_{h_1}, \ldots, w_{h_d}$, with $h_1, \ldots, h_d \in \Lambda$, are multisets (finite sets with multiplicity) of objects in Γ, describing the initial contents of each of the d regions of μ;*
- *R is a finite set of rules.*

Each membrane possesses, besides its label and position in μ, another attribute called *electrical charge*, which can be either neutral (0), positive (+) or negative (−) and is always neutral before the beginning of the computation.

The rules in R are of the following types:

(a) *Object evolution rules*, of the form $[a \to w]_h^\alpha$.

They can be applied inside a membrane labelled by h, having charge α and containing an occurrence of the object a; the object a is rewritten into the multiset w (i.e., a is removed from the multiset in h and replaced by the objects in w) without changing the charge of h.

(b) *Send-in communication rules*, of the form $a[\ ]_h^\alpha \to [b]_h^\beta$.

They can be applied to a membrane labelled by h, having charge α and such that the external region contains an occurrence of the object a; the object a is sent into h becoming b and, simultaneously, the charge of h is changed to β.

(c) *Send-out communication rules*, of the form $[a]_h^\alpha \to [\ ]_h^\beta b$.

They can be applied to a membrane labelled by h, having charge α and containing an occurrence of the object a; the object a is sent out from h to the outside region becoming b and, simultaneously, the charge of h becomes β.

(e) *Elementary division rules*, of the form $[a]_h^\alpha \to [b]_h^\beta [c]_h^\gamma$.

They can be applied to a membrane labelled by h, having charge α, containing an occurrence of the object a but having no other membrane inside (an *elementary membrane*); the membrane is divided into two membranes having label h and charges β and γ; the object a is replaced, respectively, by b and c, while the other objects of the multiset are replicated in both membranes.

(f') *Weak non-elementary division rules*, *of the form* $[a]_h^\alpha \to [b]_h^\beta [c]_h^\gamma$.

They can be applied to a membrane labelled by h, having charge α, and containing an occurrence of the object a, even if it contains further membranes; the membrane is divided into two membranes having label h and charges β and γ; the object a is replaced, respectively, by b and c, while the rest of the contents (including whole membrane substructures) is replicated in both membranes.

A computation step changes the current configuration according to the following set of principles:

- Each object and membrane can be subject to at most one rule per step, except for object evolution rules: inside each membrane, several evolution rules can be applied simultaneously.
- The application of rules is *maximally parallel*: each object appearing on the left-hand side of evolution, communication, or division rules must be subject to exactly one of them (unless the current charge of the membrane prohibits it). Analogously, each membrane can only be subject to one communication or division rule (types (b)–(f')) per computation step; these rules will be called *blocking rules* in the rest of the paper. In other words, the only objects and membranes that do not evolve are those associated with no rule, or only to rules that are not applicable due to the electrical charges.

- When several conflicting rules can be applied at the same time, a nondeterministic choice is performed; this implies that, in general, multiple possible configurations can be reached after a computation step.
- In each computation step, all the chosen rules are applied simultaneously in an atomic way. However, in order to clarify the operational semantics, each computation step is conventionally described as a sequence of micro-steps whereby each membrane evolves only after its internal configuration (including, recursively, the configurations of the membrane substructures it contains) has been updated. For instance, before a membrane division occurs, all chosen object evolution rules must be applied inside it; this way, the objects that are duplicated during the division are already the final ones.
- The outermost membrane (the root of the tree) cannot be divided and any object sent out from it cannot re-enter the system again.

A *halting computation* of the P system Π is a finite sequence $\mathcal{C} = (\mathcal{C}_0, \ldots, \mathcal{C}_k)$ of configurations, where $\mathcal{C}_0$ is the initial configuration, every $\mathcal{C}_{i+1}$ is reachable from $\mathcal{C}_i$ via a single computation step, and no rules of Π are applicable in $\mathcal{C}_k$.

P systems can be used as language *recognisers* by employing two distinguished objects yes and no: we assume that all computations are halting, and that either one copy of object yes or one of object no is sent out from the outermost membrane, and only in the last computation step, in order to signal acceptance or rejection, respectively. If all computations starting from the same initial configuration are accepting, or all are rejecting, the P system is said to be *confluent*.

In order to solve decision problems (or, equivalently, decide languages), we use *families* of recogniser P systems $\boldsymbol{\Pi} = \{\Pi_x : x \in \Sigma^\star\}$. Each input x is associated with a P system Π_x deciding the membership of x in a language $L \subseteq \Sigma^\star$ by accepting or rejecting. The mapping $x \mapsto \Pi_x$ must be efficiently computable for inputs of any length, as discussed in detail in [7].

Definition 2. *A family of P systems* $\boldsymbol{\Pi} = \{\Pi_x : x \in \Sigma^\star\}$ *is* (polynomial-time) uniform *if the mapping* $x \mapsto \Pi_x$ *can be computed by two polynomial-time deterministic Turing machines E and F as follows:*

- $F(1^n) = \Pi_n$, *where n is the length of the input x and Π_n is a common P system for all inputs of length n with a distinguished input membrane.*
- $E(x) = w_x$, *where w_x is a multiset encoding the specific input x.*
- *Finally, Π_x is simply Π_n with w_x added to a specific membrane, called the input membrane.*

The family $\boldsymbol{\Pi}$ is said to be (polynomial-time) semi-uniform if there exists a single deterministic polynomial-time Turing machine H such that $H(x) = \Pi_x$ for each $x \in \Sigma^\star$.

Any explicit encoding of Π_x is allowed as output of the construction, as long as the number of membranes and objects represented by it does not exceed the length of the whole description, and the rules are listed one by one. This restriction is enforced in order to mimic a (hypothetical) realistic process of construction of the P systems, where membranes and objects are presumably placed in a constant amount during each construction step, and require actual physical space proportional to their number; see also [7] for further details on the encoding of P systems.

2.1 Polynomial Charges

As shown in [6], it is possible to expand the traditional model of membranes with charges by using a polynomial amount of charges instead of only the usual three. When a polynomial slowdown is acceptable, like in the situation under study, the traditional and the enhanced model have the same computational power with the same membrane nesting depth. Therefore, the construction provided here assumes the presence of a polynomial amount of charges, but the results also hold for the traditional model with three charges. In particular, in this extended model the definition of a P system is enriched with a finite set Ψ that defines which charges can assume a membrane; the traditional case, $\Psi = \{-, 0, +\}$. Since a polynomial-time uniform family of this kind of P systems is still constructed using a pair of polynomial-time deterministic Turing machines, also the size of the set of charges is polynomially bounded with respect to the input size. In the rest of the paper for clarity we will represent this extended charges with tuples of various lengths. Nonetheless, each tuple is to be considered as a unique object taken from the set of charges.

3   Construction

Let $\varphi = Q_1 Q_2 \dots Q_n \varphi^\star$ be a quantified Boolean formula with n quantifiers over n variables $V = \{x_1, \dots, x_n\}$ and $\varphi^\star$ its non-quantified version in conjunctive normal form; i.e., $\varphi^\star = C_1 \wedge C_2 \wedge \dots \wedge C_m$ where each C_j, for $1 \leq j \leq m$, is a disjunctive clause. In particular, we will deal with clauses composed of exactly three literals, in order to obtain a number of possible clauses that is polynomial with respect to the number of variables [8]. Finally, we denote by $\mathsf{pos}(C_j)$ the set of variables that appear as positive literals in C_j and by $\mathsf{neg}(C_j)$ the set of variables that appears in C_j as negative literals. The **PSPACE**-complete problem that will be solved by a uniform family of P systems is the *Quantified SAT* problem in its 3-CNF variant [8], where the output is the truthiness of a quantified formula in 3-CNF.

To encode the input formula φ we employ the following encoding:

- There are $8\binom{n}{3}$ bits, one for each possible clause. The i-th bit set to one means that the i-th clause (in lexicographic order) is present in φ.
- There are then n bits, one for each variable, where the i-th bit set to one means that x_i is universally quantified. If the i-th bit is set to 0 then x_i is existentially quantified.

The previous encoding allows to know from the length of the input the number of variables present in φ; a similar encoding was already used in [11], which we refer to for additional details. Therefore, the Turing machine F of the uniformity condition is able to construct the P system with the knowledge of n and not only of the length of φ.

We are going to define a set of symbols, each one denoting a logarithmic number of quantifiers. We assume, without loss of generality, that the variables appear quantified in the order $x_1, x_2, \ldots, x_n$, so that Q_i quantifies variable x_i. If this is not true a simple renaming of the variables can provide a formula satisfying this condition. We also assume that the number of variables n is divisible by $k = \lceil \log_2 n \rceil$; if this does not hold then we apply a padding, that in any case adds no more than $2k$ variables universally quantified. Let $\ell = \frac{n}{k}$ and let $\boldsymbol{Q}_j$ for $1 \leq j \leq \ell$ be the string of quantifiers $Q_{(j-1)k+1} Q_{(j-1)k+2} \cdots Q_{jk}$ where each of the $\frac{n}{\log_2 n}$ sequences is made of k quantifiers. For example, for a formula $\exists x_1 \forall x_2 \forall x_3 \exists x_4 \forall x_5 \exists x_6 \varphi^\star$ with 6 variables, $\lceil \log_2 6 \rceil = 3$, thus $\boldsymbol{Q}_1 = \exists x_1 \forall x_2 \forall x_3$ and $\boldsymbol{Q}_2 = \exists x_4 \forall x_5 \exists x_6$.

Notice that, for a fixed $j \in \{1, \ldots, \ell\}$, the values that can be assumed by $\boldsymbol{Q}_j$ are only polynomial with respect to n: each of the quantifiers $Q_{(j-1)k+1}, \ldots, Q_{jk}$ can only be universal or existential and the variables it quantifies over are only k in number. Therefore, $\boldsymbol{Q}_j$ can assume at most $2^k < 2n$ distinct values.

3.1   Initial Configuration of the P System

The initial structure of the P system constructed by machine F of the uniformity condition consists of $\ell+1$ linearly nested membranes. The membranes are labelled from 1 (the outermost membrane) to $\ell+1$ (the innermost membrane). Intuitively, the first ℓ non-elementary membranes will be used to evaluate the formula φ, while the innermost (elementary) membrane will be used to evaluate the formula $\varphi^\star$ for a given assignment.

For each $i \in \{2, \ldots, \ell+1\}$, the membrane with label i contains objects representing all the variables quantified in $\boldsymbol{Q}_{i-1}$. For example, the membrane with label 2 contains, in the initial configuration, the objects $x_1, \ldots, x_k$, the membrane with label 3 contains $x_{k+1}, \ldots, x_{2k}$, and so on. Notice that, since the variables appear quantified in order and the number of variables can be obtained from the length of the input, this construction can be performed by machine F of the uniformity condition. Furthermore, the elementary membrane contains the object end.

The actual formula φ is encoded by two sets of symbols. The quantifiers are grouped in contiguous strings, each one containing k of them and encoded in the objects $\boldsymbol{Q}_1, \ldots, \boldsymbol{Q}_\ell$. For each clause $C_1, \ldots, C_k$ in $\varphi^\star$ the object $C_{i,i}$ is present, obtained by subscripting the clause C_i with i, its position inside the formula $\varphi^\star$. For the sake of simplicity we will use the notation C_i in both cases, when no confusion arises. Both kinds of objects are placed in the outermost membrane.

3.2 Generation of the Assignments

The generation of the assignments is performed in multiple steps. First of all, each object Q_j representing the j-th string of quantifiers must be sent into membrane j, whereas the objects $C_1, \ldots, C_m$ representing the clauses of φ^* must be sent into the innermost membrane. Finally, the objects $x_1, \ldots, x_n$ trigger the necessary membrane divisions that allow us to obtain a full 2^k-ary tree of depth ℓ. As a result there will still be 2^n elementary membranes, one for each possible assignment.

At the beginning of the computation the objects $Q_2, \ldots, Q_\ell$ are all sent in by rules of type 1. Once object Q_j enters the membrane with label j, by rules of type 2 it is rewritten to a junk object, changing the membrane charge to $(Q_j, 0)$, to record which quantifiers will be evaluated in that membrane and that at moment 0 the objects representing clauses have entered the membrane. Object Q_1 is treated differently since it is already inside membrane 1, so it sets the charge by send out instead of being sent in (rule 3):

$$Q_j\,[\,]_i^{(Q_i,0)} \to [Q_j]_i^{(Q_i,0)} \qquad\qquad \text{for } 1 < j < i \le \ell \qquad (1)$$

$$Q_j\,[\,]_j^0 \to [\#]_j^{(Q_j,0)} \qquad\qquad \text{for } 1 < j \le \ell \qquad (2)$$

$$[Q_1]_1^0 \to [\,]_1^{(Q_1,k,0,0)}\,\# \qquad (3)$$

The charge $(Q_1, k, 0, 0)$ represents the fact that the quantifiers in Q_1 need to be evaluated, and that currently the k-th one is the first that will be evaluated; the meaning of the other two values will be clarified in the following, when the evaluation procedure for the quantifiers is described.

Once all objects of type Q_j are in place, the objects $C_1, \ldots, C_m$ are sent in from the outermost to the innermost membrane in order:

$$C_i\,[\,]_j^{(Q_j,q)} \to [C_i]_j^{(Q_j,q+1)} \quad \text{for } 1 < j \le \ell, 0 \le q < m-1, \text{ and } 1 \le i \le m \quad (4)$$

$$C_i\,[\,]_{\ell+1}^q \to [C_i]_{\ell+1}^{q+1} \qquad \text{for } 1 < j \le \ell, 0 \le q < m-1, \text{ and } 1 \le i \le m \quad (5)$$

$$C_i\,[\,]_j^{(Q_j,m-1)} \to [C_i]_j^{(Q_j,k,0,0)} \qquad \text{for } 1 < j \le \ell \text{ and } 1 \le i \le m \qquad (6)$$

$$C_i\,[\,]_{\ell+1}^{m-1} \to [C_i]_{\ell+1}^{(n-k,0)} \qquad \text{for } 1 \le i \le m \qquad (7)$$

Rules of types 4 and 5 send in the objects representing the first $m-1$ clauses. When an object C_i enters a membrane, it changes the charge to record that another clause has entered. The last clause to enter, when being sent into a non-elementary membrane, modifies the charge to allow for the next phase of the assignment generation to start (rules of type 6). When it enters the innermost membrane (rules of type 7) the charge is changed to record the number of objects of type t_i and f_i that must still enter the membrane before starting the evaluation of the assignment.

Once the charges of the non-elementary membranes have been set to the form $(Q_j, k, 0, 0)$, the division process can start. Since all membranes except the outermost one already contain k objects representing the variables of φ, the charge set by the entrance of the object C_m is sufficient to trigger the applicability of the following rules:

$$[x_i]_j^{(Q_j,k,0,p)} \rightarrow [f_{i,k}]_j^{(Q_j,k,0,p)} \, [t_{i,k}]_j^{(Q_j,k,0,p+h(i,j))} \quad \text{for } 1 \leq j \leq \ell \text{ and } 1 \leq i \leq n \tag{8}$$

$$[x_i]_{\ell+1}^{(n-k,p)} \rightarrow [f_i]_{\ell+1}^{(n-k,p)} \, [t_i]_{\ell+1}^{(n-k,p+h(i,j))} \quad \text{for } 1 \leq i \leq n \tag{9}$$

where $h(i,j)$ is defined as $2^{k-(i-(j-1)k)}$. That is, p can be seen as a k-bit number, ranging from 0 to $2^k - 1$, where $h(i,j)$ sets to 1 the bit corresponding to the position of the variable x_i in the current string Q_j of quantifiers. For non-elementary membranes, rules of type 8 perform the division and update the charge to allow each membrane resulting from the division to have a unique identifier p that can be used to order all the membranes with the same label j resulting from division that are located inside the same membrane. The objects $t_{i,k}$ and $f_{i,k}$ will be rewritten $k + 1$ times before entering into the inner membranes. This allows for the division phase to be completely performed before the send-in happens. For elementary membranes, rules of type 9 perform the division, also adding the identifier p. The result of this division will be a complete tree with a branching factor of 2^k, due to the k division that happened inside each membrane.

Finally, it is necessary for the generated assignments to move into the elementary membranes to be evaluated. Since each non-elementary membrane has 2^k children, it is necessary to generate enough copies of each assignment to enter all the children membranes; this is made through rules of type 11. To avoid any conflict with the division process, each object representing the assignment waits for k steps before being duplicated using rules of type 10:

$$[\alpha_{i,t} \rightarrow \alpha_{i,t-1}]_j^{(Q_j,k,0,p)} \quad \text{for } 1 \leq t \leq k, 1 \leq i \leq n, 1 \leq j \leq \ell, \text{ and } \alpha \in \{t, f\} \tag{10}$$

$$[\alpha_{i,0} \rightarrow \underbrace{\alpha_i \cdots \alpha_i}_{2^k \text{ times}}]_j^{(Q_j,k,0,p)} \quad \text{for } 1 \leq j \leq \ell, 1 \leq i \leq n, \text{ and } \alpha \in \{t, f\} \tag{11}$$

Once the duplication process has been performed, the objects can actually be sent in, either in a non-elementary membrane (rules of type 12), where the rewriting process of rules of types 10 and 11 will be repeated, or inside an elementary membrane (rules of type 13), where the counter for the missing variable assignments present in the charge will be decremented by one:

$$\alpha_i \,[\,]_j^{(Q_j,k,0,p)} \rightarrow [\alpha_{i,k}]_j^{(Q_j,k,0,p)} \quad \text{for } 1 \le i \le k, 1 \le j \le \ell, \text{ and } \alpha \in \{\mathsf{t},\mathsf{f}\} \quad (12)$$

$$\alpha_i \,[\,]_{\ell+1}^{(n-i,p)} \rightarrow [\alpha_i]_{\ell+1}^{(n-i-1,p)} \qquad \text{for } 1 \le i \le n \text{ and } \alpha \in \{\mathsf{t},\mathsf{f}\} \quad (13)$$

Notice that since the number of objects that can be involved in send-in rules present in each membrane is 2^k, which is also the number of membranes where they can enter, they distribute uniformly (i.e., one per membrane) across all children membranes. At the end of the process, once all assignments are inside the 2^n elementary membranes, the charge of all the elementary membranes will be of the form $(0,p)$. The appearance of this charge will make it possible to start the evaluation of the assignments in the next phase.

Notice how the entire process of generating the assignments requires only polynomial time. Each membrane performs at most k divisions (requiring k time steps) and each membrane receives (via send-in) only a polynomial amount of objects (bounded above by the sum of the number of variables, the number of clauses, and the number of quantifiers). Furthermore, the number of possible types of objects and charges remains polynomial during the entire process.

3.3   Evaluation of Assignments

The assignment evaluation is performed inside the elementary membranes. The main idea is that the objects representing the assignment exit one at a time, writing their value in the charge of the membrane. The objects representing the clauses of $\varphi^\star$ are rewritten according to the different charges. If all the clauses are satisfied once the last object of the assignment has been sent out, then that assignment satisfies $\varphi^\star$. Otherwise, the assignment does not satisfy $\varphi^\star$.

For all $p \in \{0,\dots,2^k-1\}$ the following rules are present in the system:

$$[\alpha_1]_{\ell+1}^{(0,p)} \rightarrow [\,]_{\ell+1}^{(\alpha_1,p)} \,\# \qquad \text{for } \alpha \in \{\mathsf{t},\mathsf{f}\} \quad (14)$$

$$[\beta_i]_{\ell+1}^{(\alpha_{i-1},p)} \rightarrow [\,]_{\ell+1}^{(\beta_i,p)} \,\# \qquad \text{for } \alpha,\beta \in \{\mathsf{t},\mathsf{f}\} \quad (15)$$

These rules send-out as junk all the objects representing the assignment of the formula $\varphi^\star$, starting from the first one (rules of type 14), an then sending out all of them one at a time and in order (rules of type 15). This allows the following rules to "read" the assignment from the charge and rewrite an object representing a clause C_j if one of the variables has an assignment that satisfies it:

$$[C_j \rightarrow \mathsf{yes}'_p]_{\ell+1}^{(\mathsf{t}_i,p)} \qquad \text{if } x_i \in \mathsf{pos}(C_j) \quad (16)$$

$$[C_j \rightarrow \mathsf{yes}'_p]_{\ell+1}^{(\mathsf{f}_i,p)} \qquad \text{if } x_i \in \mathsf{neg}(C_j) \quad (17)$$

Once all the objects representing the assignment have been sent out, the object end is sent out to change the charge of the membrane using rules of type 18. Then the objects yes'_p, representing the clauses that have been satisfied, wait one steps by rewriting themselves in yes_p using rules of type 19. At the same time, if at least one object representing one of the clauses has not been rewritten, it exits as $\text{no}_{k,p}$, signalling that the assignment did not satisfy the formula $\varphi^\star$, and sets the charge to $\#$, inhibiting the application of any other rule (rules of type 20). If this does not happen, then one of the yes_p objects is sent out as $\text{yes}_{k,p}$, signalling that the assignment did satisfy $\varphi^\star$ (rules of type 21):

$$[\text{end}]_{\ell+1}^{(\alpha_m,p)} \rightarrow [\ ]_{\ell+1}^{\text{end}} \# \qquad\qquad \text{for } \alpha \in \{t, f\} \qquad\qquad (18)$$

$$[\text{yes}'_p \rightarrow \text{yes}_p]_{\ell+1}^{\text{end}} \qquad\qquad\qquad (19)$$

$$[C_j]_{\ell+1}^{\text{end}} \rightarrow [\ ]_{\ell+1}^{\#} \text{no}_{k,p} \qquad\qquad \text{for } 1 \leq j \leq m \qquad\qquad (20)$$

$$[\text{yes}_p]_{\ell+1}^{\text{end}} \rightarrow [\ ]_{\ell+1}^{\#} \text{yes}_{k,p} \qquad\qquad\qquad (21)$$

The evaluation of an assignment according to these rules requires a time that is linear with respect to the number of variables n. Furthermore, since all the involved quantities (e.g., possible values for p, number of clauses with three literals) are polynomial with respect to n, the number of rules to be defined is also polynomial. Therefore, the evaluation of the assignments requires a polynomial time and all rules necessary to perform it can be constructed in polynomial time.

3.4   Quantifiers

For the description of the following rules it is useful to introduce the concept of *quantification tree*, that is, the "shape" of the computation performed to actually decide if φ is a valid formula. This is a complete binary tree of depth n where to each internal level is associated a quantifier of φ. In particular Q_1 is associated to the root (depth 0), Q_2 is associated to the nodes at depth 1, and so on until the leaves are reached. The leaves are labeled with either t or f; the exact value depends on the satisfiability of $\varphi^\star$ given an assignment obtained by looking at the path from the root to the particular leaf of the tree (x_i is f if to reach depth i from depth $i-1$ the path went to the left and t if it went to the right). To establish the validity of φ each internal node acts either as an $\wedge$ gate (if the quantifier associated to that depth is a universal one) or as a $\vee$ gate (if the associated quantifier is existential). In the following, we will say that the evaluation of the quantifiers moves up a level or moves to other siblings on the same level. This is to be interpreted as a movement on this quantification tree, which is the general method employed to establish the validity of φ by this algorithm. However, while usually this entire quantification tree is explicitly represented by the membrane structure, here it is partially present in the membrane structure and partially "simulated" by the sequential application of rules inside the non-elementary membranes. Since each level of the membrane structure of this construction "compresses" $\log_2 n$ levels of a traditional construction, the resulting tree has a depth that is reduced by a factor of $\frac{1}{\log_2 n}$, thus obtaining a depth of $O\left(\frac{n}{\log_2 n}\right)$.

The evaluation of the quantifiers is performed by alternating two steps: one internal to a membrane and one where the results are sent out to the parent membrane. Each non-elementary membrane receives from its 2^k children a result, either yes or no, of a partial evaluation of the formula φ. These results are numbered from 0 to $2^k - 1$ and are treated like the leaves of a complete binary tree of depth k, each level of the tree representing a different quantifier of Q_j; that is, a fragment of the quantification tree. The results are combined two at a time in a sequential manner, according to the quantifiers of Q_j. For example the first 2^k results are combined with $\wedge$ or $\vee$ (depending on the last quantifier of Q_j) to obtain 2^{k-1} results that will be further combined until a single one is produced. This result of the evaluation of all the quantifiers in Q_j is then sent out to the parent membrane. In the case of the outermost membrane, this is actually the result of evaluating the entire formula φ. While more involved, this procedure is similar to the one usually employed for solving QSAT with P systems with a linear depth with respect to n. The main difference is that, here, instead of exploiting a deeper membrane structure, it is necessary to "compress" some levels of the membrane structure and perform part of the evaluation sequentially inside a single membrane instead of using multiple nested membranes.

In the following, we assume that $0 \leq c < 2^r - 1$ and $0 \leq p < 2^k$. Every membrane with label $j \in \{1, \dots, \ell\}$ has associated the following type of rules:

$$[\alpha_{r,c}]_j^{(Q_j, r, c, p)} \to [\,]_j^{(Q_j, r, c+1, p, \alpha)} \# \quad \text{for } 0 \leq r \leq k \text{ and } \alpha \in \{\text{yes}, \text{no}\} \quad (22)$$

Here the charge contains two indices, r and c, that indicate, respectively, that the current evaluation is of the r-th quantifier of Q_j and that the c-th result is the one that will be read. The values r and c can be interpreted as coordinates in (a fragment of) the quantification tree, where r denotes the depth and c a node among the ones at depth r. To complete the evaluation, the $(c + 1)$-th result should be combined with the c-th one, as follows:

$$[\beta_{r,c} \to \gamma_{r-1, \lfloor \frac{c}{2} \rfloor} \, \spadesuit]_j^{(Q_j, r, c, p, \alpha)} \quad \text{for } 1 \leq j \leq \ell \text{ and } \alpha, \beta \in \{\text{yes}, \text{no}\} \quad (23)$$

where γ is $\alpha \wedge \beta$ if the r-th quantifier in Q_j is a universal one and $\alpha \vee \beta$ if it is an existential one. Here α and β are two siblings in the evaluation tree and are combined to obtain the value γ of their parent. The object $\spadesuit$ appearing in rules of type 23 is used to signal (by being sent out) that the object representing $\alpha \wedge \beta$ (for a universal quantifier) or $\alpha \vee \beta$ (for an existential quantifier) has been produced and, thus, that the evaluation can continue. This action is performed by the following rules:

$$[\spadesuit]_j^{(Q_j, r, c, p, \alpha)} \to [\,]_j^{(Q_j, r, c+1, p)} \# \quad \text{for } 1 \leq j \leq \ell \text{ and } \alpha \in \{\text{yes}, \text{no}\} \quad (24)$$

$$[\spadesuit]_j^{(Q_j,r,2^r-1,p,\alpha)} \rightarrow [\,]_j^{(Q_j,r-1,0,p)} \# \quad \text{for } 1 \le j \le \ell \text{ and } \alpha \in \{\text{yes},\text{no}\} \quad (25)$$

$$[\alpha_{0,0}]_j^{(Q_j,1,1,p)} \rightarrow [\,]_j^{\#} \, \alpha_{k,p'} \quad \text{for } 1 < j \le \ell \text{ and } \alpha \in \{\text{yes},\text{no}\} \quad (26)$$

$$[\alpha_{0,0}]_1^{(Q_j,1,1,p)} \rightarrow [\,]_1^{\#} \, \alpha \quad \text{for } \alpha \in \{\text{yes},\text{no}\} \quad (27)$$

Rules of type 24 modify the charge to evaluate the next two results in the quantification tree while remaining at the same level. Once a level has been exhausted, the evaluation moves up by means of rules or type 25. Once the entire part of the quantification tree that is "simulated" inside a membrane of label j is exhausted, rules of type 26 move the result to the parent membrane. The result will be at the bottom (k-th) level of the quantification tree of the parent membrane and its position among all the other results will be given by value p that was previously stored in the membrane charge. Finally, if the membrane where the evaluation ended is the outermost one, then the produced result is actually the result of the entire computation, and it is sent out as either yes or no.

Notice that the part of the quantification tree that is "simulated" by each non-elementary membrane is polynomial in the number of nodes that it contains. Therefore, the sequential evaluation performed in this construction still requires only polynomial time. Since among membranes at the same level all evaluations are performed in parallel, the time needed to produce the result of the entire computation multiplies this time by a factor that depends only on the depth of the membrane structure. Therefore, the P system resulting from this construction is able to produce an answer in a time which is polynomial with respect to the input size.

3.5   Main Result

The construction presented here shows that QSAT in its 3-CNF variant can be solved with a nesting depth that is sublinear with respect to the number of variables. This is the first solution, as far as the authors know, that goes below a linear nesting depth. In particular:

Theorem 1. *Uniform families of P systems with active membranes with charges and weak non-elementary division rules can solve the QSAT problem in 3-CNF form, where the quantified formula given as input has n variables, using a depth of* $O(\frac{n}{\log n})$ □.

Even if the construction employed uses polynomial charges, instead of the usual 3, it has already been proved that one system can be converted into the other with only a polynomial slowdown and no increase in depth [6]. We want to remark that the availability of additional charges allowed a more compact and easier construction.

4   Conclusions

While solving **PSPACE**-complete problems, QSAT in particular, with P systems with active membranes with charges employing weak non-elementary division rules is not a new result, the construction provided here is the first one where the nesting depth of the membrane structure is sub-linear with respect to the number of variables in input. This is a first step in the direction of characterising the power of families of P systems with sublinear depth. While we have provided a construction reducing the depth needed in a specific problem (QSAT with a formula in 3-CNF), but it is still open what is the impact of this result in term of complexity classes. We want to remark that this construction cannot be directly employed to reduce the depth of the membrane structure below $O\left(\frac{n}{\log_2 n}\right)$, because we are already employing a polynomial number of charges, types of objects, and rules. Employing the same method to further reduce depth, for example to $O\left(\frac{n}{(\log_2 n)^2}\right)$, would require a superpolynomial number of charges, object types, and rules – thus violating the uniformity condition of the family.

The remaining investigation work is vast: a complete characterisation of the families of constant depth is still in the work and other classes, like the one of families of logarithmic depth, are unexplored. Charting this unknown space of complexity classes is a long-term objective that will probably be necessary to attain in order to completely understand the complex interaction between nesting depth and computational power in P systems.

References

1. Alhazov, A., Martín-Vide, C., Pan, L.: Solving a PSPACE-complete problem by recognizing P systems with restricted active membranes. Fundam. Inform. **58**(2), 67–77 (2003)
2. Leporati, A., Manzoni, L., Mauri, G., Porreca, A.E., Zandron, C.: Simulating elementary active membranes. In: Gheorghe, M., Rozenberg, G., Salomaa, A., Sosík, P., Zandron, C. (eds.) CMC 2014. LNCS, vol. 8961, pp. 284–299. Springer, Cham (2014). https://doi.org/10.1007/978-3-319-14370-5_18
3. Leporati, A., Manzoni, L., Mauri, G., Porreca, A.E., Zandron, C.: Membrane division, oracles, and the counting hierarchy. Fundam. Inform. **138**(1–2), 97–111 (2015)
4. Leporati, A., Manzoni, L., Mauri, G., Porreca, A.E., Zandron, C.: Characterising the complexity of tissue P systems with fission rules. J. Comput. Syst. Sci. **90**, 115–128 (2017)
5. Leporati, A., Manzoni, L., Mauri, G., Porreca, A.E., Zandron, C.: The counting power of P systems with antimatter. Theor. Comput. Sci. **701**, 161–173 (2017)
6. Leporati, A., Manzoni, L., Mauri, G., Porreca, A.E., Zandron, C.: A toolbox for simpler active membrane algorithms. Theor. Comput. Sci. **673**, 42–57 (2017)
7. Murphy, N., Woods, D.: The computational power of membrane systems under tight uniformity conditions. Nat. Comput. **10**(1), 613–632 (2011)
8. Papadimitriou, C.H.: Computational Complexity. Addison-Wesley, Boston (1993)
9. Păun, G.: P systems with active membranes: attacking NP-complete problems. J. Autom. Lang. Comb. **6**(1), 75–90 (2001)

10. Păun, G., Rozenberg, G., Salomaa, A.: The Oxford Handbook of Membrane Computing. Oxford University Press, Oxford (2010)
11. Porreca, A.E., Leporati, A., Mauri, G., Zandron, C.: P systems with active membranes: trading time for space. Nat. Comput. **10**(1), 167–182 (2011)
12. Sosík, P.: The computational power of cell division in P systems: beating down parallel computers? Nat. Comput. **2**(3), 287–298 (2003)
13. Zandron, C., Leporati, A., Ferretti, C., Mauri, G., Pérez-Jiménez, M.J.: On the computational efficiency of polarizationless recognizer P systems with strong division and dissolution. Fundam. Inf. **87**, 79–91 (2008)

Design of Specific P Systems Simulators on GPUs

Miguel Á. Martínez-del-Amor[✉], David Orellana-Martín,
Ignacio Pérez-Hurtado, Luis Valencia-Cabrera, Agustín Riscos-Núñez,
and Mario J. Pérez-Jiménez

Research Group on Natural Computing,
Universidad de Sevilla, Avda. Reina Mercedes S/N, 41012 Sevilla, Spain
{mdelamor,dorellana,perezh,lvalencia,ariscosn,marper}@us.es

Abstract. In order to validate P system models and to assist on their formal verification, simulators are indispensable. Moreover, having efficient simulation tools is crucial, and for this purpose, parallel platforms should be employed. So far, several parallel simulators for P systems have been developed, specifically targeting GPUs (Graphics Processing Units). Although being a hot topic within Membrane Computing, mapping P system parallelism on GPUs is still not a mature area. In the past, we have successfully accelerated the simulation of two specific families of P systems solving SAT with GPUs, and learned in the process some semantics ingredients that fit well on these parallel devices. We are extending this exploration by designing an specific simulator of a P system model for the FACTORIZATION problem. In this paper, we analyse the two main approaches for simulators, and depict some design decisions required for this case study.

Keywords: P systems · Parallel simulation · GPU computing

1 Introduction

Parallel simulation of P systems is of increasingly importance. Simulating membrane systems enable model designers to verify and validate their work, so efficient simulation tools can save time in this process. Moreover, identifying how the bioinspired parallelism of these devices can be handled by current parallel platforms can help to drive next generation technology.

Previous work in this concern has been to simulate different solutions of the same problem in order to isolate P system ingredients that fit well into the parallel architecture of GPUs. In [2], a GPU simulator for a family of P systems with active membranes and division of elementary membranes solving SAT was introduced. This was the first *specific* simulator on the GPU to be defined. In [5], a family of tissue P systems with cell division solving SAT was introduced. The former achieved an speedup of 63× compared to a sequential counterpart, while the latter obtained a 10× of acceleration. Using polarizations in the cell-like

© Springer Nature Switzerland AG 2019
T. Hinze et al. (Eds.): CMC 2018, LNCS 11399, pp. 202–207, 2019.
https://doi.org/10.1007/978-3-030-12797-8_14

model helped to reduce the amount of present objects in the membranes, and its representation has a minor impact to the GPU in terms of memory consumption.

The aforementioned simulators were designed for specific families of P systems, so tailored code was developed. There were also developments concerning *generic* simulators for P system variants, being the first one for P systems with active membranes and elementary division [1]. In this simulator, any P system for that model can be simulated (under certain pre-established restrictions), requiring to invest lot of resources for worst cases that are rare to happen in a real model. For this reason, a stressing test with toy models lead to speedups of up to 7×, but with the family solving SAT just 1.5× [4].

A new solution to the FACTORIZATION problem using computing P systems has been proposed in [6]. Let us recall that the version of FACTORIZATION problem considered in the cited paper is the following: *given a natural number which is the product of two prime numbers, find its decomposition*. A solution to this problem is provided by a family of (binary) computing polarizationless P systems with active membranes making use of minimal cooperation and minimal production (without dissolution rules and without division rules for non-elementary membranes). Minimal cooperation stands for having rules with left-hand side (LHS) length of at most 2, and minimal production means to have rules with right-hand side (RHS) lengths of at most 1.

In this paper, we present the first design decisions of a GPU simulator for the family of computing membrane systems solving the FACTORIZATION problem. This design is feasible thanks to a key feature: minimal production. In this way, it is possible to constrain the size of the membrane representation in the simulator. Furthermore, the amount of present objects can be saved by using internal counters. Moreover, binary representation of the input natural number can be natively represented using unsigned integer numbers on the GPU. This also shades a light on how to design simulators for specific models.

The rest of the paper is structured as follows: Sect. 2 introduces very briefly the key concepts of GPU computing to understand the taken decisions. Section 3 discuses the two approaches when developing parallel P system simulators. Section 4 depicts the design of the simulator while discussing the ingredients that have enabled that. Section 5 ends the paper with conclusions and future work.

2   Core Concepts of GPU Computing

When programming a GPU with CUDA, firstly, the data structures that are going to be used have to be allocated on the device. This constrains the flexibility while increasing the efficiency: reserving new memory on the fly can really slowdown the performance of the code [3]. Once all the data structures are created, the necessary data is sent from the CPU. At this point, the GPU is ready to launch threads that will execute the same code (called kernel) in parallel. The work assignation has to be carefully done by the programmer to balance the amount of threads doing actual job, and how to access the memory (which requires coalesced access to contiguous data to harness best performance). Thread execution is made hierarchically, being arranged in thread blocks. Threads within thread blocks can be synchronized and can cooperate through efficient small memory called shared memory.

3   Generic Versus Specific Parallel Simulators

There are two main approaches when developing GPU simulators for P systems: generic and specific. The former refers to simulators designed to accept a broad range of models within a variant. The latter corresponds to ad-hoc simulators for certain families or models. In CUDA, kernels run faster using static data structure without dynamic memory (i.e. allocated at the beginning of the code). For this purpose, simulators have to consider the worst cases in order to avoid memory conflicts during the simulation.

Generic simulators require to allocate GPU memory for both rule information, auxiliary data and system configurations (see Fig. 1, top-left), with enough space for all possible objects that can be generated (in the worst case, the whole alphabet). The simulation algorithm conceives two main steps: selection (Fig. 1, top-right) and execution of rules (Fig. 1, bottom-left). In order to perform selection of rules, threads need to access to rule information (to consult the LHS) and the current configuration (to seek existing objects and membrane charges), and write the result in the auxiliary data structure (executions of each rule). For execution, threads have to read the auxiliary data (rule selections) and the rule information (for the RHS) and write the new configuration. Finally, the result of the simulation is copied back to the host space for its output (Fig. 1, bottom-right).

On the contrary, specific simulators only need to allocate GPU memory for objects that are known to appear at the same time. This is normally related to the input multiset for some systems. Moreover, rule information is directly encoded in the source code. There is no need to implement a two-step algorithm given that it is known which rules are going to be executed at every step.

4   Design of a Parallel Simulator

The first step to develop a specific simulator is to design an efficient data structure: it has to be limited by containing just the required information, and has to dispose the data contiguously to enable coalesced accesses by threads. As discussed in [3, 4], one performance attribute of P system GPU simulators is object density: if we cannot estimate an upper bound for the number of different objects that can appear in a membrane, then we have to allocate space for all objects defined in the alphabet. In such a case, an array of integers stating the multiplicity of each object defined in the alphabet is required, called *unbounded* representation (see Fig. 2, top). However, if few different objects appear inside the membranes, the GPU will handle a sparse array given that the majority of multiplicities are 0. This has a negative impact in the performance, because if we use a thread to process each object, most of the threads will be idle in any case.

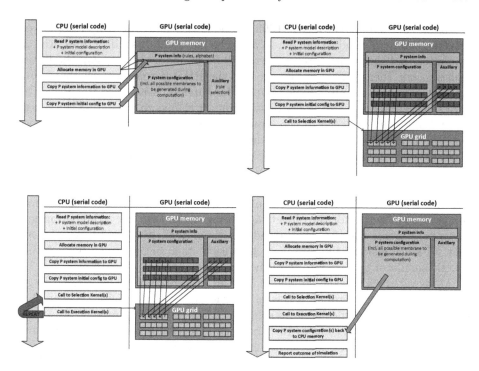

Fig. 1. Scheme of a generic P system simulator on CUDA. For all images, the left part belongs to the CPU side (host) and the right part the GPU (device). Top-left image corresponds to the initialization, where the input model is read and GPU memory is allocated. Top-right figure shows a GPU grid of threads reading information for rule selection, and annotating the outcome. Bottom-left shows the execution of rules by the threads, and the loop over selection and execution. Finally, bottom-right shows the retrieval of the result of the simulation.

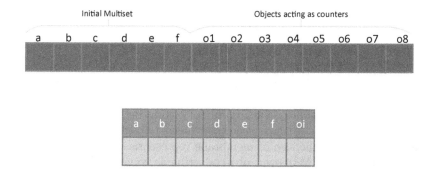

Fig. 2. Unbounded (top) vs limited (bottom) representation of membranes.

In the solution for FACTORIZATION problem, the family of computing P systems uses minimal production. Thus, and when not having send-in rules, we can guarantee that inside membranes there will be no more objects than the initial multiset, but there can be fewer because the RHS of rules can be the empty multiset. The latter causes minor impact for threads, if it is not frequent. The data structure reduces the object density impact thanks to restricting the size of membranes to just the size of the input multiset, but it has to store two values per object: the multiset value, and the corresponding object symbol or identifier. Indeed, now the objects are replaced when applying the rules, and since there is not an array position for each object, we need to annotate which object is being represented. This is called *bounded* representation, and can be seen in Fig. 2, bottom. Thus, the downside of this design is that when using minimal cooperation, a search for the objects appearing in the LHS has to be performed. However, for this specific case (an ad-hoc simulator), it is not an issue, given that we know exactly where to search in each stage beforehand. But a future generic simulator will need to implement more elaborated algorithms.

Moreover, in a specific simulator, not all objects have to be defined in an explicit way; that is, stored in the data structure for multiplicities. Given that the simulator is very specific for a solution, it is possible to represent objects as variables in the source code, or just to depend on certain variables, so the simulator can infer easily the corresponding multiplicities. This is of special interest for counters in the P system models. Normally, P system designs include objects acting as counters. Their symbols depend on subscripts, but they are different objects in any case. If they are treated as normal objects, and we cannot provide an upper bound for the size of membranes, then we would be wasting lot of resources because only one counter object appear at once while allocating a position to each of them. Moreover, specific simulators can use variables corresponding to the subscript of counter object subscripts for the simulator. That would be enough to maintain all the required information of the model, given that it is easy to infer the multiplicity of an object acting as a counter if we know the counter value.

5   Conclusions and Future Work

In this paper we show the main differences when implementing simulators for generic and specific purposes. We also briefly describe some design decisions to develop a specific simulator for a family of computing P systems solving the FACTORIZATION problem. We have seen that thanks to using minimal production, we are able to restrict the size of membrane representation in the simulator to just the input multiset. Moreover, objects acting as counters do not need to be explicitly represented in the simulator.

For future work, we plan to finalize the design and perform the implementation in order to test all the ideas and identify, if possible, more semantics ingredients that help the parallel execution of rules. Another research line would be to explore new features in GPUs that can help to the performance of the simulator, such as Dynamic Parallelism or Cooperative Groups. Moreover, kernel code compilation in runtime open doors to develop automatic CUDA code generation tailored to input models.

Acknowledgments. The authors acknowledge the support from the research project MABICAP TIN2017-89842-P, cofinanced by "Ministerio de Economa, Industria y Competitividad" (MINECO) of Spain, through the "Agencia Estatal de Investigacin" (AEI), and by "Fondo Europeo de Desarrollo Regional" (FEDER) of the European Union.

References

1. Cecilia, J.M., García, J.M., Guerrero, G.D., Martínez-del-Amor, M.A., Pérez-Hurtado, I., Pérez-Jiménez, M.J.: Simulation of P systems with active membranes on CUDA. Briefings Bioinform. **11**(3), 313–322 (2010)
2. Cecilia, J.M., García, J.M., Guerrero, G.D., Martínez-del-Amor, M.A., Pérez-Hurtado, I., Pérez-Jiménez, M.J.: Simulating a P system based efficient solution to SAT by using GPUs. J. Logic Algebraic Program. **79**(6), 317–325 (2010)
3. Martínez-del-Amor, M.A.: Accelerating membrane systems simulators using high performance computing with GPU, Ph.D. thesis, University of Seville, May 2013
4. Martínez-del-Amor, M.A., García-Quismondo, M., Macías-Ramos, L.F., Valencia-Cabrera, L., Riscos-Núñez, A., Pérez-Jiménez, M.J.: Simulating P systems on GPU devices: a survey. Fundam. Inform. **136**(3), 269–284 (2015)
5. Martínez-del-Amor, M.A., Pérez-Carrasco, J., Pérez-Jiménez, M.J.: Characterizing the parallel simulation of P systems on the GPU. Int. J. Unconventional Comput. **9**(5–6), 405–424 (2013)
6. Orellana-Martín, D., Valencia-Cabrera, L., Pérez-Jiménez, M.J.: The factorization problem: a new approach through membrane systems. In: Accepted paper in Membrane Computing Satellite Workshop of 17th International Conference on Unconventional Computation and Natural Computation, 25–29 June, Fontainebleau, France (2018)

Construction of Stable and Lightweight Technical Structures Inspired by Ossification of Bones Using Osteogenetic P Systems

Alexander Melcher[1], Ilija Vukorep[2], and Thomas Hinze[3]([✉])

[1] Niessink Engineering GmbH, Zum Osterberge 7, 31234 Edemissen, Germany
alex-melcher@gmx.de
[2] Chair of Digital Design Department, Brandenburg University of Technology,
Postfach 10 13 44, 03013 Cottbus, Germany
ilija.vukorep@b-tu.de
[3] Department of Bioinformatics, Friedrich Schiller University Jena,
Ernst-Abbe-Platz 2, 07743 Jena, Germany
thomas.hinze@uni-jena.de

Abstract. Vertebrates come with a skeleton of *bones* whose inner structure combines two contradicting properties in a fascinating way: On the one hand, bones are *stable* and robust against mechanical stress, and on the other hand they are *lightweight* to minimise the energy necessary for motion of the organism. By means of a biological process called *ossification*, the inner structure of bones becomes permanently optimised during organism's lifetime which implies a high adaptability to varying environmental and behavioural needs. An appropriate computational model of ossification provides a promising bionics tool with widespread applicability for instance in architecture for construction of technical structures. To this end, we introduce the framework of *osteogenetic P systems* able to generate and to manage the spatial inner structure of bones in a dynamical manner during ossification. Starting from an initial porous network of interwoven *filaments* surrounded by vesicles, a variety of *osteoblasts* and *osteoclasts* is placed alongside the filaments throughout the whole network. External forces, freely configurable in their intensity and effective direction, affect the outer nodes of the network inducing a spatial distribution of *mechanical stress* in its inner filamentary structure. Now, the osteoblasts move towards heavily loaded positions and strengthen the corresponding filaments while osteoclasts eliminate filamentary material wherever dispensable. Over time, the inner network structure adapts to its demands by strong filaments along the main force lines. Complementing our framework of osteogenetic P systems, we demonstrate its practicability using two case studies: The first one describes generation of a *dice-shaped cage* resistant against weights on top. The second study addresses construction of an *arched bridge* with two opposite bearings.

© Springer Nature Switzerland AG 2019
T. Hinze et al. (Eds.): CMC 2018, LNCS 11399, pp. 208–228, 2019.
https://doi.org/10.1007/978-3-030-12797-8_15

1 Introduction

Biological evolution turns out to be an astonishing toolbox of innovation, creativity, functionality, and efficiency. It results in a large number of highly effective mechanisms, operational principles, functional units, and molecular interaction systems, each of them almost perfectly adapted in order to precisely fulfill a specific task with a minimum of energy and further resources. In comparison to solutions designed by engineering, energy consumption of a biological system is diminished for up to several degrees of magnitude while its efficiency factor commonly constitutes more than 90% [1]. So, a thorough understanding of biological systems as a source for unconventional and productive ideas came into the focus of engineering more than 100 years ago. Exploitation and emulation of biological techniques and structures has been discovered as a fruitful field of applied research and development known as *bionics* [23]. In its infancy, more or less simple *mechanical* replications based on observations dominated in these attempts such as early sailplanes and gliders inspired by the flight of storks and cranes with a minimum motion of the wings [30]. Later, the outer *shape* of some animals and plants has been studied to learn about their efficient movement. Here, the boxfish (*Ostracidae*) combines outstanding aerodynamics when swimming in water with a large body volume and a small surface [20]. What stands out is that shapes and forms found in nature are primarily functional but beyond, they also convince by their *beauty* [3].

It is no surprise that engineers responsible for design of mechanical constructions and architects aiming at functional aesthetics are looking for suitable templates and inspirations within the exhaustless world of biology. Planning of *technical structures* not seldomly represents a challenging task. As an essential part of a building or a bridge, they have to guarantee the stability of the entire construction which includes its capacity of coping with mechanical stress as well as influences of the environment like storm or snow. Technical structures should fulfill their function when diverting external and internal forces into the ground. Moreover, there exists the requirement to save material without notable loss of stability and robustness. Finally, technical structures in their spatial arrangement should either be hidden to the public or they are enforced to appear as an artistic element making the construction impressive. When thinking about technical structures, its similarity to the *skeleton* of an organism becomes visible.

The skeleton of vertebrates is composed of *bones*. An adult human comprises slightly more than 200 of these supports whose mass sums up to an amount between 12 and 13 kg, most of them *long bones* [13]. Connected via joints who in turn are relatively free to move, the spatial appearance of the skeleton remains flexible while its components, the bones, feature by a rigid surface. Interestingly, each single long bone is rather lightweight, their density commonly ranges between approximately 1.7 and $2.0 \frac{g}{cm^3}$ and resembles the density of hardened concrete [26]. Although bone's density reaches merely 30% of steel, they can resist mechanical stress up to around $180 \frac{MN}{m^2}$ affecting its cross-sectional area by pressure and around $100 \frac{MN}{m^2}$ by traction [28]. In contrast, homogeneous concrete without special additions is limited to approximately $25 \frac{MN}{m^2}$ [2]. Even plain

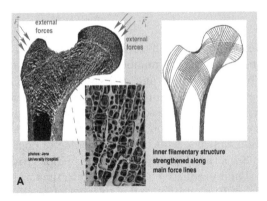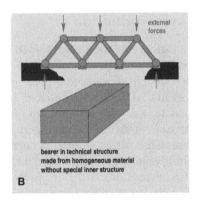

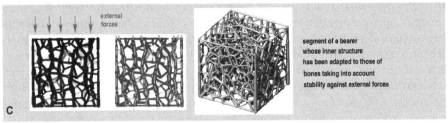

Fig. 1. (A) Sectional view of a femoral bone (put to hip joint) whose inner filamentary structure follows the main force lines providing high stability against external forces keeping a light weight. (B) Bearers in technical structures are typically made from mainly homogeneous material like concrete or steel. (C) Segment of a bearer with inner structure obtained by *artificial ossification*. For a similar stability, less material is needed.

steel typically does not exceed $260\frac{\text{MN}}{\text{m}^2}$ in average despite of its high density [14]. Unequivocally, bones can be seen as an excellent material acting as an example for construction of technical structures. The main advantage of bones consists in their inner spatial structure. While concrete and steel result in a nearly homogeneous material, the inner part of bones is formed by a porous network (tissue) of mineralised filaments (*trabeculaes*) with vesicles mainly filled with air in between. The spatial filamentary structure permanently undergoes a re-organisation in which material gets removed from filaments and, simultaneously, becomes added to strengthen other filaments or to create new ones. The process of re-organisation within the bones is called *ossification* and expresses an optimisation to keep the best possible balance between stability and light weight [12,17]. The question arises whether or not the construction of technical structures can be improved when emulating ossification in a technically reasonable way as illustrated in Fig. 1.

During the last years, *3D printers* initiated a kind of technical revolution for production of three-dimensional objects with challenging shape, complicated surface form, or irregular inner structure [7]. Controlled by a computer, a 3D printer builds the object layer by layer. Each layer is rather thin (around 0.1 mm or even less) made from a fine-grained powdered or viscous material hardened and sticked either by cooling down after short heating or by radiation using laser or ultra-violet light. At the beginning of the 3D printing era, the maximum size of objects was restricted to around 20 cm in each dimension. Likewise, only a small selection of plastic material was available in order to build an object. These early materials did not convince since their properties failed the demands for construction of technical structures. Furthermore, the material was quite expensive. In the meantime, the technique of 3D printing emerged by utilisation of many materials beyond plastics. Another important progress was made in the size of printable objects. Particularly for erection of small buildings, a new technology called *contour crafting* has been successfully developed and employed [19,27]. Here, a huge 3D printer with roboter arms arranged like a travelling crane is set into operation. The building is allowed to cover approximately 10 m × 10 m base area and two floors height. A special mixture of fast-curing concrete is laid on keeping the principle of producing one layer after the other. Having this technique at hand, it can be applied for construction of technical frames or formworks with an inner structure inspired by those found in bones. Indeed, attempts for exploitation of bone-like structures in architecture are not new. In the 1960s, the roof construction of a new lecture theatre at the University of Freiburg (Germany) has been made manually in this way but without use of 3D printing [22].

The optimisation principle of ossification for three-dimensional technical structures along with the feasibility of computer aided simulation, visualisation, and subsequent 3D printing of large-scaled objects give a strong motivation towards a new contribution to membrane computing. Incorporation of all necessary tools and methods into a common framework within the universe of P systems [24] opens a fruitful field of applications in which architecture and civil engineering can benefit from a holistic approach. In addition, P systems with their inherent capacity of coping with dynamical structures represent an ideal candidate to this objective due to their algebraic nature [10]. We introduce the framework of *osteogenetic P systems* bringing together a thoroughly selected collection of algorithmic techniques, enriched by their parameterisation and adaptation at a reasonable level of abstraction. Given the intensities and directions of affecting external forces together with the geometrical positions of bearings at the ground, a proper spatial filamentary structure is sought to be obtained by *artificial ossification* using our system. To this end, we make use of several methods, each of them reflecting the state of the art in various disciplines. The novelty and scientific value lies in the adaptation, parameterisation, and finally combination of these methods into a unique framework equipped with adjusted interfaces.

To our best knowledge, this is the first contribution addressing artificial ossification for optimisation of the inner structure of technical bearings using membrane computing. Since osteoblasts and osteoclasts might enter and leave filaments that in turn are spatially connected in a dynamical manner, a filament can be seen as a cylindrical membrane whose modifiable properties like radius, length, and orientation result from incremental interaction with agents (osteoblasts and osteoclasts) over time. Employment of membrane systems in order to figure out desired spatial structures has been studied in other contexts [8, 21], for instance to find optimal routes within a 2D map under certain constraints [15]. Complementing this achievement, walking membranes along with consideration of geometry were discussed in [16]. Beyond membrane computing, related work includes an optimisation technique for shapes and outer forms called *soft kill option*, SKO for short [5]. This approach is used to reduce the mass of a workpiece by consecutive removal of material at those positions under a low level of mechanical stress. In contrast to ossification, there is no accumulation of material and no interaction.

The paper is structured as follows: In Sect. 2, we familiarise the reader with the biological background of ossification followed by sketching the algorithmic strategy of artificial ossification in Sect. 3. We shed light on selected instruments from finite elements method (FEM) necessary for determination of the mechanical stress throughout the whole filamentary network (Sect. 4). Having all required technical knowledge at hand, the formal definition of osteogenetic P systems is given in Sect. 5. Hereafter, two case studies selected from different application scenarios demonstrate its practical use. First, as an introductory example, the generation of a dice-shaped cage resistant against weights on top with more than 3,000 filaments is taken under examination in Sect. 6. The second case study introduced in Sect. 7 is dedicated to an arched bridge consisting of nearly 1,600 filaments with two opposite bearings. In both case studies, a sufficient spatial structure could be identified in accordance with engineering experience. A final discussion concludes benefits and challenges raising open questions for future work.

2   Biological Background of Ossification

Long bones form a complex *tissue* composed of different cell types arisen from *mesenchymal stem cells*, an embryonal connective precursor [11]. Along with differentiation, mainly *osteoblasts* emerge from this starting point. These cells tend to line up and stick together during progression of cell division which ends up in completion of a *trabecula*, a filament residing at the inner part of the bone. Simultaneous generation of adjacent filaments and their growth leads to successive enrichment of filaments and their interconnection which in turn induces a spatial filamentary network called *matrix* of the bone. This process is accompanied by inclusion of other cell types like blood vessels. Gaps within the matrix structure are called *vesicles*. Due to inherent activities like production of metabolites, vesicles can be spatially robust for a while and temporarily prevent osteoblasts from penetration. The spongy shape of the inner part of a long bone turns out to be soft in the beginning. Over time, more and more *collagen* and various *minerals* incorporated into the cells consolidate its spatial structure. At the outer face called *cortical bone*, the filamentary structure becomes much more densitive since vesicles cannot persist. After maturation of the bone tissue, its constituent

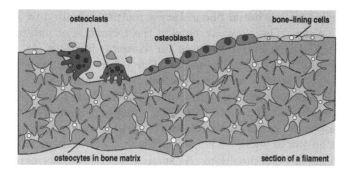

Fig. 2. Schematic representation of biological ossification.

cells have been named *osteocytes*. An adult human body accomodates around $42 \cdot 10^9$ of these in total [25].

Groups of osteoblasts maintain their mobility and resist absorption into an interconnected filamentary structure. Instead, they pass along the filaments. Filamentary regions under high pressure or mechanical stress exhibit so-called microcracks releasing signalling substances and growth factors like *bone morphogenetic proteins* (BMPs). Attracted by these messengers, osteoblasts move towards these regions and start synthesis of bone matrix to repair the microcracks by filling additional material which strengthens the corresponding filament.

Osteoclasts act as antagonists of osteoblasts. Although it seems that there is no evidence of a common cellular ancestor, osteoclasts are assumed to develop from fusions of macrophages residing in regions surrounded by growing bone matrix. An osteoclast possess at its bottom a rasp-like surface. This shape succeeds in resorption of bone matrix while the osteoclast slides along the underlying filament diminishing its mass. Interestingly, osteoclasts are attracted by microcracks in filaments and related messengers as well. Due to their large size in comparison to osteoblasts (more than 100-fold), osteoclasts often fail in reaching the microcracks keeping a certain distance. So, osteoclasts become active in regions of low pressure and low mechanical stress. Filamentary material released by osteoclasts gets recycled whenever neighboured new bone matrix is built.

The interplay of osteoblasts and osteoclasts appears as a well-balanced regulatory system known as *ossification* [29], see Fig. 2. Its re-modelling function of a control loop organises an optimisation process in which strong filamentary structures follow the main force lines inside the bone since most of the microcracks occur along these lines.

3   Idea and Approach of Artificial Ossification

Artificial ossification stands for a biologically inspired optimisation strategy to find out a spatial filamentary structure able to resist given external forces and keeping a proper balance between stability and light weight of the construction in terms of re-modelling the inner structure of long bones in vertebrates.

At the beginning, an initial filamentary structure delimited by an auxiliary outer box is needed. Therefore, we employ the technique of *natural neighbour interpolation (Lloyd's algorithm)* based on *Voronoi* diagrams [18]: A random placement of dots in a three-dimensional Cartesian coordinate system forms a seed to generate spatial regions (vesicles). Within an iterative scheme, we let spherical bubbles successively grow out of each of the dots. Whenever two neighboured bubbles start to intersect, their growth gets stopped by placing a filament in tangential orientation to both bubbles. A filament is modelled by a cylinder with an initial radius. The new filament on its own expands along its longitudinal axis in both directions. As soon as it hits another expanding filament or comes rather close to its adjacent counterparts, all concerned filaments stop further expansion into the corresponding direction and become connected forming a new filamentary junction. After all, we obtain a three-dimensional porous network of interconnected filaments, see Fig. 3. Since formation of trabecular structures in long bones results from a cluster of cells in which vesicular spots appear and expand towards vesicles by pushing the trabecular material outwards, Lloyd's algorithm provides a good approximation of the underlying biological process.

Having an initial filamentary network at hand, the given external forces affecting its outer nodes are taken into consideration. Using the *finite elements method* [9], the resulting mechanical stress within each of the filaments can be determined. To do so, each node (filamentary junction) implies a linear equation system capturing all involved moments of force and effective forces separated according to the x-, y-, and z-dimensions.

Now, the artificial ossification can be set into operation. For this purpose, a large number of *osteoblasts* and *osteoclasts* is randomly placed at the filaments of the entire network. Each osteoclast removes material from its hosting filament reducing its radius. The opposite effect is caused by osteoblasts that add material at the residential filament increasing its radius. In addition, osteoclasts and osteoblasts are able to move along the filaments. While osteoblasts successively pass towards network regions of high mechanical stress, osteoclasts avoid stressful regions. After the motion step, the artificial ossification scheme runs in a cyclic manner by iterated re-calculation of the mechanical stress throughout the whole network followed by the activity of osteoblasts and osteoclasts. Attention has to be paid to situations in which topological modifications inside the network occur: In case of a very thin filament whose radius gets more and more decreased, we remove the filament after a minimum threshold is reached. Furthermore, a junction should connect at least three filaments. If there are only two of them, both filaments become merged into one.

In principle, the artificial ossification can proceed open-end. Since the given external forces remain unchanged during the entire process, the motion of osteoblasts and osteoclasts will more and more slow down and finally stop or pass a repetitive pattern. Unmovable osteoblasts and osteoclasts lose their capability of addition or removal of material.

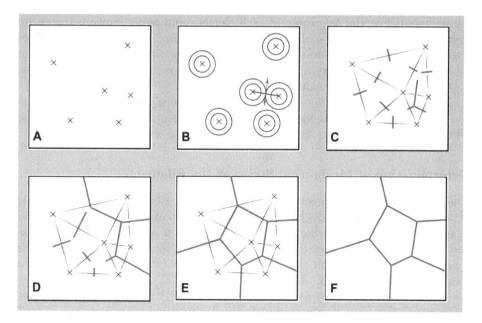

Fig. 3. Gaining an initial spatial filamentary structure using *Lloyd's algorithm.* (A) Random placement of dots. (B) Growing bubbles out of each dot. Intersecting bubbles induce generation of a new filament in tangential orientation. (C) Expansion of filaments. (D) Expanding filaments hit each other forming junctions of three or more filaments. (E) Completion of the filamentary structure. (F) Initial network of interconnected filaments. For better visualisation, a 2D structure is depicted. Within artificial ossification, we utilise 3D coordinates instead.

We found that a proper indicator for termination of the artificial ossification is the percentage of surviving filaments in comparison to its initial number. This percentage typically decreases from 100% at the beginning and converges throughout progression of ossification. By means of the ratio between osteoblasts and osteoclasts placed inside the network, the desired overall mass of the final filamentary structure forming the optimisation result can be configured.

4   Selection of Techniques from Finite Elements Method

Algorithmic handling of artificial ossification comes with adaptation of selected techniques subsumed by *finite elements method* (FEM) [9]. They have in common that a complex mechanical structure gets *decomposed* into its elementary parts. Each *element* can be seen as an impartible unit equipped with individual *parameters* like physical dimension, shape, affecting outer forces, technical conditions of the material and many others. Connection of elements is done via interfaces reflecting corresponding parameter values. Natural and geometrical *laws* modelled by mathematical equations employing the aforementioned parameters define the *behaviour* of each element and hence capture the entire *system's dynamics*. Since each element is characterised exclusively by its effective current parameter values and underlying laws without assumption of an inherent persistent memory able to reconstruct parameter values from the past, it is said to be *finite* analogously to finite automata.

In our scenario, each *filament* and each *filamentary junction* within the network of the bone matrix embodies an individual element. Hereafter, we introduce all techniques necessary to implement our concept of artificial ossification.

Determination of Mechanical Stress at the Filaments

The activities and the directions of move for the osteoblasts and osteoclasts attached to the filaments depend on the average level of mechanical stress found in each filament. The mechanical stress σ present in an element is defined as the amount of force F affecting element's cross-sectional area A by $\sigma = \frac{F}{A}$. For a filament taken as element and modelled by a *cylinder*, its cross-sectional area follows from its radius r by $A = \pi \cdot r^2$.

A *force* is expressed by a vector $\boldsymbol{F} = (F_x, F_y, F_z)^T$ with its absolute value $F = |\boldsymbol{F}| = \sqrt{F_x^2 + F_y^2 + F_z^2}$ in a three-dimensional Cartesian coordinate system. External forces – taken as input of the filamentary system to cope with – might stress all or some of its outer nodes (filamentary junctions at the outer faces of the system). Typically for technical structures, they result from weights or loads on top by means of gravity opposed to the y-axis. A weight of mass m placed on top of a node induces a *normal force* $\boldsymbol{F} = (0, -m \cdot g, 0)^T$ with gravitational acceleration $g \approx 9.81 \frac{m}{s^2}$.

The given external forces get diverted throughout the filaments and filamentary junctions inside the network towards the ground. Calculation of forces in the inner part of the network requires a strategy of successive determination from the nodes affected by external forces to adjacent filaments and junctions towards the nodes at the bottom. To this end, all filamentary junctions become ascendingly ordered by their degree of neighbourship with respect to the nodes assigned with external forces.

Now, for each filamentary junction, we obtain a linear equation system to be solved numerically. To do so, we follow the natural law of *actio = reactio* meaning that for any node within the network the sum of forces constitutes 0 in each dimension, formally $\sum F_x = 0$, $\sum F_y = 0$, and $\sum F_z = 0$. Moreover, forces affecting a junction via an adjacent filament act like a lever: The offset along the main axis of the filament with length l amplifies the effecting force $\boldsymbol{F}$ causing a torsion at the junction under study. Therefore, we must take into account resulting moments $\boldsymbol{M} = l \cdot \boldsymbol{F}$ of force $\boldsymbol{F}$ as well. They also sum up to 0 in each dimension of rotation: $\sum M_x = 0$, $\sum M_y = 0$, $\sum M_z = 0$. In total, we gain six linear equations capturing all known forces (previously calculated or given) and forces to determine for the next layer throughout the network.

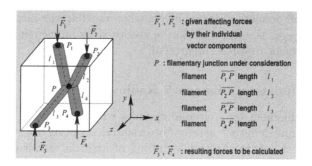

Fig. 4. Exemplary setting of filamentary junction P connected with four adjacent filaments, given affecting forces and resulting forces to be calculated.

Let us demonstrate this approach by an example depicted in Fig. 4. Here, the filamentary junction under study is node $P = (x, y, z)^T$ connecting four filaments $\overline{P_1P}$, $\overline{P_2P}$, $\overline{P_3P}$, and $\overline{P_4P}$. Their opposite junctions are $P_1 = (x_1, y_1, z_1)^T$ to $P_4 = (x_4, y_4, z_4)^T$, respectively. The length l_i of each filament $\overline{P_iP}$ is defined by $l_i = \sqrt{(x_i - x)^2 + (y_i - y)^2 + (z_i - z)^2}$, $i = 1, \ldots, 4$. Let us assume that forces $\boldsymbol{F}_1 = (0, -F_{1_y}, 0)^T$ affecting P_1 and $\boldsymbol{F}_2 = (0, -F_{2_y}, 0)^T$ affecting P_2 are given. We need to know forces $\boldsymbol{F}_3 = (F_{3_x}, F_{3_y}, F_{3_z})^T$ and $\boldsymbol{F}_4 = (F_{4_x}, F_{4_y}, F_{4_z})^T$. This implies a linear equation system as follows:

$$\sum F_x = 0 = F_{1_x} + F_{2_x} + F_{3_x} + F_{4_x} = 0 + 0 + F_{3_x} + F_{4_x}$$

$$\sum F_y = 0 = -F_{1_y} - F_{2_y} + F_{3_y} + F_{4_y}$$

$$\sum F_z = 0 = F_{1_z} + F_{2_z} + F_{3_z} + F_{4_z} = 0 + 0 + F_{3_z} + F_{4_z}$$

$$\sum M_x = 0 = l_1 \cdot F_{1_x} + l_2 \cdot F_{2_x} + l_3 \cdot F_{3_x} + l_4 \cdot F_{4_x} = 0 + 0 + l_3 \cdot F_{3_x} + l_4 \cdot F_{4_x}$$

$$\sum M_y = 0 = -l_1 \cdot F_{1_y} - l_2 \cdot F_{2_y} + l_3 \cdot F_{3_x} + l_4 \cdot F_{4_x}$$

$$\sum M_z = 0 = l_1 \cdot F_{1_z} + l_2 \cdot F_{2_z} + l_3 \cdot F_{3_z} + l_4 \cdot F_{4_z} = 0 + 0 + l_3 \cdot F_{3_z} + l_4 \cdot F_{4_z}$$

The solution to this is:

$$F_{3_x} = 0$$
$$F_{3_y} = \frac{l_1 + l_4}{l_3 + l_4} \cdot F_{1_y} + \frac{l_2 + l_4}{l_3 + l_4} \cdot F_{2_y}$$
$$F_{3_z} = 0$$
$$F_{4_x} = 0$$
$$F_{4_y} = \frac{l_1 + l_3}{l_3 + l_4} \cdot F_{1_y} + \frac{l_2 + l_3}{l_3 + l_4} \cdot F_{2_y}$$
$$F_{4_z} = 0$$

Filament $\overline{P_1P}$ is stressed by $\boldsymbol{F}_1$, filament $\overline{P_2P}$ by $\boldsymbol{F}_2$, filament $\overline{P_3P}$ by $(-F_{3_x}, -F_{3_y}, -F_{3_z})^T$, and finally filament $\overline{P_4P}$ by $(-F_{4_x}, -F_{4_y}, -F_{4_z})^T$. Please note that the components of forces invert when tackling the next layer of junctions. This is due to the fact that forces absorbed by an element in turn affect the adjacent element towards the ground.

Incremental Update of Filament's Radius

We represent a filament by a circular cylinder whose volume $V = \pi r^2 l$ subject to its radius r and length l acts as an essential property for visualisation of the filamentary structure. At the beginning of artificial ossification, each filament's radius gets initialised with an individual value. Along with activity of residing osteoblasts and osteoclasts, its radius becomes incrementally increased or decreased. To this end, we assume that within one time step an attached osteoblast adds a constant amount of ΔV to the filaments's volume while an osteoclast diminishes the volume by ΔV, respectively. We need to know the corresponding change of the underlying radius r in order to update this parameter:

$$
\begin{aligned}
V + \Delta V &= \pi \cdot (r + \Delta r)^2 \cdot l \\
&= \pi r^2 l + 2\pi r \Delta r l + \pi (\Delta r)^2 l \qquad | - V \\
\Delta V &= \pi l (\Delta r)^2 + 2\pi l r \Delta r \qquad | - \Delta V \\
0 &= (\Delta r)^2 + 2r \cdot \Delta r - \frac{\Delta V}{\pi l} \\
\Delta r &= \sqrt{r^2 + \frac{\Delta V}{\pi l}} - r
\end{aligned}
$$

In case of an osteoblast, the radius r gets increased by Δr, in case of an osteoclast decreased.

Elimination of a Filament

It might happen that the resulting amount of a radius gets smaller and smaller over time and finally falls below the minimum threshold dynamically set to Δr. If so, the corresponding filament gets completely removed and residing osteoblasts and osteoclasts will be randomly re-distributed within the entire system. There is still another reason for further elimination. In rare cases, elimination of a filament due to its vanishing radius might imply a so-called "dangling" filament. One of its ends has no connection to other filaments. So, it cannot contribute to transmission of forces and hence, it is negligible. We decided to eliminate dangling filaments as well.

Unification of two Exclusively Connected Filaments into one

We expect a junction to connect at least three filaments. Along with elimination of a filament, a situation might occur in which a junction comprises exactly two filaments. Typically, both filaments are oriented in a certain planar angle to each other. The corner makes the system less stable since it causes additional moments of force to be compensated by neighboured junctions stressing its material. Analogously to biological ossification, we "smooth" the corner by unification of two exclusively connected filaments into one, see Fig. 5.

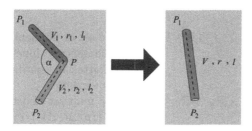

Fig. 5. Merging two cornered filaments $\overline{P_1 P}$ and $\overline{P_2 P}$ into a common filament $\overline{P_1 P_2}$.

Let node $P = (x, y, z)^T$ be the common junction of two filaments, one of them denoted $\overline{P_1 P}$ with $P_1 = (x_1, y_1, z_1)^T$, radius r_1, length $l_1 = \sqrt{(x_1 - x)^2 + (y_1 - y)^2 + (z_1 - z)^2}$, volume $V_1 = \pi r_1^2 l_1$ and the other one named $\overline{P_2 P}$ with $P_2 = (x_2, y_2, z_2)^T$, radius r_2, length $l_2 = \sqrt{(x_2 - x)^2 + (y_2 - y)^2 + (z_2 - z)^2}$, and volume $V_2 = \pi r_2^2 l_2$, respectively. Either filaments to merge form a planar angle α specified by

$$\cos \alpha = \frac{(x - x_1) \cdot (x - x_2) + (y - y_1) \cdot (y - y_2) + (z - z_1) \cdot (z - z_2)}{l_1 \cdot l_2}.$$

Both filaments $\overline{P_1 P}$ and $\overline{P_2 P}$ are removed from the system and replaced by the unified filament $\overline{P_1 P_2}$ with length $l = \sqrt{l_1^2 + l_2^2 - 2 l_1 l_2 \cos \alpha}$, volume $V = V_1 + V_2$, and radius $r = \sqrt{\frac{V}{\pi \cdot l}}$. In addition, we eliminate junction P.

5   Osteogenetic P Systems

Let A and B be arbitrary sets, $\emptyset$ the empty set, $\mathbb{N}$ the set of natural numbers including zero, $\mathbb{R}$ the set of real numbers, and $\mathbb{R}_+$ the set of non-negative real numbers. The Cartesian product $A \times B = \{(a, b) \mid a \in A \wedge b \in B\}$ collects all tuples from A and B. $\wp(A)$ symbolises the power set of A. A multiset over A is a mapping $\mathcal{F} : A \longrightarrow \mathbb{N} \cup \{+\infty\}$. Multisets in general can be written as an elementwise enumeration of the form $\{(a_1, \mathcal{F}(a_1)), (a_2, \mathcal{F}(a_2)), \dots\}$ since $\forall (a, b_1), (a, b_2) \in \mathcal{F} : b_1 = b_2$. A multiset can also be specified by unordered enumeration of multiple elements like for instance $\{a, a, b, a, b\}$ instead of $\{(a, 3), (b, 2)\}$. The support $\mathrm{supp}(\mathcal{F}) \subseteq A$ of $\mathcal{F}$ is defined by $\mathrm{supp}(\mathcal{F}) = \{a \in A \mid \mathcal{F}(a) > 0\}$. Let $\mathcal{F}$ and $\mathcal{G}$ be multisets. The multiset sum $\mathcal{F} \uplus \mathcal{G}$ is defined by $\mathcal{F} \uplus \mathcal{G} = \{(a, h) \mid a \in \mathrm{supp}(\mathcal{F}) \cup \mathrm{supp}(\mathcal{G}) \wedge h = \mathcal{F}(a) + \mathcal{G}(a)\}$.

Definition of Systems Components

An osteogenetic P system Π_O is a construct

$$\Pi_O = (J, B, C, M, m, (\boldsymbol{F}_1, P_1), \ldots, (\boldsymbol{F}_m, P_m))$$

with its components

$J \subset \mathbb{R} \times \mathbb{R} \times \mathbb{R}$ finite set of filamentary junctions
A filamentary junction is specified by its Cartesian coordinates in x-, y-, and z-dimension.

$B : [0, 1] \times \mathbb{R}_+ \times \mathbb{R}_+ \longrightarrow \mathbb{N}$ finite multiset of osteoblasts
Let $((p, \Delta l, \Delta V), 1) \in B$ be an individual osteoblast. p marks its relative position at the longitudinal axis of the hosting filament ($0 \le p \le 1$). Δl gives the motility of the osteoblast which means the distance it moves within one time step along the hosting filament's longitudinal axis. This might include transition to an adjacent filament. ΔV defines the volume of bone matrix synthesised by the osteoblast within one time step and added to the volume of the hosting filament.

$C : [0, 1] \times \mathbb{R}_+ \times \mathbb{R}_+ \longrightarrow \mathbb{N}$ finite multiset of osteoclasts
Let $((p, \Delta l, \Delta V), 1) \in C$ be an individual osteoclast. p marks its relative position at the longitudinal axis of the hosting filament ($0 \le p \le 1$). Δl gives the motility of the osteoclast which means the distance it moves within one time step along the hosting filament's longitudinal axis. This might include transition to an adjacent filament. ΔV defines the volume of bone matrix resorbed by the osteoclast within one time step and removed from the volume of the hosting filament.

$M \subset J \times J \times \mathbb{R}_+ \times \mathbb{R}_+ \times \wp(B) \times \wp(C)$ finite set of membranes (filaments)
Let $(j_1, j_2, r, \sigma, B_M, C_M) \in M$ be a membrane. j_1 and j_2 define the filamentary junctions at the opposite ends. r stands for the average radius of the membrane. σ denotes the amount of

mechanical stress affecting the membrane. $B_M \subseteq B$ indicates the residing osteoblasts and $C_M \subseteq C$ the osteoclasts, respectively. Over all membranes, $\biguplus_M B_M = B$ and $\biguplus_M C_M = C$ is required.

$m \in \mathbb{N} \setminus \{0\}$ number of force vectors

$\boldsymbol{F}_i \in \mathbb{R} \times \mathbb{R} \times \mathbb{R}$ force vector with its components in x-, y-, and z-dimension and index $i \in \{1, \ldots, m\}$. A force vector describes intensity and direction of an external force affecting a filamentary junction of the system.

$P_i \in J$ point of impact of force vector $\boldsymbol{F}_i$.

In addition, we define for auxiliary use a *neighbourship function* $E : J \longrightarrow \wp(M)$ which assigns all adjacent membranes (filaments) to a filamentary junction, formally $E(j) = \{m \in M \mid m = (j_1, j_2, r, \sigma, B_m, C_m) \wedge ((j_1 = j) \vee (j_2 = j))\}$.

Systems Behaviour

The components of an osteogenetic P system Π_O make available a data structure in order to capture all initial parameter values and trace their course by stepwise incremental modifications over time. Here, the tuple (J, B, C, M) represents the systems configuration since its constituents have been updated within a time step.

When set into operation, the system carries out an initialisation phase in order to create a starting filamentary network structure. Using *Lloyd's algorithm*, we obtain a set J of filamentary junctions together with their geometrical connections by membranes (filaments) as components of M. Additionally, the initial radius r is set for all membranes. The next step concerns placement of given external forces $\boldsymbol{F}_i$ with respect to filamentary junctions P_i. Afterwards, the mechanical stress σ for each membrane in M is calculated. This in turn is based on determination of affecting forces for each membrane. Starting from the filamentary junctions located at the impact positions of external forces, each individual filamentary junction implies a linear equation system to be solved numerically using *Gaussian elimination method* [4]. This comes along with checking the validity of the underlying initial network structure to exclude crossing, garbled, or widely intersecting membranes. Those rare cases typically imply under- or over-determined equation systems with no numerical solution. If so, corresponding filamentary junctions and adjacent membranes get removed. Now, a number of osteoblasts B and osteoclasts C is generated and randomly attached to membranes at random positions along the hosting membranes. For appropriate optimisation results, osteoblasts and osteoclasts should penetrate most or all spatial regions of the filamentary network avoiding larger gaps. Now, we have the entire setting of initial data at hand.

The dynamical systems behaviour is organised by an iterative update scheme for artificial ossification. In an incremental manner, the systems components B, C, M, and J have been evaluated and modified whereas each pass represents one time step. More in detail, following actions are consecutively carried out:

- **Synthesis activity of osteoblasts:** For all membranes and for each residing osteoblast, the addition of bone volume ΔV results in an increase of the radius r of the hosting membrane (filament) by Δr.
- **Resorption activity of osteoclasts:** For all membranes and for each residing osteoclast, the reduction of bone volume ΔV is done by decrease of the radius r of the hosting membrane (filament) by Δr.
- **Elimination of thin filaments:** If the remaining radius of a membrane falls below the threshold of Δr, it is removed from the system. All hosting osteoblasts and osteoclasts become released and randomly re-distributed among the surviving membranes of the entire system.
- **Removal of dangling filaments:** A filamentary junction connected with merely one membrane (filament) gets removed from the system and the corresponding membrane as well.
- **Unification of two exclusively connected filaments (Smoothing of corners):** Filamentary junctions connected with two membranes get removed and membranes are merged into one. Residing osteoblasts and osteoclasts are placed at random relative positions of the unified membrane.
- **Move of osteoblasts:** For all membranes and for each residing osteoblast, its move along the longitudinal filament's axis gets emulated. Let $(j_1, j_2, r, \sigma, B_M, C_M)$ be the hosting membrane with length l and $(p, \Delta l, \Delta V)$ the osteoblast under study. First, the direction of move is obtained. To do so, the mechanical stress σ within adjacent membranes is used. If the stress in a membrane connected via j_1 is higher than in the hosting membrane and higher than those connected via j_2, the osteoblast moves towards j_1, its new relative position is $\frac{p \cdot l - \Delta l}{l}$. In case of a negative value, the osteoblast is eliminated from the hosting membrane and attached to the adjacent membrane with maximum mechanical stress. Otherwise, if the stress in an adjacent membrane via j_2 is higher, the new relative position of the osteoblast is $\frac{p \cdot l + \Delta l}{l}$, respectively. A value >1 indicates removal of the osteoblast from its hosting membrane, and it joins the adjacent membrane via j_2 with maximum mechanical stress. If all neighboured membranes possess lower levels of mechanical stress than the hosting membrane, the osteoblast is removed from its hosting membrane and randomly attached to an arbitrary membrane within the entire system.
- **Move of osteoclasts:** Conducted analogously to move of osteoblasts with the only difference that the move is directed towards adjacent membranes with minimum mechanical stress instead of maximum.
- **Re-calculation of mechanical stress** for all membranes (filaments).

Iterations of the update scheme terminate as soon a previously given number of passes is reached or the number of remaining membranes falls below a predefined threshold. The implementation of osteogenetic P systems and their dynamical behaviour has been done using the software tool *Rhinoceros 3D* by Robert McNeel and Associates [6] equipped with extensions *grasshopper – algorithmic modeling for Rhino* (http://www.grasshopper3d.com), *Karamba parametric engineering* (https://www.karamba3d.com), and *HoopSnake* (http://www.grasshopper3d.com/group/hoopsnake). This software collection brings together a strong modelling engine for data management with the required algorithms, a toolbox of finite elements methods, and a graphical engine to generate animated visualisations of filamentary structures evolved during artificial ossification. The model files for all case studies introduced in the following sections are available from the authors upon request. They contain all technical details and act as formal representations of the corresponding systems as a whole.

6   Case Study Dice-shaped Cage

In an introductory example, we employ artificial ossification using an osteogenetic P system for computer-aided construction of a dice-shaped cage able to resist weights on top. This prototype of an element for technical structures is intended to mimic a small brickstone in a frost-protected environment. In comparison to its counterpart made of homogeneous concrete, our cube with inner filamentary structure saves around 30% of the material.

For the outer box of the cube, we choose an edge length of 5 cm which implies a total volume of $125\,cm^3$ representing a well-balanced compromise between an applicable size on the one hand and affordability in its need of computational resources and 3D-printability on the other. The initial filamentary structure comprises $|M| = 3,128$ membranes interconnected via $|J| = 2,096$ filamentary junctions. Out of these, $m = 91$ nodes on top have been affected by vertical external forces $F_i = (0,-1,0)^T$ with $i = 1,\ldots,m$ which means 1N per force vector. A total amount of $|B| = 300$ osteoblasts and $|C| = 300$ osteoclasts complement the initial systems setting. The parity between these agents enables a progression of artificial ossification in which the total mass of all filaments undergoes merely slight changes to have an approximate mass conservation. All membranes (filaments) share an initial radius of 1 mm. Each osteoblast and each osteoclast is capable of processing a filamentary bone volume of $\Delta V = 1\,mm^3$ per iteration (one time step).

Figure 6 illustrates the spatial structure of the cube under study. For visualisation, we set two arbitrarily chosen sectional planes in parallel to each other throughout the filamentary network. After 300, 900, and finally 1,500 iterations we observe the depicted inner structure of the cube emerged during progression of artificial ossification. It becomes visible that mainly vertically oriented filaments get more and more strengthened along the main force lines from top to the ground. In contrast, filaments located in horizontal, diagonal, or inclined orientation have been eliminated or unburdened. After 1,500 iterations, the number

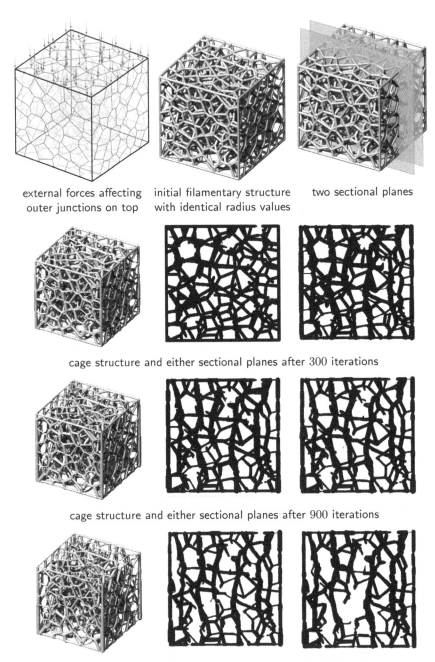

external forces affecting outer junctions on top

initial filamentary structure with identical radius values

two sectional planes

cage structure and either sectional planes after 300 iterations

cage structure and either sectional planes after 900 iterations

cage structure and either sectional planes after 1,500 iterations

Fig. 6. Case study dice-shaped cage – progression and results of artificial ossification

of membranes (filaments) is reduced to $2,058$. The inner filamentary structure successively approximates a cage with many strong vertical columns and holes in between which is in accordance with the expectations from support structure planning. When employing our cage as a brickstone within walls of a building model, its orientation matters. We are aware of the fact that the inner cage structure obtained by artificial ossification is not perfect in terms of a global optimum but it gives an inspirational imagination of the shape strived for.

7   Case Study Arched Bridge

Bridges belong to the most impressive constructions in architecture. They appear in a large variety of shapes and exemplify a close relationship between form and function. The spatial arrangement of support structures witnesses numerous approaches for diversion of forces into the ground. The challenge when constructing a bridge consists in the requirement that all forces have to be bundled since only few bearings exist to connect the bridge with the ground. Most of the area underneath a bridge needs to be free from any construction elements. Hence, this case study was motivated by the question how artificial ossification is able to figure out a sufficient support structure for a bridge with two bearings at the opposite ends and no further connections to the ground. A standard engineering solution to this is called arched bridge, see Fig. 7 upper right part.

For the underlying osteogenetic P system, we initiate an outer box of $8\,cm \times 2\,cm \times 2\,cm$ in size. At the beginning, $|M| = 1,559$ membranes (filaments) and $|J| = 904$ filamentary junctions form a fine-grained initial structure. A number of $m = 400$ force vectors, each of them with intensity of 1N and uniformly placed on top in vertical orientation express the weight to cope with. $|B| = 200$ osteoblasts and $|C| = 200$ osteoclasts have been set into operation. A radius of $1\,mm$ is assigned to all initial filaments, $\Delta V = 1\,mm^3$ holds for all osteoblasts and osteoclasts.

We let the artificial ossification process run for 500 iterations, see Fig. 7. Indeed, the filamentary structure converges into an arched shape with particular strong filaments in horizontal direction in the middle upper part of the bridge. Alongside the main force lines, the filaments exhibit a high density. Underneath the arch, large holes indicate that the material is dispensable. Due to the limited operating range of osteoblasts and osteoclasts, a cluster of filaments got lost at a centered position of the bottom. These filaments are very loosely connected to the rest of the bridge. Osteoblasts and osteoclasts acting here have been more or less locally caught and prevent this cluster of filaments from extinction. Except for this local cluster, the obtained filamentary structure reveals the desired form.

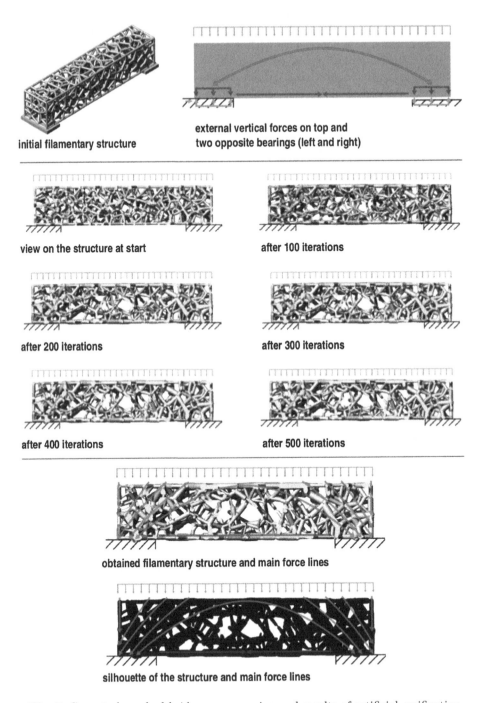

Fig. 7. Case study arched bridge – progression and results of artificial ossification

8   Conclusions

Our concept of osteogenetic P systems for artificial ossification is mainly focused on applications in architecture and civil engineering to figure out suitable spatial structures for frameworks under the influence of freely configurable external forces. In terms of computer science, our approach can be seen as a heuristical strategy since osteoblasts and osteoclasts have been initially placed by random and the geometrical positions of filamentary junctions are randomly set as well. Optimisation of spatial structures turns out to be an advantageous field of employment for P systems in general due to its consistently algebraic and set-based nature complemented by auxiliary algorithmic techniques like selected finite elements methods in our project. Both case studies demonstrated the practicability of our framework. Although the spatial structures emerged from artificial ossification do not represent a perfect solution, their close adaptation to the main force lines becomes apparent. So, inspirations are given and prototypes produced whose final form can be made by finetuning. There exists several ideas for further work: In a next stage, the number of osteoblasts and osteoclasts could vary throughout the ossification process instead of kept constant. In this way, a structure modelling from "coarse" at the beginning towards "fine" at the end is envisioned but it needs an appropriate strategy of control that is still missing. Another open question concerns the "best" point in time in which the ossification should terminate. A final percentage of surviving filaments taken as a threshold is a first indicator but further criteria could be more precise.

References

1. Albanese, A., et al.: The effect of nanoparticle size, shape, and surface chemistry on biological systems. Annu. Rev. Biomed. Eng. **14**, 1–16 (2012)
2. van Amsterdam, E.: Construction Materials for Civil Engineering. Juta & Company (2000)
3. Ananthanatayanan, A., Azadi, M., Kim, S.: Towards a bio-inspired leg design for high-speed running. Bioinspiration Biomimetics **7**(4), 046005 (2012)
4. Bathe, K.J., Wilson, E.L.: Numerical Methods in Finite Element Analysis. Prentice Hall, Upper Saddle River (1976)
5. Baumgartner, A., et al.: Soft kill option: the biological way to find an optimum structure topology. Int. J. Fatigue **14**(6), 387–393 (1992)
6. Becker, M., Golay, P.: Rhino NURBS 3D Modeling. Updog Publishers (2009)
7. Bose, S., Vahabzadeh, S., Bandyopadhyay, A.: Bone tissue engineering using 3D printing. Mater. Today **16**(12), 496–504 (2013)
8. Cacciagrano, D., Corradini, F., Merelli, E., Tesei, L.: Multiscale bone remodelling with spatial P systems. EPTCS **40**, 70–84 (2010)
9. Desai, Y.M., Eldho, T.I., Shah, A.H.: Finite Element Method with Applications in Engineering. Person, London (2011)
10. Frisco, P., Gheorghe, M., Pérez-Jiménez, M.J. (eds.): Applications of Membrane Computing in Systems and Synthetic Biology. ECC, vol. 7. Springer, Cham (2014). https://doi.org/10.1007/978-3-319-03191-0

11. Frost, H.M.: From Wolff's law to the Utah paradigm: insights about bone physiology and its clinical applications. Anat. Rec. **262**, 398–419 (2001)

12. Gerhard, F., et al.: In silico biology of bone modelling and remodelling: adaptation. Philos. Trans. R. Soc. **367**, 2011–2030 (2009)

13. McGinnis, P.M.: Biomechanics of Sport and Exercise. Human Kinetics, Champaign (2005)

14. Hibbeler, R.C.: Engineering Mechanics: Statics. Pearson Prentice Hall, Upper Saddle River (2007)

15. Hinze, T., Grützmann, K., Höckner, B., Sauer, P., Hayat, S.: Categorised counting mediated by blotting membrane systems for particle-based data mining and numerical algorithms. In: Gheorghe, M., Rozenberg, G., Salomaa, A., Sosík, P., Zandron, C. (eds.) CMC 2014. LNCS, vol. 8961, pp. 241–257. Springer, Cham (2014). https://doi.org/10.1007/978-3-319-14370-5_15

16. Hinze, T., Weber, L.L., Hatnik, U.: Walking membranes: grid-exploring P systems with artificial evolution for multi-purpose topological optimisation of cascaded processes. In: Leporati, A., Rozenberg, G., Salomaa, A., Zandron, C. (eds.) CMC 2016. LNCS, vol. 10105, pp. 251–271. Springer, Cham (2017). https://doi.org/10.1007/978-3-319-54072-6_16

17. Huiskes, R., et al.: Effects of mechanical forces on maintenance and adaptation of form in trabecular bone. Nature **405**, 704–706 (2000)

18. Kanungo, T., et al.: An efficient k-means clustering algorithm: analysis and implementation. IEEE Trans. Pattern Anal. Mach. Intell. **24**(7), 881–892 (2002)

19. Khoshnevis, B., et al.: Mega-scale fabrication by contour crafting. Int. J. Ind. Syst. Eng. **1**(3), 301–320 (2006)

20. Kozlov, A., et al.: Bio-inspired design: aerodynamics of boxfish. Procedia Eng. **105**, 323–328 (2015)

21. Lian, Q., Wu, Z.: Membrane computing based virtual network embedding algorithm with path splitting. Appl. Mech. Mater. **687**, 2997–3002 (2014)

22. Nachtigall, W., Pohl, G.: Bau-Bionik. Springer, Heidelberg (2013). https://doi.org/10.1007/978-3-540-88995-3

23. Nachtigall, W., Wisser, A.: Bionics by Examples: 250 Scenarios from Classical to Modern Times. Springer, Cham (2014). https://doi.org/10.1007/978-3-319-05858-0

24. Paun, G., Rozenberg, G., Salomaa, A. (eds.): The Oxford Handbook of Membrane Computing. Oxford University Press, Oxford (2009)

25. Robling, A.G., Castillo, A.B., Turner, C.H.: Biomechanical and molecular regulation of bone remodeling. Annu. Rev. Biomed. Eng. **8**, 455–498 (2006)

26. Trotter, M., et al.: Densities of bones of white and negro skeletons. J. Bone Joint Surg. **42a**, 50–58 (1960)

27. Vukorep, I.: Autonomous big-scale additive manufacturing using cable-driven robots. In: Proceedings 34th International Symposium on Automation and Robotics in Construction (ISARC 2017), Taipeh, pp. 254–259 (2017)

28. Weinkamer, R., Fratzl, P.: Mechanical adaptation of biological materials - the examples of bone and wood. Mater. Sci. Eng. **31**, 1164–1173 (2011)

29. Wolff, J.: Das Gesetz der Transformation der Knochen. Hirschwald, Berlin (1892)

30. Yongxiang, L.U.: Significance and progress of bionics. Springer J. Bionic Eng. **1**(1), 1–3 (2004)

On Small Universality of Spiking Neural P Systems with Multiple Channels

Xiaoxiao Song[1,2(✉)], Hong Peng[3], Jun Wang[1,2], Guimin Ning[4], Tao Wang[1,2], Zhang Sun[1,2], and Yankun Xia[1,2]

[1] Key Laboratory of Fluid and Power Machinery, Ministry of Education, Xihua University, Chengdu 610039, People's Republic of China
songxx_xhu@163.com
[2] School of Electrical Engineering and Electronic Information, Xihua University, Chengdu 610039, People's Republic of China
[3] School of Computer and Software Engineering, Xihua University, Chengdu 610039, People's Republic of China
[4] Department of Information Engineering, Chengdu Industry and Trade College, Chengdu 611731, People's Republic of China

Abstract. SN P systems with multiple channels are a new variant of spiking neural P systems (SN P systems, in short), which introduce channel labels into spiking rules. The computational power of SN P systems with multiple channels in computing Turing computable function is investigated, and two small SN P systems with multiple channels are constructed in this work. We obtain two universal systems with 57 neurons using standard spiking rules and 39 neurons using extended spiking rules, respectively.

Keywords: Membrane computing · Spiking neural P systems · Multiple channels · Small universal systems · Computing function

1 Introduction

Membrane computing was initiated by Păun [1] in 1998, which is a branch of natural computing. It aims to abstract computing ideas from the function and structure of cells and their cooperations. P systems are parallel and distributed computing devices. Mainly, three kinds of P systems are investigated, including cell-like P systems [2], tissue-like P systems [3] and neural-like P systems. [4] gave the overview of P systems.

Supported by the Chunhui Project Foundation of the Education Department of China (Nos. Z2017082, Z2016143 and Z2016148), Foundation of Sichuan Province Key Laboratory of Power Electronics Energy-saving Technologies & Equipment (No. szjj2015-065), National Natural Science Foundation of China (Nos. 61472328 and 61703345), Sichuan Province Key Laboratory of Power Electronics Energy-saving Technologies & Equipment (No. szjj2016-048) and Research Foundation of the Education Department of Sichuan province (No. 17TD0034), China.

T. Hinze et al. (Eds.): CMC 2018, LNCS 11399, pp. 229–245, 2019.
https://doi.org/10.1007/978-3-030-12797-8_16

SN P systems (spiking neural P systems), which belong to neural-like P systems, were first proposed in [5] as a class of computing devices. Spikes and rules could be contained in every neuron. The computing result is represented by the spikes sent to the environment. The systems work in parallel way with all neurons and in sequential way in each neuron.

Many SN P systems and their variants have been investigated. SN P systems were proven to be universal as number generators/acceptors [5–7], function computing devices [8–10], and language generators [11,12]. In [13] and [14] SN P systems with weights and thresholds were presented respectively, and they were proven to be universal as natural number generators and acceptors. Then, weighted systems were proven to be Turing universal as function computing devices [15–17] and language generators [18]. By moving the rules from neurons to synapses, SN P systems with rules on synapses were proposed [19], and they can also simulate Turing machines [20,21]. According to the principle of inhibitory impulses in neurons, inhibitory synapses and anti-spikes were introduced in SN P systems, and these variants can generate any Turing computable number [22] and recursively enumerable languages [23]. SN P systems with astrocytes were proposed according to their excitatory and inhibitory role [23], which can work as number generators and acceptors [24]. SN P systems with white hole neurons were proven to be universal as number generators [25] and axon P systems were proven to be universal with only 4 neurons to generate sets of numbers and 9 neurons to compute functions [26]. By considering the homogeneity of the cells, SN P systems with homogeneous neurons were proven to be universal as number generators/acceptors [27–30]. Most of the SN P systems are working in parallel mode, however, some sequential SN P systems have been discussed [31–34], and all of them were proven to be universal in generating numbers. Without considering the global clock, asynchronous SN P systems were discussed and proven to be Turing universal in number generating [35] and function computing [36,37].

Moreover, some applications of SN P systems are shown in the existing literatures, such as fault diagnosis [38–42], knowledge representation [43,44], image processing [45] and combinatorial optimization problems [46]. As well, some NP-hard problems can be solved by SN P systems in a polynomial time [47–49].

Recently, SN P systems with multiple channels were proposed in [50]. In these systems, the synapses of each neuron have some channels which are marked with channel labels. The SN P systems with multiple channels can accept and generate sets of Turing computable natural numbers. However, can SN P systems with multiple channels be used as a universal device to compute Turing computable functions? It is listed as an open problem in [50], i.e., small universality of SN P systems with multiple channels. In order to answer this open problem, the computational power of these systems is investigated in computing the sets of Turing computable functions in this work. In this regard, we construct two universal SN P systems with multiple channels using standard and extended spiking rules respectively for computing functions.

In Sect. 2 we introduce some necessary prerequisites related to universality and register machines. The definition of SN P systems with multiple channels is given in Sect. 3. Then two small universal SN P systems with multiple channels for computing functions are given in Sect. 4 and Sect. 5, using standard spiking rules and extended spiking rules respectively. Some improvements of the systems are also given in these two sections. The conclusion is drawn in the last section.

2 Prerequisites

To make it easier for readers to understand the universal register machines, some notions and notations are introduced in this section. More details about membrane computing and formal languages could be found in [2] and [51] respectively.

For an alphabet Σ, the set of all nonempty strings and finite strings over Σ are denoted by Σ^+ and Σ^* respectively, and λ denotes the empty string. Specifically, a^+ and a^* are used instead of $\{a\}^+$ and $\{a\}^*$ when $\Sigma = \{a\}$ is a singleton.

Over an alphabet Σ, the set of regular expressions are defined: (i) $a \in \Sigma$ and λ are regular expressions; (ii) $(E_1)^+$, $(E_1)(E_2)$ and $(E_1) \cup (E_2)$ are regular expressions, if E_1 and E_2 are regular expressions over Σ; (iii) nothing else is a regular expression over Σ. E^* represents $(E)^+ \cup \{\lambda\}$. Any regular expression E is associated with a language $L(E)$ as follows: (i) $L(a) = \{a\}$ for all $a \in \Sigma$ and $L(\lambda) = \{\lambda\}$; (ii) for all E_1 and E_2, $L((E_1)^+) = (L(E_1))^+$, $L((E_1) \cup (E_2)) = L(E_1) \cup L(E_2)$ and $L((E_1)(E_2)) = L(E_1)L(E_2)$.

A register machine can be denoted by $M = (m, H, l_0, l_h, I)$. m is the number of registers. H and I denote the set of instruction labels and instructions respectively. Each label from H is associated with only one instruction from I. l_0 and l_h denote the start and halt labels. Three kinds of instructions are shown as follows:

(1) $l_i: (ADD(r), l_j, l_k)$ (the system simulates instruction l_j or l_k non-deterministically after adding 1 to register r),
(2) $l_i: (SUB(r), l_j, l_k)$ (when register r is not empty, the system subtracts 1 from register r and then simulates instruction l_j; otherwise simulates instruction l_k without any operation in register r),
(3) $l_h: HALT$ (the halt instruction).

We call M_u is universal, when $\varphi_x(y) = M_u(g(x), y)$, where x and y are natural numbers and g is a recursive function. A universal register machine M_u from [52] is adopted to compute Turing computable functions in this paper. $M_u = (8, H, l_0, l_h, I)$ includes 8 registers and 23 instructions. At the beginning of the computation, the inputs are introduced in registers labeled 1 and 2, and when M_u halts, the computing result is placed in the first register labeled with 0.

Before using M_u in computing functions with SN P systems with multiple channels, a modification should be made. Because the computing result is stored in register 0, it can't contain any SUB instruction. Therefore, an additional register labeled with 8 is adopted, where the result is stored and no SUB instruction acts on it. Moreover, the halt instruction l_h is replaced by the following three instructions:

$$l_{22} : (SUB(0), l_{23}, l'_h), \quad l_{23} : (ADD(8), l_{22}), \quad l'_h : HALT.$$

Then we obtain a universal register machine M'_u, shown in Fig. 1, which has 9 registers and 25 labels. The added register stores the computation result of M'_u. Register machines are considered to be deterministic when computing model is adopted, which means $l_i : (ADD(r), l_j))$ can be used to replace $l_i : (ADD(r), l_j, l_k)$ as the ADD instruction. The construction of universal SN P systems with multiple channels both in Sects. 4 and 5 is based on M'_u.

$$
\begin{array}{ll}
l_0 : (SUB(1),\ l_1,\ l_2), & l_1 : (ADD(7),\ l_0), \\
l_2 : (ADD(6),\ l_3), & l_3 : (SUB(5),\ l_2,\ l_4), \\
l_4 : (SUB(6),\ l_5,\ l_3), & l_5 : (ADD(5),\ l_6), \\
l_6 : (SUB(7),\ l_7,\ l_8), & l_7 : (ADD(1),\ l_4), \\
l_8 : (SUB(6),\ l_9,\ l_0), & l_9 : (ADD(6),\ l_{10}), \\
l_{10} : (SUB(4),\ l_0,\ l_{11}), & l_{11} : (SUB(5),\ l_{12},\ l_{13}), \\
l_{12} : (SUB(5),\ l_{14},\ l_{15}), & l_{13} : (SUB(2),\ l_{18},\ l_{19}), \\
l_{14} : (SUB(5),\ l_{16},\ l_{17}), & l_{15} : (SUB(3),\ l_{18},\ l_{20}), \\
l_{16} : (ADD(4),\ l_{11}), & l_{17} : (ADD(2),\ l_{21}), \\
l_{18} : (SUB(4),\ l_0,\ l_{22}), & l_{19} : (SUB(0),\ l_0,\ l_{18}), \\
l_{200} : (ADD(0),\ l_0), & l_{21} : (ADD(3),\ l_{18}), \\
l_{22} : (SUB(0),\ l_{23},\ l'_h), & l_{23} : (ADD(8),\ l_{22}), \\
l'_h : HALT
\end{array}
$$

Fig. 1. The universal register machine M'_u

3   SN P Systems with Multiple Channels

Here we recall the definition of an SN P system with multiple channels.

SN P systems with multiple channels were proposed in [50]. The system $(m \geq 1)$ is a construct

$$\Pi = (O, L, \sigma_1, \sigma_2, \ldots, \sigma_m, syn, in, out), \text{ where}$$

(1) $O = \{a\}$ is the alphabet, where the only symbol a is called spike;

(2) $L = \{1, 2, ..., N\}$ is channel labels;
(3) $\sigma_1, \sigma_2, ..., \sigma_m$ are neurons of the form $\sigma_i = (n_i, R_i)$, $1 \leq i \leq m$. $n_i \geq 0$ is the number of spikes initially stored in σ_i, and R_i is a finite set of rules used in neuron σ_i, which have two forms:
   • $E/a^c \rightarrow a^p(l)$, where E is a regular expression over O and $c \geq p \geq 1$, $l \in L_i$, $L_i \subseteq L$ is a finite set of channel labels used in σ_i;
   • $a^s \rightarrow \lambda$, for some $s \geq 1$;
(4) $syn \subseteq \{1, 2, ..., m\} \times \{1, 2, ..., m\} \times L$ with the form (i, j, l), $i \neq j$ for $1 \leq i, j \leq m$ and $l \in L$, which denotes the synapses;
(5) in indicates the input neuron;
(6) out indicates the output neuron.

The spiking rules have the form of $E/a^c \rightarrow a^p(l)$ with $p = 1$ called standard spiking rules or $p > 1$ called extended spiking rules. The neuron fires, when n spikes are contained in it, and $a^n \in L(E)$, $n \geq c$. After consuming c spikes from σ_i, p spikes are sent immediately to all neurons $\sigma_j \in \{\sigma_j | (i, j, l) \in syn\}$ along synapses labeled by l.

The forgetting rules are used to remove some spikes without any other operation in neurons. If s spikes are contains in neuron σ_i, rule $b^s \rightarrow \lambda$ can be used to remove all the spikes from it.

In each step, a rule from R_i must be used if some rules in neuron σ_i can be used. If more than one rule can be used, only one of them is chosen non-deterministically to be used. In contrary to one neuron, all neurons in a system Π work in parallel manner with an assumed global clock.

The number of spikes in neurons is the initial configuration of the system, which can be denoted by $(n_1, n_2, ..., n_m)$. The configuration of the system can be transformed by using rules in neurons. A computation is consisted of any sequence of transitions starting from the initial configuration. When no rule can be used, the computation halts. At the end of the computation, the result is sent out by output neuron. When a spike is emitted, we mark that time instance with 1; otherwise mark it with 0. The result of a computation is defined as the total number of spikes or the time distance between the first two spikes sent to the environment.

SN P systems with multiple channels start to compute $f : N^k \rightarrow N$ by reading a binary sequence, which is denoted by a spike train in an environment. Here we use input neuron to receive k natural numbers $n_1, n_2, ..., n_k$ by reading a spike train $z = 10^{n_1}10^{n_2}1...10^{n_k}1$. It means a spike is received by the input neuron at ith step if the ith bit of z is 1, otherwise nothing is received. So the input neuron receives $k+1$ spikes totally. After that, no spike comes to the input neuron. In this work, the result of the computation is defined by the number of spikes sent by the output neuron to the environment, which is denoted by a spike train 0^b1^r0, for $b \geq 0$ and $r = f(n_1, n_2, ..., n_k)$. No spike is sent out in the first b steps from beginning of the computation.

In Sects. 4 and 5, SN P systems with multiple channels are represented graphically. The neurons are represented by the rounded rectangles, and the synapses are represented by the arrows between these rounded rectangles. All the initial spikes and rules are in neurons. The incoming arrow on the input neuron suggests receiving spikes from environment, and the outgoing arrow on output neuron suggests emitting spikes to environment.

4   Small Universal Computing with Standard Spiking Rules

A small universal SN P system with multiple channels using standard spiking rules for computing functions is constructed in this section.

Theorem 1. There is a small universal SN P system with multiple channels Π for computing functions using standard spiking rules having 57 neurons.

Proof. We design an SN P system with multiple channels Π using standard spiking rules to simulate the computation of the universal register machine M'_u. The main framework of the system is shown in Fig. 2, and consists of ADD, SUB, INPUT, OUTPUT and some composite modules. If n is the number contained in register r, neuron σ_r contains $2n$ spikes.

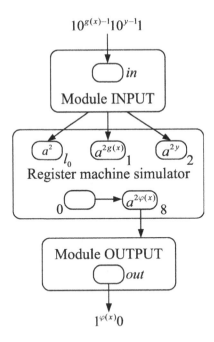

Fig. 2. The framework of the small universal SN P system with multiple channels

Figure 3 shows the module INPUT. With all neurons empty, the spike train $10^{g(x)-1}10^{y-1}1$ from the environment is read by INPUT module, and load $2g(x)$ and $2y$ spikes in neurons σ_1 and σ_2, respectively. At the beginning, neuron σ_{in}

receives the first spike from environment. $a \rightarrow a(1)$ is enabled and sends a spike to both neurons σ_{c_1} and σ_{c_2}. By receiving one spike, rule $a \rightarrow a(1)$ in neurons σ_{c_1} and σ_{c_2} can be used. From this moment until the second spike arrives in neurons σ_{c_1} and σ_{c_2}, they emit one spike to each other in each step, and also send one spike to σ_1 via channel (1) in each step. Neuron σ_{in} receives the second spike after $g(x) - 1$ steps, and neurons σ_{c_1} and σ_{c_2} contain two spikes one step later. At this moment, $2g(x)$ spikes have been loaded in neuron σ_1 and rule $a \rightarrow a(1)$ is not enable, which means no further spikes are sent to neuron σ_1.

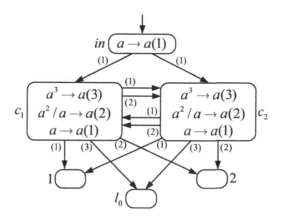

Fig. 3. Module INPUT

With two spikes in neurons σ_{c_1} and σ_{c_2}, $a^2/a \rightarrow a(2)$ can be used. It means neurons σ_{c_1} and σ_{c_2} send one spike to each other and also send one spike to σ_2 via channel (2) in each step, until the third spike is sent from neuron σ_{in} to both of them. Then $2y$ spikes have been loaded in neuron σ_2.

When neuron σ_{in} receives the third spike, it sends the third spike to both neurons σ_{c_1} and σ_{c_2}. With three spikes, only rule $a^3 \rightarrow a(3)$ in neurons σ_{c_1} and σ_{c_2} can be used. After that, neuron σ_{l_0} gets one spike from neurons σ_{c_1} and σ_{c_2} via channel (3) respectively, which means the work of module INPUT is finished and the system starts to compute the functions.

Figure 4 shows the ADD module simulating $l_i : (ADD(r), l_j)$ which works as follows. Suppose $l_i : (ADD(r), l_j)$ has to be simulated at step t. $a^2 \rightarrow a(1)$ is enabled, when two spikes are contained in neuron σ_{l_i}. Then neurons $\sigma_{l_i^{(1)}}$ and $\sigma_{l_i^{(2)}}$ get one spike from σ_{l_i} via channel (1), respectively. With one spike, rule $a \rightarrow a(1)$ in both neurons $\sigma_{l_i^{(1)}}$ and $\sigma_{l_i^{(2)}}$ can be used, sending a spike to both σ_j and σ_r. Therefore, the number of spikes in σ_r increases by two, which means the number in register r adds 1. And the system is ready to simulate instruction l_j.

Figure 5 shows the module SUB simulating $l_i : (SUB(r), l_j, l_k)$. Suppose an SUB instruction has to be simulated at step t. The rule $a^2 \rightarrow a(1)$ is enabled when two spikes are contained in neuron σ_{l_i}. Then neurons $\sigma_{l_i^{(1)}}$ and σ_r get one

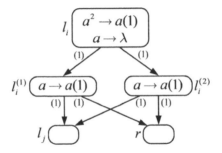

Fig. 4. Module ADD simulating ADD instruction $l_i : (ADD(r), l_j)$

spike from σ_{l_i} via channel (1), respectively. The rest of the computation can be divided into two cases according to the number of spikes contained in σ_r:

(1) If there are $2n + 1(n \geq 1)$ spikes in σ_r, which means the number stored in register r is n (the single spike is retrieved from neurons σ_{l_i} via channel (1)). Then the rule $a(a^2)^+/a^3 \rightarrow a(1)$ can be used. Thus, three spikes in neuron σ_r are consumed (only $2n - 2$ remained in register r, which means the number stored in register r is reduced by 1) and a spike is sent to neuron σ_{l_j} via channel (1). Because $\sigma_{l_i^{(1)}}$ receives a spike from neuron σ_{l_i} in the previous step, its rule $a \rightarrow a(1)$ becomes enabled. So, in this step, $\sigma_{l_i^{(1)}}$ sends one spike to both σ_{l_k} and σ_{l_j}. Neuron σ_{l_j} receives two spikes and the system is ready to simulate instruction l_j.
(2) If only one spike is contained in neuron σ_r, which means the number stored in register r is zero (the only one spike is retrieved from neuron σ_{l_i} via channel (1)). Then the rule $a \rightarrow a(2)$ can be used. Thus, the only spike in σ_r is consumed and a spike is sent to neuron σ_{l_k} via channel (2). In same step, $\sigma_{l_i^{(1)}}$ sends one spike to both neurons σ_{l_j} and σ_{l_k}. Neuron σ_{l_k} receives two spikes and the system is ready to simulate instruction l_k.

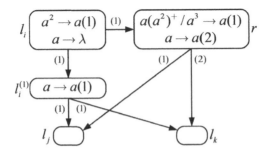

Fig. 5. Module SUB simulating SUB instruction $l_i : (SUB(r), l_j, l_k)$

Note that, there are some SUB instructions acting on same register, like register 5 which is involved in four SUB instructions: l_3, l_{11}, l_{12}, and l_{14}. For example, while simulating instruction $l_3 : (SUB(5), l_2, l_4)$, the neurons σ_2, σ_{12}, σ_{14}, σ_{16} (if the spikes in register 5 is greater than 0) or σ_4, σ_{13}, σ_{15}, σ_{17} (if the number of spikes in register 5 equals 0) receive one spike from register 5 respectively. All of the spikes are removed by the forgetting rule $a \to \lambda$, except for neurons σ_2 (receives another spike from neuron $\sigma_{l_i^{(1)}}$ at the same step, if the spikes in register 5 is greater than 0) or σ_4 (receives another spike from neuron $\sigma_{l_i^{(1)}}$ at the same step, if the number of spikes in register 5 equals 0). So no undesired effect appears.

The module OUTPUT, with the function of outputting the result of computation, is shown in Fig. 6. The register 8 emits spikes to the environment acting as the output neuron. Assume at step t the computation halts, which means the system Π starts to output the result and neuron $\sigma_{l_h'}$ gets two spikes. Register 8 receives a spike from $\sigma_{l_h'}$ fired by $a^2 \to a(1)$. Then $2n + 1$ spikes are contained in neuron σ_8. The rule $a(a^2)^+/a^2 \to a(1)$ is enabled and can be used for n times. Thus, n spikes are sent to environment, which is the computation result.

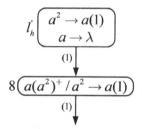

Fig. 6. Module OUTPUT

The constructed SN P system with multiple channels using standard spiking rules uses: 9 neurons for 9 registers, 25 neurons for 25 labels, 20 auxiliary neurons in ADD modules, 14 auxiliary neurons in SUB modules, 3 neurons in INPUT module, which comes to a total of 71 neurons.

The neuron numbers can be decreased by exploring relationships between some instructions of register machine M_u'.

There is only one consecutive ADD-ADD instructions in M_u':

$$l_{17} : (ADD(2), l_{21}), \quad l_{21}(ADD(3), l_{18}).$$

The module shown in Fig. 7 can simulate the two instructions, then $\sigma_{l_{21}}$ and two auxiliary neurons are saved.

There is still one sequence of SUB-SUB instructions:

$$l_{11} : (SUB(5), l_{12}, l_{13}), \quad l_{13} : (SUB(2), l_{18}, l_{19}).$$

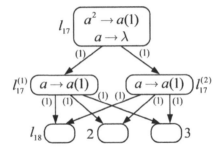

Fig. 7. The module simulating consecutive ADD-ADD instructions l_{17} : $(ADD(2), l_{21})$, $l_{21}(ADD(3), l_{18})$

The module shown in Fig. 8 can simulate the SUB-SUB instructions. More complicated, there are four cases in this module: $\{n > 0, k > 0\}$, $\{n > 0, k = 0\}$, $\{n = 0, k > 0\}$ and $\{n = 0, k = 0\}$, where register 5 has $2n$ spikes and register 2 has $2k$ spikes respectively. The evolution of the spike numbers in SUB-SUB module during the computation is shown in Tables 1, 2, 3 and 4.

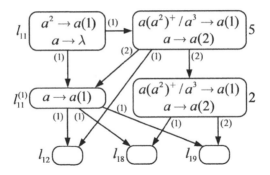

Fig. 8. The module simulating consecutive SUB-SUB instructions l_{11} : $(SUB(5), l_{12}, l_{13})$, $l_{13}(SUB(2), l_{18}, l_{19})$

In this way, $\sigma_{l_{13}}$ and a auxiliary neuron can be saved.

There could be a common neuron for SUB instructions which address different registers. An example of two SUB instructions sharing one common neuron is shown in Fig. 9, which address different registers. When neuron $\sigma_{l_{i_1}}$ has two spikes, the rule $a^2 \to a(1)$ is enabled. Then neurons $\sigma_{l_i^{(1)}}$ and σ_{r_1} get one spike from $\sigma_{l_{i_1}}$ via channel (1), respectively. The neurons $\sigma_{r_1}, \sigma_{l_{j_1}}$ and $\sigma_{l_{k_1}}$ work in the same way as in the SUB module shown in Fig. 5. But one addition spike is sent to both neurons $\sigma_{l_{j_2}}$ and $\sigma_{l_{k_2}}$ respectively. Without any other spike arrives in $\sigma_{l_{j_2}}$ and $\sigma_{l_{k_2}}$ at the same time, the two spikes will be removed by the forgetting rule. In this way, the instruction l_{i_1} is correctly simulated l_{i_1} : $(SUB(r_1), l_{j_1}, l_{k_1})$ and

Table 1. The evolution of numbers of spikes in neurons of SUB-SUB module during the simulation of SUB-SUB instructions with the case that $n > 0$ and $k > 0$

	step			
	t	$t+1$	$t+2$	$t+3$
σ_{11}	2	0	0	0
σ_5	$2n$	$2n+1$	$2n-2$	$2n-2$
σ_2	$2k$	$2k$	$2k$	$2k$
$\sigma_{l_{11}^{(1)}}$	0	1	0	0
σ_{12}	0	0	2	2
σ_{18}	0	0	1	0
σ_{19}	0	0	1	0

Table 2. The evolution of numbers of spikes in neurons of SUB-SUB module during the simulation of SUB-SUB instructions with the case that $n > 0$ and $k = 0$

	step			
	t	$t+1$	$t+2$	$t+3$
σ_{11}	2	0	0	0
σ_5	$2n$	$2n+1$	$2n-2$	$2n-2$
σ_2	0	0	0	0
$\sigma_{l_{11}^{(1)}}$	0	1	0	0
σ_{12}	0	0	2	2
σ_{18}	0	0	1	0
σ_{19}	0	0	1	0

Table 3. The evolution of numbers of spikes in neurons of SUB-SUB module during the simulation of SUB-SUB instructions with the case that $n = 0$ and $k > 0$

	step				
	t	$t+1$	$t+2$	$t+3$	$t+4$
σ_{11}	2	0	0	0	0
σ_5	0	1	0	0	0
σ_2	$2k$	$2k$	$2k+1$	$2k-2$	$2k-2$
$\sigma_{l_{11}^{(1)}}$	0	1	1	0	0
σ_{12}	0	0	1	1	0
σ_{18}	0	0	1	2	2
σ_{19}	0	0	1	1	0

Table 4. The evolution of numbers of spikes in neurons of SUB-SUB module during the simulation of SUB-SUB instructions with the case that $n = 0$ and $k = 0$

	step				
	t	$t+1$	$t+2$	$t+3$	$t+4$
σ_{11}	2	0	0	0	0
σ_5	0	1	0	0	0
σ_2	0	0	1	0	0
$\sigma_{l_{11}^{(1)}}$	0	1	1	0	0
σ_{12}	0	0	1	1	0
σ_{18}	0	0	1	1	0
σ_{19}	0	0	1	2	2

no undesired effect appears on other instructions. By using this results, instructions l_0, l_3, l_4, l_6, l_{10}, l_{15} and l_{19}, which address registers 1, 5, 6, 7, 4, 3 and 0 respectively, can share a common neuron, thus 6 neurons are saved.

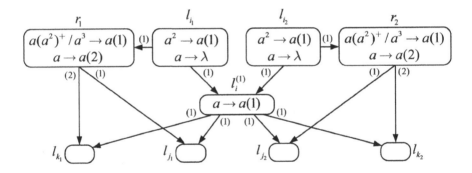

Fig. 9. A module simulating two SUB instructions with $r_1 \neq r_2$

Instructions l_8, l_{11}, l_{13}, l_{18} and l_{22}, which address registers 6, 5, 2, 4 and 0 respectively, can also share another common neuron. For instructions l_{11} and l_{13} are simulated by the SUB-SUB module, they have already share a common neuron. Figure 10 shows the module, which simulates instructions l_{11} and l_{13} with another instruction (l_8, l_{18} or l_{22}). The evolution of the module is similar to the module shown in Fig. 9. So, the second group of instructions can save 3 neurons.

Therefore, by using the above optimization modules, we can save 14 neurons in total. The number of neurons used by the constructed SN P system with multiple channels using standard spiking rules, can be decremented from 71 to 57. This completes the proof.

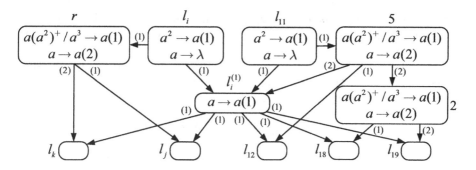

Fig. 10. A module simulating instructions l_{11} and l_{13} with other instruction with $r \neq 2$ and $r \neq 5$

5   Small Universal Computing with Extended Spiking Rules

Different from Sect. 4, in this section a smaller universal SN P system with multiple channels using extended spiking rules is constructed for computing functions.

Theorem 2. There is a small universal SN P system with multiple channels using extended spiking rules computing functions having 39 neurons for Π'.

Proof. The SN P system with multiple channels using extended spiking rules is constructed to simulate universal register machine M'_u. The framework of Π' is same with Π, shown in Fig. 2, and consists of ADD, SUB, INPUT, OUTPUT and some composite modules. Still in registers, $2n$ spikes represent number n.

The modules SUB, SUB-SUB, INPUT and OUTPUT in Π' are same with Π.

Figure 11 shows the ADD module used in system Π'. With two spikes in σ_{l_i}, the rule $a^2 \rightarrow a^2(1)$ is enabled. Two spikes are sent from σ_{l_i} to both σ_{l_j} and σ_r, respectively. Therefore, the number of spikes in σ_r increases by 2, which means the number in register r adds 1. Then the system begins to simulate instruction l_j.

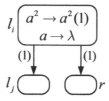

Fig. 11. Module ADD in Π'

So, we have 9 neurons for 9 registers, 25 neurons for 25 labels, 14 auxiliary neurons in SUB modules, 3 neurons in INPUT module, which comes to a total of 51 neurons.

The number of neurons can also be decreased by exploring relationships between some instructions of register machine M_u'.

The module simulating ADD-ADD instructions

$$l_{17} : (ADD(2), l_{21}), \quad l_{21} : (ADD(3), l_{18})$$

in system Π' is shown in Fig. 12, and the neuron associated with label l_{21} can be saved.

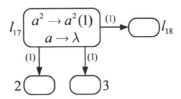

Fig. 12. Module simulating consecutive ADD-ADD instructions in Π'

Since the modules SUB and SUB-SUB in Π' are same with Π, the modules in Figs. 8, 9 and 10 can also be used in Π'. In this way, 11 neurons are saved (2 neurons from SUB-SUB module, 6 from the first group of instructions and 3 from the second group of instructions).

Therefore, 12 neurons are saved, and the number of neurons can be decremented from 51 to 39 in system Π'. The theorem holds.

6   Conclusion

SN P systems with multiple channels were introduced in [50]. In this work, we investigated the problem of small universality of these variant SN P systems in computing Turing computable function. Two small universal systems are constructed, using standard spiking rules and extended spiking rules, respectively. In case of using standard spiking rules, a universal SN P system with multiple channels in functions computing needs 57 neurons; while using extended spiking rules, only 39 neurons are needed.

Comparing with traditional extended spiking rules, $E/a^c \rightarrow a^p; d$, channel labels are added in SN P systems with multiple channels, but the delay time d is not used. It is interesting to investigate whether the required number of neurons can be reduced or the ability of dealing with complex problems can be improved when the feature of delay is used in SN P systems with multiple channels.

How to integrate other strategies and models in SN P systems with multiple channels is worth to investigate, such as anti-spikes, exhaustive use of rules, white hole neurons, homogeneous neurons, request rules, asynchronous mode, local synchronous mode and sequential mode.

Recently, cell-like SN P system, as a new kind of SN P system, was proposed [53], which look like a cell-like P system but works in the manner of SN P systems. If channel labels are introduced into cell-like SN P systems, the corresponding computational power could be a good further research topic.

References

1. Păun, G.: Computing with membranes. J. Comput. Syst. Sci. **61**(1), 108–143 (2000)
2. Păun, G.: Membrane Computing: An Introduction. Springer, Berlin (2002). https://doi.org/10.1007/978-3-642-56196-2
3. Martín-Vide C., Păun G., Pazos J., Rodríguez-Patón A.: Tissue P systems. Theor. Comput. Sci. **296**, 295–326 (2003)
4. Păun, G., Rozenberg, G., Salomaa, A.: The Oxford Handbook of Membrane Computing. Oxford University Press, Oxford (2010)
5. Ionescu, M., Păun, G., Yokomori, T.: Spiking neural P systems. Fundam. Informaticae **71**, 279–309 (2006)
6. Păun, A., Păun, G.: Small universal spiking neural P systems. BioSystems **90**(1), 48–60 (2007)
7. Neary, T.: A universal spiking neural P system with 11 neurons. In: Proceedings of the Eleventh International Conference on Membrane Computing, pp. 327–346. Springer, Jena (2010)
8. Neary, T.: Three small universal spiking neural P systems. Theor. Comput. Sci. **567**, 2–20 (2008)
9. Zhang, X., Zeng, X., Pan, L.: Smaller universal spiking neural P systems. Fundam. Informaticae **87**(1), 117–136 (2008)
10. Neary, T.: A boundary between universality and non-universality in extended spiking neural P systems. In: Dediu, A.-H., Fernau, H., Martín-Vide, C. (eds.) LATA 2010. LNCS, vol. 6031, pp. 475–487. Springer, Heidelberg (2010). https://doi.org/10.1007/978-3-642-13089-2_40
11. Chen, H., Freund, R., Ionescu, M., Păun, G., Pérez-Jiménez, M.: On string languages generated by spiking neural P systems. Fundam. Informaticae **75**(1), 141–162 (2007)
12. Păun, G., Pérez-Jiménez, M., Rozenberg, G.: Spike trains in spiking neural P systems. Int. J. Found. Comput. Sci. **17**(4), 975–1002 (2006)
13. Wang, J., Hoogeboom, H.J., Pan, L., Păun, G., Pérez-Jiménez, M.J.: Spiking neural P systems with weights. Neural Comput. **22**(10), 2615–2646 (2010)
14. Zeng, X., Zhang, X., Song, T., Pan, L.: Spiking neural P systems with thresholds. Neural Comput. **26**(7), 1340–1361 (2014)
15. Pan, L., Zeng, X., Zhang, X., Jiang, Y.: Spiking neural P systems with weighted synapses. Neural Process. Lett. **35**(1), 13–27 (2012)
16. Zeng, X., Pan, L., Pérez-Jiménez, M.J.: Small universal simple spiking neural P systems with weights. Sci. China Inf. Sci. **57**(9), 1–11 (2014)
17. Zhang, X., Zeng, X., Pan, L.: Weighted spiking neural P systems with rules on synapses. Fundam. Informaticae **134**(1–2), 201–218 (2014)
18. Zeng, X., Xu, L., Liu, X., Pan, L.: On languages generated by spiking neural P systems with weights. Inf. Sci. **278**(10), 423–433 (2014)

19. Song, T., Pan, L., Păun, G.: Spiking neural P systems with rules on synapses. Theor. Comput. Sci. **529**(4), 82–95 (2014)

20. Song, T., Xu, J., Pan, L.: On the universality and non-universality of spiking neural P systems with rules on synapses. IEEE Trans. Nanobiosci. **14**(8), 960–966 (2015)

21. Song, T., Pan, L.: Spiking neural P systems with rules on synapses working in maximum spiking strategy. Theor. Comput. Sci. **14**(1), 38–44 (2015)

22. Pan, L., Păun, G.: Spiking neural P systems with anti-spikes. Int. J. Comput. Commun. Control **IV**(3), 273–282 (2009)

23. Krithivasan, K., Metta, V.P., Garg, D.: On string languages generated by spiking neural P systems with anti-spikes. Int. J. Found. Comput. Sci. **22**(1), 15–27 (2011)

24. Pan, L., Wang, J., Hoogeboom, H.J.: Spiking neural P systems with astrocytes. Neural Comput. **24**(3), 805–825 (2014)

25. Song, T., Gong, F., Liu, X., Zhao, Y., Zhang, X.: Spiking neural P systems with white hole neurons. IEEE Trans. Nanobiosci. **15**(7), 666–673 (2016)

26. Zhang, X., Pan, L., Păun, A.: On the universality of axon P systems. IEEE Trans. Neural Netw. Learn. Syst. **26**(11), 2816–2829 (2015)

27. Zeng, X., Zhang, X., Pan, L.: Homogeneous spiking neural P systems. Fundam. Informaticae **97**(1), 275–294 (2009)

28. Song, T., Wang, X., Zhang, Z., Chen, Z.: Homogeneous spiking neural P systems with anti-spikes. Neural Comput. Appl. **24**(7–8), 1833–1841 (2014)

29. Jiang, K., Chen, W., Zhang, Y., Pan, L.: Spiking neural P systems with homogeneous neurons and synapses. Neurocomputing **171**(C), 1548–1555 (2015)

30. Song, T., Zheng, P., Wong, M.L.D., Wang, X.: Design of logic gates using spiking neural P systems with homogeneous neurons and astrocytes-like control. Inf. Sci. **372**, 380–391 (2016)

31. Ibarra, O.H., Păun, A., Rodríguez-Patón, A.: Sequential SNP systems based on min/max spike number. Theor. Comput. Sci. **410**(30), 2982–2991 (2009)

32. Song, T., Pan, L., Jiang, K., Song, B., Chen, W.: Normal forms for some classes of sequential spiking neural P systems. IEEE Trans. NanoBiosci. **12**(3), 255–264 (2013)

33. Zhang, X., Zeng, X., Luo, B., Pan, L.: On some classes of sequential spiking neural P systems. Neural Comput. **26**(5), 974–997 (2014)

34. Zhang, X., Luo, B., Fang, X., Pan, L.: Sequential spiking neural P systems with exhaustive use of rules. BioSystems **108**(1–3), 52–62 (2012)

35. Cavaliere, M., Ibarra, O.H., Păun, G., Egecioglu, O., Ionescu, M., Woodworth, S.: Asynchronous spiking neural P systems. Theor. Comput. Sci. **410**(24), 2352–2364 (2009)

36. Song, T., Pan, L., Păun, G.: Asynchronous spiking neural P systems with local synchronization. Inf. Sci. **219**(24), 197–207 (2013)

37. Song, T., Zou, Q., Liu, X., Zeng, X.: Asynchronous spiking neural P systems with rules on synapses. Neurocomputing **151**(3), 1439–1445 (2015)

38. Peng, H., Wang, J., Pérez-Jiménez, M.J., Wang, H., Shao, J., Wang, T.: Fuzzy reasoning spiking neural P system for fault diagnosis. Inf. Sci. **235**(6), 106–116 (2013)

39. Wang, J., Peng, H.: Adaptive fuzzy spiking neural P systems for fuzzy inference and learning. Int. J. Comput. Math. **90**(4), 857–868 (2013)

40. Wang, T., Zhang, G., Zhao, J., He, Z., Wang, J., Pérez-Jiménez, M.J.: Fault diagnosis of electric power systems based on fuzzy reasoning spiking neural P systems. IEEE Trans. Power Syst. **30**(3), 1182–1194 (2015)

41. Tu, M., Wang, J., Peng, H., Shi, P.: Application of adaptive fuzzy spiking neural P systems in fault diagnosis of power systems. Chin. J. Electron. **23**(1), 87–92 (2014)

42. Wang, T., Zhang, G., Pérez-Jiménez, M.J., Cheng, J.: Weighted fuzzy reasoning spiking neural P systems: application to fault diagnosis in traction power supply systems of high-speed railways. J. Comput. Theor. Nanosci. **12**(7), 1103–1114 (2015)

43. Wang, J., Shi, P., Peng, H., Pérez-Jiménez, M.J., Wang, T.: Weighted fuzzy spiking neural P systems. IEEE Trans. Fuzzy Syst. **21**(2), 209–220 (2013)

44. Wang, T., Zhang, G., Pérez-Jiménez, M.J.: Fuzzy membrane computing: theory and applications. Int. J. Comput. Commun. Control **10**(6), 904–935 (2015)

45. Díaz-Pernil, D., Peña-Cantillana, F., Gutiérrez-Naranjo, M.A.: A parallel algorithm for skeletonizing images by using spiking neural P systems. Neurocomputing **115**, 81–91 (2013)

46. Zhang, G., Rong, H., Neri, F., Pérez-Jiménez, M.J.: An optimization spiking neural P system for approximately solving combinatorial optimization problems. Int. J. Neural Syst. **24**(5), 1440006 (2014)

47. Ishdorj, T.O., Leporati, A., Pan, L., Zeng, X., Zhang, X.: Deterministic solutions to QSAT and Q3SAT by spiking neural P systems with pre-computed resources. Theor. Comput. Sci. **411**(25), 2345–2358 (2010)

48. Leporati, A., Mauri, G., Zandron, C., Păun, G., Pérez-Jiménez, M.J.: Uniform solutions to SAT and Subset Sum by spiking neural P systems. Nat. Comput. **8**(4), 681–702 (2009)

49. Pan, L., Păun, G., Pérez-Jiménez, M.J.: Spiking neural P systems with neuron division and budding. Sci. China Inf. Sci. **54**(8), 1596–1607 (2011)

50. Peng, H., Yang, J., Wang, J., Wang, T., Sun, Z., Song, X., Lou, X., Huang, X.: Spiking neural P systems with multiple channels. Neural Netw. **95**, 66–71 (2017)

51. Rozenberg, G., Salomaa, A.: Handbook of Formal Languages. Springer, Berlin (1997). https://doi.org/10.1007/978-3-642-59136-5

52. Korec, I.: Small universal register machines. Theor. Comput. Sci. **168**(2), 267–301 (1996)

53. Wu, T., Zhang, Z., Păun, G., Pan, L.: Cell-like spiking neural P systems. Theor. Comput. Sci. **623**(11), 180–189 (2016)

Modeling Plant Development
with M Systems

Petr Sosík[2(✉)], Vladimír Smolka[2], Jaroslav Bradík[2], and Max Garzon[1]

[1] The University of Memphis, Memphis, TN, USA
[2] Research Institute of the IT4Innovations Centre of Excellence,
Faculty of Philosophy and Science, Silesian University, Opava, Czech Republic
petr.sosik@fpf.slu.cz

Abstract. Morphogenetic systems (M systems) have been recently introduced as a computational model aiming at a deeper understanding of morphogenetic phenomena such as growth, self-reproduction, homeostasis and self-healing of evolving systems. M systems hybridize principles common in membrane computing and abstract self-assembly. The model unfolds in a 3D (or generally, dD) space, growing structures that are self-assembled from generalized tiles using shape and location sensitive local rules. The environment provides mutually reacting atomic particles that contribute to growth control. Initial studies of M systems demonstrated their computational universality and efficiency, as well as their robustness to injuries through their self-healing capabilities. Here, we make a systematic comparison of their generativity power with Lindenmayer systems, the best known model of pattern and shape assembly.

1 Introduction

Morphogenesis, i.e. the biological process of development of an organism with specific shape and functionality, is among the fundamental aspects of developmental biology. Morphogenesis is also a classical area in biology, computational studies and mathematical models, or even art (digital morphogenesis). Its importance was realized already by the early founding fathers of computer science [5,11]. Turing's paper [11] is perhaps the original most famous attempt at producing a model to explain the memory pattern formation and their resilience in biological organisms.

A morphogenetic (M) system is a formal model attempting to address the general question whether morphogenesis can be, at some level, meaningfully understood from the perspective of information processing. There have been two notable attempts to address this topic, namely membrane computing and virtual cells [10]. The original inspiring idea of *membrane computing* [7], was to develop models focusing on the role of membranes in the process of morphogenesis of the living cell, while obtaining new insights and approaches to solving difficult problems in computer science. (The introductory section of [8] gives a survey of results in membrane computing specifically related to morphogenesis).

© Springer Nature Switzerland AG 2019
T. Hinze et al. (Eds.): CMC 2018, LNCS 11399, pp. 246–257, 2019.
https://doi.org/10.1007/978-3-030-12797-8_17

However, all of these models assume that a cell as an atomic assembly unit of an abstract nature. Here, we are interested in exploring the developmental process from scratch, i.e., through self-assembly of 1D or 2D primitives allowing for self-assembly of 3D (multi-)cell-like forms. To be sure, we are not interested in faithful models of biological organisms, but in revealing potential mechanisms or strategies whereby they may be achieved through a complexification process distributed in space and time, emerging from the bottom-up through local interactions among atomic components available in an environment. Specifically, the objective is to explore higher functions such as internal dynamical homeostasis, self-reproduction, and self-healing, for example, and their mutual relationships.

The fundamental ingredient of P systems is the membrane that separates a virtual cell from the external world or the various parts of it. M systems extend this concept with spatial relationships and constraints in the organization of biological systems, including the role of *geometric shape*. An attempt at a general approach to formalization of spatial and geometrical interaction in complex (biological) systems is the 3π calculus [1] based on process algebra. To implement space and geometry in M systems, we have employed and generalized another bio-inspired approach – abstract tile assembly originated in DNA computing [2,12]. The goal of the resulting model of M systems is to reflect, to some degree, the corresponding macroscopic observables of growth of biological organisms (independently of whether they faithfully describe factual atomic processes in biological organisms), while maintaining their computational feasibility, by using an appropriate level of granularity in both time and resources. Initial studies published in [9] and [8] demonstrated that the model is powerful enough from the computational point of view, exhibiting the Turing-universal computational power even under severe restrictions, and a capability of trading space for time when interpreted as an NP-hard problems solver. More importantly, these studies also showed robustness of the model under injuries and its self-healing capabilities.

Since the most interesting model of shape and pattern generation through a kind of morphogenetic system is the Lindermayer systems (L-systems), it is a natural question to address the relation between M systems and L-systems [3]. Section 2 recalls the definition of M systems, while referring to [8,9] for examples. In Sect. 3 we discuss similarities and differences between the growth mechanisms of the two kinds of systems. We show that, under certain restrictions, the generative mechanism of L systems, as interpreted by turtle graphics, can be stepwise simulated by L systems. We also provide an example of such simulation of a classical L system modelling growth of a tree. Finally, in Sect. 4, we present discussion on the achieved results and open questions. We further conjecture that M systems extend the capabilities of L systems to address interactions among individual plants and their parts with the environment. Thus, morphogenetic processes in complex environments could be modeled by M systems as well.

2   Morphogenetic Systems

This section summarizes the definition of M system and its basic properties. The reader is referred to consult [8,9] for a complete specification and examples, as some details are omitted in the following description.

Principles of M systems are based on ideas of abstract self-assembly systems on one hand, and membrane systems with proteins on membranes [6] on the other. In the latter, the term "protein" denotes an abstract object freely imitating some aspects of biological protein. To distinguish between these and similar objects in M systems, we have introduced a new term "protion."

M systems extend the concept of P systems with explicit geometric features and self-assembly capabilities, that may help to realize the potential of the original idea of membrane computing. The whole system unfolds in an dD Euclidean space $\mathbb{R}^d$ in *discrete time steps*, although here we will assume 3D space throughout. There are three types of objects present in the system: *protions*, *tiles* and *floating objects*.

Floating objects are small shapeless atomic objects floating freely within the environment, but with a nonzero volume, and having at every moment their specified position in space. They can be carried through protion channels and participate in mutual reactions with other types of objects.

Tiles have their predefined size and shape, together with specified position and orientation in space at each moment. Tiles can stick together along their edges or at selected points. These edges/points are called *connectors* and they are covered with *glues*. Their connection is controlled by a pre-defined *glue relation*. Thus the tiles can self-assemble into interconnected structures.

Protions are placed on tiles and, apart from acting as protion channels letting floating objects pass through, they can also catalyze their reactions.

Unlike typical membrane systems, *membranes* are not present even implicitly, but they can only be self-assembled from tiles during the evolution of the M system. The connected tiles can be also disconnected and/or destroyed under certain conditions.

2.1   Polytopic Tiling

Basic element of the tiling is a d-dimensional tile shaped as a bounded convex polytope (d-polytope) [13], with faces of dimension $d-1$ called *facets*. Hence, a 1D tile is a segment/rod whose facets are its endpoints, a 2D tile is a convex polygon with its edges as facets, a 3D tile is a convex polyhedron with polygons as facets. A polytope is defined by an ordered list of its vertices in $\mathbb{R}^3$. Formally, an *m-dimensional tile* is defined as

$$t = (\Delta, \{c_1, \ldots, c_k\}, g_s), \text{ for } k \geq 0, \text{ where}$$

Δ is a bounded convex m-polytope,

$c_1, \ldots, c_k$ are its connectors,

$g_s \in G$ is the *surface glue*, where G is a finite set of *glues*.

Connectors define possible connections of the tile to other tiles. Informally, a *connector* is a site on the surface of a tile specified by its shape, glue and connecting angle. A connector may be shaped as a point, a segment or a polygon. Generally, two connectors on neighboring tiles can connect together if they have identical shapes and their glues match in the glue relation defined bellow.

Definition 1. *A* polytopic tile system *in* $\mathbb{R}^d$ *is a construct* $T = (Q, G, \gamma, d_g, S)$, *where*

Q *is the set of tiles of dimensions* $\leq d$;

G *is the set of glues;*

$\gamma \subseteq G \times G$ *is the glue relation;*

$d_g \in \mathbb{R}_0^+$ *is the* gluing radius *(assumed to be small compared to tile sizes);*

S *is a finite multiset of seed tiles from* Q *randomly distributed in space.*

2.2   M System

Geometrical structure and growth of an M system is determined by its underlying polytopic tile system. Unlike ordinary tiling assembly systems, new tiles attaching to an existing structure can only be created by the application of rules of the M system.

Formally, for a finite alphabet O we denote by O^* the free monoid generated by O by the operation of concatenation and identity λ. As usual, $O^+ = O^* \setminus \{\lambda\}$. For a string or a multiset S and $a \in O$, $|S|_a$ denotes the multiplicity of occurrences of a in S. A multiset S over alphabet O can be represented by a string $x \in O^*$ such that $|x|_a = |S|_a$.

Definition 2. *A* morphogenetic system *(M system) in* $\mathbb{R}^d$ *is a tuple*

$$\mathcal{M} = (F, P, T, \mu, R, \sigma),$$

where

$F = (O, m, \rho, \epsilon)$ *is a catalogue of floating objects, where*

O *is a set of floating objects;*

$m : O \longrightarrow \mathbb{R}^+$ *is the* mean mobility *of each floating object;*

$\rho : O \longrightarrow \mathbb{R}_0^+$ *is* radius *of each floating object;*

$\epsilon : O \longrightarrow \mathbb{R}_0^+$ *is the* concentration *of each floating object in the environment;*

P *is a set of protions;*

$T = (Q, G, \gamma, d_g, S)$ *is a polytopic tile system in* $\mathbb{R}^d$, *with* O, P, Q, G *all pairwise disjoint;*

μ is the mapping assigning to each tile $t \in Q$ a multiset of protions placed on t together with their positions: $\mu(t) \subset P \times \Delta$ where Δ is the underlying polytope of t;

R is a finite set of reaction rules;

$\sigma : \gamma \longrightarrow O^*$ is the mapping assigning to each glue pair $(g_1, g_2) \in \gamma$ a multiset of floating objects which are released to the environment when a connection with glues (g_1, g_2) is established.

A *reaction rule* from the set R has the form $u \rightarrow v$, where u and v are strings/multisets which may contain floating objects, protions, glues and/or tiles as specified below. A rule $u \rightarrow v$, is applied when each floating object $o \in u$ is located within the distance $m(o)$ from the reaction site, and eventual further conditions specified by the rule type are also met. Reaction rules can be of four types: metabolic, creative, destructive and dividing.

Metabolic Rules
Let $u, v \in O^+$ be non-empty multisets of floating objects and $p \in P$ be a protion placed on a tile.

Type	Rule	Effect
Simple	$u \rightarrow v$	Objects in multiset u react to produce v
Catalytic	$pu \rightarrow pv$	Objects in u react in presence of p to produce v
	$u[p \rightarrow v[p$	This variant requires both u, v at the side "out"
	$[pu \rightarrow [pv$	This variant requires both u, v at the side "in"
Symport	$u[p \rightarrow [pu$	Passing of u through protion channel p
	$[pu \rightarrow u[p$	To the other side of the tile
Antiport	$u[pv \rightarrow v[pu$	Interchange of u and v through protion channel p

Creation Rules $u \rightarrow t$,
where $t \in Q$ and $u \in O^+$, can create a tile t while consuming the floating objects in u. Furthermore, t must be able to connect to an existing fixed object by some of its connector.

Destruction Rules $ut \rightarrow v$,
where $t \in Q$, $u, v \in O^+$ would destroy a tile t, while consuming the floating objects in u and producing floating objects in v.

Division Rules $g \xrightarrow{u} h \rightarrow g, h$,
where $g—h$ is a pair of glues on connectors of two connected tiles, and $u \in O^+$. As an effect of application of the rule, the two connectors disconnect and the multiset u is consumed.

Computation of the M system

A *configuration* of an M system is determined by

- set of all tiles in the environment and their relative positions;
- an interconnection graph of connectors on these tiles;
- positions for all floating objects modulo their mobility.

Configurations with any two objects (tiles or floating objects) in the same or overlapping positions in space are not allowed. The *initial* configuration contains only (unconnected) seed tiles in S and a random distribution of floating objects given by a concentration ϵ_0.

An M system transits from configuration to configuration in discrete time steps by applying rules in its set R. At each step, each floating object can be subject to at most one rule, each connector can be subject to at most one creation or division rule, and each tile can be subject to at most one destruction rule. The rules are chosen and applied in the maximally parallel manner. Finally, each floating object o changes randomly its position due to its mean mobility $m(o)$.

3   M Systems Modelling Growth of Lindenmayer Systems

In this section we compare mechanisms simulating morphogenesis of living things in M systems and L systems. Let us recall that an L system is a parallel rewriting system, a simple type of parallel formal grammar. Many variants of L systems have been studied, including deterministic, interactionless, extended or tabled L systems, as well as L systems with interactions. L systems were introduced in 1968 by Aristid Lindenmayer, and further developed in many following works. They were frequently used to model the growth of living organisms, especially plants.

Definition 3. *An* 0L *system is a triple* $G = (\Sigma, \omega, P)$, *where* Σ *is a nonempty finite alphabet,* $\omega \in \Sigma^+$ *is the axiom, and* $P \subset \Sigma \times \Sigma^*$ *is a finite set of rewriting rules.*

Strings generated by L systems are often graphically interpreted using so-called *turtle graphics*. The alphabet contains a subset $V \subseteq \Sigma$ of variables (usually denoted by letters or numbers) corresponding to elements drawn by the turtle. They may adopt different colors and sizes; line segments are frequently used. Another part of the alphabet are constants serving as controls of the turtle. The most frequent constants are:

- $+$ turn left by a pre-defined angle;
- $-$ turn right by a pre-defined angle;
- $[$ push current position and angle;
- $]$ pop position and angle.

More detailed explanation and examples of L systems with turtle graphics can be found, e.g., at Wikipedia, under the term "L system". There are plenty implementations and applications of L systems in graphics and art. For instance, more than 2000 trees and plants were modeled by L systems in the Avatar movie (2009).

3.1   A Comparison of L Systems and M Systems Growth Mechanism

A straightforward observation is that L systems are more abstract in several ways:

– any number of shape elements can be generated in L systems without any limitation, while the growth in an M system depends on the presence of surrounding floating objects, hence on the "richness" of the environment;
– during the generation process, each string is graphically interpreted independently on the others, hence there may be discontinuity in the growing shapes, their metamorphosis, connections, angles and sizes; but in an M system, each new shape is derived from the previous one only by adding/inserting/connecting new elements, or disconnecting/deleting/pushing existing ones;
– the graphical interpretation is separated from the generation mechanism so that the same generated string can be interpreted in different ways, while the M system contains explicit geometric shapes and their connection rules which determine the growth process (together with other control mechanisms) from the beginning to the end.

Therefore, many growth processes generated by L systems might be impossible to simulate step-by-step in M systems. The famous L system generating Sierpinski triangles is a simple example. As M systems are universal in the Turing sense, it is probable that they could, in principle, generate any shape including the Sierpinski triangles, but the process may be very complicated. On the other hand, L systems simulating growth of living things, especially of plants, where existing parts do not change too much (they may prolong, for instance), may be realized smoothly also in the M systems world.

3.2   Simulation of L Systems by M Systems

Now we focus on the cases when a "direct" simulation of an L system (under their graphical interpretation) by an M system is possible, and define a restricted class of L systems which can be stepwise simulated by M systems. To this end, we extend the original definition of the M systems of a fifth type

Insertion Rules $u \to t$,

where $t \in Q$ and $u \in O^+$. The rule creates tile t while consuming the floating objects in u. It can be applied if there is a pair of tiles t_1, t_2 connected with connectors c_1–c_2 such that t contains at its opposite end two connectors compatible with c_1 and c_2, respectively (with matching shapes and glues). Furthermore, each floating object $o \in u$ must exist within the radius $m(o)$ from c_1–c_2. Then u is consumed, t is created and inserted between c_1 and c_2. The tiles t_1 and t_2 are pushed in opposite directions to make room for t. If the pushing is impossible (blocked by a structure of tiles interconnecting t_1 and t_2), the rule cannot be applied.

Proposition 1. *Consider an L system $G = (\Sigma, \omega, P)$ with turtle graphics, with a set of variables $V \subseteq \Sigma$, where each rule in P is the form*

$$A \to \{[\{+, -\}V^*] \cup V\}^* \{A\} \{[\{+, -\}V^*] \cup V\}^*$$

for some $A \in V$. Further, let each variable in V be interpreted by turtle graphics as a bounded convex polytope. Then the growth of G can be stepwise simulated by an M system, i.e., each step of the L system is simulated by a fixed number of steps of the M system.

Proof. The basic idea is that each variable of the simulated L system, materialized as a bounded convex polytope, corresponds in M system to an equally-sized tile (or to a set of tiles, as suggested in Sect. 3.3 where symbol S is simulated by tiles s_1, s_2 and s_3). The major issues with a simulation of an L system by an M system, imposing restrictions on the form of L system's rules, are summarized as follows:

- An existing tile A should not be altered by an application of a rule. A change of A could possibly be resolved in an M system by its destruction and then creation of a replacement tile, but the new tile should have equal size and connectors. It might be difficult to provide a general solution. Therefore, in a rule $A \to w$ of L system, the string w should also contain A out of any control parentheses, which guarantees that A remains unchanged.
- Erasing rules $A \to \lambda$ are generally not allowed since their effect under the turtle graphics would be not only the destruction of A, but also the attraction all other (structures of) tiles attached to it to a single point.
- All constants $+, -$ at the right-hand side of a rule must be closed in push-pop parentheses $[\ ]$. Otherwise such a constant could be inserted into the string representing an existing interconnected structure of tiles, which would mean its bending by the angle assigned to $+$ or $-$, respectively. Such a bending is hard to achieve and even, perhaps, generally impossible in M systems.

The resulting restricted format of rewriting L system rules may require an attachment of new structures of tiles (under various angles) to an existing tile corresponding to the left-hand side of the rule. Furthermore, insertion of one or more new tiles between the existing tile and its neighbours could be required. This can be achieved in the simulating M system via creation and insertion rules. An M system, however, can attach/insert to every connector only one convex object at a time. Therefore, simulation of a rewriting rule $A \to w$ must be done in k steps where k is less than or equal to the number of occurrences of symbols from V in w. At each step, one or more tiles are attached to the growing structure under necessary angles.

This can be achieved by timing the environment of the simulating M system in k-steps cycles. Let there be floating objects $a_1, \ldots, a_k$ in the M system, and let $\epsilon(a_1)$ be high, while $\epsilon(a_2) = \epsilon(a_3) = \cdots = \epsilon(a_k) = 0$. Furthermore, let there be metabolic rules

$$a_1 \to a_2, \quad a_2 \to a_3, \quad \ldots \ a_{k-1} \to a_k \quad \text{and} \quad a_k \to a_1.$$

Then j-th step may allow only creation/insertion of a certain kind of tiles t_j, using a creation/insertion rule $a_j^+ \rightarrow t_j$. For each such tile t_j, the previous tile in the structure must contain a corresponding connector to which t_j is attached. The angle of the connector is determined by symbols $\pm$ eventually preceding t_j in the string w. This way, the growth of a structure corresponding to the string w is controlled.   □

3.3   Example: A Tree Growth by an M System

Consider the L system $G_t = (\Sigma, M, P)$, where $\Sigma = \{M, S, +, -, [,]\}$ and P contains two rules $M \rightarrow S[+M][-M]SM$ and $S \rightarrow SS$. Variables are M (green segment) and S (brown segment.) The turn angle is $45°$. The two rules can be interpreted graphically as follows:

The L system G_t generates a simple tree illustrated below (source: Wikipedia, https://cs.wikipedia.org/wiki/L-syst%CA9m):

We construct an M system $\mathcal{M}_t$ such that each step of G_t is simulated by two steps of $\mathcal{M}_t$. It is based on a two-dimensional polytopic tile system $T = (Q, G, \gamma, d_g, S)$, where:

$G = \{\, \bullet, \triangledown, \blacksquare, \bigcirc, \square, \mathrm{x}\}$
$Q = \{m, s_1, s_2, s_3\}$ are rods with surface glue x:
$\gamma = \{(\triangledown, \blacksquare), (\triangledown, \bullet), (\square, \bigcirc), (\square, \bullet), (\square, \blacksquare)\}$
$d_g = 0.1$
$S = \{m\}$

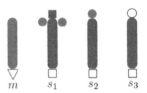

Now we complete the description of the M system $\mathcal{M}_t = (F, P, T, \mu, R, \sigma)$, where

F contains small floating objects a, b with a high mobility, a is present in the environment with a high concentration and b with zero concentration;
P is an empty set of protions;
σ assigns to each glue pair $(g_1, g_2) \in \gamma$ an empty multiset;
R contains the following rules:
  Metabolic rules: $a \to b$, $b \to a$
  Creation rules: $aaa \to s_1$, $aaa \to s_3$, $bbb \to m$
  Insertion rules: $aaa \to s_1$, $aaa \to s_3$, $bbb \to s_2$

The environment of $\mathcal{M}_t$ passes cyclically between two states, one with objects a and the other with objects b. Therefore, rods s_1 and s_3 can be created only at each odd step, while rods s_2 and m at each even step. Each transition of the L system G_t is simulated by two steps of $\mathcal{M}_t$ as illustrated at Fig. 1:

1. Each brown rod s_1, s_2 or s_3 is prolonged by attaching the rod s_3, which simulates an application of the rewriting rule $S \to SS$ of G_t. Simultaneously, each green rod m has attached the brown rod s_1 with fork-arranged connectors.
2. The fork-arranged connectors of each rod s_1 grow new green rods m under angle 45° and, simultaneously, s_1 is prolonged with s_2, which completes the simulation of the rule $M \to S[+M][-M]SM$ of G_t.

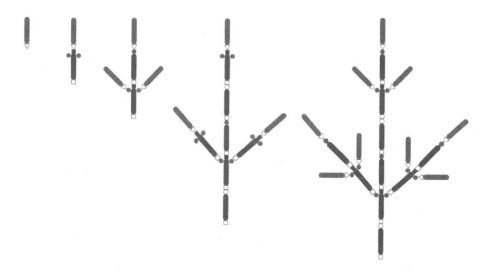

Fig. 1. Growth of M system $\mathcal{M}_t$ simulating two steps of "tree growing" L system L_t.

4   Conclusions

The paper deals with a geometric models of morphogenesis, *M systems*, that exhibit properties of self-assembly and controlled growth akin to those observed in cell biology. The model extends the membrane computing approach with explicit geometric concepts of shape and arrangement of atomic objects at specific locations. Basic abstract operations in the model include reactions among objects, their transport through protion channels, and mutual interconnection of generalized tiles in 3D, leading to construction and destruction of complex geometric structures, which are plant-inspired in the examples we have provided, but which can adopt virtually any geometric forms.

We have studied the relation of M systems to Lindenmayer (L) systems, which are generally recognized as an algorithmic (grammatical) model of development of cells and plants. This is usually achieved by interpreting the generated strings via turtle graphics. The two models differ in many aspects. We show that L systems are more abstract in several senses, which allows them to generate sequences of shapes with strong discontinuities between them. This is impossible in the framework of M systems where each new shape is derived from the previous one just by adding, deleting or pushing tiles. Therefore, we impose certain restrictions on the form of L system's rules, stating thus a *sufficient condition* for their stepwise simulation in the framework of M systems. Both a formal proof of this statement and an example application are provided. A *necessary condition* for such a simulation remains an *open problem*.

M systems could significantly extend the growth and modelling capacity of L systems by exploiting communication between parts of the growing structures by floating objects. These can be both produced and consumed during development of growth, (dis)connection and destruction of tiles, providing an effective tool for their growth control. The relation between the capability of M systems and that of L systems interacting with their environment [4] is a question left open for further research. Another open question is the applicability of M systems in the ecosystem of *digital morphogenesis*. From this point of view, the *self-healing properties* of M systems [8] and their applicability in the framework of L systems are of a special interest. A further research avenue could be pursued by equipping the model with a kind of abstract genetic code defining shapes of tiles and placement of connectors and other protions on them, allowing their digital evolution.

Acknowledgements. This work was supported by The Ministry of Education, Youth and Sports Of the Czech Republic from the National Programme of Sustainability (NPU II) project IT4Innovations Excellence in Science - LQ1602, and by the Silesian University in Opava under the Student Funding Scheme, project SGS/13/2016.

References

1. Cardelli, L., Gardner, P.: Processes in space. In: Ferreira, F., Löwe, B., Mayordomo, E., Mendes Gomes, L. (eds.) CiE 2010. LNCS, vol. 6158, pp. 78–87. Springer, Heidelberg (2010). https://doi.org/10.1007/978-3-642-13962-8_9

2. Krasnogor, N., Gustafson, S., Pelta, D., Verdegay, J.: Systems Self-Assembly: Multidisciplinary Snapshots. Studies in Multidisciplinarity. Elsevier Science, Amsterdam (2011)

3. Lindenmayer, A., Prusinkiewicz, P., et al.: The Algorithmic Beauty of Plants. Springer, New York (1991). https://doi.org/10.1007/978-1-4613-8476-2

4. Mech, R., Prusinkiewicz, P.: Visual models of plants interacting with their environment. In: Blau, B., et al. (eds.) Proceedings of SIGGRAPH 1996, Computer Graphics Proceedings, Annual Conference Series, pp. 397–410. ACM (1996)

5. von Neumann, J.: Probabilistic logics and the synthesis of reliable organisms from unreliable components. Ann. Math. Stud. **34**, 43–98 (1956)

6. Păun, A., Popa, B.: P systems with proteins on membranes. Fundam. Inform. **72**(4), 467–483 (2006)

7. Păun, G., Rozenberg, G., Salomaa, A. (eds.): The Oxford Handbook of Membrane Computing. Oxford University Press, Oxford (2010)

8. Sosík, P., Smolka, V., Drastík, J., Bradík, J., Garzon, M.: On the robust power of morphogenetic systems for time bounded computation. In: Gheorghe, M., Rozenberg, G., Salomaa, A., Zandron, C. (eds.) CMC 2017. LNCS, vol. 10725, pp. 270–292. Springer, Cham (2018). https://doi.org/10.1007/978-3-319-73359-3_18

9. Sosík, P., Smolka, V., Drastík, J., Moore, T., Garzon, M.: Morphogenetic and homeostatic self-assembled systems. In: Patitz, M.J., Stannett, M. (eds.) UCNC 2017. LNCS, vol. 10240, pp. 144–159. Springer, Cham (2017). https://doi.org/10.1007/978-3-319-58187-3_11

10. Tomita, M.: Whole-cell simulation: a grand challenge of the 21st century. Trends Biotechnol. **19**(6), 205–210 (2001)

11. Turing, A.: The chemical basis of morphogenesis. Philos. Trans. R. Soc. Lond. B **237**, 7–72 (1950)

12. Winfree, E.: Self-healing tile sets. In: Chen, J., Jonoska, N., Rozenberg, G. (eds.) Nanotechnology: Science and Computation. Natural Computing Series, pp. 55–78. Springer, Heidelberg (2006). https://doi.org/10.1007/3-540-30296-4_4

13. Ziegler, G.: Lectures on Polytopes. Graduate Texts in Mathematics. Springer, New York (1995)

An Improved Quicksort Algorithm Based on Tissue-Like P Systems with Promoters

Shuo Yan, Jie Xue$^{(\boxtimes)}$, and Xiyu Liu

School of Management Science and Engineering,
Shandong Normal University, Jinan 250014, China
`jiexue@sdnu.edu.cn`

Abstract. P systems are distributed and parallel computing models. In this paper, we proposed an improved Quicksort algorithm, called ECTPP-Quicksort, which is based on evolution-communication tissue-like P systems with promoters. ECTPP-Quicksort, taking advantage of the parallel nature, allows objects to be sorted to evolve according to instructions or rules simultaneously. In this way, the time complexity of Quicksort is improved greatly to $O(log_2n)$ compared to $O(nlog_2n)$ of the conventional Quicksort algorithm. We designed the rules, objects, membrane structures and some other characteristics of ECTPP-Quicksort P system in detail. It is meaningful to the development of membrane computing.

Keywords: Quicksort algorithm · P systems · Improved

1 Introduction

Quicksort is a popular sorting algorithm which has a better time complexity on average than most other sorting algorithms. However, its calculated performance is unstable and not so good, hence how to implement Quicksort algorithm in parallel to improve its efficiency is still an ongoing research topic [1].

There are many previous attempts to enhance its efficiency. One feasible approach is to assign one another processor for every new sub-sequence so that each sub-sequence can execute in parallel in a sense. However, the algorithm still cannot reach an ideal efficiency as the computing inside every sub-sequence is not parallel. Also, the additional processors bring extra spaces costs which are not expected [2]. Another way is to divide each sequence into blocks which are distributed dynamically to spare processors. However, the vast extra atomic synchronization instructions make the costs to be much more expensive [3]. Besides, in [4] Blelloch attempted to improve Quicksort based on prefix sums, but its post-study showed a poor performance when the improved arithmetic executing.

On the other hand, there have some reasonable and preferable attempts on this work. For example, Wagar proposed a powerful quicksort algorithm called hyperquicksort. With its improvement and development, it has achieved a satisfactory efficiency [5]. Also, David Powers et al. described a parallelized quicksort

© Springer Nature Switzerland AG 2019
T. Hinze et al. (Eds.): CMC 2018, LNCS 11399, pp. 258–274, 2019.
https://doi.org/10.1007/978-3-030-12797-8_18

that can operate with a less time complexity on a CRCW (concurrent read and concurrent write) and PRAM (parallel random-access machine) with n processors by performing partitioning implicitly [6].

Despite these jobs, there was no more surprise on improving the efficiency of Quicksort. At this time, a kind of distributed and parallel computing model called P system was introduced to solve sorting problems. The theory of P systems (also called membrane computing) is a new branch of natural computing, which abstracts computing concepts from the constructions and functions of cells or the cooperation of cells in living bodies. In P systems, each cell is composed of two parts, multisets of objects and evolution rules. Multisets of objects in a membrane system are equivalent to biological materials in a living body and evolution rules are equivalent to chemical reactions. Rules which are executed in the maximally parallel way determine how objects evolve. P system is becoming a powerful and efficient computing tool because of its unique parallel nature. P systems with symbol objects and evolution rules are powerful computing models.

At the very beginning, in [7] Arulanandham presented a way to realize the conventional bead-sort by using tissue-like P systems. In [8] Ceterchi et al. showed a way to realize insertion sort by using P systems with symport and antiport rules. Besides, in [9] Ceterchi et al. introduced how P systems with promoters improve the static sort. Also, in [10] Ceterchi et al. simulated the bitonic sort using P systems with only rewriting rules. After then, in [11] Ceterchi and Tomescu showed a way to implement sorting networks with P systems. Also, some other sorting algorithms could be improved by using P systems, Alhazov et al. provided good examples [12,13]. These researches above improved the efficiency of sorting algorithms by using P systems with its nature of distributed and parallel. However, many of them had not designed the direct membrane algorithms with detailed evolution rules and the whole steps which are easy to execute but difficult to design. Instead, they designed the coupled membrane algorithms which integrate the characteristic of sorting algorithms and P systems to create membrane frames and partial rules. Also, in spite of the fact that Quicksort is a popular sorting algorithm with a better algorithm complexity on average than most other sorting algorithms, no research dedicates to improve Quicksort algorithm with P systems until now.

In this paper, an improved Quicksort algorithm, called ECTPP-Quicksort, using evolution-communication tissue-like P systems with promoters, is proposed. One contribution of this study is that we have decreased the time complexity to $O(log_2 n)$ therefore its efficiency has improved a lot by using P systems. In ECTPP-Quicksort, instructions can be executed in parallel both in every subsequence inside and between different sub-sequence so that it is time-saving. Another contribution is that we have designed the direct membrane algorithms with rules, objects, membrane structures and some other characteristics in detail. It has a positive effect on the direct membrane algorithms whose design is difficult and applications are limited.

This paper is organized as follows. In Sect. 2, we introduce some preliminaries about tissue-like P systems with promoters and Quicksort algorithm. Section 3 proposes and introduces the ECTPP-Quicksort algorithm using a parallel mechanism. Also, the efficiency of ECTPP-Quicksort is shown in this section. In Sect. 4, we propose one illustrative example which is used to explain how the ECTPP-Quicksort algorithm works concretely. Finally, Sect. 5 gives conclusions of this paper and the direction of future research.

2   Preliminaries

2.1   Tissue-Like P Systems with Promoters

In this section, we introduce Evolution-Communication Tissue-like P Systems with promoters.

Tissue-like P systems were derived from a kind of fundamental P systems called cell-like P systems, by considering the construction of tissues and the relationship between different cells. Tissue-like P systems were made up of several cells, which are placed in a common environment and linked by communication channels. The communication channels can be given both in advance and established dynamically during the process of computing. Objects can be transported from one cell to another cell through communication channels using relevant rules. Also, tissue-like P systems can exchange objects with the environment in an even better fashion by using evolution-communication rules. These rules execute with a maximal parallelism. That is, one applies rules which are maximal and no more object can evolve at the same time by any rule. Evolution-communication rules are often used in tissue-like P systems [14].

There is a class of evolution-communication tissue-like P systems called evolution-communication tissue-like P systems with promoters (ECTPP). In tissue-like P systems with promoters, rules are also controlled by some particular objects called promoters. Only when the corresponding promoters exist can the rules with its unique promoters be executed. Furthermore, promoters need not change itself both in species and amounts during the process when rules are performing, and they can evolve by utilizing several different rules concurrently [15, 16].

2.2   Quicksort Algorithm

Quicksort, serving as a systematic method for placing elements in order, is an efficient sorting algorithm. The basic idea of Quicksort is dividing a large array into two small sub-arrays by comparing the value of elements, then it will sort the two sub-arrays recursively by the same way.

The result of Quicksort can be shown efficiently by a binary search tree. Binary search tree, sometimes called ordered or sorted binary tree, is a rooted binary tree whose internal nodes can store keys. Each node has two different sub-trees, generally denoted by the left tree and the right tree. There is a particular property of binary search tree that the key in each node must be bigger than or equal to any key stored in its left sub-tree, and smaller than or equal to any key stored in its right sub-tree. Each execution of Quicksort corresponds the following binary search tree: the initial pivot key in Quicksort is the root node of the binary search tree; the pivot key of the left half is the root of the left sub-tree, in the same way, the pivot key of the right half is the root of the right sub-tree, and so on. In this study, we obtain the final result of an ordered array by building a binary search tree in our system.

Mathematical analysis of a conventional Quicksort algorithm shows that it takes $O(nlog_2n)$ comparisons to sort n items on average. And in the worst case, when it degrades into Bead Sort, it takes $O(n^2)$ comparisons. In the best case, it takes $O(logn)$ comparisons to sort n items.

3   The ECTPP-Quicksort Algorithm

3.1   Membrane Structures for the ECTPP-Quicksort Algorithm

Now we describe membrane structures for the ECTPP-Quicksort algorithm. In the beginning, we describe the membranes. First, we need one membrane labeled by 0 as the input membrane into which we input the objects to be sorted. Then we need n membranes labeled by $1 \cdots n$, and n is the amount of the types of objects to be sorted. After that, other $n-1$ membranes labeled by $n+2 \cdots 2n$ are used as comparing comparators. Besides, there is an output membrane labeled by $n+1$. Then, we need two membranes receiving the two sub-arrays of objects. One membrane labeled by $2n+1$ is used to receive objects whose amounts are less than the current pivot object. Similarly, another membrane labeled by $2n+2$ is used to receive objects whose amounts are more than the current pivot object. We call these $5n-2$ membranes the computing membranes. Finally, there are 2^n-1 membranes labeled by $T1 \cdots T2^{n-1}$ which act as a binary search tree. The binary search is our finally result and we call these n membranes the binary search tree membranes. Consequently, the total number of membranes is $2^n + 5n - 3$ in this ECTPP-Quicksort algorithm.

Now we describe the channels between cells in this ECTPP-Quicksort algorithm. N links start from the input membrane 0 to membranes j for $1 \leq j \leq n$, wherefore objects can be sent from the input membrane 0 to membranes j through these n links. Then other $n-1$ links starting from the membrane labeled by 1 to membranes labeled by $n+j$ for $2 \leq j \leq n$ are used to send the current pivot object to membrane $n+j$ to take part in a comparison with object j. Similarly, there are $n-1$ links starting from the other $n-1$ membranes labeled by j for $2 \leq j \leq n$ to these $n-1$ membranes labeled by $n+j$ for $2 \leq j \leq n$ each to each, thus we can send the normal objects to compare with the current pivot object. On the other hand, there is a link starting from membrane labeled by 1 to membrane labeled by $n+1$ to send all current pivot objects to be outputted. Therefore, there is a link starting from membrane $n+1$ to the environment to output all the current pivot as a result. Then, there are two links starting from every membrane labeled by $n+j$ for $2 \leq j \leq n$ to membranes labeled by $2n+1$ and $2n+2$. The link starting from membrane $n+j$ for $2 \leq j \leq n$ to membrane $2n+1$ is used to transport objects with lesser amounts than the current pivot object, and the link from membrane labeled $n + j$ for $2 \leq j \leq n$ to membrane labeled $2n + 2$ is used to transport objects with larger amounts than the current pivot object.

To show it more clearly, the membrane structure for the ECTPP-Quicksort algorithm is shown in Figs. 1 and 2.

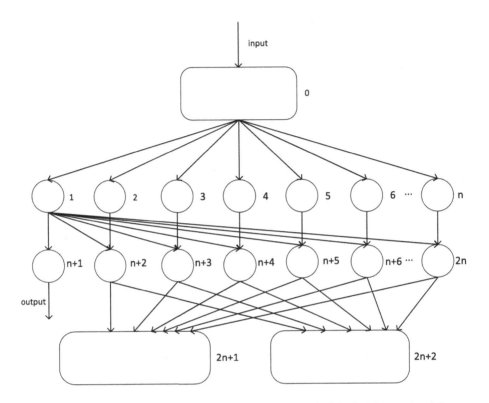

Fig. 1. The computing membrane structure for the ECTPP-Quicksort algorithm.

3.2   Objects for the ECTPP-Quicksort Algorithm

The ECTPP-Quicksort tissue-like P system is as follows.

$$\Pi_{ECTPP-Quicksort} = (O, \sigma_O, \sigma_1, \cdots, \sigma_{2n+2}, syn, \rho, i_{out}) \tag{1}$$

where:

1. O is the alphabets of all objects in the ECTPP-Quicksort P system and $O = \{a_{ij}, H_{ij}, O_{i1}, O_{i2}\}$;
2. syn represents all synapses between cells in the ECTPP-Quicksort P system and $syn = \{\{0,1\}, \{0,2\}, \cdots, \{0,n\}; \{1, n+1\}, \{1, n+2\}, \cdots, \{1, 2n\}; \{2, n+2\}, \{3, n+3\}, \cdots, \{n, 2n\}; \{n+1, E\}; \{n+2, 2n+1\}, \{n+3, 2n+1\}, \cdots, \{2n, 2n+1\}; \{n+2, 2n+2\}$;

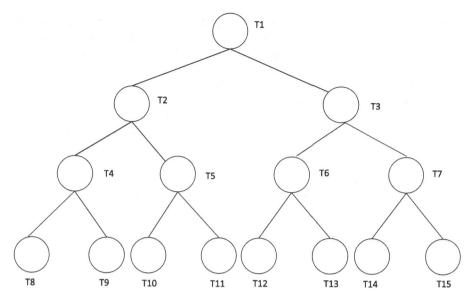

Fig. 2. The binary search tree membrane structure for the ECTPP-Quicksort algorithm.

3. $\rho = \{r_i > r_j \mid i < j\}$ defines the partial ordering relationship of rules; It means that rules with the higher order will be executed with higher priority;
4. $\sigma_0 = (w_{0,0}, R_0), \sigma_1 = (G_{1,0}, R_1), \sigma_2 = (G_{2,0}, R_2), \sigma_{2n+2} = (w_{2n+2,0}, R_{2n+2})$;

Where:

(a) σ_i for $1 \leq i \leq 2n + 2$ represents a cell or membrane;
(b) R_h for $1 \leq h \leq 2n + 2$ is a finite set of rules in cell h, of the following forms:

(1) $(G)_z \rightarrow (xy, go_q)$, where G is the multiset of objects consumed by this rule, z is the promoter and x or y are the multisets of objects produced by this rule, and go_q represents that x or y are emitted immediately to cell q;
(2) $(G)_z \rightarrow (xy, go)$, where x and y are emitted to all cells σ_q such that $(q, p) \subseteq syn$;
(3) $(G)_z \rightarrow xy$, where x and y will not be emitted to any cells. Only G and the promoter z exist in a cell can a rule be carried out. Also, the symbol of r_{hv} stands for the vth subset of rules in cell h, and $\cup$ is used to connected the rules in the same subset.

5. $i_{out} = n + 1$ indicates that the membrane labeled by $n + 1$ is the output cell in where the objects are to go to the binary search tree membranes.

In this ECTPP-Quicksort algorithm, object a_{ij} represents that the computing process of a_{ij} happened during the ith recursion of the whole computing process, and the subscript j is used to distinguish different types of objects. Assume that the kind of elements to be sorted is n. That is to say, the array to be sorted is $n_1, n_2, \cdots, n_n$. Consequently, the input objects are n_1 copies of a_{11}, n_2 copies of a_{12}, n_3 copies of a_{13},,n_n copies of a_{1n}.

We need additional objects H_{ij} for $1 \leq i \leq n$ and $1 \leq j \leq n$ acting as intermediate objects in comparisons between a_{ij} and the pivot objects a_{i1}. Moreover, we need additional objects O_{i1} and O_{i2} which are promoters during comparisons. The function of O_{i1} or O_{i2} is selecting a transport direction between subrules for each object. If the amounts of objects are larger than the current object, they will use the rule with promoter O_{i2} so that these objects will be sent to membrane $2n + 2$. Similarly, objects will use the rule with promoter O_{i1} to be sent to membrane $2n+1$, if their amounts are less than the current pivot object.

ECTPP-Quicksort is a recursive algorithm that is why we need select a pivot object in each recursion. In the 1st recursion, we choose the first object a_{i1} as the pivot object, then we compare the number of each object with the current pivot object concurrently. After these comparisons, we get two sub-arrays of objects and we send objects whose amounts are less than the current pivot object to one membrane as well as send objects whose amounts are larger than the current pivot object to another membrane. Then the ECTPP-Quicksort algorithm executes with these sub-arrays of objects recursively and simultaneously. In each recursion, we send all copies of the current pivot object to the environment and we can obtain the result by building a binary sorting tree according to the subscript i of every pivot objects.

3.3   Rules for the ECTPP-Quicksort Algorithm

Rules of ECTPP-Quicksort tissue-like P system is as follows.

For $1 \leq i \leq n$:

R_0:

$$r_{01} = \{(a_{i\theta})_{\neg a_{11}} \rightarrow a_{i1}\}, 1 \leq \theta \leq n, 2 \leq i \leq n;$$
$$r_{02} = \{a_{ij} \rightarrow (a_{ij}, go_j)\}, 1 \leq j \leq n;$$
$R_j = \{a_{ij} \rightarrow (a_{ij}, go)\}, 1 \leq j \leq n; \ R_{n+1} = \{a_{i1} \rightarrow (a_{i1}, go_{Ti})\}; \ R_{n+j}:$

For $2 \leq j \leq n$:

$$r_{(n+j),1} = \{a_{i1}a_{ij} \rightarrow H_{ij}\};$$
$$r_{(n+j),2} = \{a_{i1} \rightarrow O_{i1}\} \cup \{a_{ij} \rightarrow O_{i2}\};$$
$$r_{(n+j),3} = \{H_{ij} \rightarrow a_{ij}\};$$
$$r_{(n+j),4} = \{(a_{ij})_{O_{i1}} \rightarrow (a_{ij}, go_{2n+1})\} \cup \{(a_{ij})_{O_{i2}} \rightarrow (a_{ij}, go_{2n+2})\};$$
$$r_{(n+j),5} = \{O_{i1} \rightarrow \lambda\} \cup \{O_{i2} \rightarrow \lambda\};$$
$R_{2n+1} = \{a_{ij} \rightarrow (a_{(2i)j}, go_0)\};$
$R_{2n+2} = \{a_{ij} \rightarrow (a_{(2i+1)j}, go_0)\};$

The operating mechanism of these rewriting rules are similar to chemical reactions. Objects are transformed into other objects and sent to other cells by using these rewriting rules.

3.4   Computing Process for the ECTPP-Quicksort Algorithm

The steps are as follows. In these following steps, the range of i is $1 \leq i \leq n$ unless otherwise specified.

Step 1. In this ECTPP-Quicksort tissue-like P system, Cell 0 is the input cell. We input several types of objects with different amounts to be sorted to cell 0. Rule r_{01} will be executed in this step to select one type of object a_{ij} randomly and transform it into a_{i1} when $i \geq 2$, as a result that this P system always have a current pivot object in every recursion. Then rule r_{02} will be executed to send all copies of a_{ij} for $1 \leq j \leq n$ from cell 0 to cell j.

Step 2. In this step, rule r_{j1} is executed in cell j for $1 \leq j \leq n$ so that all copies of a_{ij} are sent to cell $n+j$ as well as all copies of the current pivot object a_{i1} are sent to every cells a_{n+j} for $2 \leq j \leq n$ to compare with other objects.

Step 3. One operation of *Step* 3 is outputting which takes place in cell $n+1$ using rule R_{n+1}. In every recursion, all copies of the current pivot object a_{i1} will be transported from cell $n+1$ into membrane labeled by Ti of the binary search tree as the final result. Another operation of *Step* 3 conducting in cell $n+j$ for $2 \leq j \leq n$ is shown as follows. Rule $r_{(n+j),1}$ will be executed to consume a_{ij} and a_{i1} equably using an internal flat maximally parallel mechanism. At the same time, H_{ij} will be generated as an intermediate object with the same copies of a_{ij} or $ai1$ which will be burned up firstly. That is, object with fewer numbers of a_{ij} and a_{i1} will be exhausted with rule $r_{(n+j),1}$, and $r_{(n+j),1}$ will create the same copies of H_{ij} in this step.

Step 4. Rule $r_{(n+j),2}$ will be executed in cell $n+j$ for $2 \leq j \leq n$ during this step. Sub-rule $\{a_{i1} \rightarrow O_{i1}\}$ will be executed if the number of a_{i1} is larger than a_{ij}. That is, if a_{i1} exists in cell $n+j$, rule $\{a_{i1} \rightarrow O_{i1}\}$ will be executed to clean out all copies of a_{i1} and generate the same copies of promoter O_{i1}. On the other hand, sub-rule $\{a_{ij} \rightarrow O_{i2}a_{ij}\}$ will be executed if the number of a_{ij} is larger than a_{i1}. That is, if a_{ij} exists in cell $n+j$, rule $\{a_{ij} \rightarrow O_{i2}a_{ij}\}$ will be executed to generate the same copies of promoter O_{i2}, but a_{ij} does not change itself. Therefore, the generation of O_{i1} means that the amount of a_{i1} is larger than a_{ij} and the generation of O_{i2} has an opposite meaning.

Step 5. Rule $r_{(n+j),3}$ will be executed in cell $n+j$ for $2 \leq j \leq n$ to transform all copies of H_{ij} into a_{ij} with the same copies in this step. Therefore, the amount of a_{ij} will revert to its initial amount after this step.

Step 6. Rule $r_{(n+j),4}$ will be executed in cell $n+j$ for $2 \leq j \leq n$ during this step. If promoter O_{i1} exists in cell $n+j$, sub-rule $\{(a_{ij})_{O_{i1}} \rightarrow (a_{ij}, go_{2n+1})\}$ will be executed for the reason that all copies of a_{ij} will be sent to cell $2n+1$. Similarly, if promoter O_{i2} exists in cell $n+j$ rather than O_{i1}, sub-rule $\{(a_{ij})_{O_{i2}} \rightarrow (a_{ij}, go_{2n+2})\}$ will be executed and all copies of a_{ij} will be sent to cell $2n+2$. After this step, all initial objects are divided into two sub-arrays of objects existing in two different cells.

Step 7. In this step, rule $r_{(n+j),5}$ will be executed in cell $n+j$ for $2 \leq j \leq n$, all copies of promoters O_{i1} or O_{i2} will be exhausted. After this step, all current objects expect the pivot object in this ECTPP-Quicksort tissue-like P system exist in cell $2n+1$ or $2n+2$.

Step 8. The initial array composed of different objects has been divided into two sub-arrays after step 7. One of the two sub-arrays is composed of objects whose amounts are less than the current pivot object, and these objects exist in cell $2n + 1$ now. Another sub-array is composed of objects whose amounts are larger than the pivot object and these objects exist in cell $2n + 2$. In this step, subscript i of objects in cell $2n + 1$ should be instead of $2i$. Only do this can the output objects be built into a binary search tree according to their subscript i. Then objects in cell $2n + 1$ will enter to cell 0 by using rule $R_{2n+1} = \{a_{ij} \to a_{(2i)j}, go_0\}$ for $2 \le j \le n$. On the other hand, subscript i of objects in cell $2n+2$ should be instead of $2i+1$, and objects in cell $2n+2$ will enter to cell 0 by using rule $R_{2n+2} = \{a_{ij} \to a_{(2i+1)j}, go_0\}$ for $2 \le j \le n$. Therefore, the recursion for the first time is finished now and the two sub-arrays composed of objects will exist in cell 0 after this step and the second time of recursion will start.

Step 9. When there is no objects enter to cell 0, the recursion stops. Objects transported from the output cell $n + 1$ are all entering the binary search tree membranes according to rule $R_{n+1} = \{a_{i1} \to (a_{i1}, go_{Ti})\}$. Now, we get the final result, that is the binary search tree.

ECTPP-Quicksort uses a parallel mechanism of tissue-like P Systems with promoters introduced above to execute in parallel. Table 1 shows a pseudo-code of ECTPP-Quicksort algorithm.

3.5   Interpretation of the Result and Algorithm Efficiency for ECTPP-Quicksort

In *step* 10, we have built a binary search tree as our final result. Now we explain why the pivot objects go to the binary search tree membranes with rule R_{n+1}. According to the unique nature of binary search tree and the rule i changing in ECTPP-Quicksort, we put object a_{11} as the root node of the tree. Then a_{21} is the left-sub-node of a11 and a_{31} is the right-sub-node of it. Similarly, a_{41} is the left-sub-node of a_{21} and a_{51} is the right-sub-node of it. Also, a_{61} is the left-sub-node of a_{31} and a_{71} is the right-sub-node of it. By parity of reasoning, we can build the whole binary search tree as shown in Fig. 2. Consequently, rule R_{n+1} is $R_{n+1} = a_{i1} \to (a_{i1}, go_{Ti})$. Then we can get the whole ordered array from the binary search tree according to that the key in each node must be greater than or equal to any key stored in the left sub-tree, and less than or equal to any key stored in the right sub-tree.

Now we need to explain one thing. In the case when two type of objects have the same amounts, the O_{ij} can not appear when the two kind of objects react together. At this time, we will use another rule $a_{ij} \to (a_{ij}, go_E)$ where E is the environment. Finally, a_{ij} will be treated have the same amounts with a_{i1}.

ECTPP-Quicksort algorithm takes t time units to sort n items because of its parallelism, and t is the height of its binary search tree. In every time units, eleven rules will be executed. Consequently, this improved Quicksort algorithm takes $11t$ times to solved n items. Mathematical analysis of ECTPP-Quicksort algorithm shows that the time complexity is $O(log_2 n)$ on average which is improved a

Table 1. Algorithm for ECTPP-Quicksort.

Algorithm

Input :

N copies of objects a_{ij} which represents the array to be sorted.

Output :

A binary search tree with a_{i1}.

Method :

For $1 \leq i \leq n$,

Rule r_{01}: If $i1$, select a type of object a_{ij} randomly and make all copies of it to be replaced by a_{i1} so that we have a type of pivot object in every recursion;

Rule r_{02}: Transport all copies of a_{ij} to cell j, $1 \leq j \leq n$;

Rule R_j: Transport all copies of a_{ij} to cell $n + j$ and all copies of a_{i1} to cell $n + 1 \cdot 2n$, $2 \leq j \leq n$;

Rule R_{n+1}: In cell $n + 1$, every current pivot object in each recursion will be transported into binary search tree membranes as the final result by using R_{n+1};

Rule $r_{(n+j),1}$: Consume a_{ij} and a_{i1} equably and H_{ij} will be generated as intermediate species. And the amount of H_{ij} is same with object a_{ij} or a_{i1} which is burned up firstly in cell $n + j$, $2 \leq j \leq n$;

Rule $r_{(n+j),2}$: If there exists a_{i1} in cell $n + j$, O_{i1} will be generated and a_{i1} will be burned up. If there exists a_{ij}, O_{i2} will be generated in cell $n + j$, $2 \leq j \leq n$;

Rule $r_{(n+j),3}$: Transform all H_{ij} into a_{ij} so that the number of a_{ij} is same as its initial number in cell $n + j$, $2 \leq j \leq n$;

Rule $r_{(n+j),4}$: If there exists O_{i1}, send all copies of a_{ij} from cell $n + j$ to cell $2n + 1$; If there exists O_{i2}, send all copies of a_{ij} from cell $n + j$ to cell $2n + 2$, $2 \leq j \leq n$;

Rule $r_{(n+j),5}$: All copies of O_{i1} and O_{i2} will be exhausted in cell $n + j$, $2 \leq j \leq n$;

Rule R_{2n+1}: One of the subscript i of objects a_{ij} in cell $2n + 1$ should be instead of $2i$ and all objects enter to cell 0;

Rule R_{2n+2}: One of the subscript i of objects a_{ij} in cell $2n + 2$ should be instead of $2i + 1$ and all objects enter to cell 0.

---

lot than the conventional Quicksort algorithm with $O(nlog_2n)$. Obviously, the algorithm efficiency of ECTPP-Quicksort is substantially improved from that of the conventional Quicksort algorithm.

4 Implementation of ECTPP-Quicksort

We present an illustrative example in this section in order to demonstrate how ECTPP-Quicksort works. In this case, we consider the following array to be sorted: three, one, four, five and two. Therefore, our initial objects in the P system are three copies of a_{11}, one copy of a_{12}, four copies of a_{13}, five copies of a_{14} and two copies of a_{15}. The whole execution process of this computing is recursive. We explain the process of the 1st recursion in detail as follows, then we show the current objects after executing every step of the following recursions in tables. Now we consider the 1st recursion of the computing process.

Step 1. We have transformed the array to be sorted into several types of objects a_{11}, a_{12}, a_{13}, a_{14}, a_{15}. And we input the following objects to cell 0: three copies of a_{11}, one copy of a_{12}, four copies of a_{13}, five copies of a_{14} and two copies of a_{15}. Rule cannot be executed because $i = 1$, then it does not meet its execution condition. Rule $r_{02} = \{a_{1j} \rightarrow (a_{1j}, go_j)\}$ can be executed to put all copies of a_{1j} for $1 \leq j \leq 5$ in cell 0 to cell j simultaneously and respectively. After this execution, there are three copies of a_{11} in cell 1, one copy of a_{12} in cell 2, four copies of a_{13} in cell 3, five copies of a_{14} in cell 4 and two copies of a_{15} in cell 5.

Step 2. In cell j for $1 \leq j \leq 5$, rule $R_j = \{a_{ij} \rightarrow (a_{ij}, go)\}$ is executed firstly during *step* 2. As a result, a_{1j} is sent to cell $5 + j$ for $2 \leq j \leq 5$ simultaneously and respectively to compare with other objects. Besides, all copies of $a11$ are sent to cell 6 to be transported into the environment. Put it more concretely, all copies of a_{11} are sent to cell $6 \cdots 10$. At the same time, all copies of a_{12} are sent from cell 2 to cell 7. Also, all copies of a_{13} are sent from cell 3 to cell 8, and all copies of a_{14} are sent from cell 4 to cell 9 as well as all copies of a_{15} are sent from cell 5 to cell 10. It means that there are three copies of a_{11} in cell 6, three copies of a_{11} and one copy of a_{12} in cell 7, three copies of a_{11} and four copies of a_{13} in cell 8, three copies of a_{11} and five copies of a_{14} in cell 9, three copies of a_{11} and two copies of a_{15} in cell 10 after this step.

Step 3. One operation of Step 3 is outputting which takes place in cell 6 using rule R_6. In every recursion, the current pivot objects will be transported into the environment as a part of the result to be recorded. In this operation, rule $R_6 = \{a_{11} \rightarrow a_{11}, go_{T1}\}$ is executed so that all copies of $a11$ are sent to one of the binary search tree membrane labeled by $T1$ as the final result. Another operation of *Step* 3 is shown as follows. Rule $r_{(5+j),1} = \{a_{11}a_{1j} \rightarrow H_{1j}\}$ for $2 \leq j \leq 5$ is executed to consume a_{1j} and a_{11} equably using the internal flat maximally parallel mechanism. At the same time, H_{1j} is generated as an intermediate specie with the same copies of a_{1j} or a_{i1} which is burned up firstly. The process during this step in cell $7 \cdots 10$ is shown as following.

In cell 7, rule $r_{71} = \{a_{11}a_{12} \rightarrow H_{13}\}$ is executed, as a result, one copy of a_{11} and one copy of a_{12} evolve using rule r_{71} in cell 7 so that one copy of H_{12} is generated and two copies of a_{11} is remaining. After this step, the existing objects in cell 7 are two copies of a_{11} and one copy of H_{12}. Using the same mechanism and rule $r_{(5+j),1} = \{a_{11}a_{1j} \rightarrow H_{1j}\}$ for $3 \leq j \leq 5$ simultaneously, after the 3rd step, other objects in this ECTPP-Quicksort P system are three copies of a_{13} in cell $T1$, three copies of H_{13} and one copy of a_{13} in cell 8, three copies of H_{14} and two copies of a_{14} in cell 9, two copies of H_{15} and one copy of a_{15} in cell 10.

Step 4. Rule $r_{(5+j),2} = \{a_{11} \rightarrow O_{11}\} \cup \{a_{1j} \rightarrow O_{12}\}$ is executed in this step. Specifically, a_{11} will disappear in cell $7 \cdots 10$ after this step. The process in cell $7 \cdots 10$ is shown as following.

In cell 7, the sub-rule $\{a_{11} \rightarrow O_{11}\}$ of rule $r_{72} = \{a_{11} \rightarrow O_{11}\} \cup \{a_{12} \rightarrow O_{12}\}$ is executed for the reason that there are two copies of a_{11} in cell 7 and no remaining copies of a_{12}. Consequently, all copies of a_{11} are transformed into O_{11} with the same copies in cell 7. After this step, the current objects in cell 7 are two copies of O_11 and one copy of H_{12}. Using the similar mechanism and rules at the same time, after the 4th step, other objects in this ECTPP-Quicksort P system are three copies of a_{13} in cell $T1$, one copy of O_{12}, one copy of a_{13} and three copies of H_{13} in cell 8, two copies of O_{12}, two copies of a_{14} and three copies of H_{14} in cell 9, one copy of O_{11} and two copies of H_{15} in cell 10.

Step 5. In this step, rule $r_{(5+j),3} = \{H_{1j} \rightarrow a_{1j}\}$ for $2 \leq j \leq 5$ is executed to transform all copies of H_{ij} into a_{ij} with the same copies in cell j. The evolving process in cell $7 \cdots 10$ is shown as following.

In cell 7, $ruler_{73} = \{H_{12} \rightarrow a_{12}\}$ is executed to transform a_{ll} copies of H_{12} into a_{12} with the same copies. Therefore, after this step, objects in cell 7 are two copies of O_{11} and one copy of a_{12}. Using the similar mechanism and rule $r_{(5+j),3} = \{H_{1j} \rightarrow a_{1j}\}$ for $3 \leq j \leq 5$, other objects in this ECTPP-Quicksort P system after this step includes three copies of a_{13} in cell $T1$, four copies of $a13$ and one copy of O_{12} in cell 8, five copies of a_{14} and two copies of O_{12} in cell 9, two copies of a_{15} and one copy of O_{11} in cell 10.

Step 6. Rule $r_{(5+j),4} = \{(a_{1j})O_{11} \rightarrow (a_{1j}, go_{11})\} \cup \{(a_{1j})O_{12} \rightarrow (a_{1j}, go_{12})\}$ is executed in this step to send all copies of objects whose amount is larger than a_{11} to membrane 12, and send all copies of objects whose amount is less than a_{11} to membrane 11. The evolving process in cell $7 \cdots 10$ is shown as following.

In cell 7, the current objects are two copies of O_{11} and one copy of a_{12} so that it meet the execution condition of sub-rule $\{(a_{12})O_{11} \rightarrow (a_{12}, go_{11})\}$ to send one copy of a_{12} to cell 11. After this step, objects in cell 7 are two copies of O_{11} and object in cell 11 is one copy of a_{12}. Using the same mechanism, other objects in this P system includes one copy of O_{12} in cell 8 and four copies of a_{13} in cell 12, five copies of a_{14} in cell 12 and two copies of O_{12} in cell 9, two copies of a_{15} in cell 11 and one copy of O_{11} in cell 10 after this step. That is, all existing objects in this P system are three copies of a_{13} in cell $T1$, two copies of O_{11} in cell 7, one copy of O_{12} in cell 8, two copies of O_{12} in cell 9, one copy of O_{11} in cell 10, one copy of a_{12} and two copies of a_{15} in cell 11, four copies of a_{13} and five copies of a_{14} in cell 12.

Step 7. In this step, $r_{(5+j),5} = \{O_{11} \to \lambda\} \cup \{O_{12} \to \lambda\}$ for $2 \leq j \leq 5$ is executed and all copies of promoters O_{11} or O_{12} are exhausted. The evolving process in cell $7 \cdots 10$ is shown as following.

In cell 7, all copies of O_{11} are exhausted by executing sub-rule $\{O_{11} \to \lambda\}$ so that no objects exist in cell 7 now. Similarly, after this step, no objects exist in cell $8 \cdots 10$. Now, all current objects in this ECTPP-Quicksort P system are three copies of a_{13} in cell $T1$, one copy of a_{12} and two copies of a_{15} in cell 11, and four copies of a_{13} and five copies of a_{14} in cell 12.

Step 8. In this step, the subscript 1 of objects a_{1j} in cell 11 is instead of 2 and all copies of objects enter to cell 0 by using rule $R_{11} = \{a_{1j} \to (a_{(2i)j}, go_0)\}$, and the subscript 1 of objects a_{1j} in cell 12 is instead of 3 and all copies of objects enter to cell 0 by using rule $R_{12} = \{a_{1j} \to (a_{(2i)j}, go_0)\}$. As a result, all current objects in this ECTPP-Quicksort P system are one copy of a_{22}, two copies of a_{25}, four copies of a_{33} and five copies of a_{34} in cell 0. Now, the recursion for the first time is finishing. Then the next recursion will be executed next.

Step 9. When there is no objects enter to cell 0, the recursion stops. Objects transported from the output cell 6 are all entering the binary search tree membranes according to rule $R_6 = \{a_{i1} \to (a_{i1}, go_{Ti})\}$. And we get the final result, that is the binary search tree.

Now we describe every state after each step in tables. Tables 2, 3 and 4 show the process of the first recursion.

Table 2. Current objects in cell 0 to cell 12 after *step* 1 and *step* 2 in the 1st recursion.

Step	r	Cell0	Cell1	Cell2	Cell3	Cell4	Cell5	Cell6	Cell7	Cell8	Cell9	Cell10
1	01	$a_{11}^3 a_{12} a_{13}^4 a_{14}^5 a_{15}^2$										
1	02		a_{11}^3	a_{12}	a_{13}^4	a_{14}^5	a_{15}^2					
2	j							a_{11}^3	$a_{11}^3 a_{12}$	$a_{11}^3 a_{13}^4$	$a_{11}^3 a_{14}^5$	$a_{11}^3 a_{15}^2$

Then the algorithm starts its 2nd recursion. In the beginning, rule r_{01} is executed to choose one type of object a_{ij} as the current pivot object randomly. We suppose that it selects objects a_{25} and a_{33} randomly. Tables 5, 6 and 7 show the process of the 2nd recursion.

Table 3. Current objects in cell 0 to cell 12 after *step* 3 to *step* 9 in the 1st recursion.

Step	r	Cell7	Cell8	Cell9	Cell10	Cell11	Cell12	Output
3	$(5+j),1$	$a_{11}^2 H_{12}$	$a_{13} H_{13}^3$	$a_{14} H_{14}^3$	$a_{11} H_{15}^2$			a_{11}^3
4	$(5+j),2$	$O_{11}^2 H_{12}$	$O_{13} a_{13} H_{13}^3$	$O_{14} a_{14} H_{14}^3$	$O_{11} H_{15}^2$			
5	$(5+j),3$	$O_{11}^2 a_{12}$	$O_{13} a_{13}^4$	O_{14}^5	$O_{11} a_{15}^2$			
6	$(5+j),4$	O_{11}^2	O_{13}	O_{14}	O_{11}	$a_{12} a_{15}^2$	$a_{13}^4 a_{14}^5$	
7	$(5+j),5$					$a_{12} a_{15}^2$	$a_{13}^4 a_{14}^5$	
8	$2n+1$					$a_{22} a_{25}^2$	$a_{33}^4 a_{34}^5$	
9	$2n+2$					$a_{22} a_{25}^2$	$a_{33}^4 a_{34}^5$	

Table 4. Current objects in cell Ti in the 1st recursion.

Step	CellT1	CellT2	CellT3	...	CellT15
1					
2					
3	a_{11}^3				
4	a_{11}^3				
5	a_{11}^3				
6	a_{11}^3				
7	a_{11}^3				
8	a_{11}^3				
9	a_{11}^3				

Table 5. Current objects in cell 0 to cell 12 after *step* 1 and *step* 2 in the 2st recursion.

Step	r	Cell0	Cell1	Cell2	Cell3	Cell4	Cell5	Cell6	Cell7	Cell8	Cell9	Cell10
1	01	$a_{22}a_{33}^4a_{34}^5a_{25}^2$										
1	02		$a_{21}^2a_{31}^4$	a_{22}		a_{34}^5						
2	j								a_{21}^2	a_{31}^4	$a_{21}^2a_{31}^4a_{22}$	$a_{21}^2a_{31}^4a_{34}^5$	$a_{21}^2a_{31}^4$

Table 6. Current objects in cell 0 to cell 12 after *step* 3 to *step* 9 in the 2st recursion.

Step	r	Cell7	Cell8	Cell9	Cell10	Cell11	Cell12	Output
3	$(5+j),1$	$a_{21}a_{31}^4H_{22}$	$a_{21}^2a_{31}^4$	$a_{21}^2a_{34}H_{34}^4$	$a_{21}^2a_{31}^4$			$a_{21}^2a_{31}^4$
4	$(5+j),2$	$O_{21}O_{31}^4H_{22}$	$O_{21}^2O_{31}^4$	$O_{21}^2O_{32}a_{34}H_{34}^4$	$O_{21}^2O_{31}^4$			
5	$(5+j),3$	$O_{21}O_{31}^4a_{22}$	$O_{21}^2O_{31}^4$	$O_{21}^2O_{32}a_{34}^5$	$O_{21}^2O_{31}^4$			
6	$(5+j),4$	$O_{21}O_{31}^4$	$O_{21}^2O_{31}^4$	$O_{21}^2O_{32}$	$O_{21}^2O_{31}^4$	a_{22}	a_{34}	
7	$(5+j),5$					a_{22}	a_{34}^5	
8	$2n+1$					a_{42}	a_{74}^5	
9	$2n+2$					a_{42}	a_{74}^5	

Table 7. Current objects in cell Ti in the 2st recursion.

Step	CellT1	CellT2	CellT3	...	CellT15
1					
2					
3	a_{11}^3	a_{21}^2	a_{31}^4		
4	a_{11}^3	a_{21}^2	a_{31}^4		
5	a_{11}^3	a_{21}^2	a_{31}^4		
6	a_{11}^3	a_{21}^2	a_{31}^4		
7	a_{11}^3	a_{21}^2	a_{31}^4		
8	a_{11}^3	a_{21}^2	a_{31}^4		
9	a_{11}^3	a_{21}^2	a_{31}^4		

Table 8. Current objects in cell 0 to cell 12 after *step* 1 and *step* 2 in the 3st recursion.

Step	r	Cell0	Cell1	Cell2	Cell3	Cell4	Cell5	Cell6	Cell7	Cell8	Cell9	Cell10
1	01	$a_{42}a_{74}^5$										
1	02		$a_{41}a_{71}^5$									
2	j							$a_{41}a_{71}^5$	$a_{41}a_{71}^5$	$a_{41}a_{71}^5$	$a_{41}a_{71}^5$	$a_{41}a_{71}^5$

Table 9. Current objects in cell 0 to cell 12 after *step* 3 to *step* 9 in the 3st recursion.

Step	r	Cell7	Cell8	Cell9	Cell10	Cell11	Cell12	Output
3	$(5+j),1$	$a_{41}a_{71}^5$	$a_{41}a_{71}^5$	$a_{41}a_{71}^5$	$a_{21}^2a_{31}^4$			$a_{41}a_{71}^5$
4	$(5+j),2$	$a_{41}a_{71}^5$	$a_{41}a_{71}^5$	$a_{41}a_{71}^5$	$a_{41}a_{71}^5$			
5	$(5+j),3$	$a_{41}a_{71}^5$	$a_{41}a_{71}^5$	$a_{41}a_{71}^5$	$a_{41}a_{71}^5$			
6	$(5+j),4$	$a_{41}a_{71}^5$	$a_{41}a_{71}^5$	$a_{41}a_{71}^5$	$a_{41}a_{71}^5$			
7	$(5+j),5$							
8	$2n+1$							
9	$2n+2$							

Table 10. Current objects in cell Ti in the 3st recursion.

Step	CellT1	CellT2	CellT3	CellT4	CellT5	CellT6	CellT7	...	CellT15
1									
2									
3	a_{11}^3	a_{21}^2	a_{31}^4	a_{41}			a_{71}^5		
4	a_{11}^3	a_{21}^2	a_{31}^4	a_{41}			a_{71}^5		
5	a_{11}^3	a_{21}^2	a_{31}^4	a_{41}			a_{71}^5		
6	a_{11}^3	a_{21}^2	a_{31}^4	a_{41}			a_{71}^5		
7	a_{11}^3	a_{21}^2	a_{31}^4	a_{41}			a_{71}^5		
8	a_{11}^3	a_{21}^2	a_{31}^4	a_{41}			a_{71}^5		
9	a_{11}^3	a_{21}^2	a_{31}^4	a_{41}			a_{71}^5		

Then algorithm starts its 3rd recursion. Logically speaking, the number of sub-arrays to be sorted simultaneously in this recursion should be four. However, the number is two in this example because the computing is going to finish. The objects selected to be the current pivot objects are a_{42} and a_{74} surely because there is only one type of object in each sub-array. Tables 8, 9 and 10 show the process of the 3rd recursion.

The final result as the whole binary search tree we have got is shown in Fig. 3.

This binary search tree shows that the number of a_{21} and the number of a_{41} is less than the number of a_{11}, a_{31}, a_{71}. Also, the number of a_{41} is less than the number of a_{21} and the end the number of a_{31} is less than the number of a_{71}. Therefore, The order of every amount is $|a_{41}| \leq |a_{21}| \leq |a_{11}| \leq |a_{31}| \leq |a_{71}|$. That is $1 \leq 2 \leq 3 \leq 4 \leq 5$.

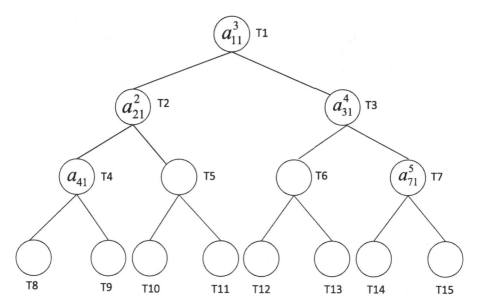

Fig. 3. The binary search tree membrane structure for the ECTPP-Quicksort algorithm.

5   Conclusions

We proposed an improved Quicksort algorithm which is called ECTPP-Quicksort, using a distributed and parallel mechanism in this paper. In ECTPP-Quicksort, we first designed the direct membrane algorithms with membrane structures, objects, rules and some other characteristics in detail.Therefore, we can use this algorithm directly and expediently. Then we implemented ECTPP-Quicksort by a calculate instance to show the feasibility and effectiveness of this improved Quicksort algorithm. For further research, it is meaningful to improve Quicksort algorithm using some other neural-like membrane computing models. Particularly, spiking neural P systems (SN P system) is hoped to be applied to improving Quicksort algorithm. By this work, the efficiency of sorting algorithms will be improved greatly.

References

1. Evans, D.J., Dunbar, R.C.: Quicksort. Comput. J. **5**(1), 10–15 (1962)
2. Evans, D.J., Dunbar, R.C.: The parallel quicksort algorithm part I-run time analysis. Int. J. Comput. Math. **12**(1), 19–55 (1982)
3. Cederman, D., Tsigas, P.: GPU-Quicksort: a practical quicksort algorithm for graphics processors. J. Exp. Algorithmics **14**, 4 (2010)
4. Reif, J.H.: Synthesis of Parallel Algorithms. Morgan Kaufmann Publishers Inc., Burlington (1993)

5. Wagar, B.: Hyperquicksort: a fast sorting algorithm for hypercubes. In: Heath, M. (ed.) Hypercube Multiprocessors, pp. 292–299. SIAM, Philadelphia (1987)
6. Powers, D.M.W.: Informatik: Universitt Kaiserslautern. Parallelized QuickSort with Optimal Speedup (1991)
7. Arulanandham, J.J.: Implementing bead-sort with P systems. In: Calude, C.S., Dinneen, M.J., Peper, F. (eds.) UMC 2002. LNCS, vol. 2509, pp. 115–125. Springer, Heidelberg (2002). https://doi.org/10.1007/3-540-45833-6_10
8. Ceterchi, R., Martin-Vide, C.: Dynamic P Systems. Revised Papers from the International Workshop on Membrane Computing **24**(4), 146–186 (2002)
9. Ceterchi, R., Martin-Vide. C.: P systems with communication for static sortings. In: Brainstorming Week on Membrane Computing, pp. 5–11 (2003)
10. Ceterchi, R., Pérez-Jiménez, M.J., Tomescu, A.I.: Simulating the bitonic sort using P systems. In: Eleftherakis, G., Kefalas, P., Păun, G., Rozenberg, G., Salomaa, A. (eds.) WMC 2007. LNCS, vol. 4860, pp. 172–192. Springer, Heidelberg (2007). https://doi.org/10.1007/978-3-540-77312-2_11
11. Ceterchi, R., Tomescu, A.I.: Implementing sorting networks with spiking neural P systems. Fundam. Inf. **87**(1), 35–48 (2008)
12. Alhazov, A., Sburlan, D.: Static sorting P systems. In: Ciobanu, G., Pâun, G., Pérez-Jiménez, M.J. (eds.) Applications of Membrane Computing. NCS, pp. 215–252. Springer, Heidelberg (2005). https://doi.org/10.1007/3-540-29937-8_8
13. Ceterchi, R., Pérez-Jiménez, M.D.J., Tomescu, A.I.: Sorting omega networks simulated with P systems optimal data layouts. Daniel Díaz-Pernil, pp. 79–92 (2010)
14. Freund, R., Păun, G., Pérez-Jiménez, M.J.: Tissue P systems with channel states. Theor. Comput. Sci. **330**(1), 101–116 (2005)
15. Song, B., Zhang, C., Pan, L.: Tissue-like P systems with evolutional symport/antiport rules. Inf. Sci. **378**, 177–193 (2017)
16. Giavitto, J., Michel, O.: The topological structures of membrane computing. Fundam. Inf. **49**(1–3), 123–145 (2002)

Author Index

Printed in the United States
By Bookmasters